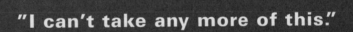

"I can't take any more of this."

"Look, can you just have your nervous breakdown
after we've saved the world?"

— from "In the Wonderful Land of Clockwork"

doom
PATROL
planet love

writer   **Grant Morrison**

pencillers   **Richard Case**
Sean Phillips
Steve Pugh
Ian Montgomery
Paris Cullins
Duke Mighten
Ken Steacy

original series covers   **Simon Bisley**
Tom Taggart
Jamie Hewlett
Duncan Fegredo
Richard Case
Keith Giffen
Mike Mignola

inkers   **Stan Woch**
Sean Phillips
Steve Pugh
Brad Vancata
Walter Simonson
Ray Kryssing
Mark McKenna
Ken Steacy

colorist   **Daniel Vozzo**

letterers   **John Workman**
Ken Steacy

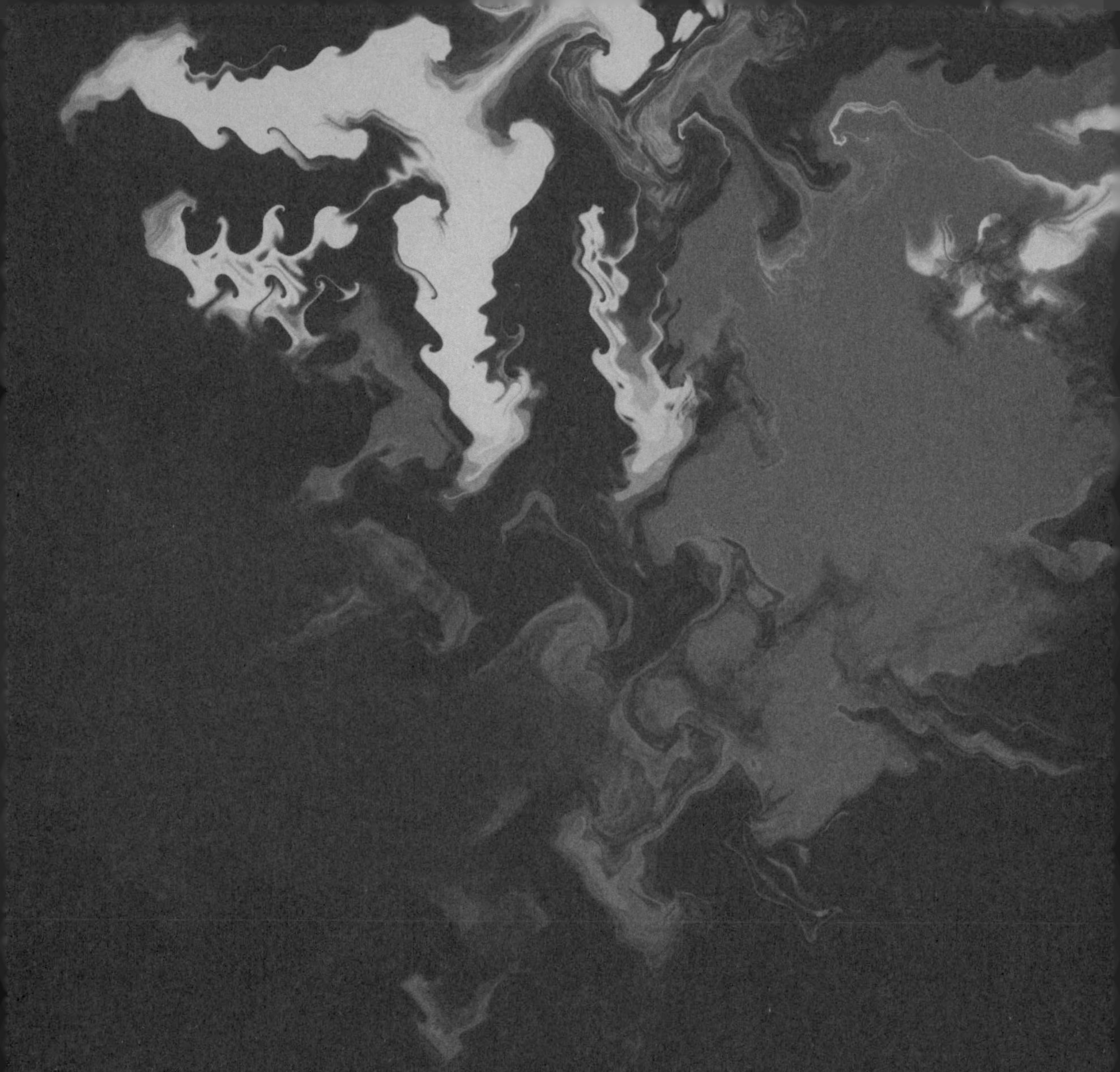

Karen Berger Senior VP-Executive Editor / **Tom Peyer** Editor-original series / **Scott Nybakken** Editor-collected edition
Robbin Brosterman Senior Art Director / **Paul Levitz** President & Publisher / **Georg Brewer** VP-Design & DC Direct Creative
Richard Bruning Senior VP-Creative Director / **Patrick Caldon** Executive VP-Finance & Operations / **Chris Caramalis** VP-Finance
John Cunningham VP-Marketing / **Terri Cunningham** VP-Managing Editor / **Alison Gill** VP-Manufacturing / **David Hyde** VP-Publicity
Hank Kanalz VP-General Manager, WildStorm / **Jim Lee** Editorial Director-WildStorm / **Paula Lowitt** Senior VP-Business & Legal Affairs
MaryEllen McLaughlin VP-Advertising & Custom Publishing / **John Nee** Senior VP-Business Development
Gregory Noveck Senior VP-Creative Affairs / **Sue Pohja** VP-Book Trade Sales / **Steve Rotterdam** Senior VP-Sales & Marketing
Cheryl Rubin Senior VP-Brand Management / **Jeff Trojan** VP-Business Development, DC Direct / **Bob Wayne** VP-Sales

Cover illustration by Brian Bolland. Publication design by Amelia Grohman.

DOOM PATROL: PLANET LOVE
Published by DC Comics.

DC Comics, 1700 Broadway, New York, NY 10019
A Warner Bros. Entertainment Company
Printed in Canada. First Printing. ISBN: 978-1-4012-1624-5

CONTENTS

8   **in the wonderful land of clockwork**
from DOOM PATROL #58 — August 1992
cover art by Simon Bisley

34   **dying inside**
from DOOM PATROL #59 — September 1992
cover art by Tom Taggart

60   **brief candles**
from DOOM PATROL #60 — October 1992
cover art by Jamie Hewlett

86   **" ..."**
from DOOM PATROL #61 — November 1992
cover art by Tom Taggart

112   **planet love**
from DOOM PATROL #62 — December 1992
cover art by Duncan Fegredo

138   **the empire of chairs**
from DOOM PATROL #63 — January 1993
cover art by Richard Case

164   **judgment day**
from DOOM FORCE SPECIAL #1 — July 1992
cover art pencilled by Keith Giffen, inked by Mike Mignola
and colored by Daniel Vozzo

"This is the sound you'd hear at night in lonely places.

It's the sound of the secret machinery at the center of the world."

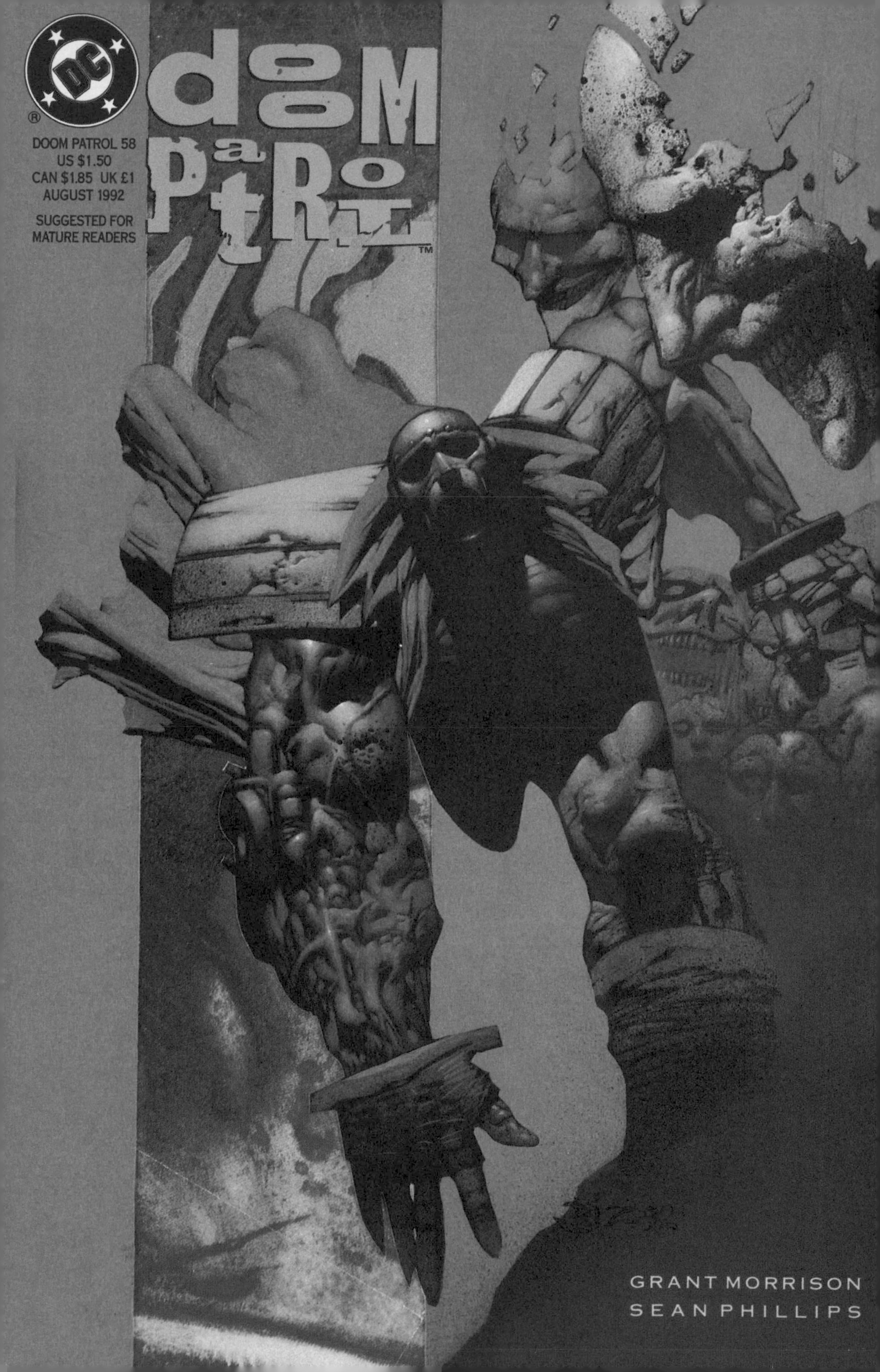
DC
DOOM PATROL
DOOM PATROL 58
US $1.50
CAN $1.85 UK £1
AUGUST 1992
SUGGESTED FOR
MATURE READERS
GRANT MORRISON
SEAN PHILLIPS

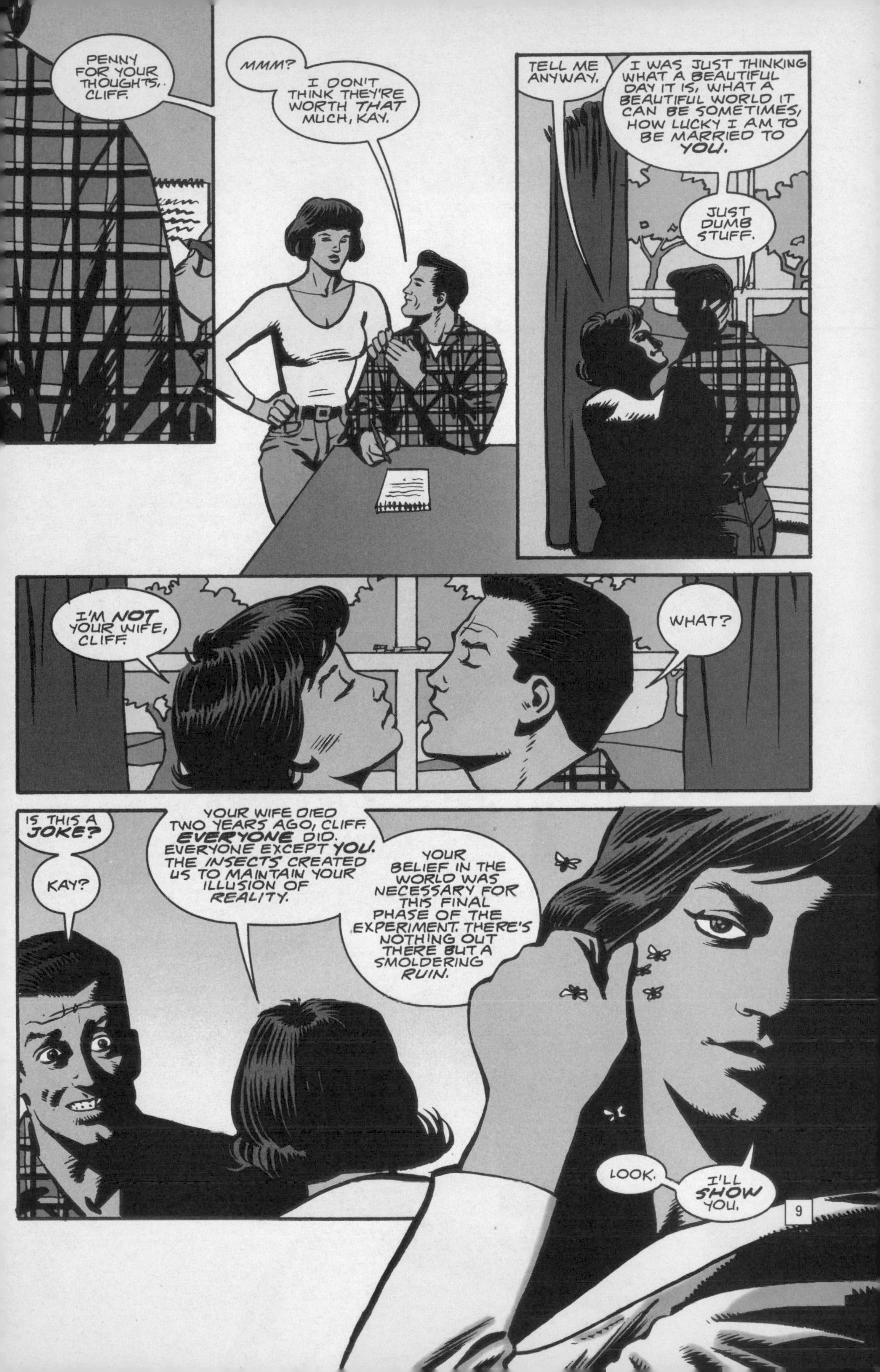

PENNY FOR YOUR THOUGHTS, CLIFF.
MMM?
I DON'T THINK THEY'RE WORTH THAT MUCH, KAY.
TELL ME ANYWAY.
I WAS JUST THINKING WHAT A BEAUTIFUL DAY IT IS, WHAT A BEAUTIFUL WORLD IT CAN BE SOMETIMES, HOW LUCKY I AM TO BE MARRIED TO YOU.
JUST DUMB STUFF.
I'M NOT YOUR WIFE, CLIFF.
WHAT?
IS THIS A JOKE?
KAY?
YOUR WIFE DIED TWO YEARS AGO, CLIFF. EVERYONE DID. EVERYONE EXCEPT YOU. THE INSECTS CREATED US TO MAINTAIN YOUR ILLUSION OF REALITY.
YOUR BELIEF IN THE WORLD WAS NECESSARY FOR THIS FINAL PHASE OF THE EXPERIMENT. THERE'S NOTHING OUT THERE BUT A SMOLDERING RUIN.
LOOK.
I'LL SHOW YOU.

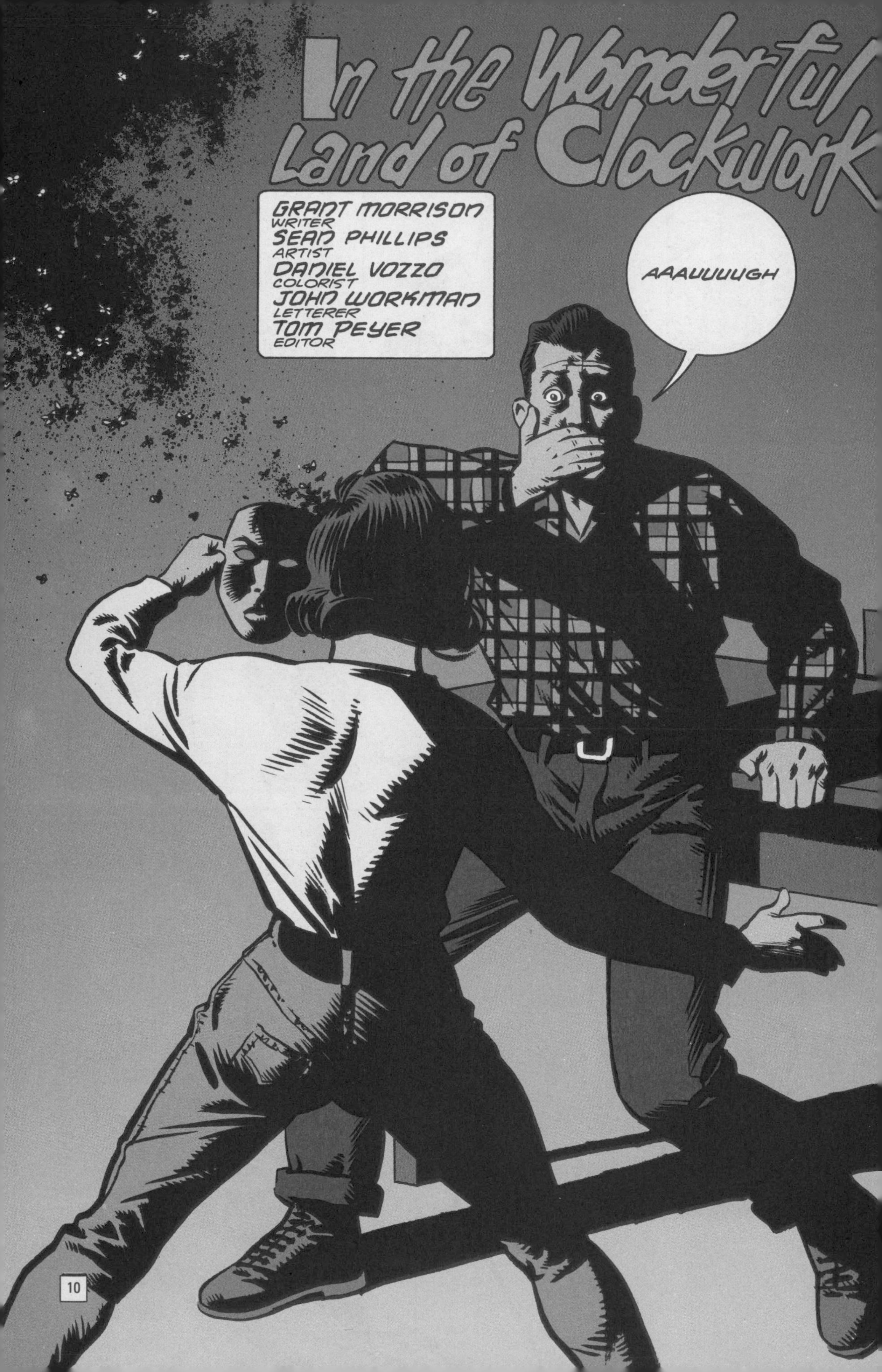
In the Wonderful Land of Clockwork
GRANT MORRISON
WRITER
SEAN PHILLIPS
ARTIST
DANIEL VOZZO
COLORIST
JOHN WORKMAN
LETTERER
TOM PEYER
EDITOR
AAAUUUUGH

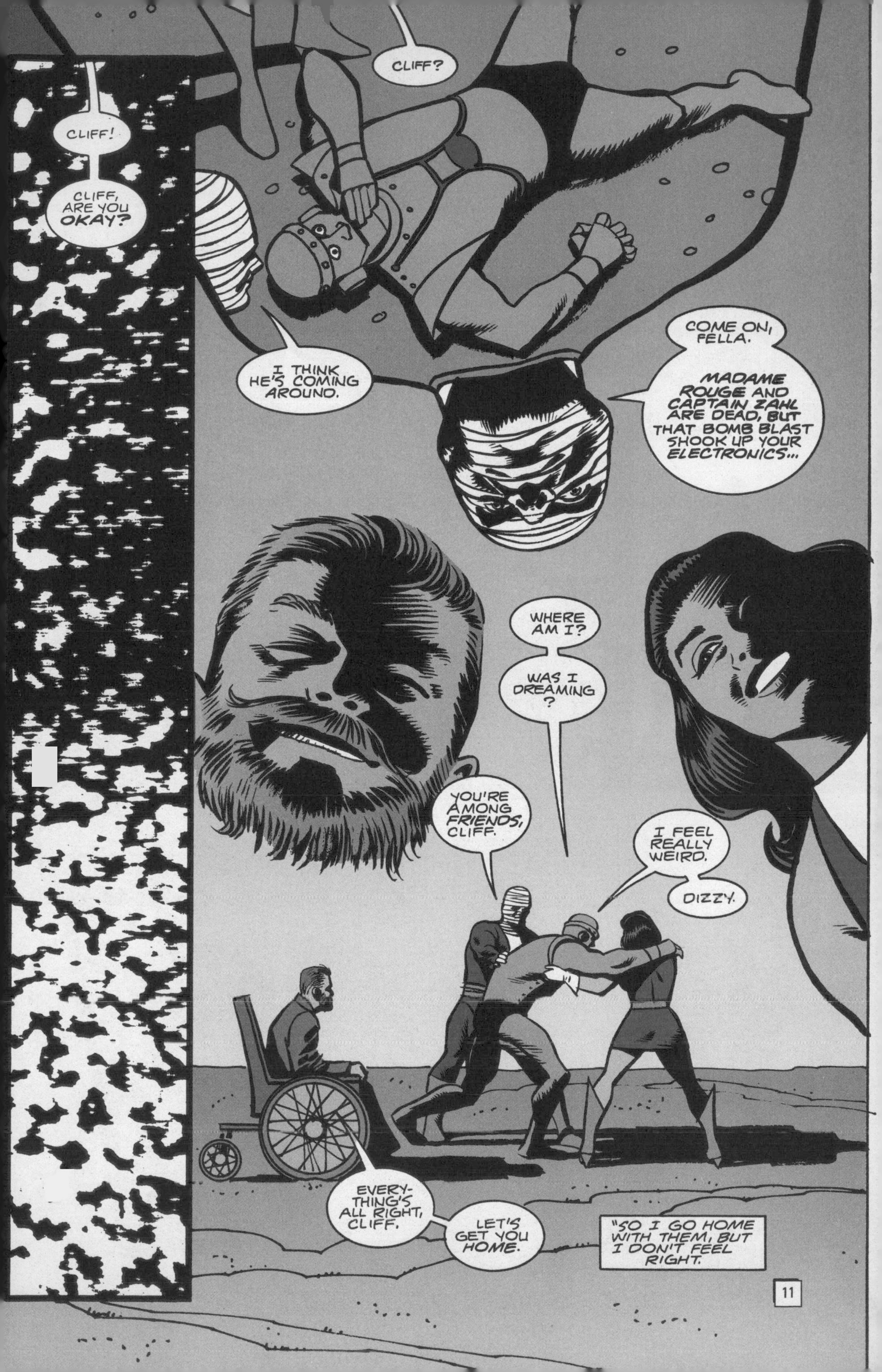
CLIFF?
CLIFF!
CLIFF, ARE YOU OKAY?
I THINK HE'S COMING AROUND.
COME ON, FELLA.
MADAME ROUGE AND CAPTAIN ZAHL ARE DEAD, BUT THAT BOMB BLAST SHOOK UP YOUR ELECTRONICS...
WHERE AM I?
WAS I DREAMING?
YOU'RE AMONG FRIENDS, CLIFF.
I FEEL REALLY WEIRD.
DIZZY.
EVERY-THING'S ALL RIGHT, CLIFF.
LET'S GET YOU HOME.
"SO I GO HOME WITH THEM, BUT I DON'T FEEL RIGHT.

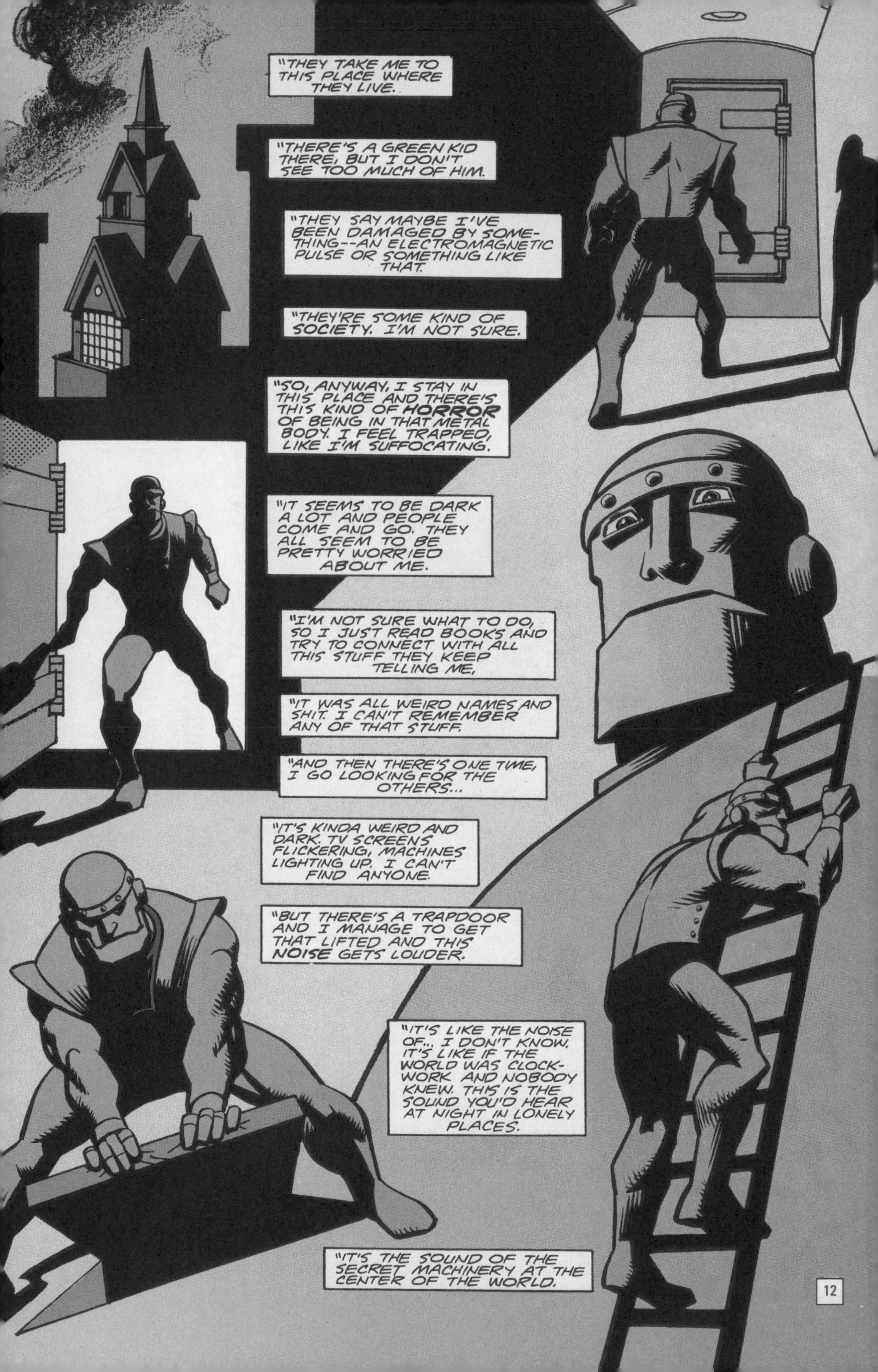
"THEY TAKE ME TO THIS PLACE WHERE THEY LIVE.
"THERE'S A GREEN KID THERE, BUT I DON'T SEE TOO MUCH OF HIM.
"THEY SAY MAYBE I'VE BEEN DAMAGED BY SOME-THING--AN ELECTROMAGNETIC PULSE OR SOMETHING LIKE THAT.
"THEY'RE SOME KIND OF SOCIETY. I'M NOT SURE.
"SO, ANYWAY, I STAY IN THIS PLACE AND THERE'S THIS KIND OF HORROR OF BEING IN THAT METAL BODY. I FEEL TRAPPED, LIKE I'M SUFFOCATING.
"IT SEEMS TO BE DARK A LOT AND PEOPLE COME AND GO. THEY ALL SEEM TO BE PRETTY WORRIED ABOUT ME.
"I'M NOT SURE WHAT TO DO, SO I JUST READ BOOKS AND TRY TO CONNECT WITH ALL THIS STUFF THEY KEEP TELLING ME.
"IT WAS ALL WEIRD NAMES AND SHIT. I CAN'T REMEMBER ANY OF THAT STUFF.
"AND THEN THERE'S ONE TIME, I GO LOOKING FOR THE OTHERS...
"IT'S KINDA WEIRD AND DARK. TV SCREENS FLICKERING, MACHINES LIGHTING UP. I CAN'T FIND ANYONE.
"BUT THERE'S A TRAPDOOR AND I MANAGE TO GET THAT LIFTED AND THIS NOISE GETS LOUDER.
"IT'S LIKE THE NOISE OF... I DON'T KNOW. IT'S LIKE IF THE WORLD WAS CLOCK-WORK AND NOBODY KNEW. THIS IS THE SOUND YOU'D HEAR AT NIGHT IN LONELY PLACES.
"IT'S THE SOUND OF THE SECRET MACHINERY AT THE CENTER OF THE WORLD.

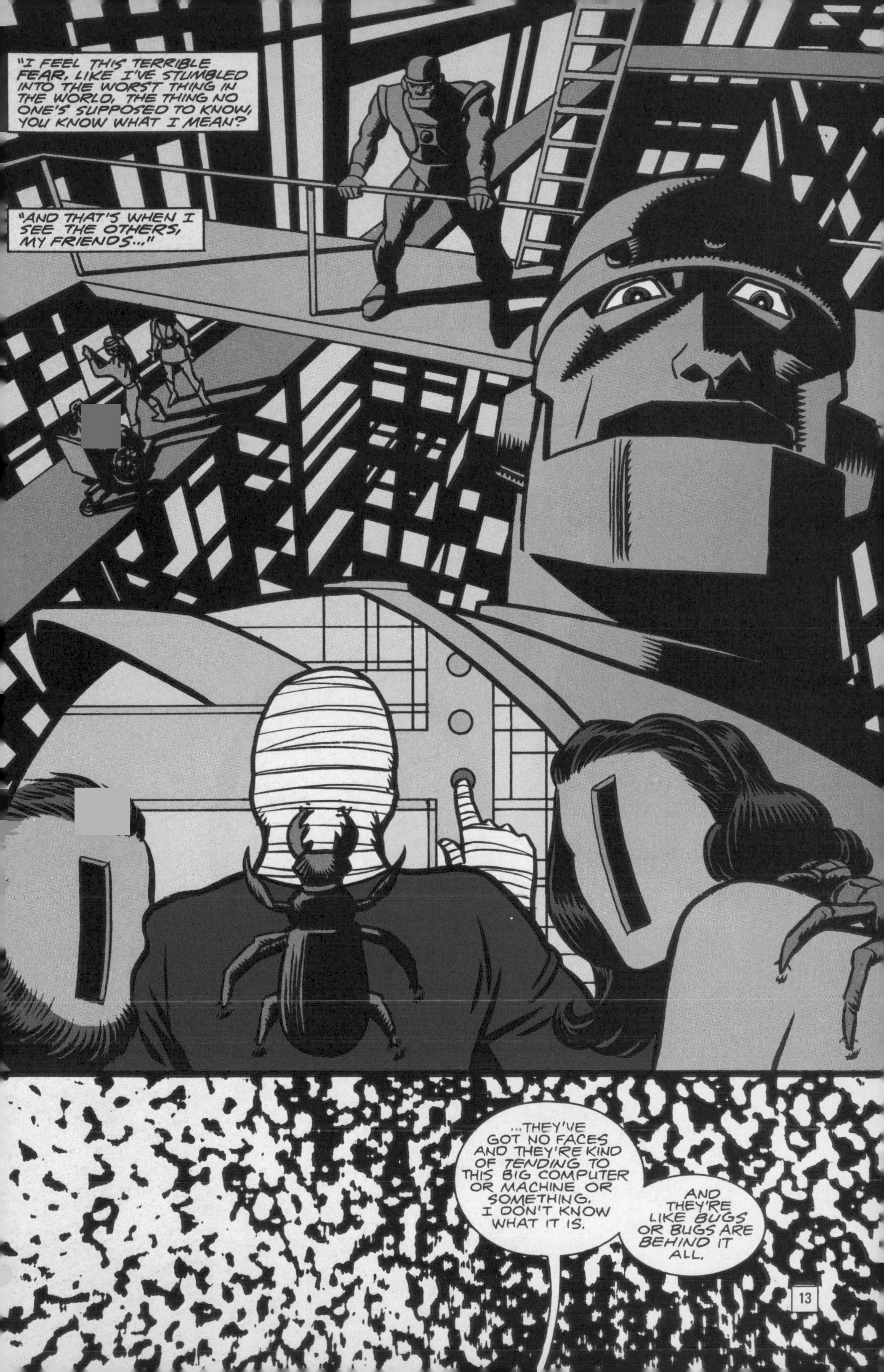
"I FEEL THIS TERRIBLE FEAR, LIKE I'VE STUMBLED INTO THE WORST THING IN THE WORLD, THE THING NO ONE'S SUPPOSED TO KNOW, YOU KNOW WHAT I MEAN?
"AND THAT'S WHEN I SEE THE OTHERS, MY FRIENDS..."
...THEY'VE GOT NO FACES AND THEY'RE KIND OF TENDING TO THIS BIG COMPUTER OR MACHINE OR SOMETHING. I DON'T KNOW WHAT IT IS.
AND THEY'RE LIKE BUGS OR BUGS ARE BEHIND IT ALL.

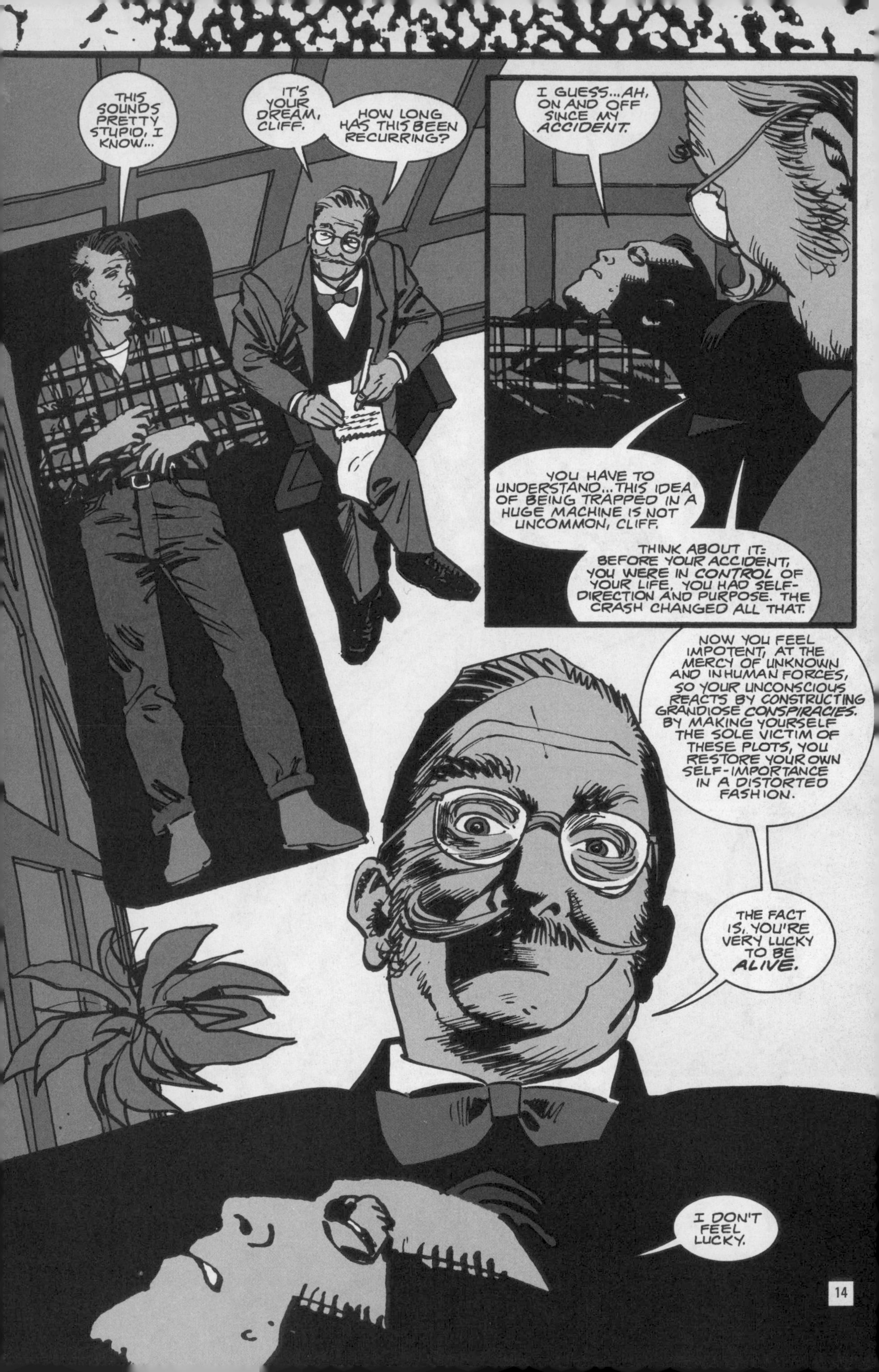
THIS SOUNDS PRETTY STUPID, I KNOW...
IT'S YOUR DREAM, CLIFF.
HOW LONG HAS THIS BEEN RECURRING?
I GUESS...AH, ON AND OFF SINCE MY ACCIDENT.
YOU HAVE TO UNDERSTAND...THIS IDEA OF BEING TRAPPED IN A HUGE MACHINE IS NOT UNCOMMON, CLIFF.
THINK ABOUT IT: BEFORE YOUR ACCIDENT, YOU WERE IN CONTROL OF YOUR LIFE, YOU HAD SELF-DIRECTION AND PURPOSE. THE CRASH CHANGED ALL THAT.
NOW YOU FEEL IMPOTENT, AT THE MERCY OF UNKNOWN AND INHUMAN FORCES, SO YOUR UNCONSCIOUS REACTS BY CONSTRUCTING GRANDIOSE CONSPIRACIES. BY MAKING YOURSELF THE SOLE VICTIM OF THESE PLOTS, YOU RESTORE YOUR OWN SELF-IMPORTANCE IN A DISTORTED FASHION.
THE FACT IS, YOU'RE VERY LUCKY TO BE ALIVE.
I DON'T FEEL LUCKY.

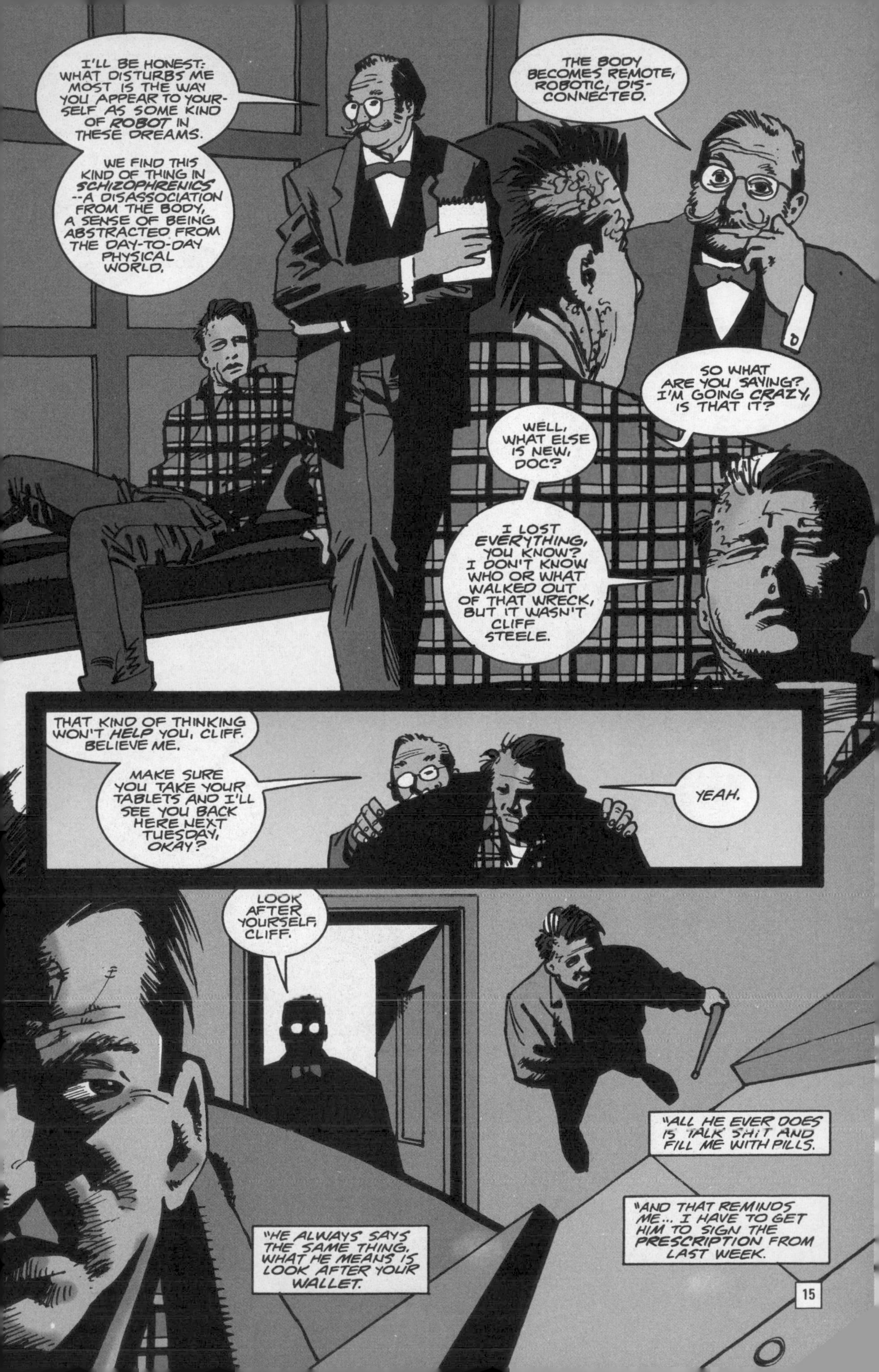
I'LL BE HONEST: WHAT DISTURBS ME MOST IS THE WAY YOU APPEAR TO YOURSELF AS SOME KIND OF ROBOT IN THESE DREAMS.
WE FIND THIS KIND OF THING IN SCHIZOPHRENICS --A DISASSOCIATION FROM THE BODY, A SENSE OF BEING ABSTRACTED FROM THE DAY-TO-DAY PHYSICAL WORLD.
THE BODY BECOMES REMOTE, ROBOTIC, DISCONNECTED.
SO WHAT ARE YOU SAYING? I'M GOING CRAZY, IS THAT IT?
WELL, WHAT ELSE IS NEW, DOC?
I LOST EVERYTHING, YOU KNOW? I DON'T KNOW WHO OR WHAT WALKED OUT OF THAT WRECK, BUT IT WASN'T CLIFF STEELE.
THAT KIND OF THINKING WON'T HELP YOU, CLIFF. BELIEVE ME.
MAKE SURE YOU TAKE YOUR TABLETS AND I'LL SEE YOU BACK HERE NEXT TUESDAY, OKAY?
YEAH.
LOOK AFTER YOURSELF, CLIFF.
"HE ALWAYS SAYS THE SAME THING. WHAT HE MEANS IS LOOK AFTER YOUR WALLET.
"ALL HE EVER DOES IS TALK SHIT AND FILL ME WITH PILLS.
"AND THAT REMINDS ME... I HAVE TO GET HIM TO SIGN THE PRESCRIPTION FROM LAST WEEK.

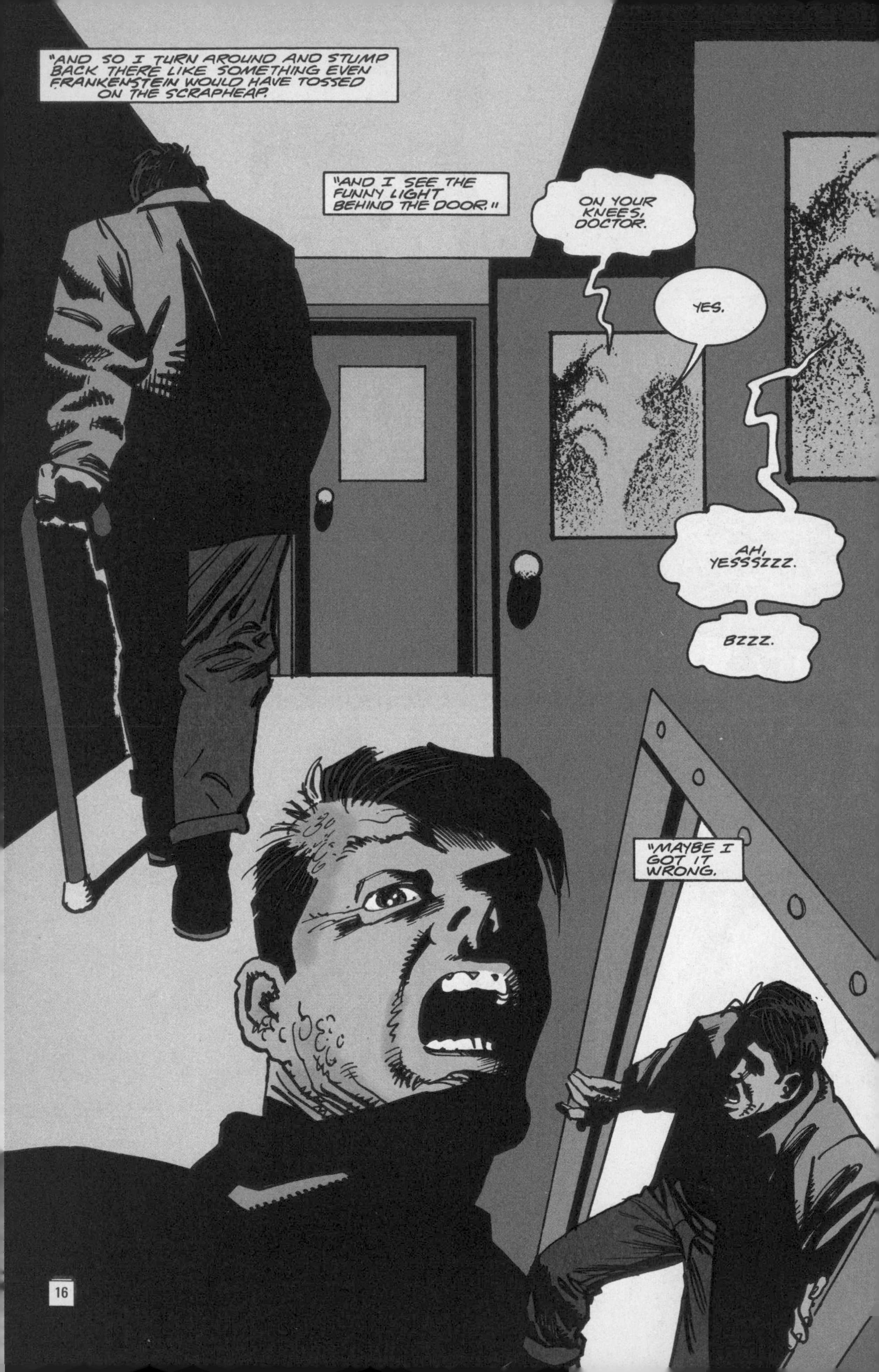
"AND SO I TURN AROUND AND STUMP BACK THERE LIKE SOMETHING EVEN FRANKENSTEIN WOULD HAVE TOSSED ON THE SCRAPHEAP.
"AND I SEE THE FUNNY LIGHT BEHIND THE DOOR."
ON YOUR KNEES, DOCTOR.
YES.
AH, YESSSZZZ.
BZZZ.
"MAYBE I GOT IT WRONG.

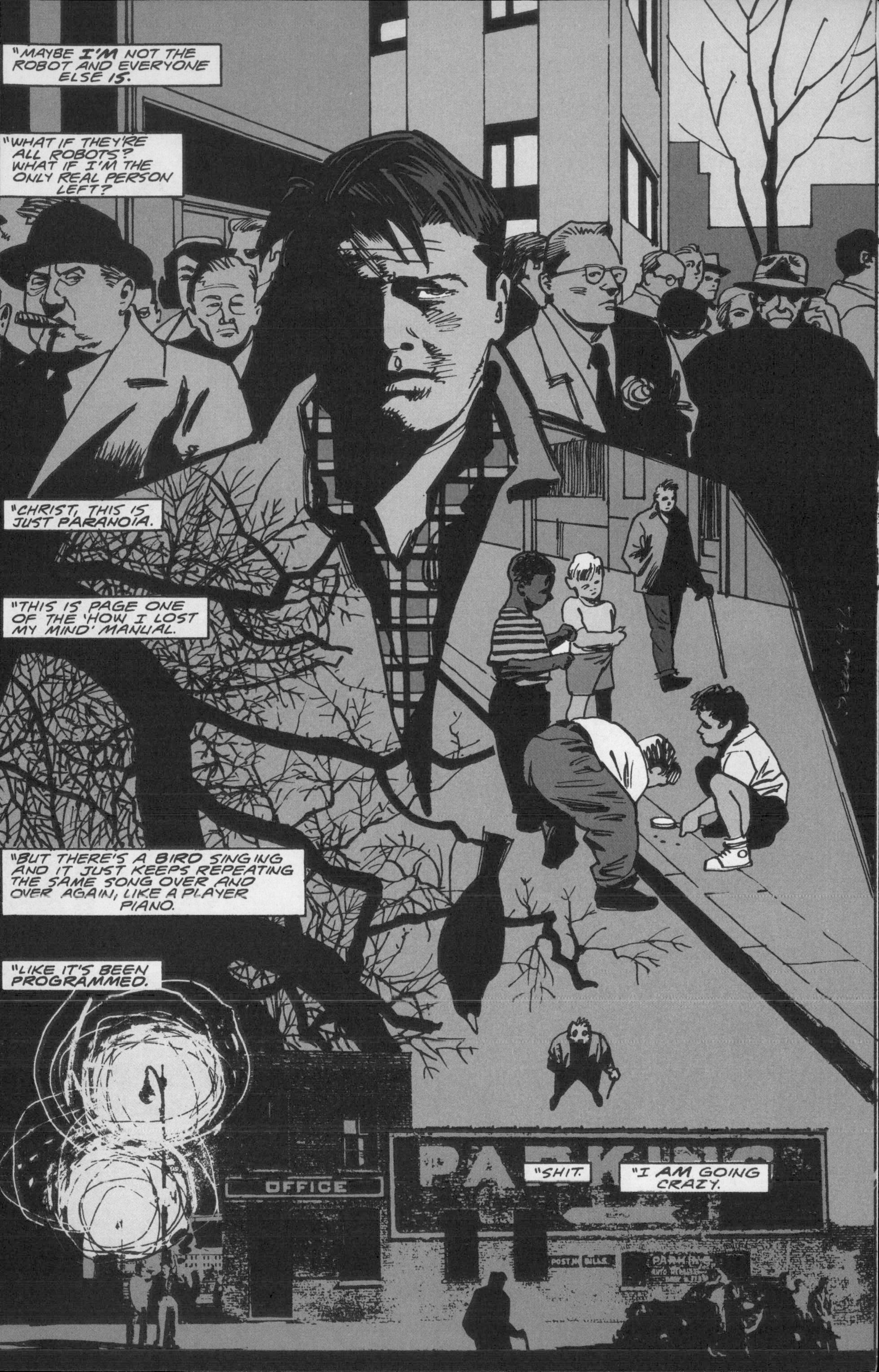
"MAYBE I'M NOT THE ROBOT AND EVERYONE ELSE IS.
"WHAT IF THEY'RE ALL ROBOTS? WHAT IF I'M THE ONLY REAL PERSON LEFT?
"CHRIST, THIS IS JUST PARANOIA.
"THIS IS PAGE ONE OF THE 'HOW I LOST MY MIND' MANUAL.
"BUT THERE'S A BIRD SINGING AND IT JUST KEEPS REPEATING THE SAME SONG OVER AND OVER AGAIN, LIKE A PLAYER PIANO.
"LIKE IT'S BEEN PROGRAMMED.
OFFICE
"SHIT.
"I AM GOING CRAZY.

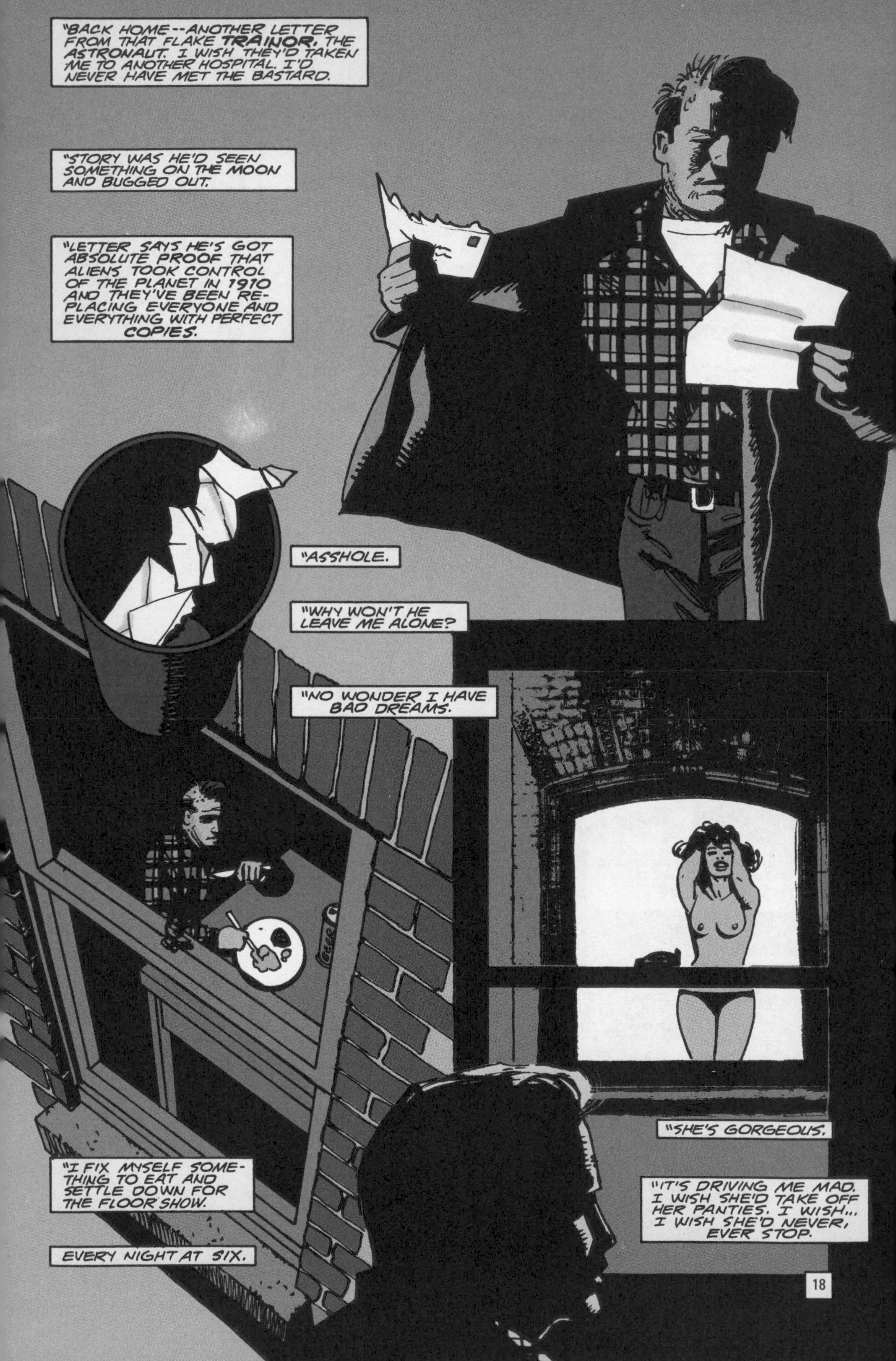
"BACK HOME--ANOTHER LETTER FROM THAT FLAKE TRAINOR. THE ASTRONAUT. I WISH THEY'D TAKEN ME TO ANOTHER HOSPITAL. I'D NEVER HAVE MET THE BASTARD.
"STORY WAS HE'D SEEN SOMETHING ON THE MOON AND BUGGED OUT.
"LETTER SAYS HE'S GOT ABSOLUTE PROOF THAT ALIENS TOOK CONTROL OF THE PLANET IN 1910 AND THEY'VE BEEN REPLACING EVERYONE AND EVERYTHING WITH PERFECT COPIES.
"ASSHOLE.
"WHY WON'T HE LEAVE ME ALONE?
"NO WONDER I HAVE BAD DREAMS.
"I FIX MYSELF SOMETHING TO EAT AND SETTLE DOWN FOR THE FLOOR SHOW.
EVERY NIGHT AT SIX.
"SHE'S GORGEOUS.
"IT'S DRIVING ME MAD. I WISH SHE'D TAKE OFF HER PANTIES. I WISH... I WISH SHE'D NEVER, EVER STOP.

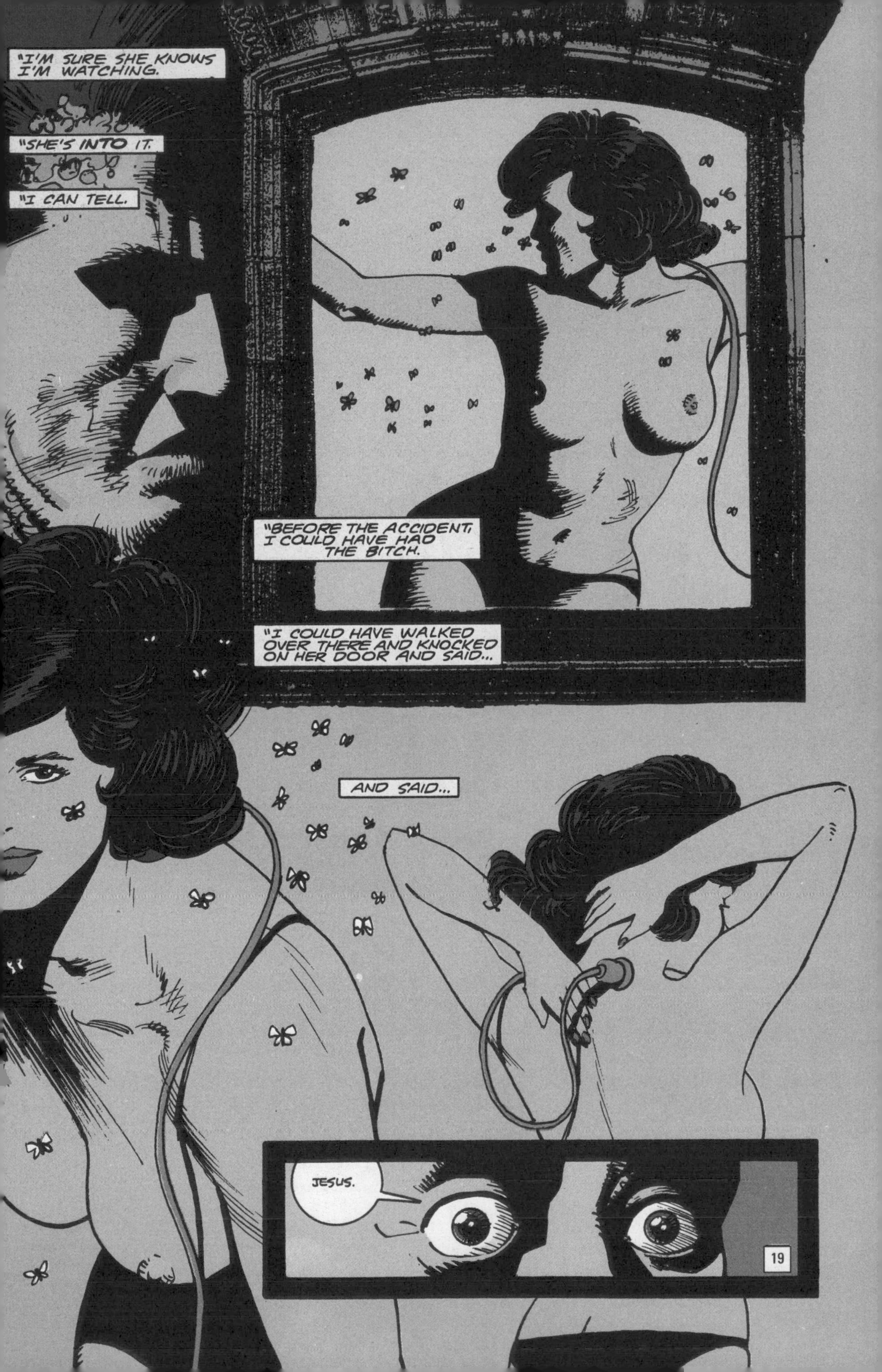

"I'M SURE SHE KNOWS I'M WATCHING.
"SHE'S INTO IT.
"I CAN TELL.
"BEFORE THE ACCIDENT, I COULD HAVE HAD THE BITCH.
"I COULD HAVE WALKED OVER THERE AND KNOCKED ON HER DOOR AND SAID...
AND SAID...
JESUS.

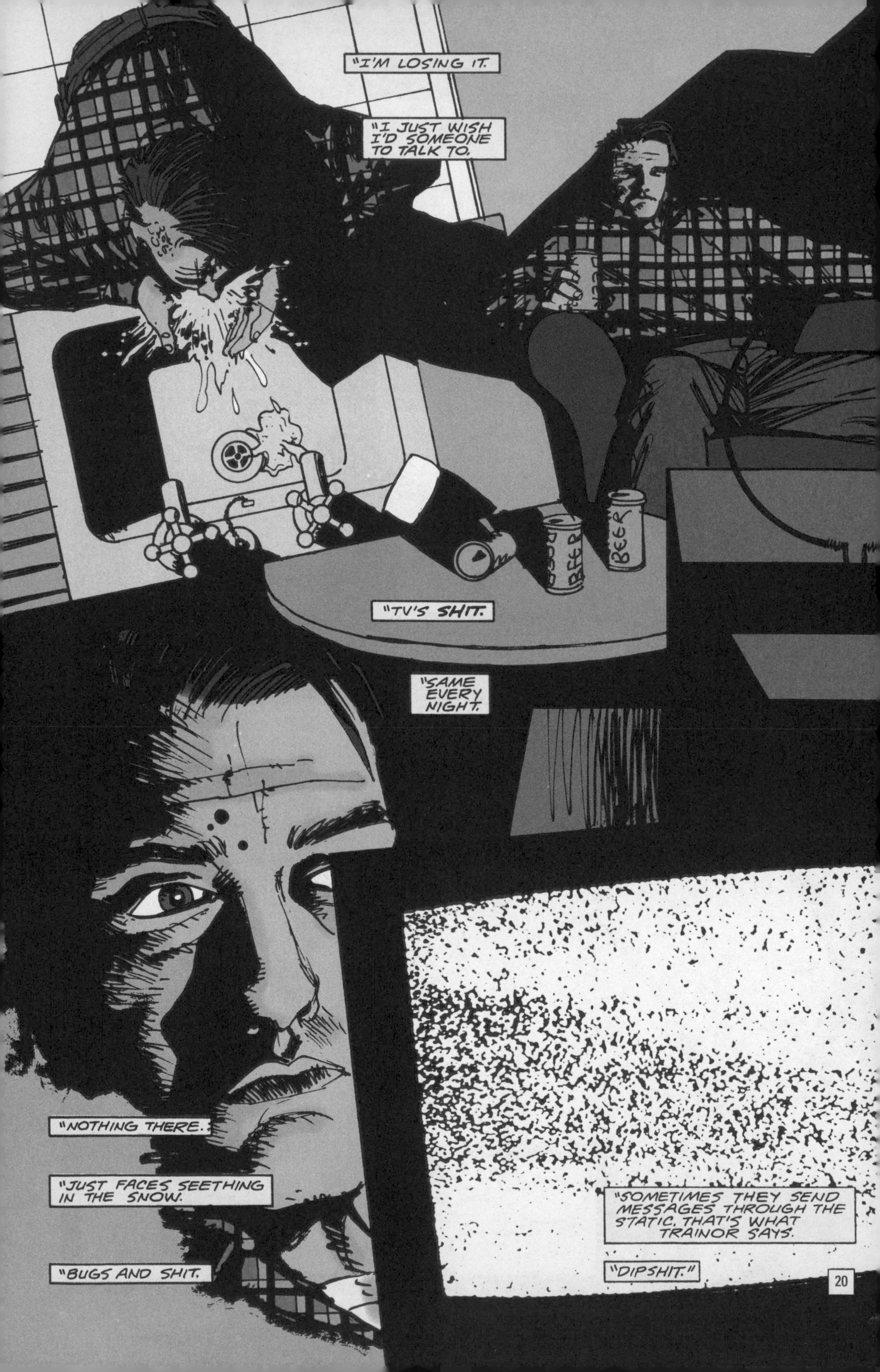
"I'M LOSING IT.
"I JUST WISH I'D SOMEONE TO TALK TO.
GOOD BEER
BEER
"TV'S SHIT.
"SAME EVERY NIGHT.
"NOTHING THERE.
"JUST FACES SEETHING IN THE SNOW.
"BUGS AND SHIT.
"SOMETIMES THEY SEND MESSAGES THROUGH THE STATIC. THAT'S WHAT TRAINOR SAYS.
"DIPSHIT."

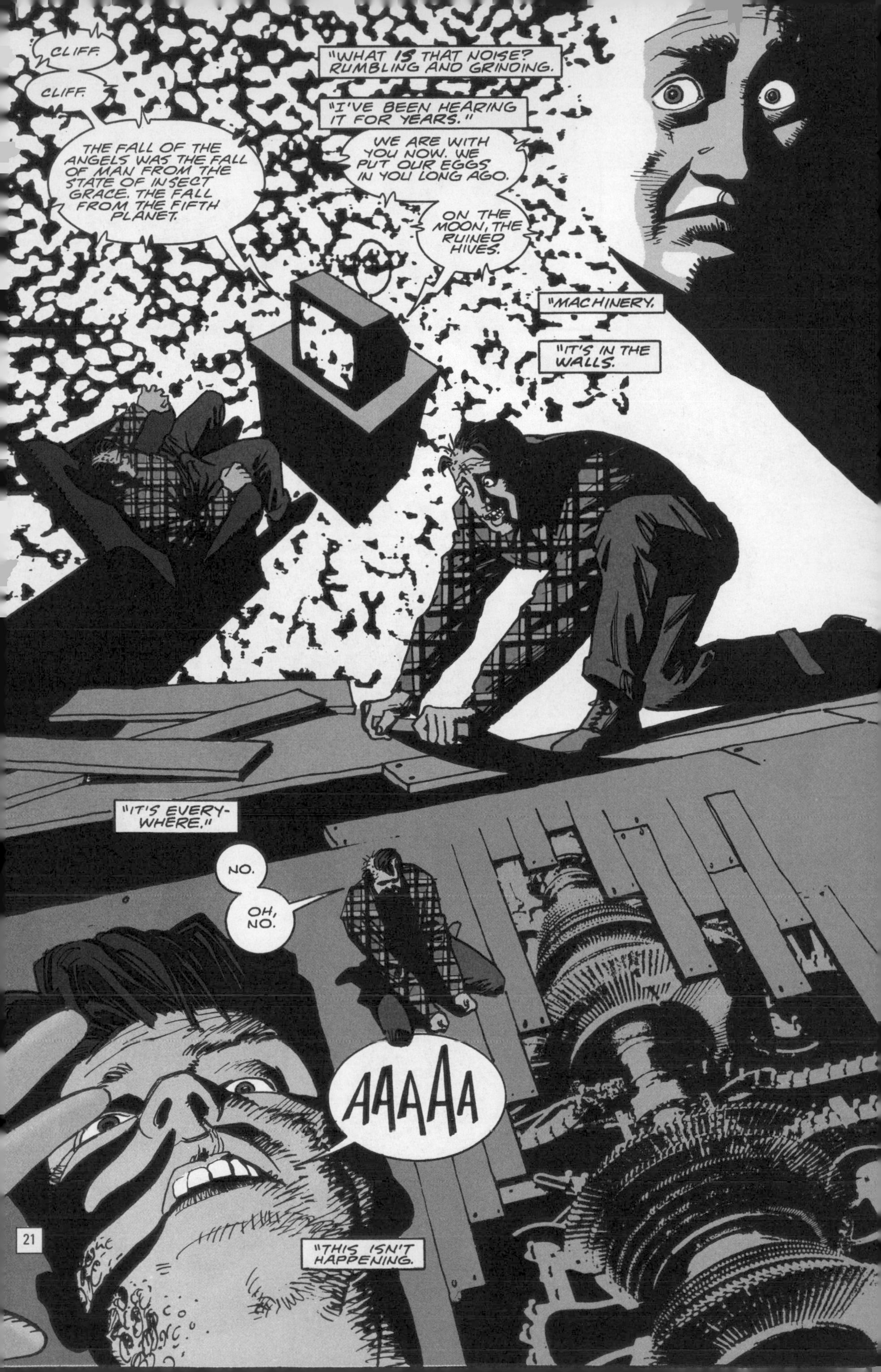

CLIFF.
CLIFF.
"WHAT IS THAT NOISE? RUMBLING AND GRINDING.
"I'VE BEEN HEARING IT FOR YEARS."
THE FALL OF THE ANGELS WAS THE FALL OF MAN FROM THE STATE OF INSECT GRACE. THE FALL FROM THE FIFTH PLANET.
WE ARE WITH YOU NOW. WE PUT OUR EGGS IN YOU LONG AGO.
ON THE MOON, THE RUINED HIVES.
"MACHINERY.
"IT'S IN THE WALLS.
"IT'S EVERY-WHERE."
NO.
OH, NO.
AAAAA
"THIS ISN'T HAPPENING.

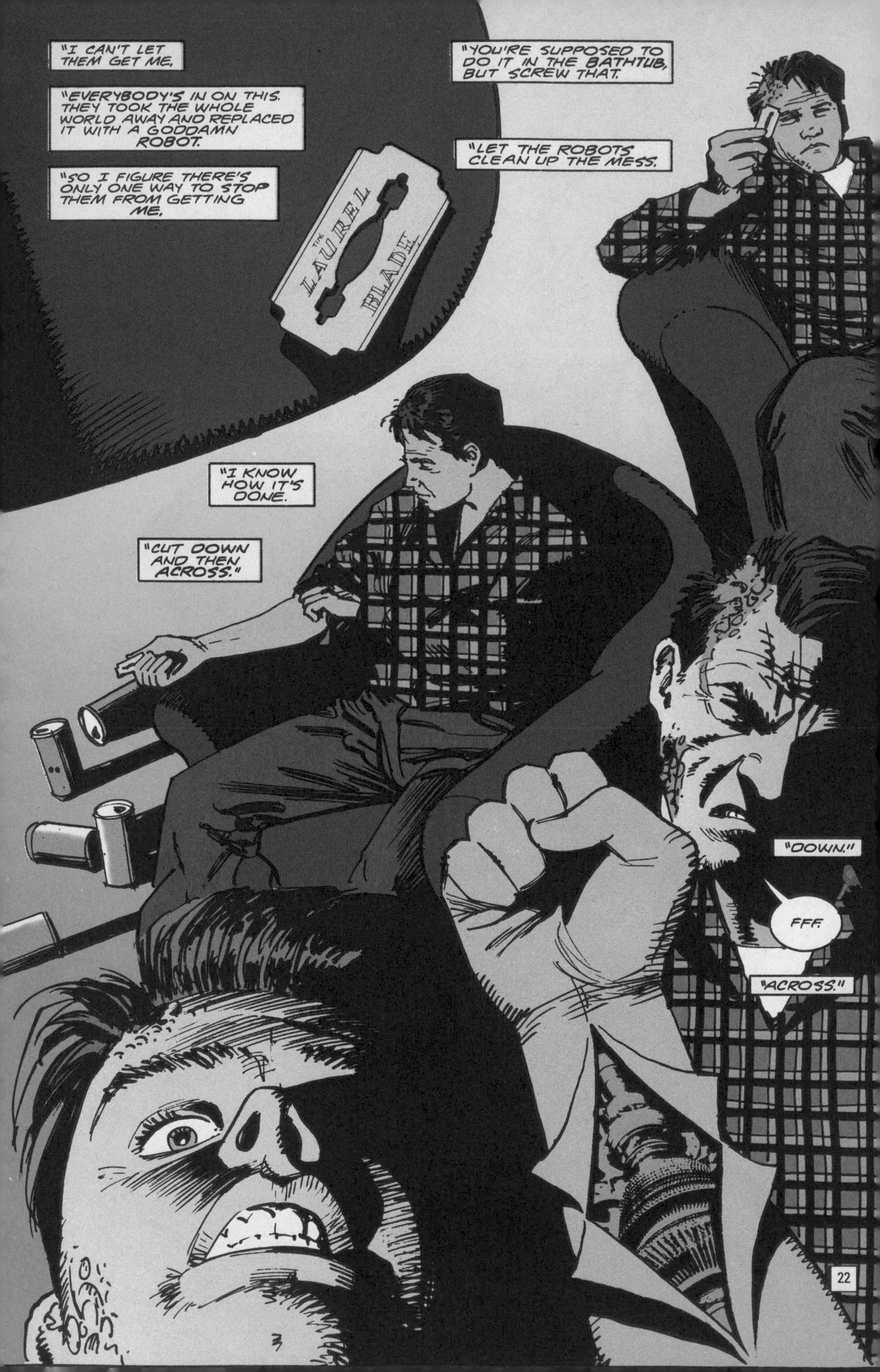
"I CAN'T LET THEM GET ME.
"EVERYBODY'S IN ON THIS. THEY TOOK THE WHOLE WORLD AWAY AND REPLACED IT WITH A GODDAMN ROBOT.
"SO I FIGURE THERE'S ONLY ONE WAY TO STOP THEM FROM GETTING ME.
THE LAUREL BLADE
"YOU'RE SUPPOSED TO DO IT IN THE BATHTUB, BUT SCREW THAT.
"LET THE ROBOTS CLEAN UP THE MESS.
"I KNOW HOW IT'S DONE.
"CUT DOWN AND THEN ACROSS."
"DOWN."
FFF.
"ACROSS."

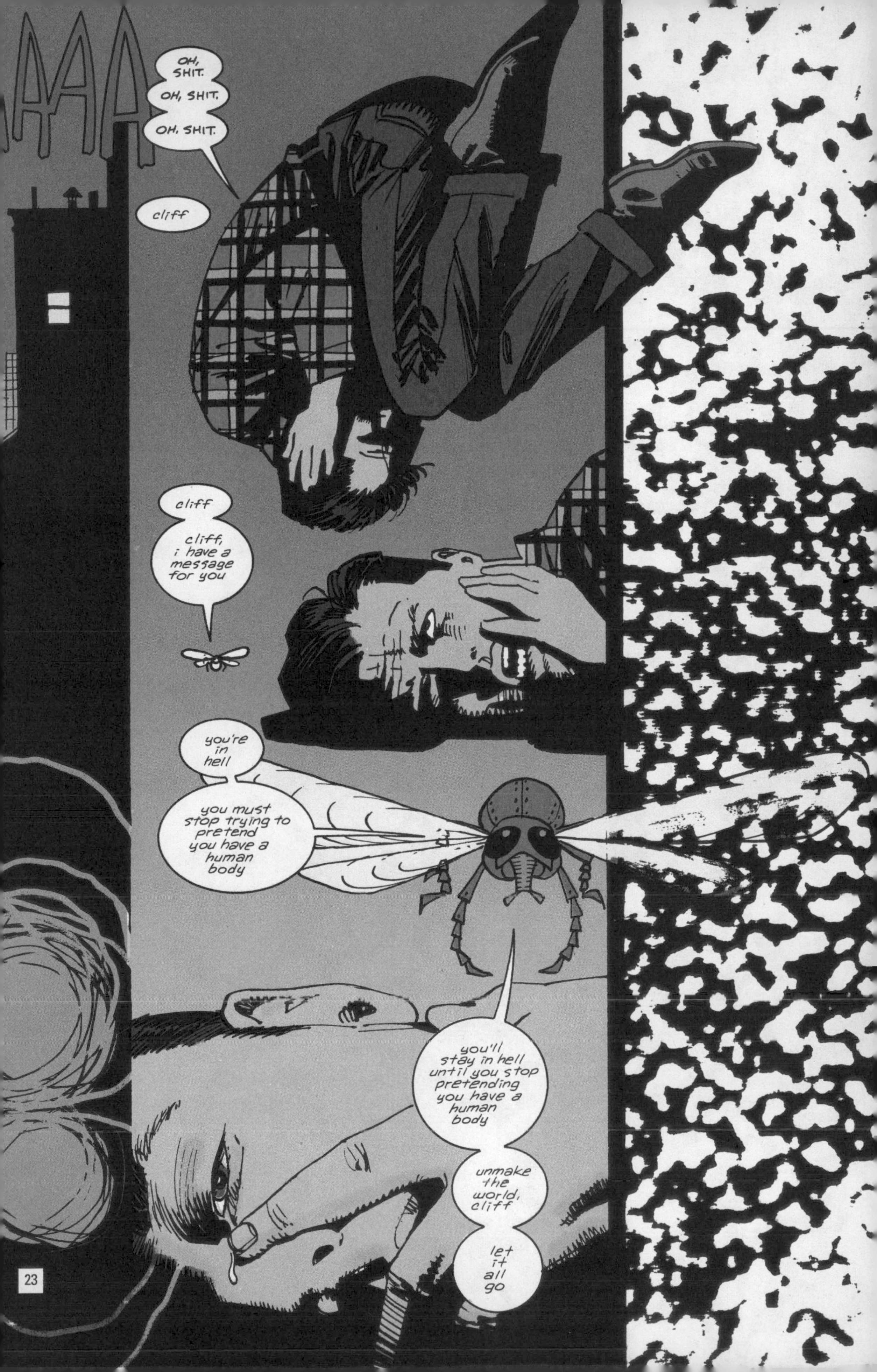
AAA
OH, SHIT.
OH, SHIT.
OH, SHIT.
cliff
cliff
cliff, i have a message for you
you're in hell
you must stop trying to pretend you have a human body
you'll stay in hell until you stop pretending you have a human body
unmake the world, cliff
let it all go

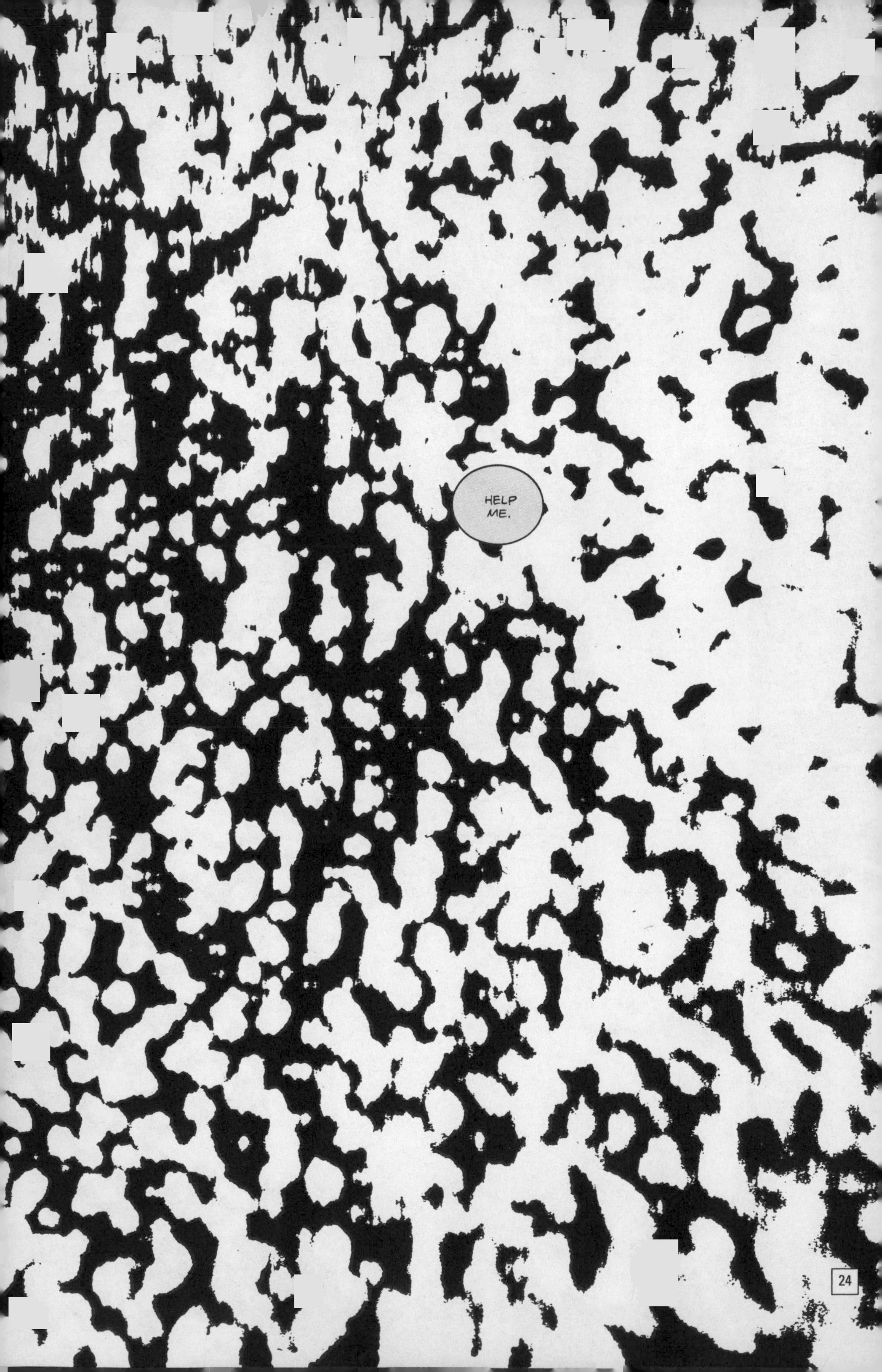
HELP ME.

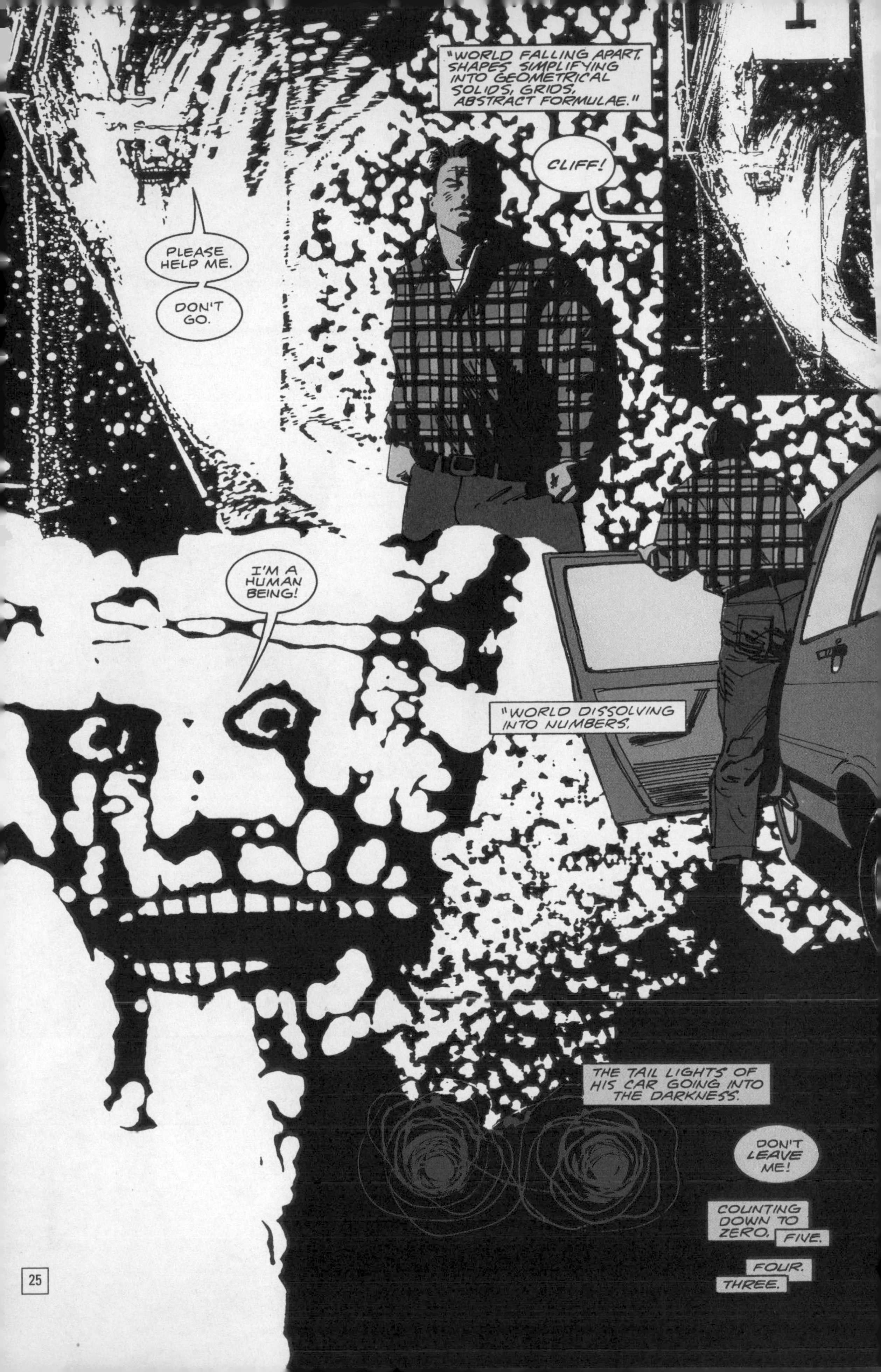

"WORLD FALLING APART. SHAPES SIMPLIFYING INTO GEOMETRICAL SOLIDS, GRIDS, ABSTRACT FORMULAE."
CLIFF!
PLEASE HELP ME.
DON'T GO.
I'M A HUMAN BEING!
"WORLD DISSOLVING INTO NUMBERS."
THE TAIL LIGHTS OF HIS CAR GOING INTO THE DARKNESS.
DON'T LEAVE ME!
COUNTING DOWN TO ZERO.
FIVE.
FOUR.
THREE.

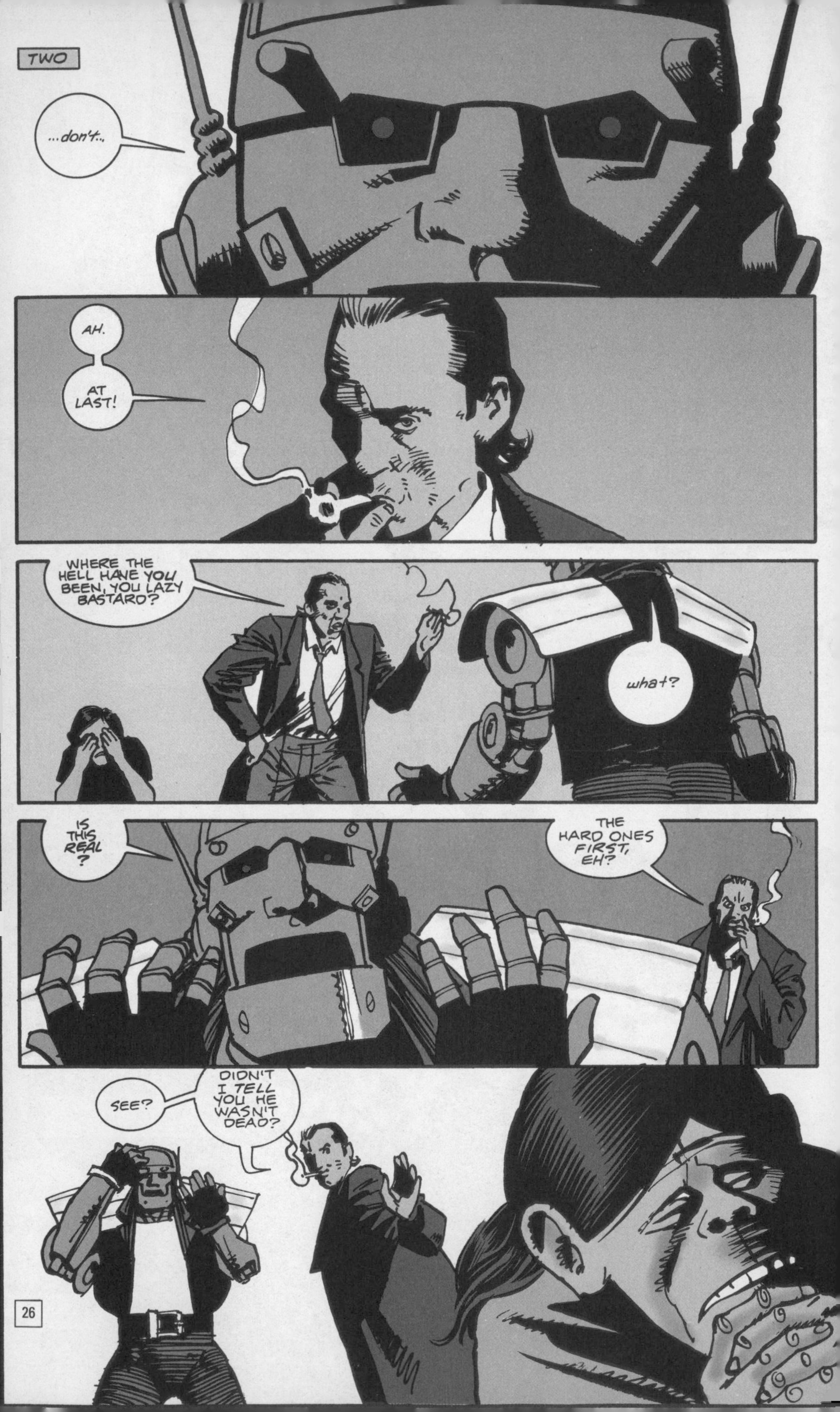
TWO
...don't...
AH.
AT LAST!
WHERE THE HELL HAVE YOU BEEN, YOU LAZY BASTARD?
what?
IS THIS REAL ?
THE HARD ONES FIRST, EH?
SEE?
DIDN'T I TELL YOU HE WASN'T DEAD?

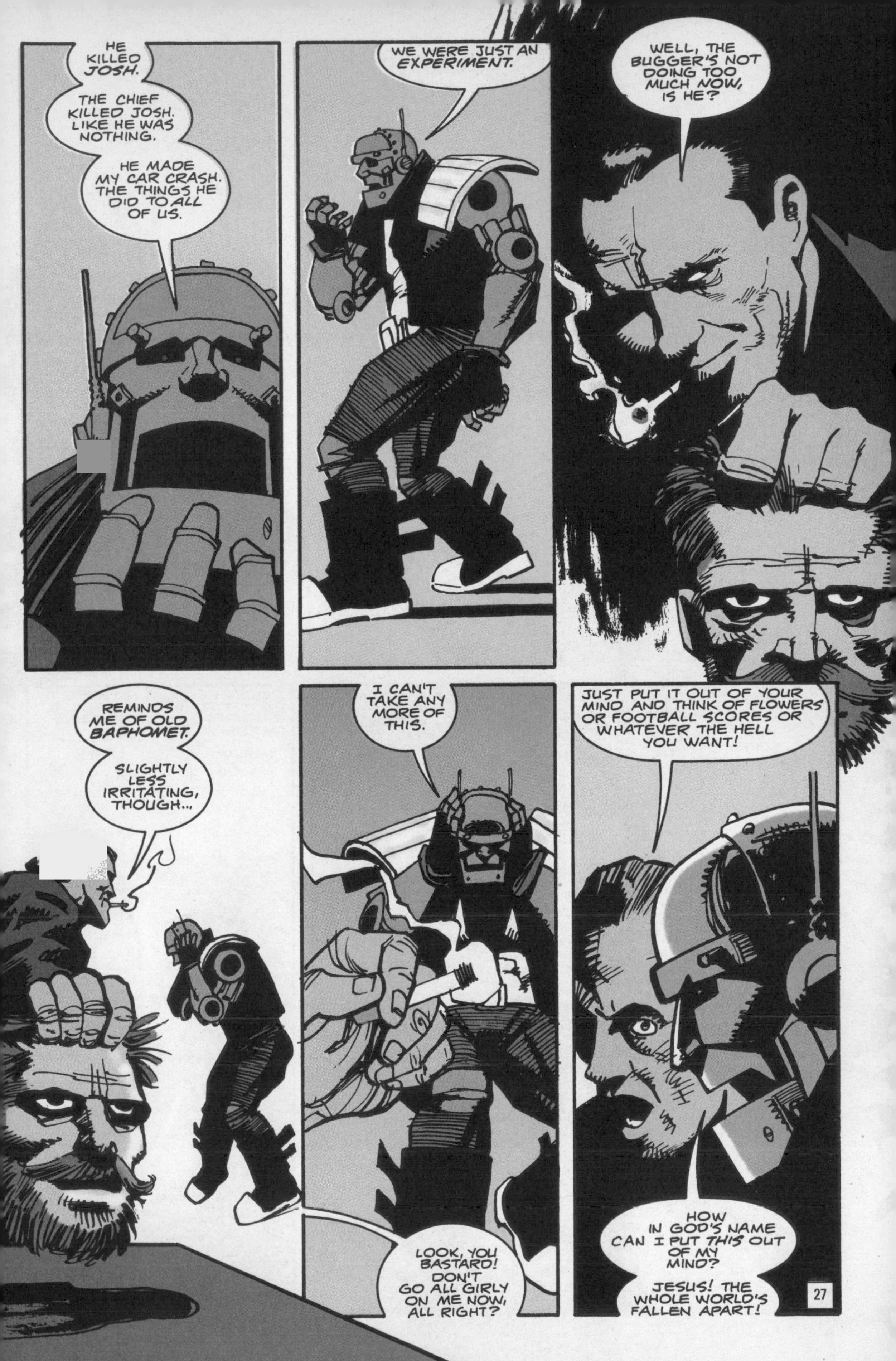
HE KILLED JOSH.
THE CHIEF KILLED JOSH. LIKE HE WAS NOTHING.
HE MADE MY CAR CRASH. THE THINGS HE DID TO ALL OF US.
WE WERE JUST AN EXPERIMENT.
WELL, THE BUGGER'S NOT DOING TOO MUCH NOW, IS HE?
REMINDS ME OF OLD BAPHOMET.
SLIGHTLY LESS IRRITATING, THOUGH...
I CAN'T TAKE ANY MORE OF THIS.
LOOK, YOU BASTARD! DON'T GO ALL GIRLY ON ME NOW, ALL RIGHT?
JUST PUT IT OUT OF YOUR MIND AND THINK OF FLOWERS OR FOOTBALL SCORES OR WHATEVER THE HELL YOU WANT!
HOW IN GOD'S NAME CAN I PUT THIS OUT OF MY MIND?
JESUS! THE WHOLE WORLD'S FALLEN APART!

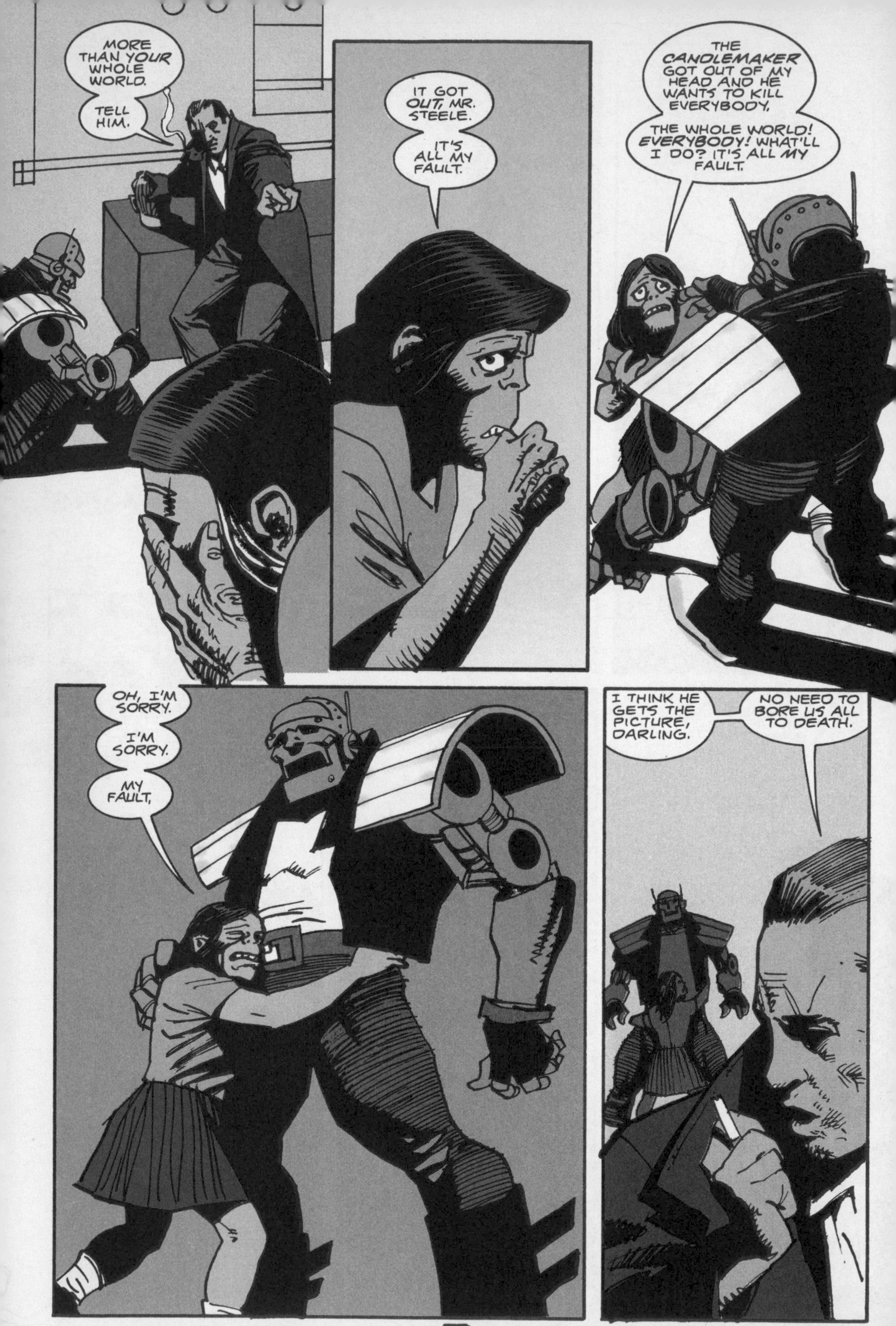
MORE THAN YOUR WHOLE WORLD.
TELL HIM.
IT GOT OUT, MR. STEELE.
IT'S ALL MY FAULT.
THE CANDLEMAKER GOT OUT OF MY HEAD AND HE WANTS TO KILL EVERYBODY.
THE WHOLE WORLD! EVERYBODY! WHAT'LL I DO? IT'S ALL MY FAULT.
OH, I'M SORRY.
I'M SORRY.
MY FAULT.
I THINK HE GETS THE PICTURE, DARLING.
NO NEED TO BORE US ALL TO DEATH.

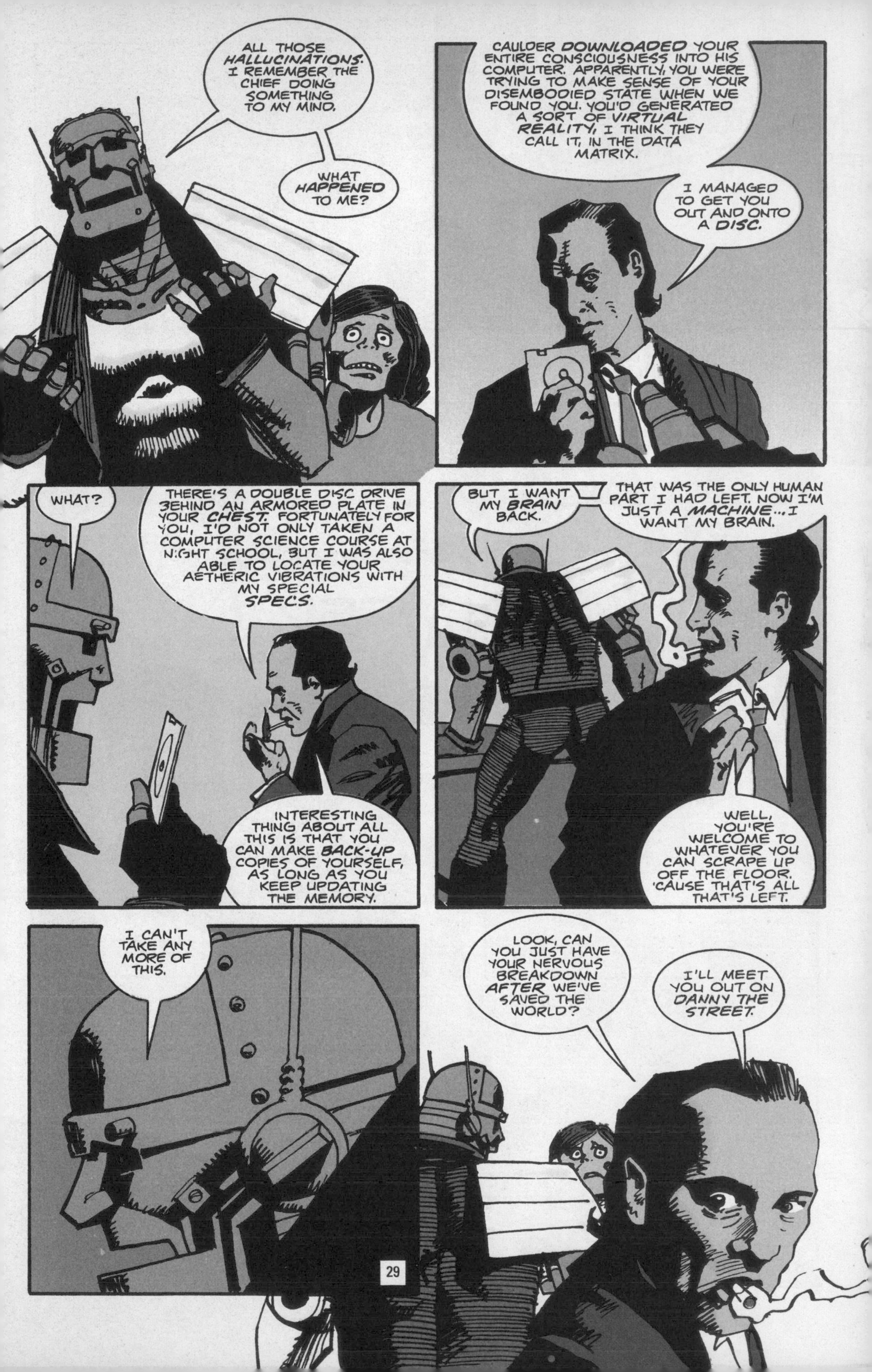
ALL THOSE HALLUCINATIONS. I REMEMBER THE CHIEF DOING SOMETHING TO MY MIND.
WHAT HAPPENED TO ME?
CAULDER DOWNLOADED YOUR ENTIRE CONSCIOUSNESS INTO HIS COMPUTER. APPARENTLY, YOU WERE TRYING TO MAKE SENSE OF YOUR DISEMBODIED STATE WHEN WE FOUND YOU. YOU'D GENERATED A SORT OF VIRTUAL REALITY, I THINK THEY CALL IT, IN THE DATA MATRIX.
I MANAGED TO GET YOU OUT AND ONTO A DISC.
WHAT?
THERE'S A DOUBLE DISC DRIVE BEHIND AN ARMORED PLATE IN YOUR CHEST. FORTUNATELY FOR YOU, I'D NOT ONLY TAKEN A COMPUTER SCIENCE COURSE AT NIGHT SCHOOL, BUT I WAS ALSO ABLE TO LOCATE YOUR AETHERIC VIBRATIONS WITH MY SPECIAL SPECS.
INTERESTING THING ABOUT ALL THIS IS THAT YOU CAN MAKE BACK-UP COPIES OF YOURSELF, AS LONG AS YOU KEEP UPDATING THE MEMORY.
BUT I WANT MY BRAIN BACK.
THAT WAS THE ONLY HUMAN PART I HAD LEFT. NOW I'M JUST A MACHINE... I WANT MY BRAIN.
WELL, YOU'RE WELCOME TO WHATEVER YOU CAN SCRAPE UP OFF THE FLOOR. 'CAUSE THAT'S ALL THAT'S LEFT.
I CAN'T TAKE ANY MORE OF THIS.
LOOK, CAN YOU JUST HAVE YOUR NERVOUS BREAKDOWN AFTER WE'VE SAVED THE WORLD?
I'LL MEET YOU OUT ON DANNY THE STREET.

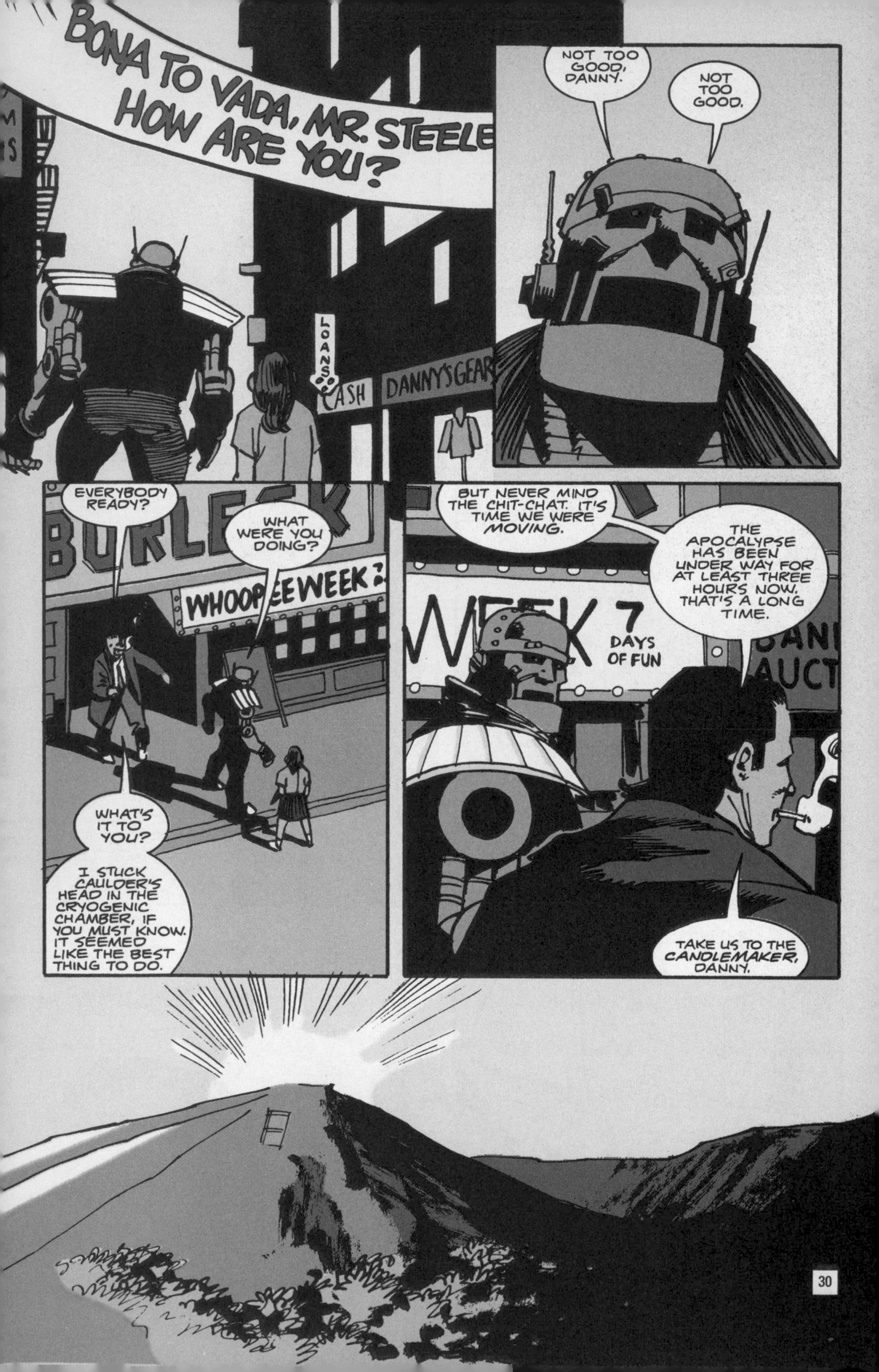
BONA TO VADA, MR. STEELE. HOW ARE YOU?
LOANS
CASH
DANNY'S GEAR
NOT TOO GOOD, DANNY.
NOT TOO GOOD.
BURLESK
WHOOPEE WEEK
EVERYBODY READY?
WHAT WERE YOU DOING?
WHAT'S IT TO YOU?
I STUCK CAULDER'S HEAD IN THE CRYOGENIC CHAMBER, IF YOU MUST KNOW. IT SEEMED LIKE THE BEST THING TO DO.
WEEK 7 DAYS OF FUN
BUT NEVER MIND THE CHIT-CHAT. IT'S TIME WE WERE MOVING.
THE APOCALYPSE HAS BEEN UNDER WAY FOR AT LEAST THREE HOURS NOW. THAT'S A LONG TIME.
TAKE US TO THE CANDLEMAKER, DANNY.

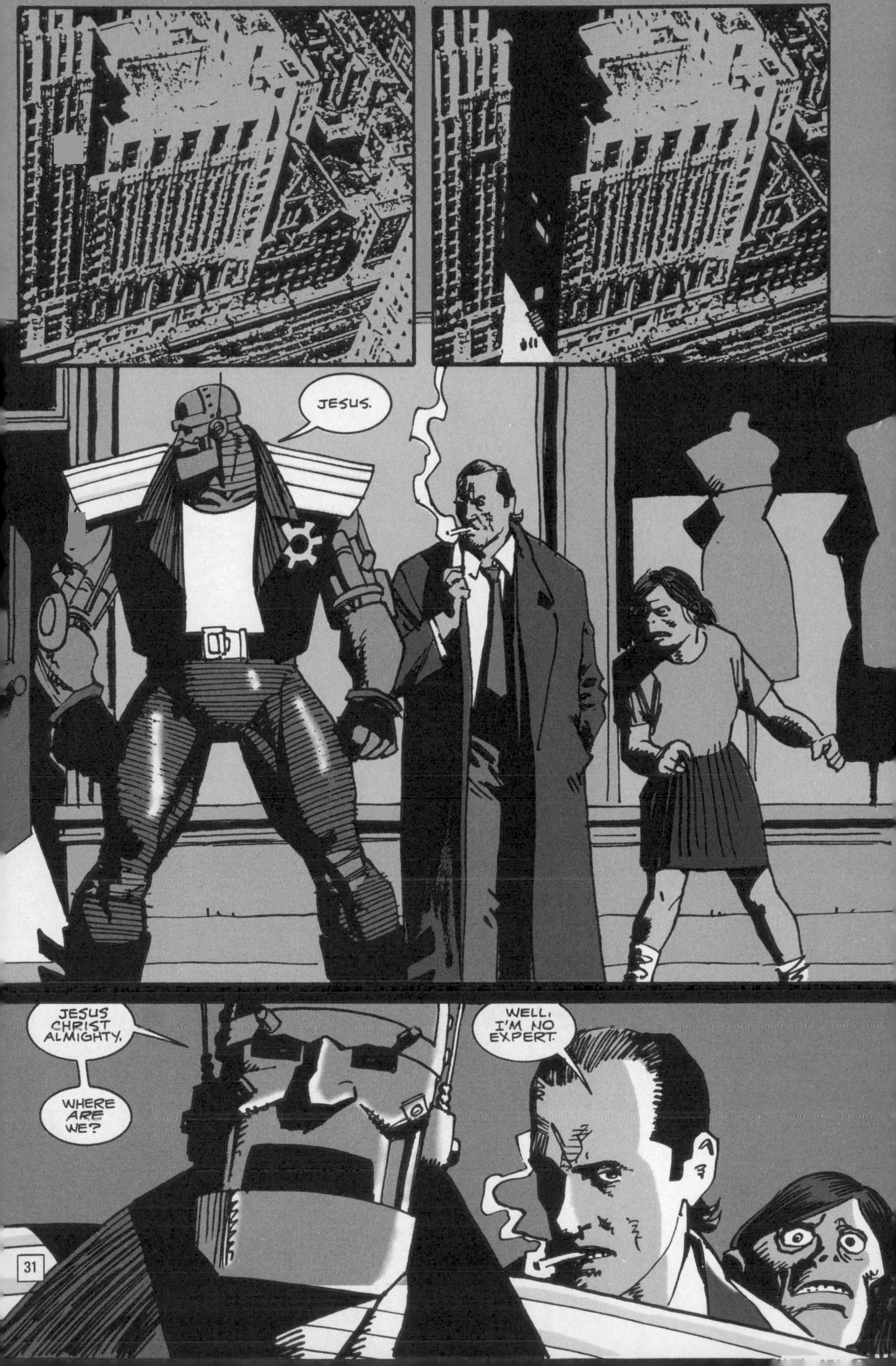
JESUS.
JESUS CHRIST ALMIGHTY.
WHERE ARE WE?
WELL, I'M NO EXPERT.

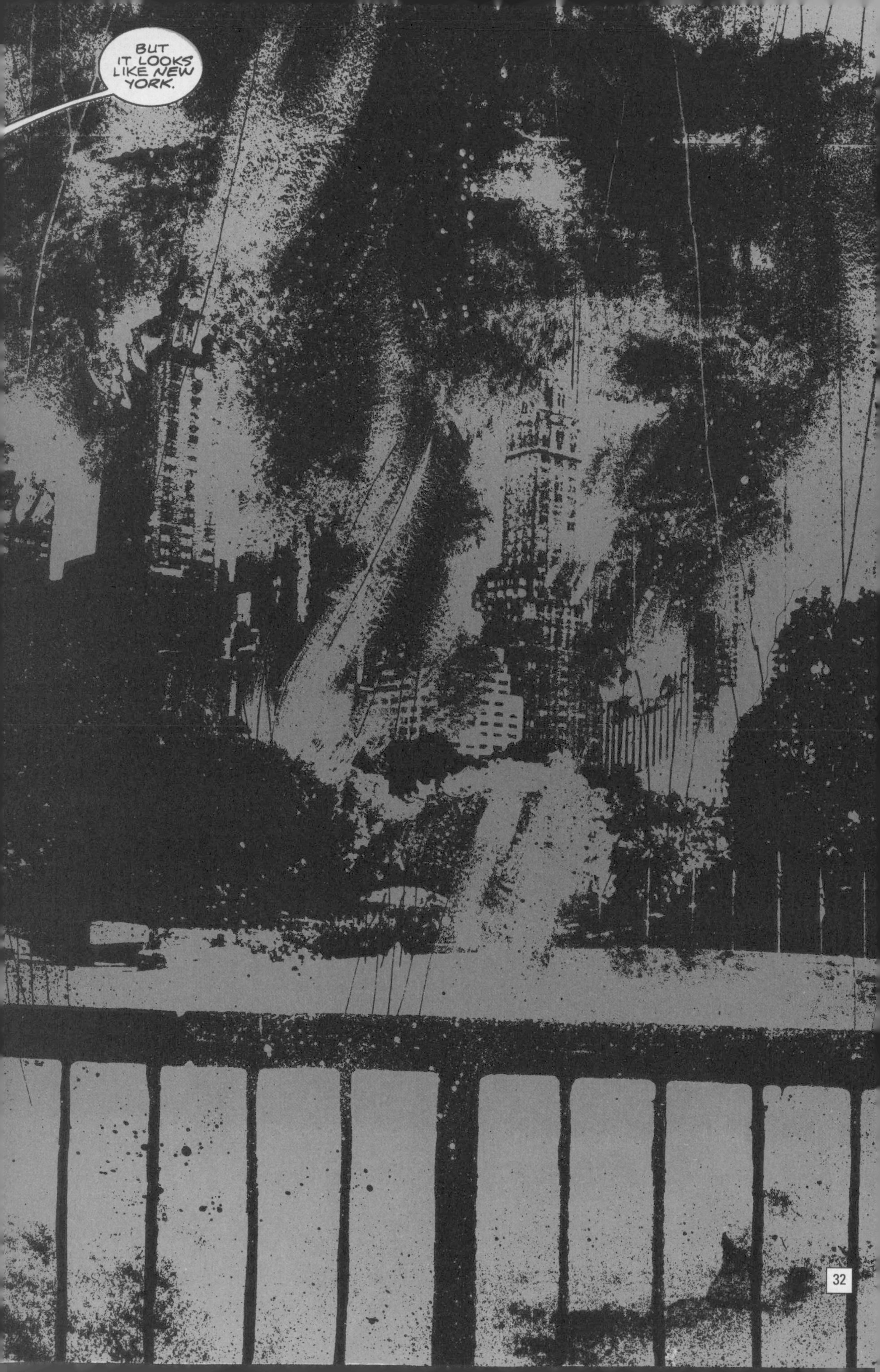
BUT IT LOOKS LIKE NEW YORK.

Nothing."

"How dare you approach me. You're nothing. You're like the rest. Not real.

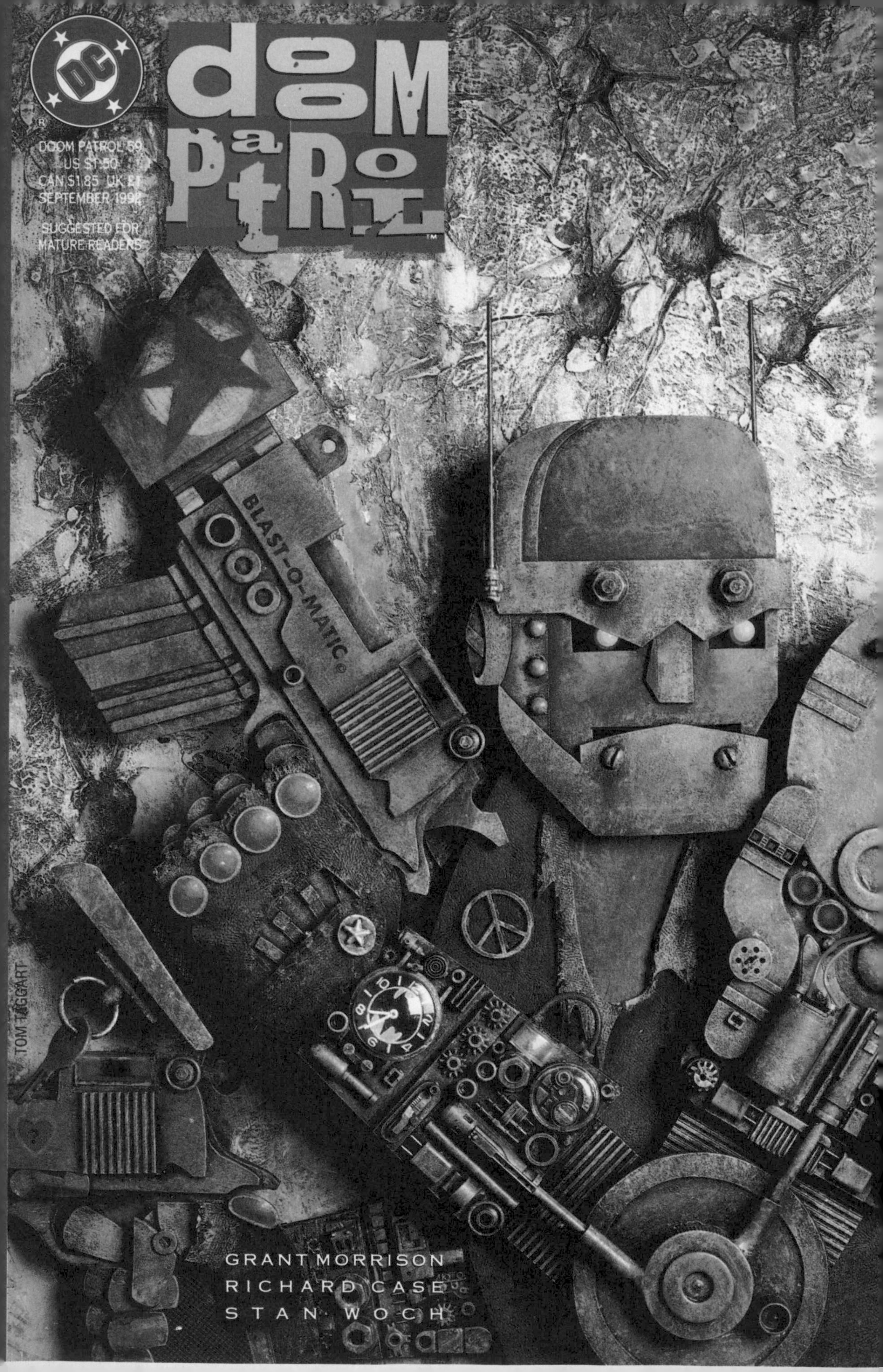
DOOM PATROL
DOOM PATROL 59
US $1.50
CAN $1.85 UK £1
SEPTEMBER 1992
SUGGESTED FOR MATURE READERS
BLAST-O-MATIC
TOM TAGGART
GRANT MORRISON
RICHARD CASE
STAN WOCH

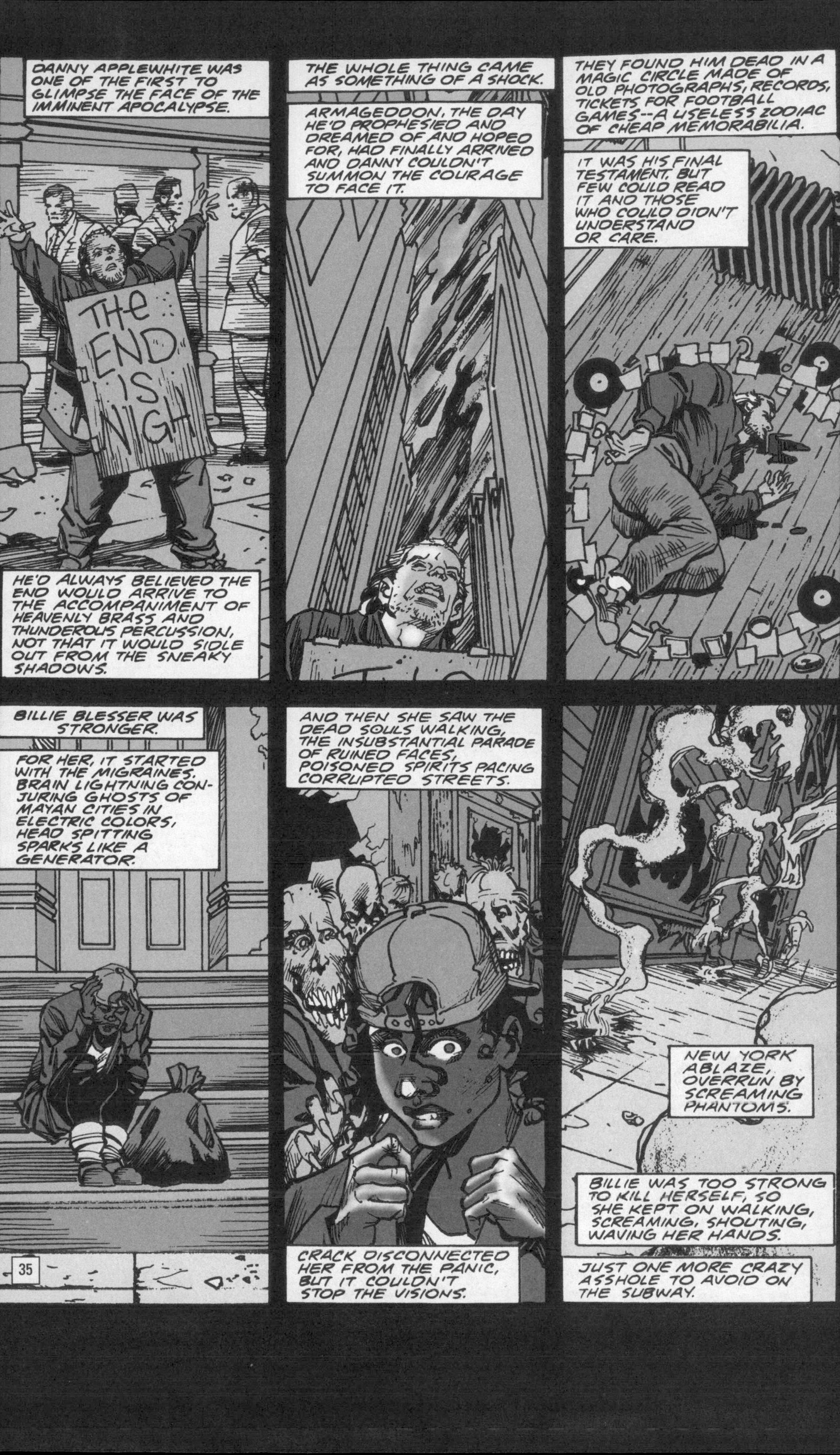
DANNY APPLEWHITE WAS ONE OF THE FIRST TO GLIMPSE THE FACE OF THE IMMINENT APOCALYPSE.
THE END IS NIGH
HE'D ALWAYS BELIEVED THE END WOULD ARRIVE TO THE ACCOMPANIMENT OF HEAVENLY BRASS AND THUNDEROUS PERCUSSION, NOT THAT IT WOULD SIDLE OUT FROM THE SNEAKY SHADOWS.
THE WHOLE THING CAME AS SOMETHING OF A SHOCK.
ARMAGEDDON, THE DAY HE'D PROPHESIED AND DREAMED OF AND HOPED FOR, HAD FINALLY ARRIVED AND DANNY COULDN'T SUMMON THE COURAGE TO FACE IT.
THEY FOUND HIM DEAD IN A MAGIC CIRCLE MADE OF OLD PHOTOGRAPHS, RECORDS, TICKETS FOR FOOTBALL GAMES--A USELESS ZODIAC OF CHEAP MEMORABILIA.
IT WAS HIS FINAL TESTAMENT, BUT FEW COULD READ IT AND THOSE WHO COULD DIDN'T UNDERSTAND OR CARE.
BILLIE BLESSER WAS STRONGER.
FOR HER, IT STARTED WITH THE MIGRAINES. BRAIN LIGHTNING CONJURING GHOSTS OF MAYAN CITIES IN ELECTRIC COLORS, HEAD SPITTING SPARKS LIKE A GENERATOR.
AND THEN SHE SAW THE DEAD SOULS WALKING, THE INSUBSTANTIAL PARADE OF RUINED FACES, POISONED SPIRITS PACING CORRUPTED STREETS.
CRACK DISCONNECTED HER FROM THE PANIC, BUT IT COULDN'T STOP THE VISIONS.
NEW YORK ABLAZE, OVERRUN BY SCREAMING PHANTOMS.
BILLIE WAS TOO STRONG TO KILL HERSELF, SO SHE KEPT ON WALKING, SCREAMING, SHOUTING, WAVING HER HANDS.
JUST ONE MORE CRAZY ASSHOLE TO AVOID ON THE SUBWAY.

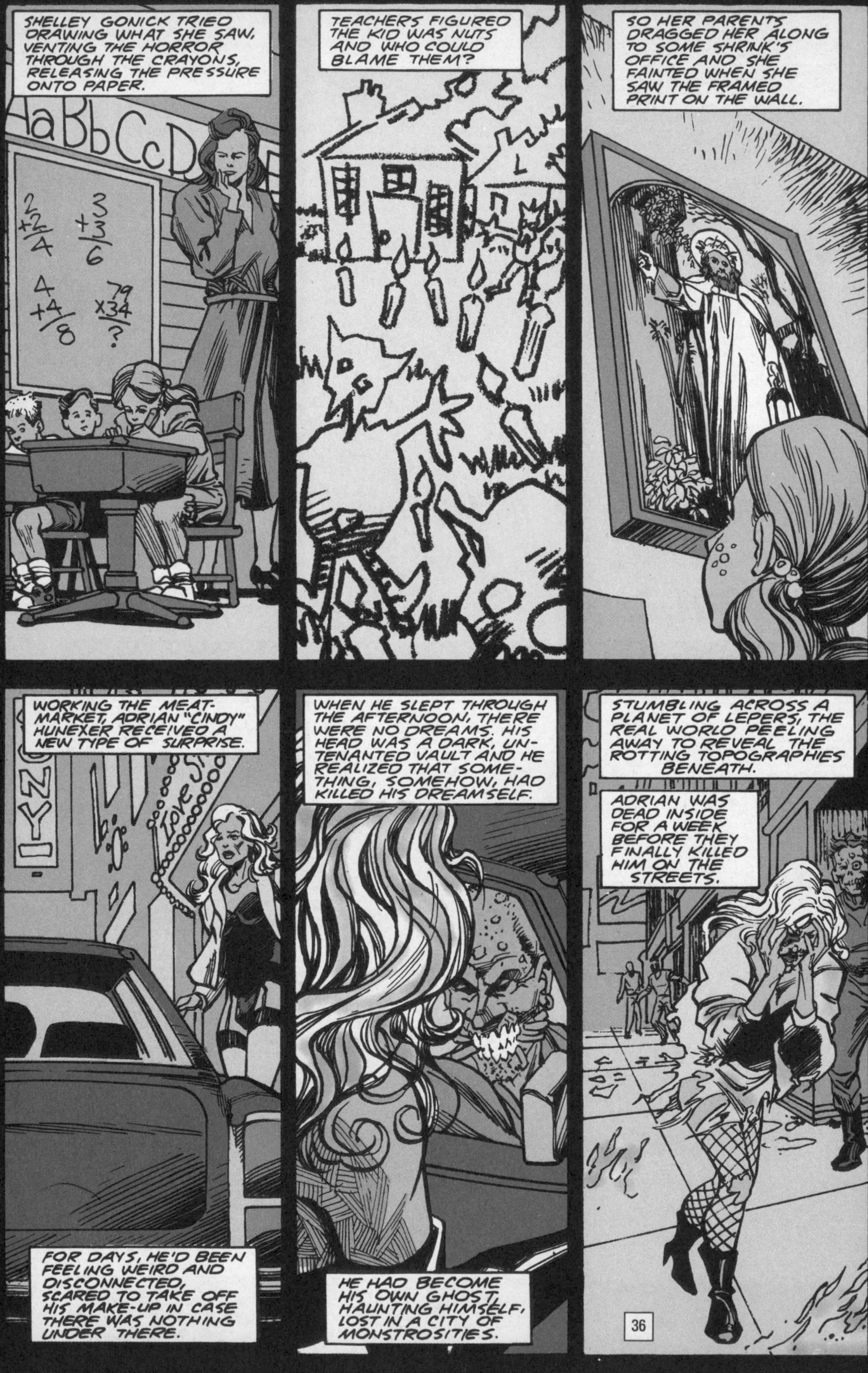

SHELLEY GONICK TRIED DRAWING WHAT SHE SAW, VENTING THE HORROR THROUGH THE CRAYONS, RELEASING THE PRESSURE ONTO PAPER.
AaBbCcD
2 +2 4
3 +3 6
4 +4 8
79 x34 ?
TEACHERS FIGURED THE KID WAS NUTS AND WHO COULD BLAME THEM?
SO HER PARENTS DRAGGED HER ALONG TO SOME SHRINK'S OFFICE AND SHE FAINTED WHEN SHE SAW THE FRAMED PRINT ON THE WALL.
WORKING THE MEAT-MARKET, ADRIAN "CINDY" HUNEXER RECEIVED A NEW TYPE OF SURPRISE.
FOR DAYS, HE'D BEEN FEELING WEIRD AND DISCONNECTED, SCARED TO TAKE OFF HIS MAKE-UP IN CASE THERE WAS NOTHING UNDER THERE.
WHEN HE SLEPT THROUGH THE AFTERNOON, THERE WERE NO DREAMS. HIS HEAD WAS A DARK, UN-TENANTED VAULT AND HE REALIZED THAT SOME-THING, SOMEHOW, HAD KILLED HIS DREAMSELF.
HE HAD BECOME HIS OWN GHOST, HAUNTING HIMSELF, LOST IN A CITY OF MONSTROSITIES.
STUMBLING ACROSS A PLANET OF LEPERS, THE REAL WORLD PEELING AWAY TO REVEAL THE ROTTING TOPOGRAPHIES BENEATH.
ADRIAN WAS DEAD INSIDE FOR A WEEK BEFORE THEY FINALLY KILLED HIM ON THE STREETS.

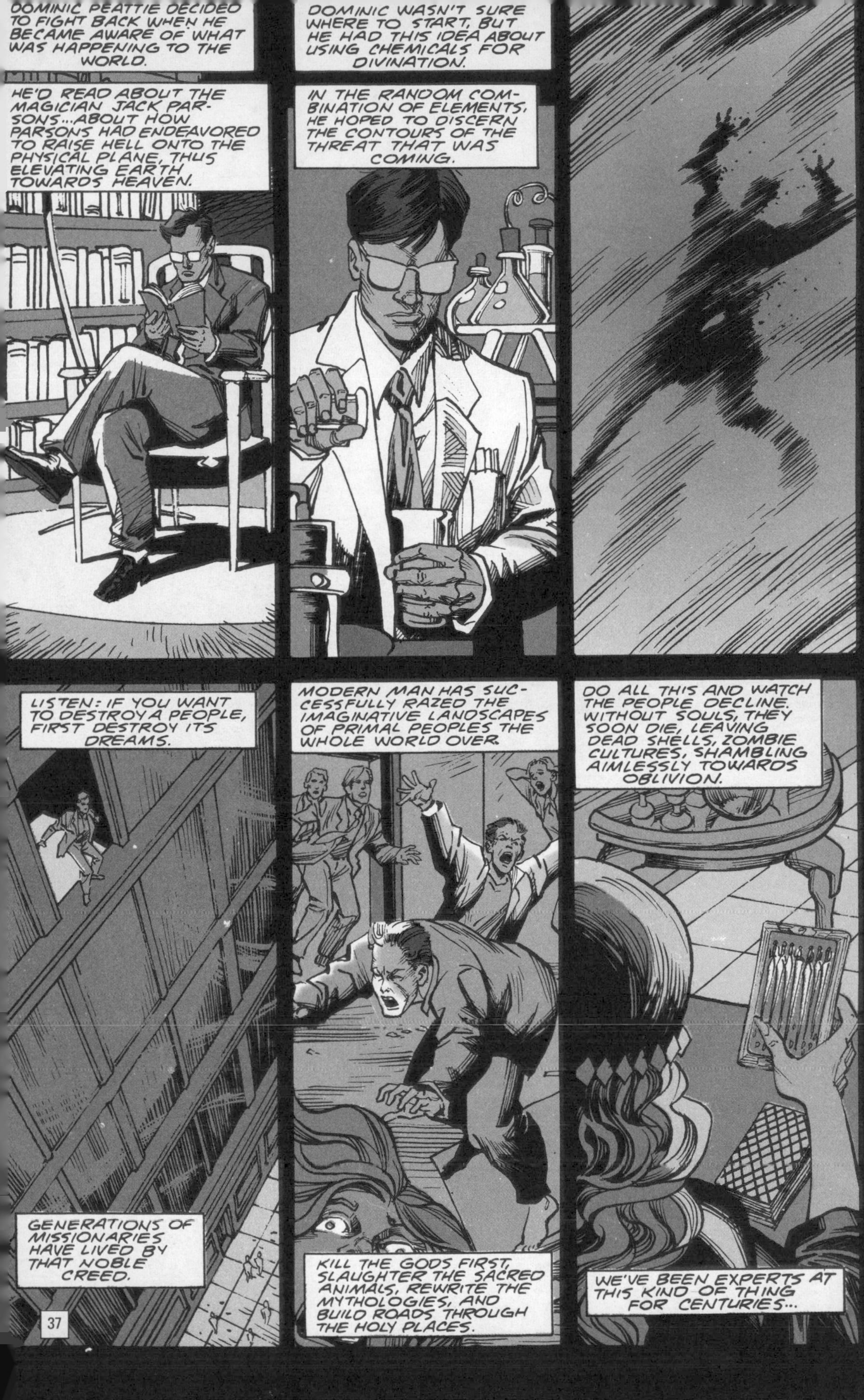
DOMINIC PEATTIE DECIDED TO FIGHT BACK WHEN HE BECAME AWARE OF WHAT WAS HAPPENING TO THE WORLD.
HE'D READ ABOUT THE MAGICIAN JACK PARSONS...ABOUT HOW PARSONS HAD ENDEAVORED TO RAISE HELL ONTO THE PHYSICAL PLANE, THUS ELEVATING EARTH TOWARDS HEAVEN.
DOMINIC WASN'T SURE WHERE TO START, BUT HE HAD THIS IDEA ABOUT USING CHEMICALS FOR DIVINATION.
IN THE RANDOM COMBINATION OF ELEMENTS, HE HOPED TO DISCERN THE CONTOURS OF THE THREAT THAT WAS COMING.
LISTEN: IF YOU WANT TO DESTROY A PEOPLE, FIRST DESTROY ITS DREAMS.
GENERATIONS OF MISSIONARIES HAVE LIVED BY THAT NOBLE CREED.
MODERN MAN HAS SUCCESSFULLY RAZED THE IMAGINATIVE LANDSCAPES OF PRIMAL PEOPLES THE WHOLE WORLD OVER.
KILL THE GODS FIRST, SLAUGHTER THE SACRED ANIMALS, REWRITE THE MYTHOLOGIES, AND BUILD ROADS THROUGH THE HOLY PLACES.
DO ALL THIS AND WATCH THE PEOPLE DECLINE. WITHOUT SOULS, THEY SOON DIE, LEAVING DEAD SHELLS, ZOMBIE CULTURES, SHAMBLING AIMLESSLY TOWARDS OBLIVION.
WE'VE BEEN EXPERTS AT THIS KIND OF THING FOR CENTURIES...

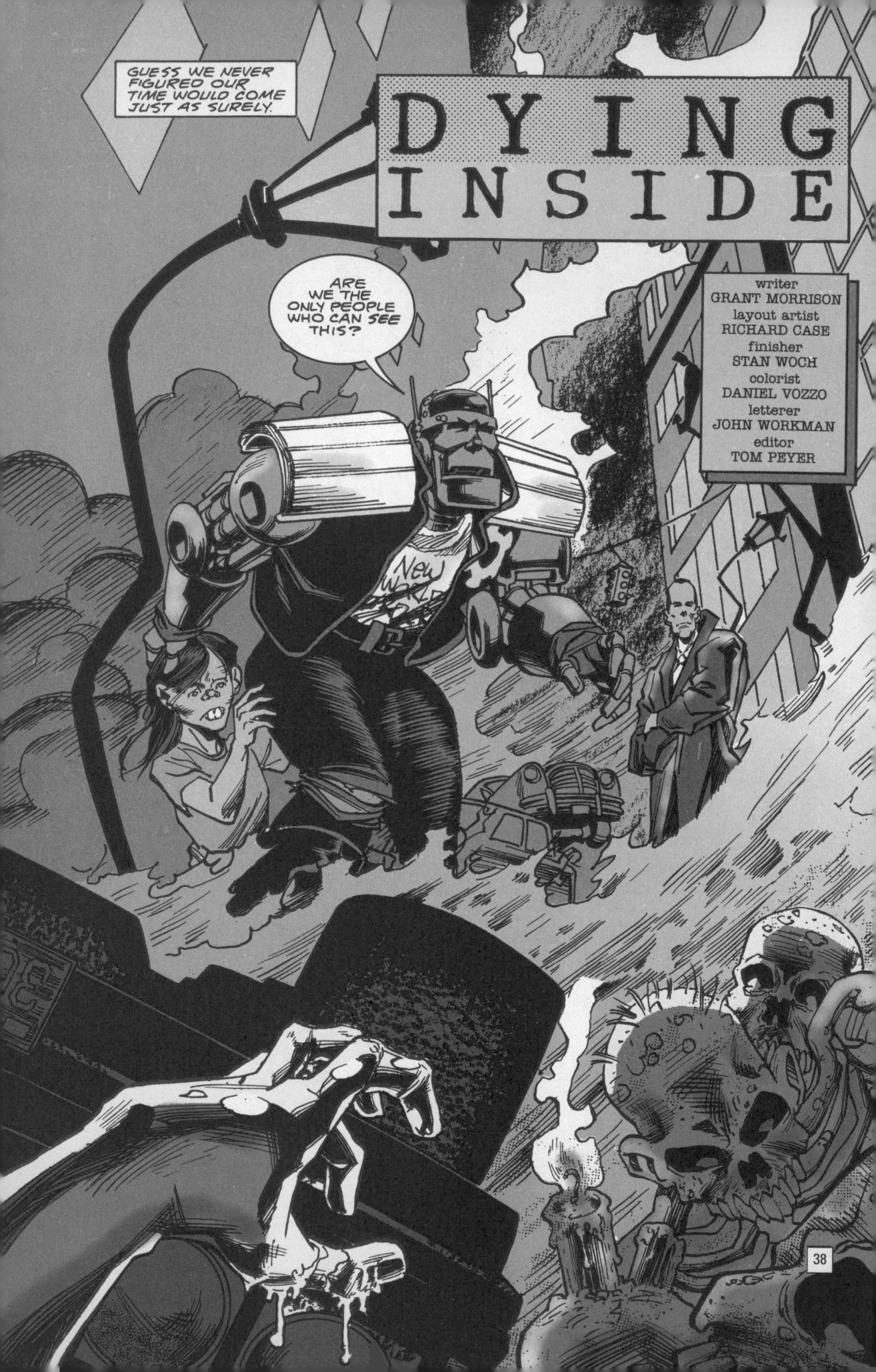
GUESS WE NEVER FIGURED OUR TIME WOULD COME JUST AS SURELY.
DYING INSIDE
ARE WE THE ONLY PEOPLE WHO CAN SEE THIS?
writer GRANT MORRISON
layout artist RICHARD CASE
finisher STAN WOCH
colorist DANIEL VOZZO
letterer JOHN WORKMAN
editor TOM PEYER

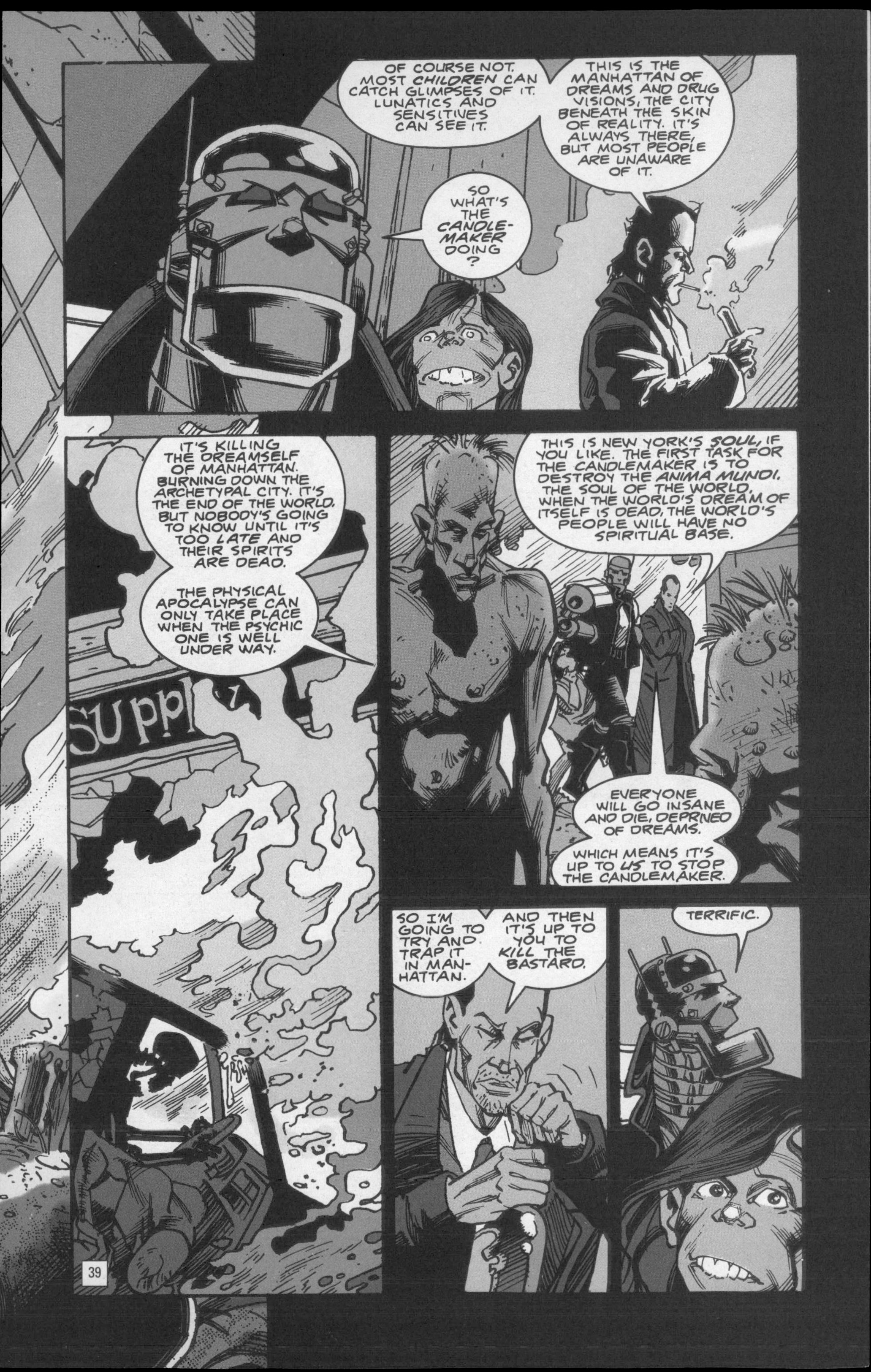
OF COURSE NOT. MOST CHILDREN CAN CATCH GLIMPSES OF IT. LUNATICS AND SENSITIVES CAN SEE IT.
THIS IS THE MANHATTAN OF DREAMS AND DRUG VISIONS, THE CITY BENEATH THE SKIN OF REALITY. IT'S ALWAYS THERE, BUT MOST PEOPLE ARE UNAWARE OF IT.
SO WHAT'S THE CANDLE-MAKER DOING?
IT'S KILLING THE DREAMSELF OF MANHATTAN. BURNING DOWN THE ARCHETYPAL CITY. IT'S THE END OF THE WORLD, BUT NOBODY'S GOING TO KNOW UNTIL IT'S TOO LATE AND THEIR SPIRITS ARE DEAD.
THE PHYSICAL APOCALYPSE CAN ONLY TAKE PLACE WHEN THE PSYCHIC ONE IS WELL UNDER WAY.
SUPPI
THIS IS NEW YORK'S SOUL, IF YOU LIKE. THE FIRST TASK FOR THE CANDLEMAKER IS TO DESTROY THE ANIMA MUNDI, THE SOUL OF THE WORLD. WHEN THE WORLD'S DREAM OF ITSELF IS DEAD, THE WORLD'S PEOPLE WILL HAVE NO SPIRITUAL BASE.
EVERYONE WILL GO INSANE AND DIE, DEPRIVED OF DREAMS.
WHICH MEANS IT'S UP TO US TO STOP THE CANDLEMAKER.
SO I'M GOING TO TRY AND TRAP IT IN MAN-HATTAN.
AND THEN IT'S UP TO YOU TO KILL THE BASTARD.
TERRIFIC.

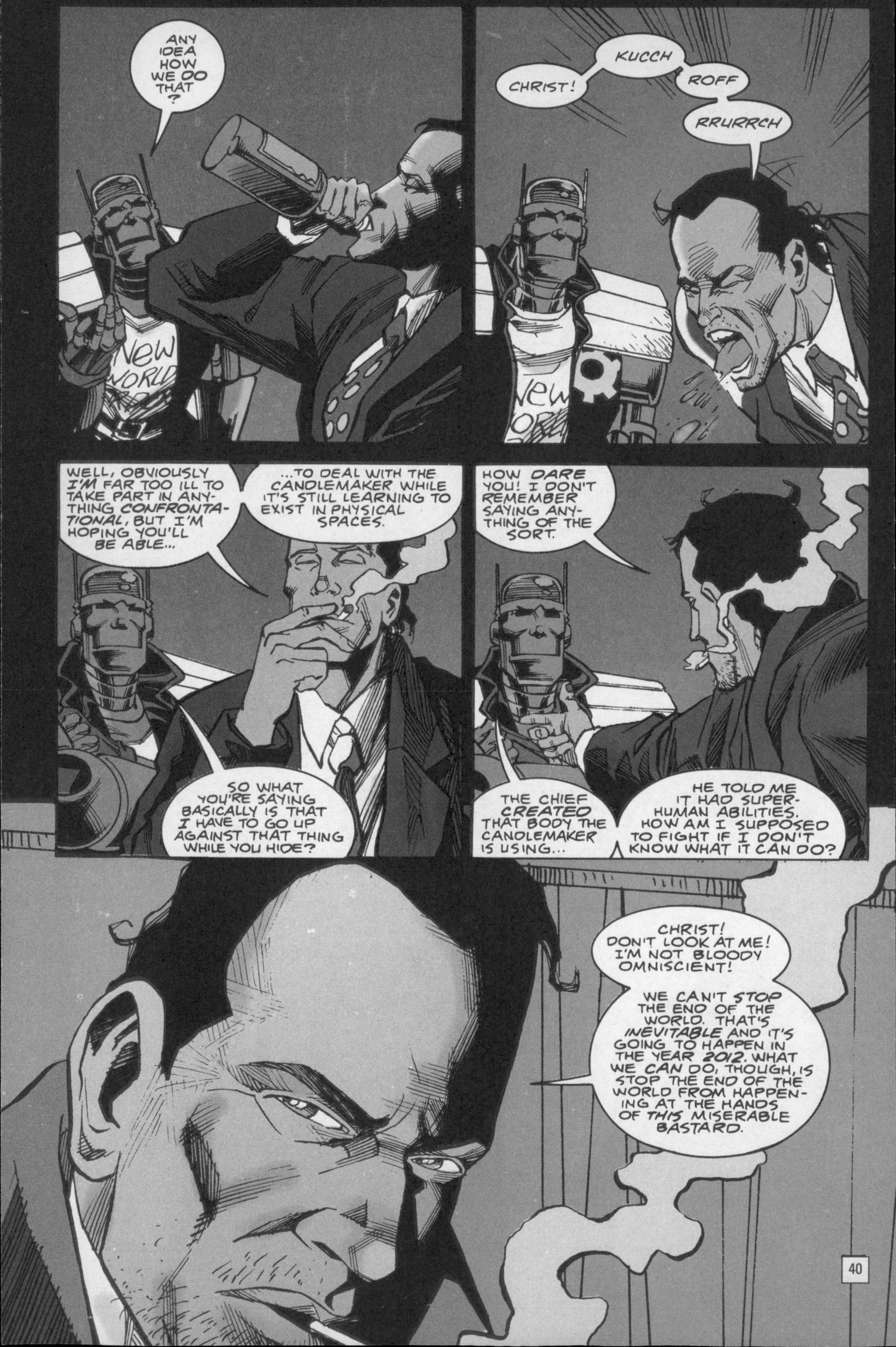
ANY IDEA HOW WE DO THAT?
CHRIST!
KUCCH
ROFF
RRURRCH
WELL, OBVIOUSLY I'M FAR TOO ILL TO TAKE PART IN ANYTHING CONFRONTATIONAL, BUT I'M HOPING YOU'LL BE ABLE...
...TO DEAL WITH THE CANDLEMAKER WHILE IT'S STILL LEARNING TO EXIST IN PHYSICAL SPACES.
SO WHAT YOU'RE SAYING BASICALLY IS THAT I HAVE TO GO UP AGAINST THAT THING WHILE YOU HIDE?
HOW DARE YOU! I DON'T REMEMBER SAYING ANYTHING OF THE SORT.
THE CHIEF CREATED THAT BODY THE CANDLEMAKER IS USING...
HE TOLD ME IT HAD SUPER-HUMAN ABILITIES. HOW AM I SUPPOSED TO FIGHT IF I DON'T KNOW WHAT IT CAN DO?
CHRIST! DON'T LOOK AT ME! I'M NOT BLOODY OMNISCIENT!
WE CAN'T STOP THE END OF THE WORLD. THAT'S INEVITABLE AND IT'S GOING TO HAPPEN IN THE YEAR 2012. WHAT WE CAN DO, THOUGH, IS STOP THE END OF THE WORLD FROM HAPPENING AT THE HANDS OF THIS MISERABLE BASTARD.

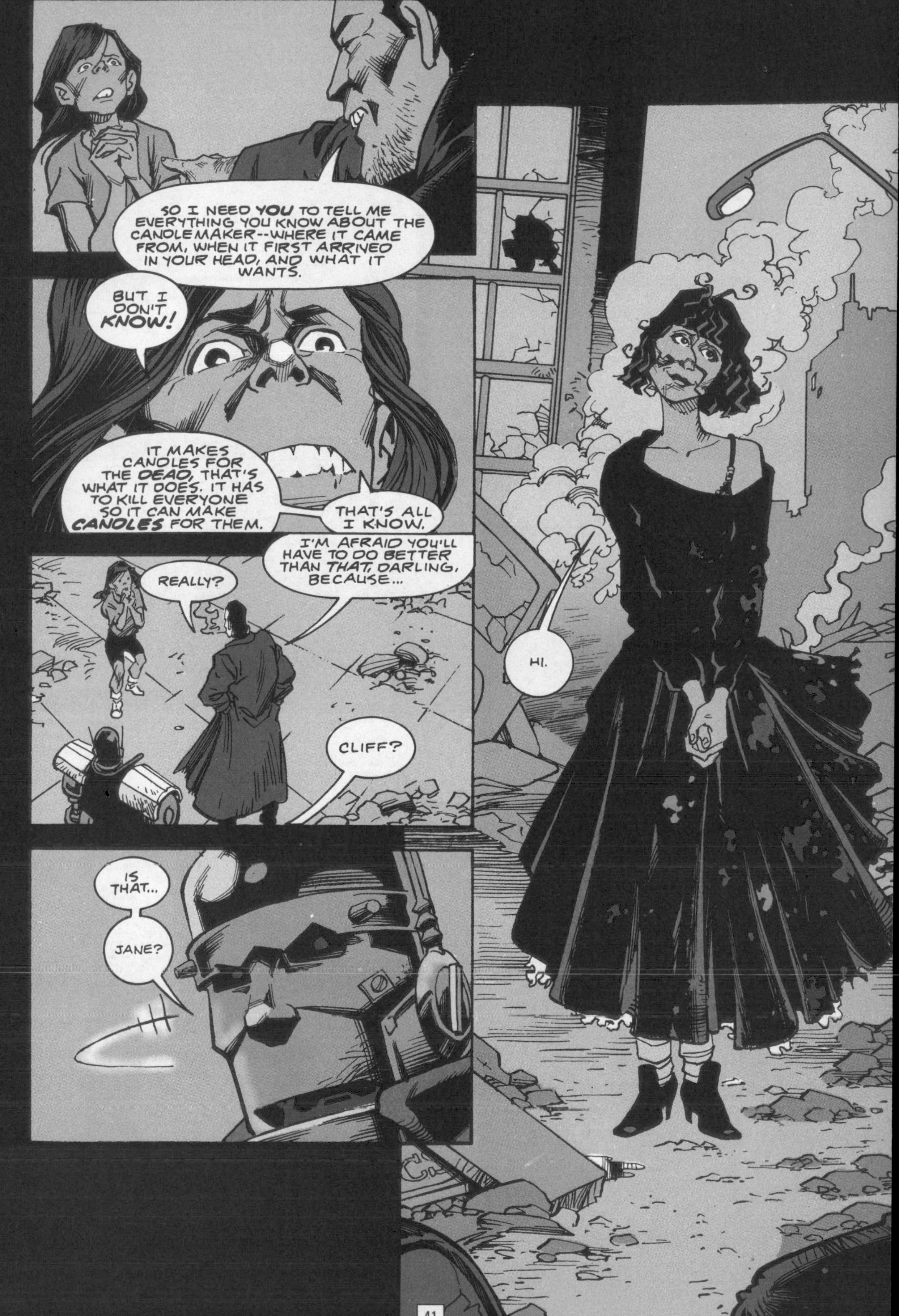
SO I NEED YOU TO TELL ME EVERYTHING YOU KNOW ABOUT THE CANDLEMAKER--WHERE IT CAME FROM, WHEN IT FIRST ARRIVED IN YOUR HEAD, AND WHAT IT WANTS.
BUT I DON'T KNOW!
IT MAKES CANDLES FOR THE DEAD, THAT'S WHAT IT DOES. IT HAS TO KILL EVERYONE SO IT CAN MAKE CANDLES FOR THEM.
THAT'S ALL I KNOW.
REALLY?
I'M AFRAID YOU'LL HAVE TO DO BETTER THAN THAT, DARLING, BECAUSE...
CLIFF?
IS THAT...
JANE?
HI.

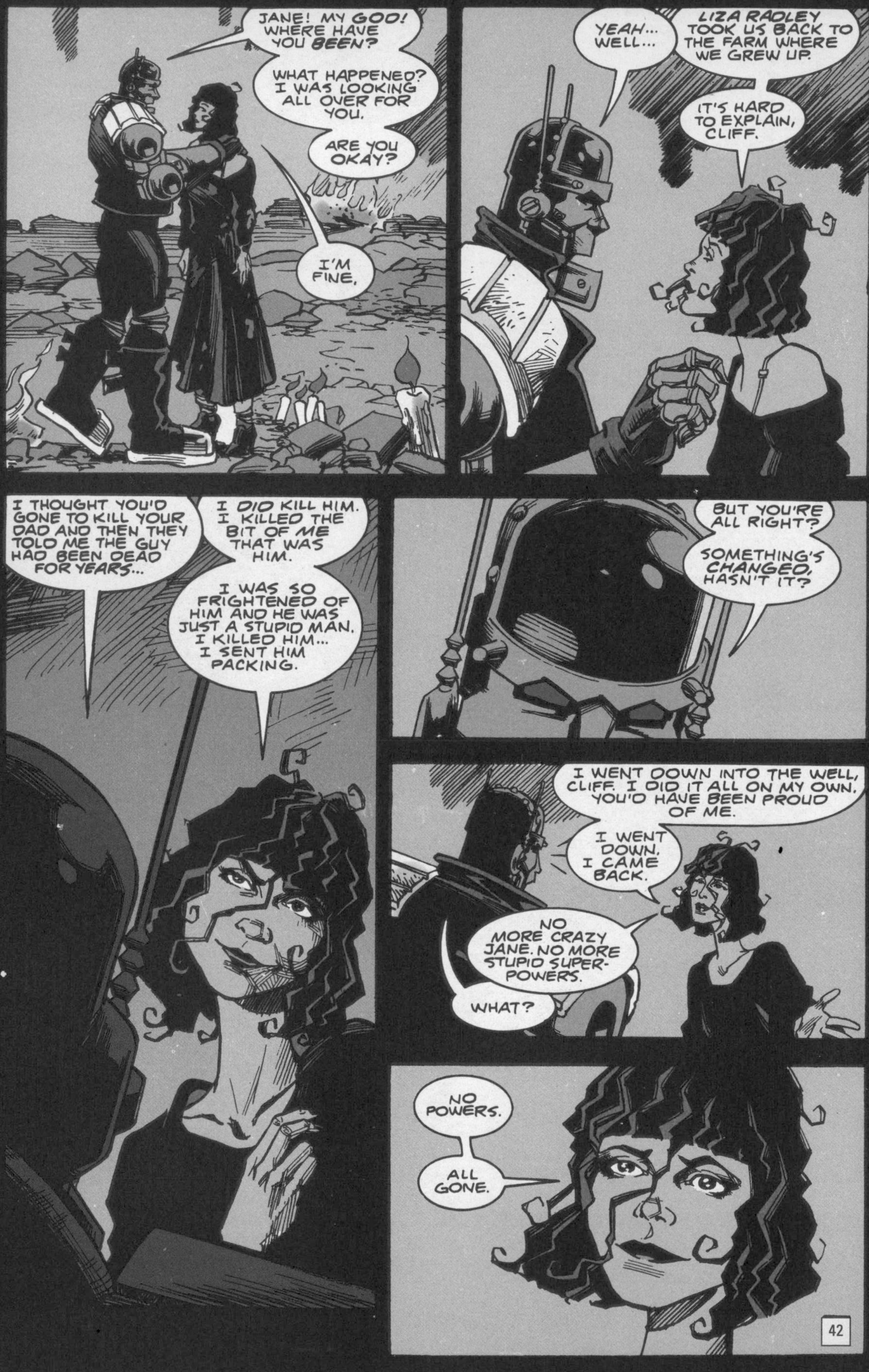
JANE! MY GOD! WHERE HAVE YOU BEEN?
WHAT HAPPENED? I WAS LOOKING ALL OVER FOR YOU.
ARE YOU OKAY?
I'M FINE.
YEAH... WELL...
LIZA RADLEY TOOK US BACK TO THE FARM WHERE WE GREW UP.
IT'S HARD TO EXPLAIN, CLIFF.
I THOUGHT YOU'D GONE TO KILL YOUR DAD AND THEN THEY TOLD ME THE GUY HAD BEEN DEAD FOR YEARS...
I DID KILL HIM. I KILLED THE BIT OF ME THAT WAS HIM.
I WAS SO FRIGHTENED OF HIM AND HE WAS JUST A STUPID MAN. I KILLED HIM... I SENT HIM PACKING.
BUT YOU'RE ALL RIGHT?
SOMETHING'S CHANGED, HASN'T IT?
I WENT DOWN INTO THE WELL, CLIFF. I DID IT ALL ON MY OWN. YOU'D HAVE BEEN PROUD OF ME.
I WENT DOWN. I CAME BACK.
NO MORE CRAZY JANE. NO MORE STUPID SUPER-POWERS.
WHAT?
NO POWERS.
ALL GONE.

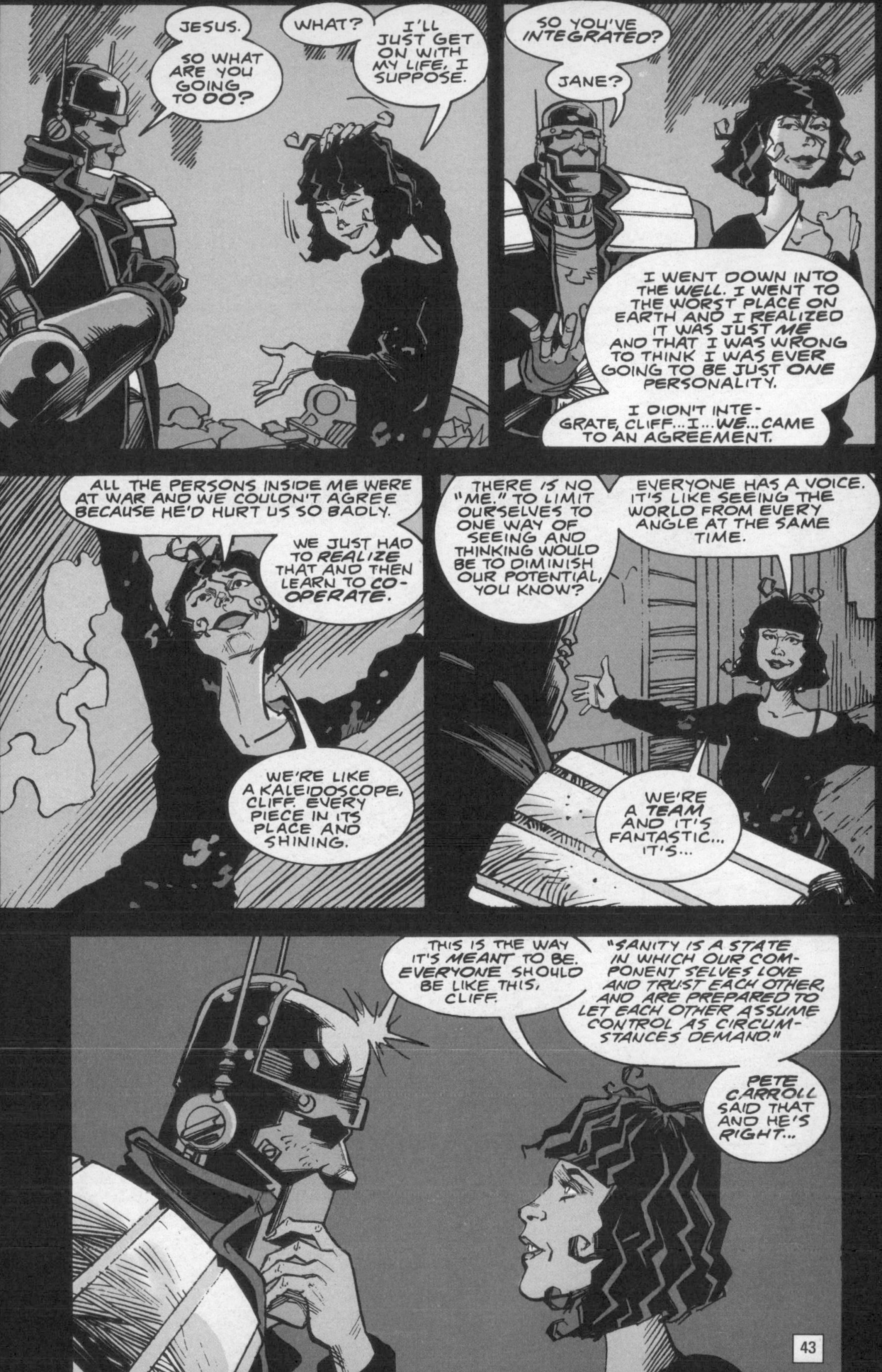

JESUS.
SO WHAT ARE YOU GOING TO DO?
WHAT?
I'LL JUST GET ON WITH MY LIFE, I SUPPOSE.
SO YOU'VE INTEGRATED?
JANE?
I WENT DOWN INTO THE WELL. I WENT TO THE WORST PLACE ON EARTH AND I REALIZED IT WAS JUST ME AND THAT I WAS WRONG TO THINK I WAS EVER GOING TO BE JUST ONE PERSONALITY.
I DIDN'T INTEGRATE, CLIFF... I... WE... CAME TO AN AGREEMENT.
ALL THE PERSONS INSIDE ME WERE AT WAR AND WE COULDN'T AGREE BECAUSE HE'D HURT US SO BADLY.
WE JUST HAD TO REALIZE THAT AND THEN LEARN TO CO-OPERATE.
WE'RE LIKE A KALEIDOSCOPE, CLIFF. EVERY PIECE IN ITS PLACE AND SHINING.
THERE IS NO "ME." TO LIMIT OURSELVES TO ONE WAY OF SEEING AND THINKING WOULD BE TO DIMINISH OUR POTENTIAL, YOU KNOW?
EVERYONE HAS A VOICE. IT'S LIKE SEEING THE WORLD FROM EVERY ANGLE AT THE SAME TIME.
WE'RE A TEAM AND IT'S FANTASTIC... IT'S...
THIS IS THE WAY IT'S MEANT TO BE. EVERYONE SHOULD BE LIKE THIS, CLIFF.
"SANITY IS A STATE IN WHICH OUR COMPONENT SELVES LOVE AND TRUST EACH OTHER, AND ARE PREPARED TO LET EACH OTHER ASSUME CONTROL AS CIRCUMSTANCES DEMAND."
PETE CARROLL SAID THAT AND HE'S RIGHT...

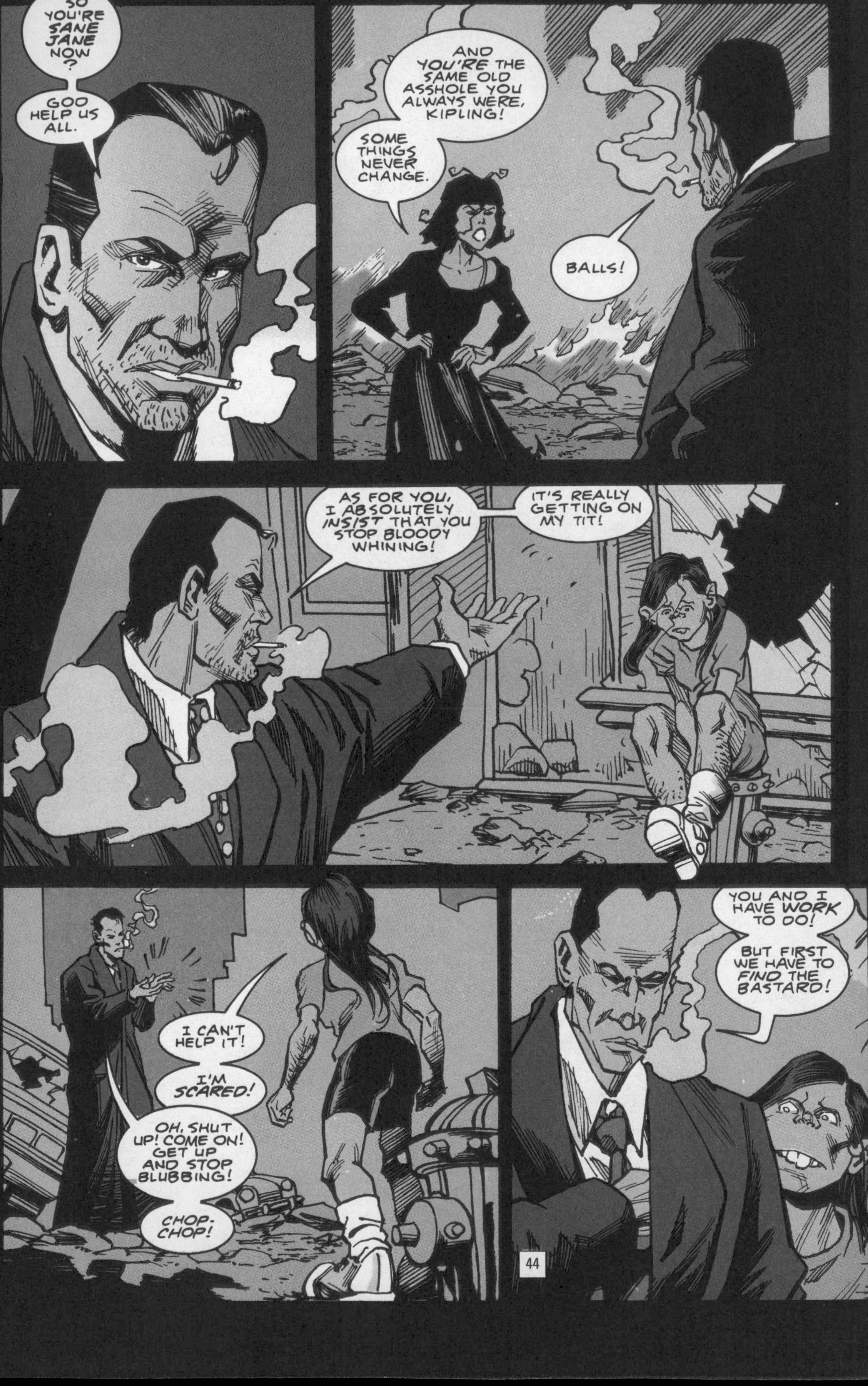
SO YOU'RE SANE JANE NOW?
GOD HELP US ALL.
AND YOU'RE THE SAME OLD ASSHOLE YOU ALWAYS WERE, KIPLING!
SOME THINGS NEVER CHANGE.
BALLS!
AS FOR YOU, I ABSOLUTELY INSIST THAT YOU STOP BLOODY WHINING!
IT'S REALLY GETTING ON MY TIT!
I CAN'T HELP IT!
I'M SCARED!
OH, SHUT UP! COME ON! GET UP AND STOP BLUBBING!
CHOP-CHOP!
YOU AND I HAVE WORK TO DO!
BUT FIRST WE HAVE TO FIND THE BASTARD!

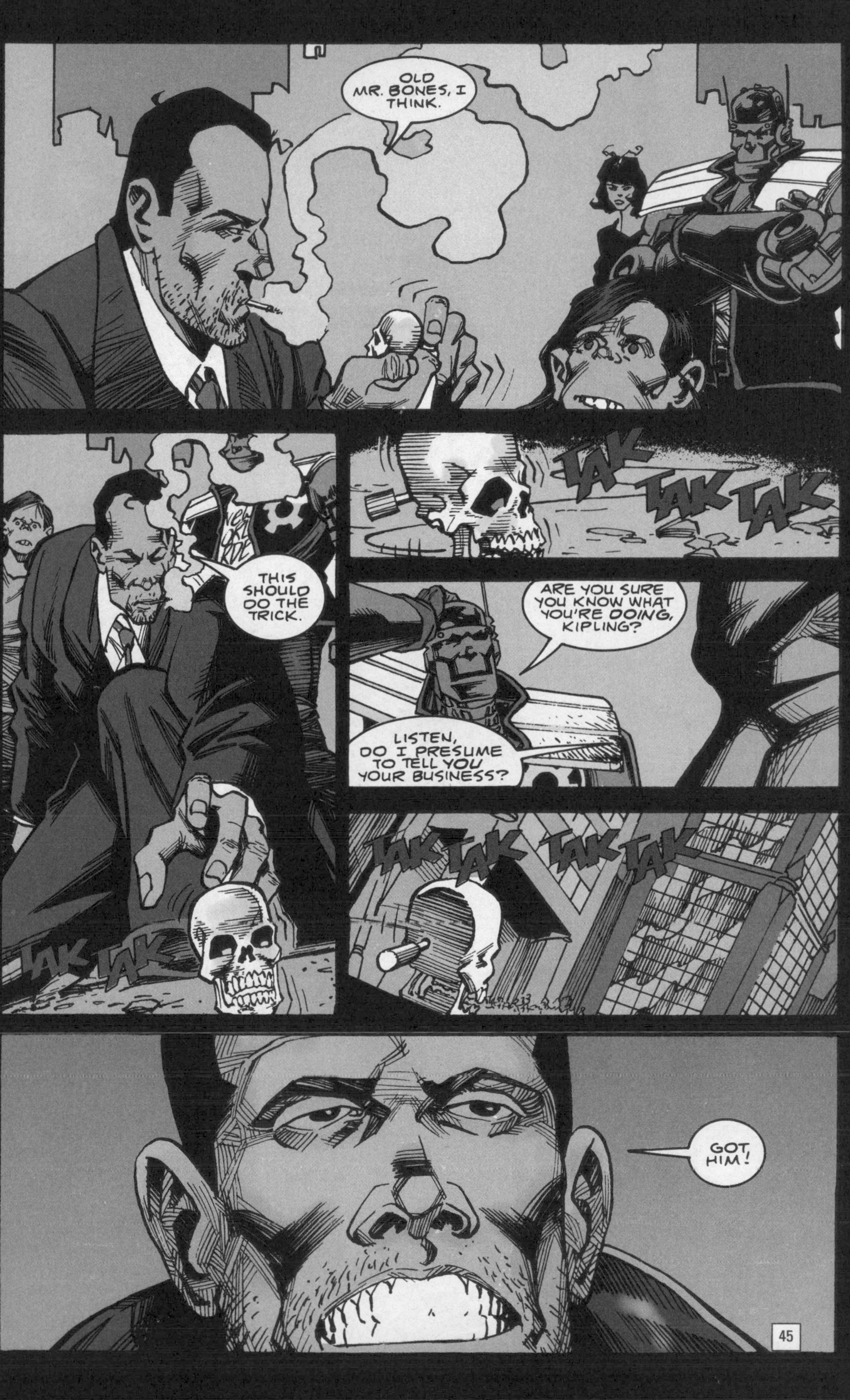
OLD MR. BONES, I THINK.
THIS SHOULD DO THE TRICK.
TAK TAK TAK TAK
ARE YOU SURE YOU KNOW WHAT YOU'RE *DOING*, KIPLING?
LISTEN, DO I PRESUME TO TELL *YOU* YOUR BUSINESS?
TAK TAK
TAK TAK TAK TAK
GOT HIM!

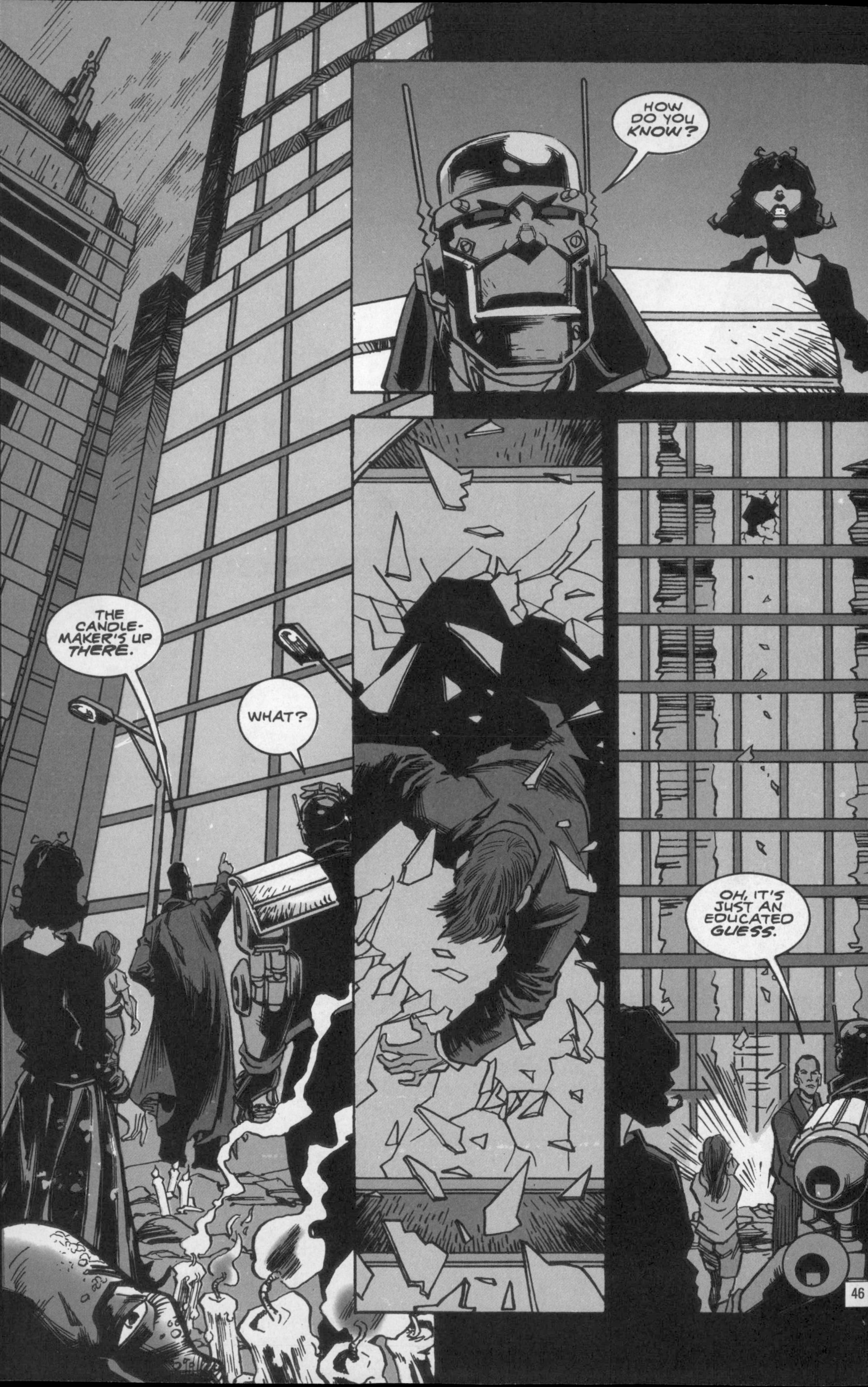

HOW DO YOU KNOW?
THE CANDLE-MAKER'S UP THERE.
WHAT?
OH, IT'S JUST AN EDUCATED GUESS.

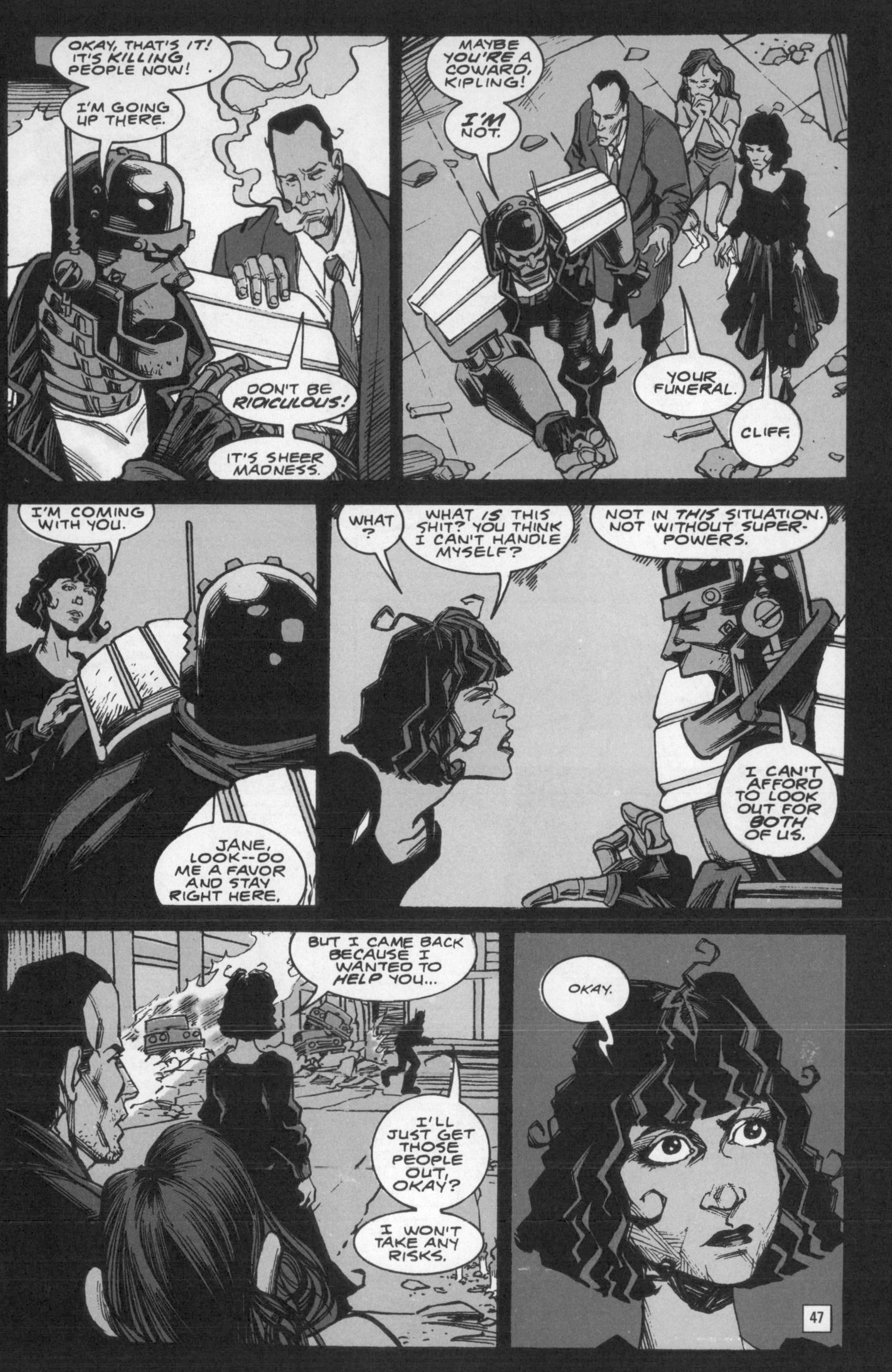
OKAY, THAT'S IT! IT'S KILLING PEOPLE NOW!
I'M GOING UP THERE.
DON'T BE RIDICULOUS!
IT'S SHEER MADNESS.
MAYBE YOU'RE A COWARD, KIPLING!
I'M NOT.
YOUR FUNERAL.
CLIFF.
I'M COMING WITH YOU.
JANE, LOOK--DO ME A FAVOR AND STAY RIGHT HERE.
WHAT?
WHAT IS THIS SHIT? YOU THINK I CAN'T HANDLE MYSELF?
NOT IN THIS SITUATION. NOT WITHOUT SUPER-POWERS.
I CAN'T AFFORD TO LOOK OUT FOR BOTH OF US.
BUT I CAME BACK BECAUSE I WANTED TO HELP YOU...
I'LL JUST GET THOSE PEOPLE OUT, OKAY?
I WON'T TAKE ANY RISKS.
OKAY.

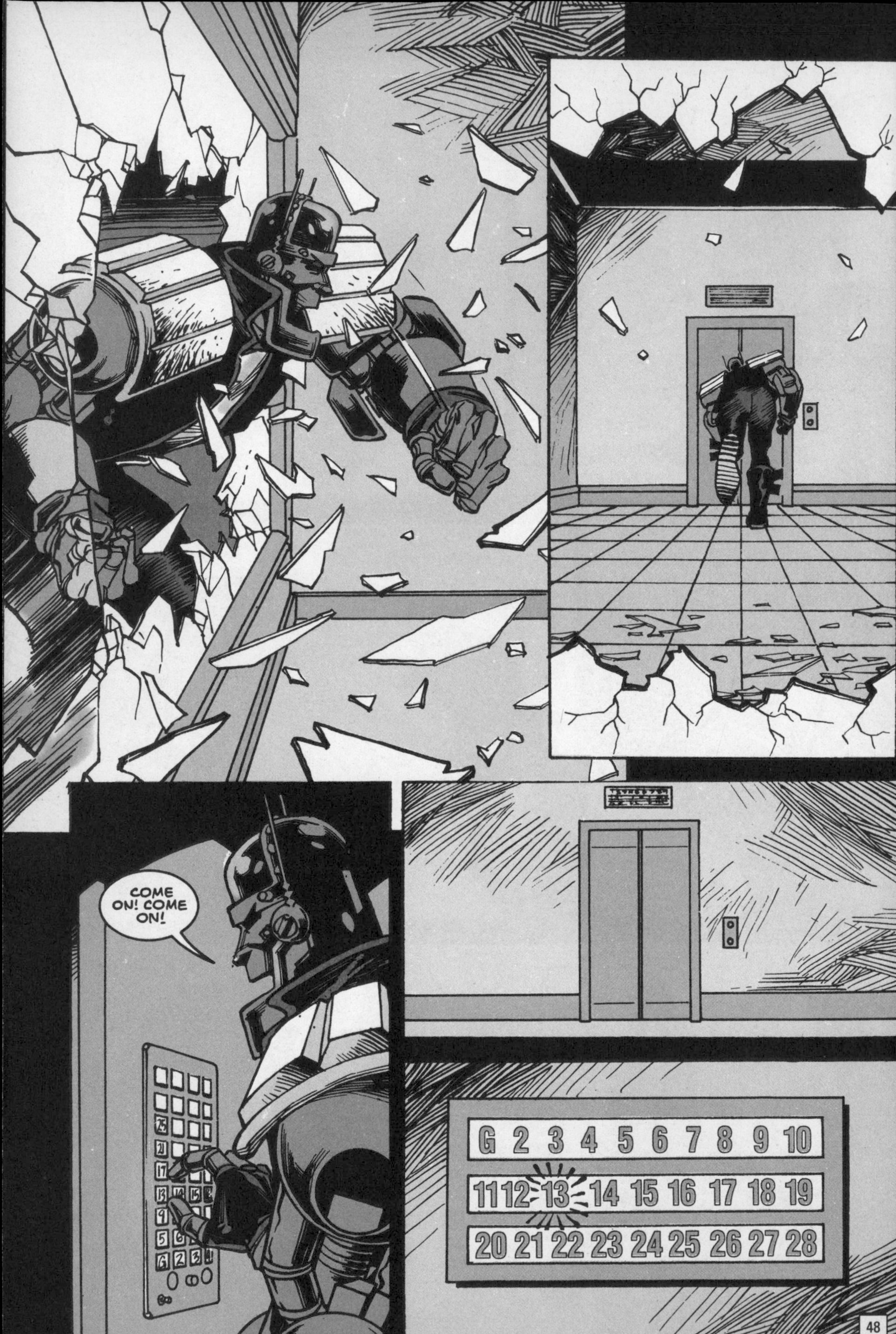
COME ON! COME ON!
G 2 3 4 5 6 7 8 9 10
11 12 13 14 15 16 17 18 19
20 21 22 23 24 25 26 27 28

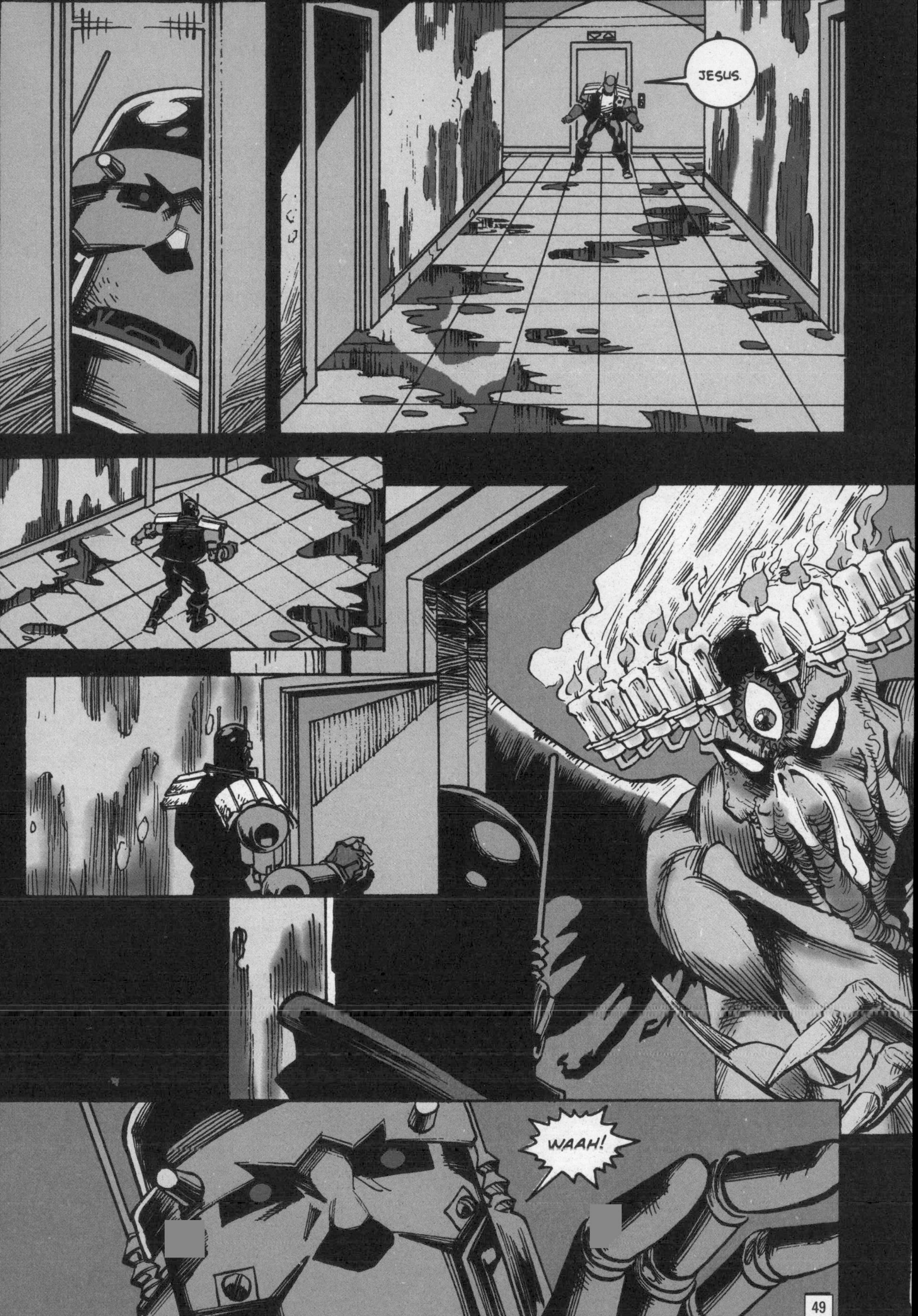
JESUS.
WAAH!

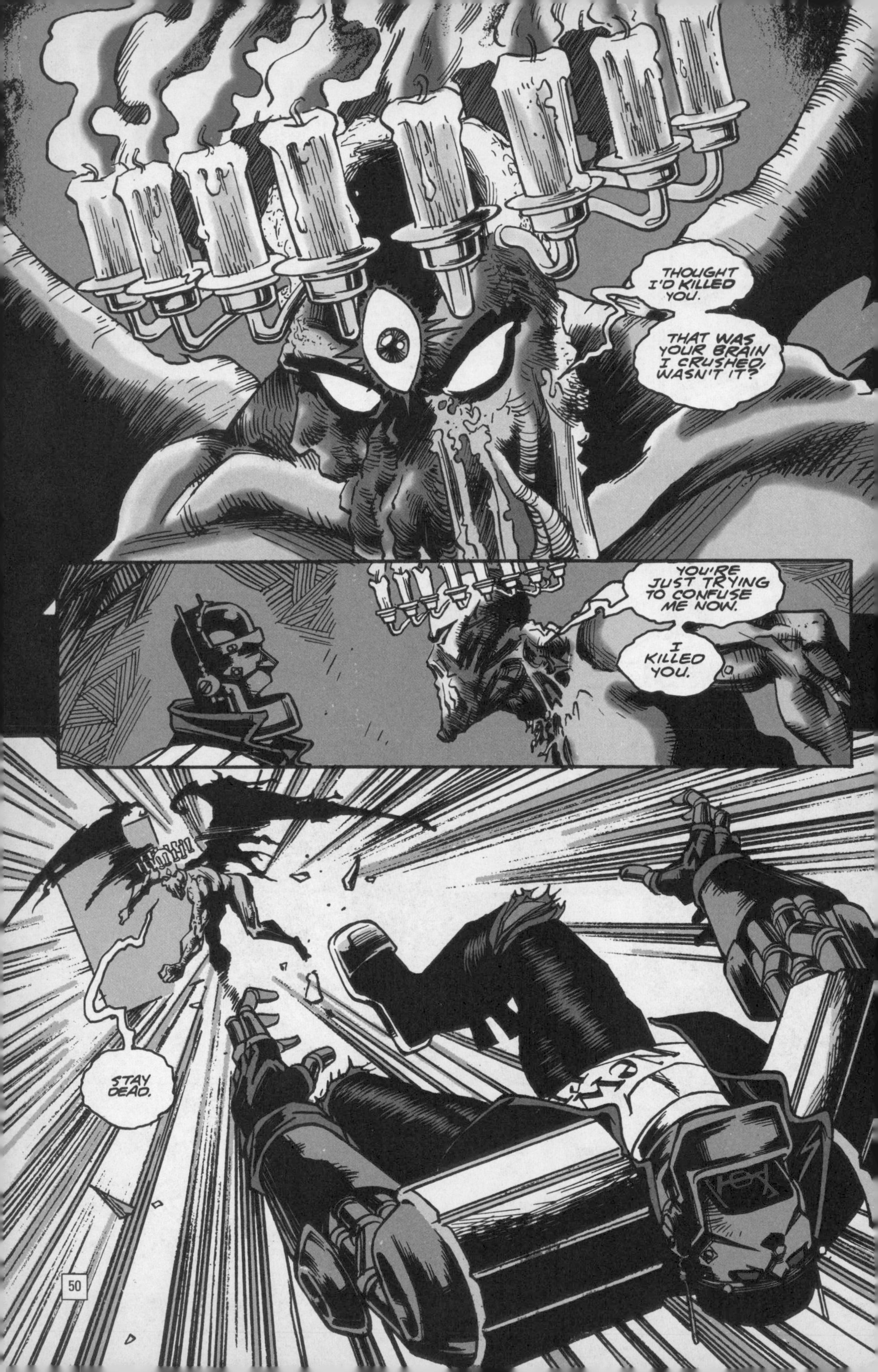
THOUGHT I'D KILLED YOU.
THAT WAS YOUR BRAIN I CRUSHED, WASN'T IT?
YOU'RE JUST TRYING TO CONFUSE ME NOW.
I KILLED YOU.
STAY DEAD.

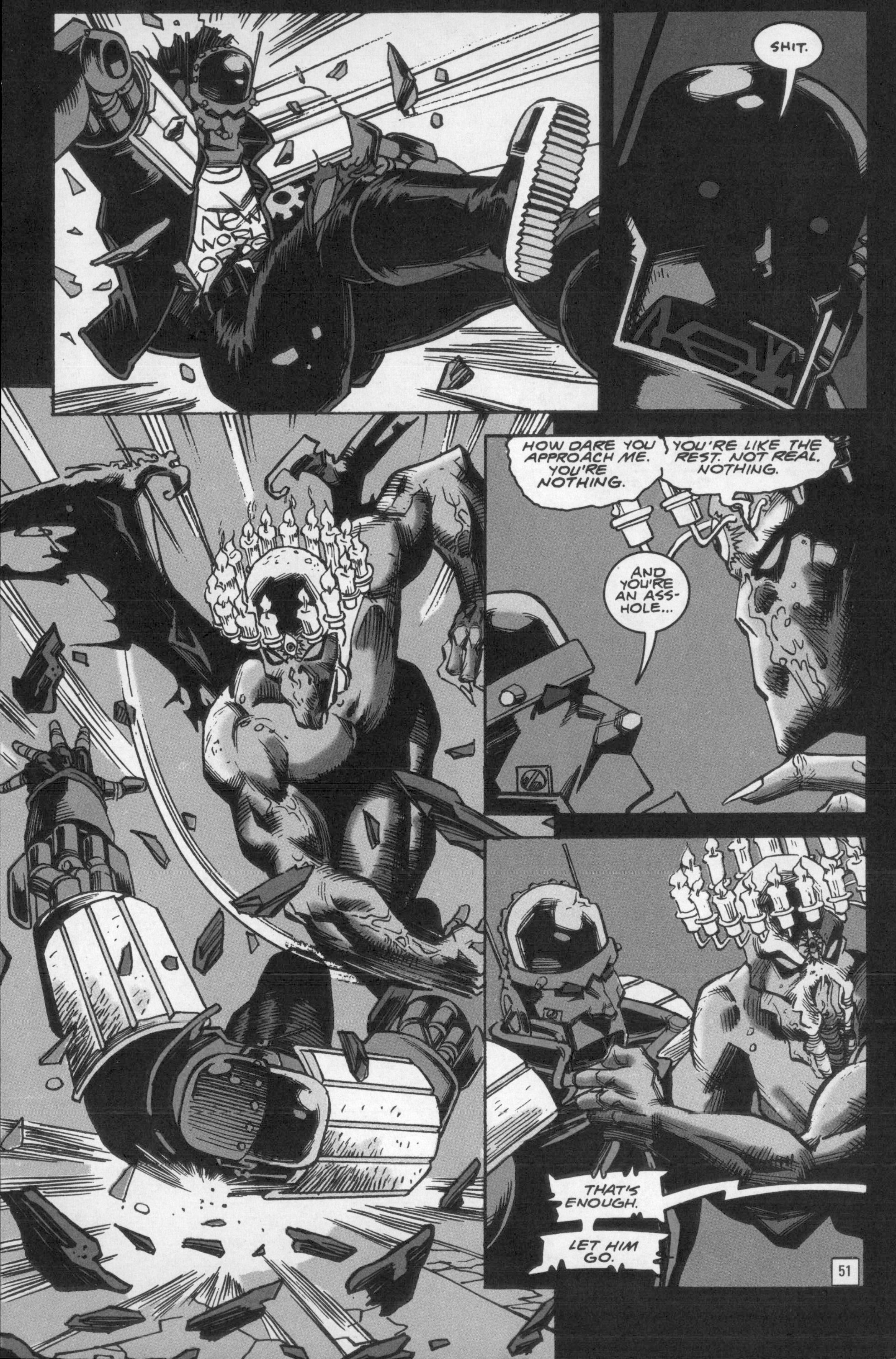
SHIT.
HOW DARE YOU APPROACH ME. YOU'RE NOTHING.
YOU'RE LIKE THE REST. NOT REAL. NOTHING.
AND YOU'RE AN ASS-HOLE...
THAT'S ENOUGH.
LET HIM GO.

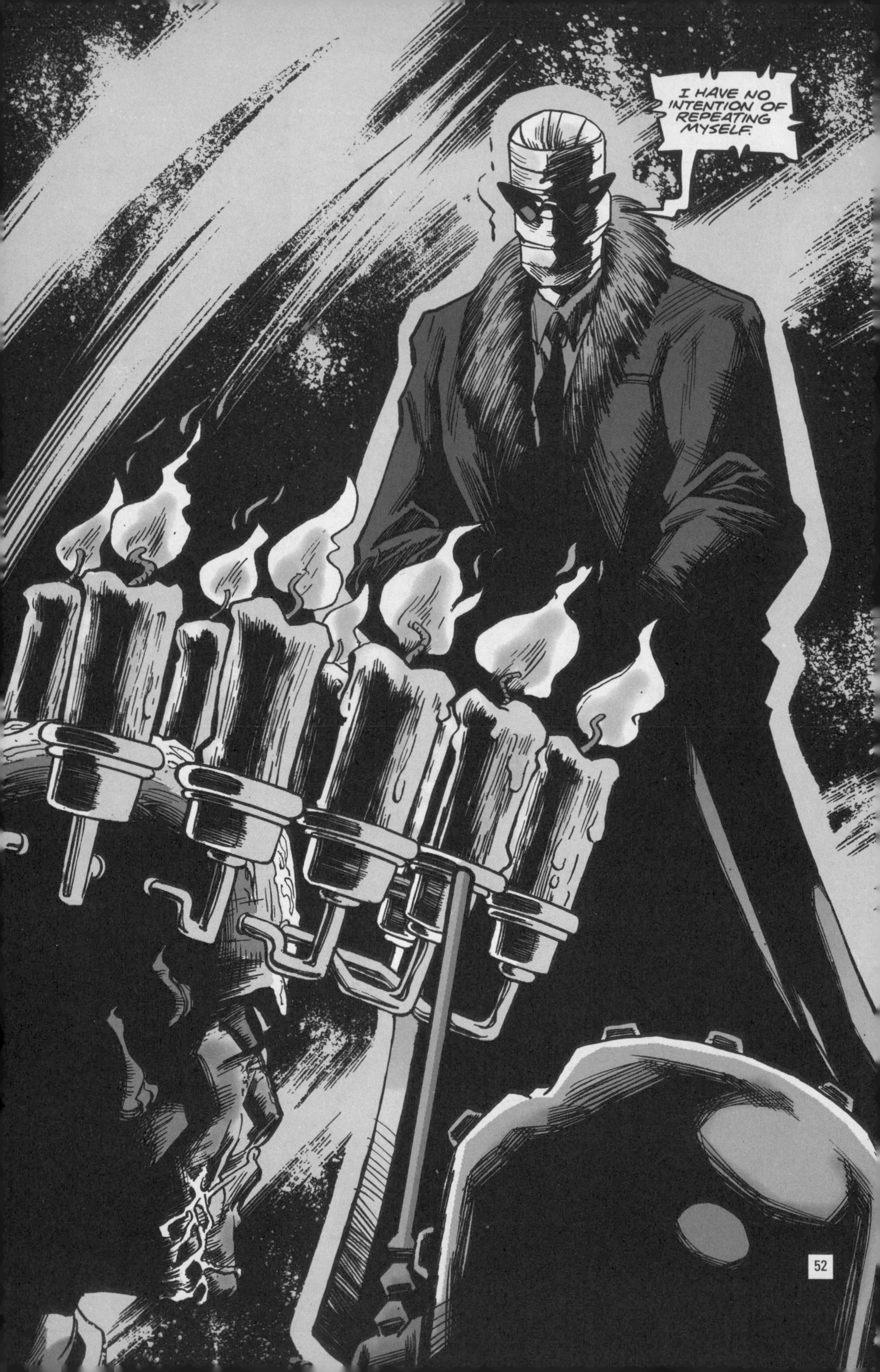
I HAVE NO INTENTION OF REPEATING MYSELF.

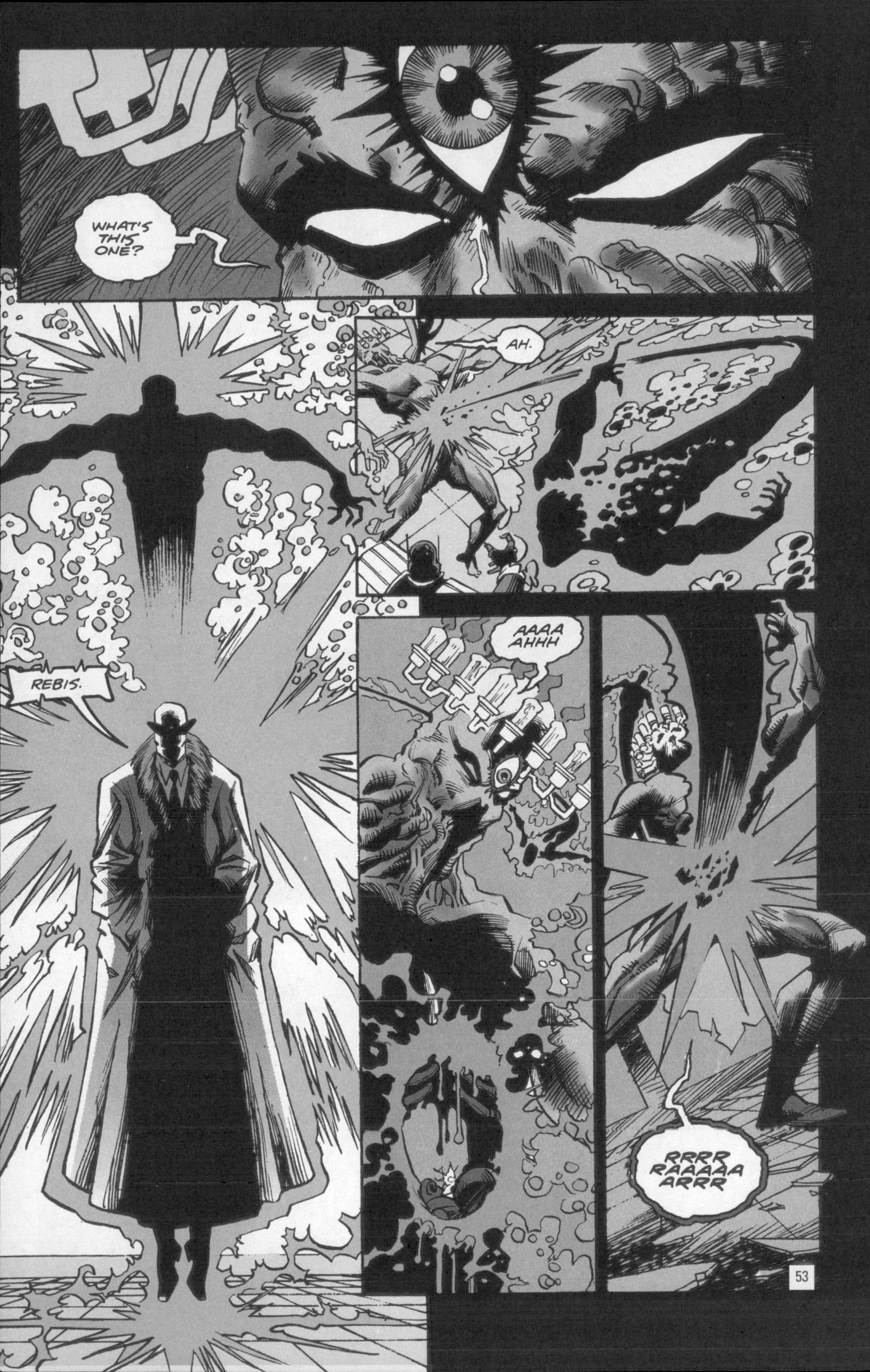
WHAT'S THIS ONE?
AH.
REBIS.
AAAA AHHH
RRRR RAAAAA ARRR

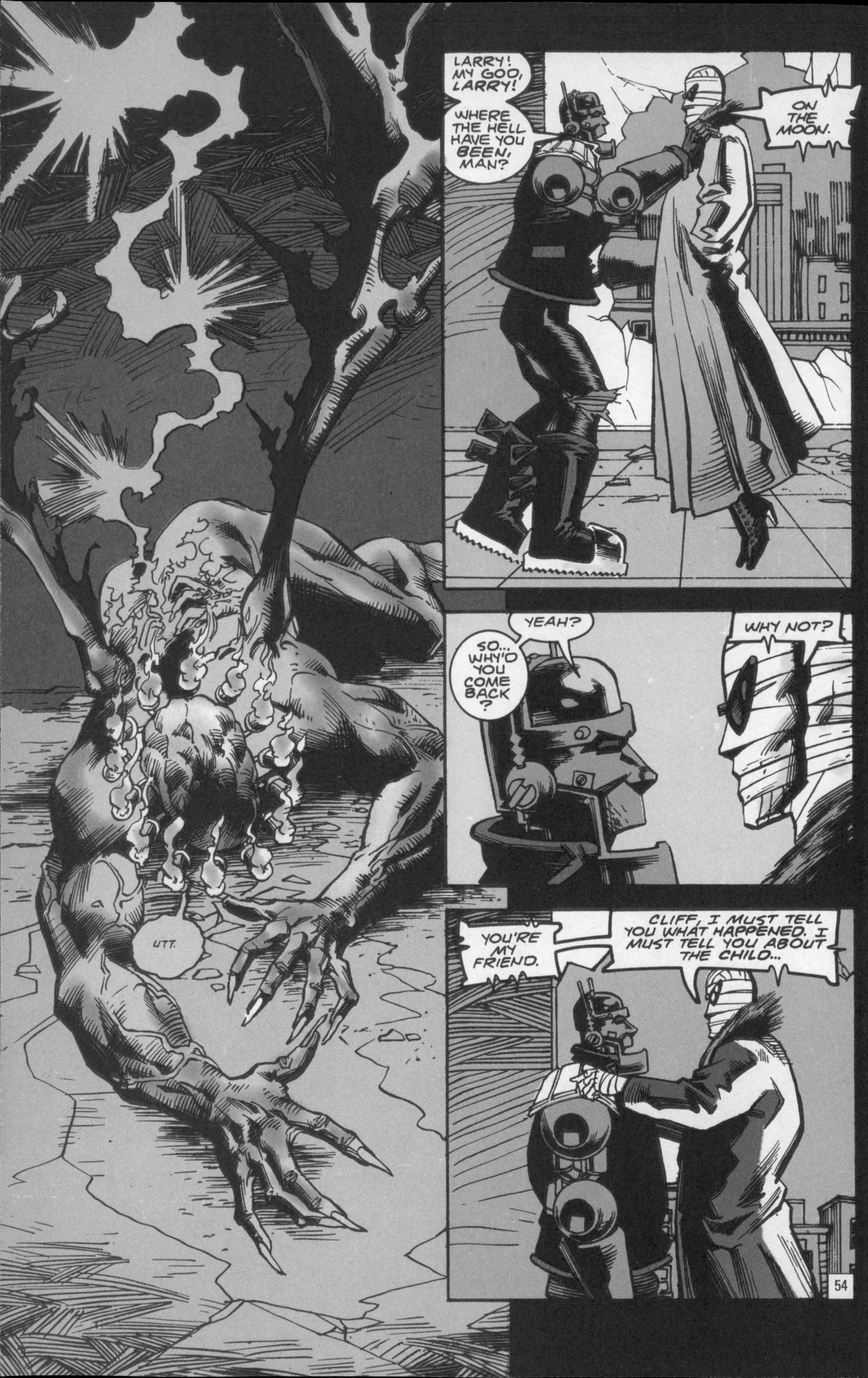

UTT.
LARRY! MY GOD, LARRY!
WHERE THE HELL HAVE YOU BEEN, MAN?
ON THE MOON.
YEAH?
SO... WHY'D YOU COME BACK?
WHY NOT?
YOU'RE MY FRIEND.
CLIFF, I MUST TELL YOU WHAT HAPPENED. I MUST TELL YOU ABOUT THE CHILD...

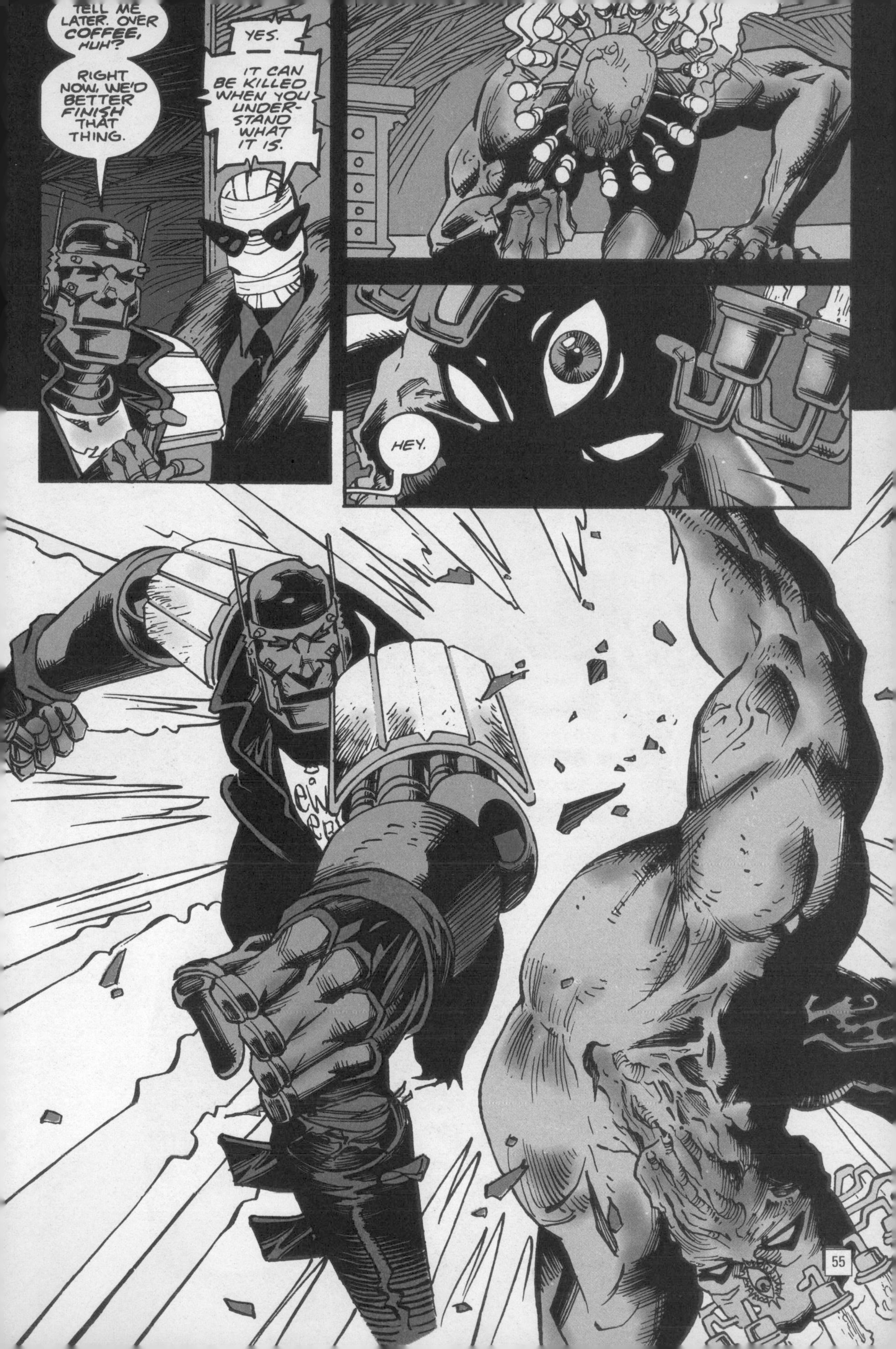

TELL ME LATER. OVER COFFEE, HUH?
RIGHT NOW, WE'D BETTER FINISH THAT THING.
YES.
IT CAN BE KILLED WHEN YOU UNDER-STAND WHAT IT IS.
HEY.

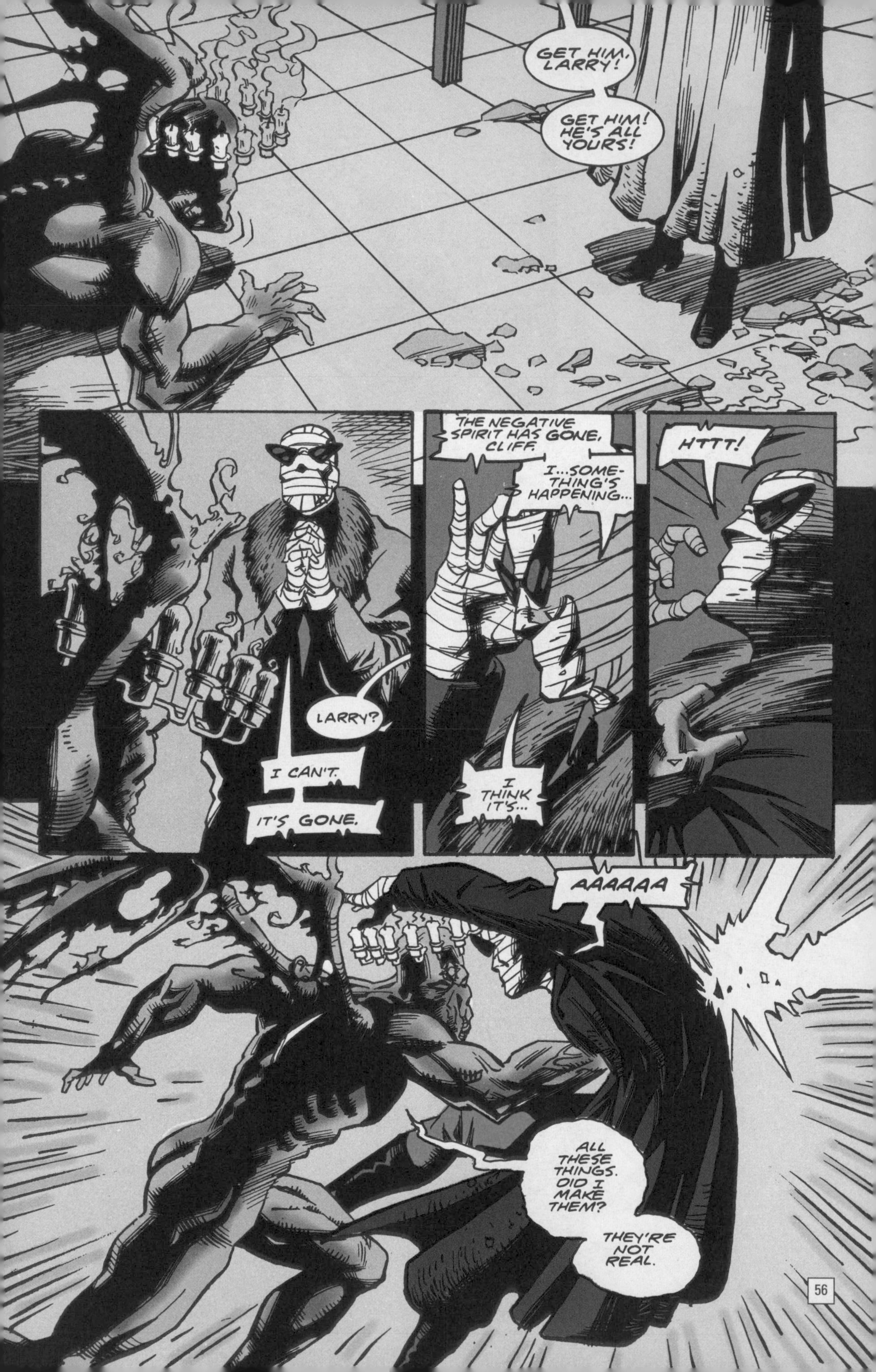
GET HIM, LARRY!
GET HIM! HE'S ALL YOURS!
LARRY?
I CAN'T.
IT'S GONE.
THE NEGATIVE SPIRIT HAS GONE, CLIFF.
I...SOME-THING'S HAPPENING...
I THINK IT'S...
HTTT!
AAAAAA
ALL THESE THINGS. DID I MAKE THEM?
THEY'RE NOT REAL.

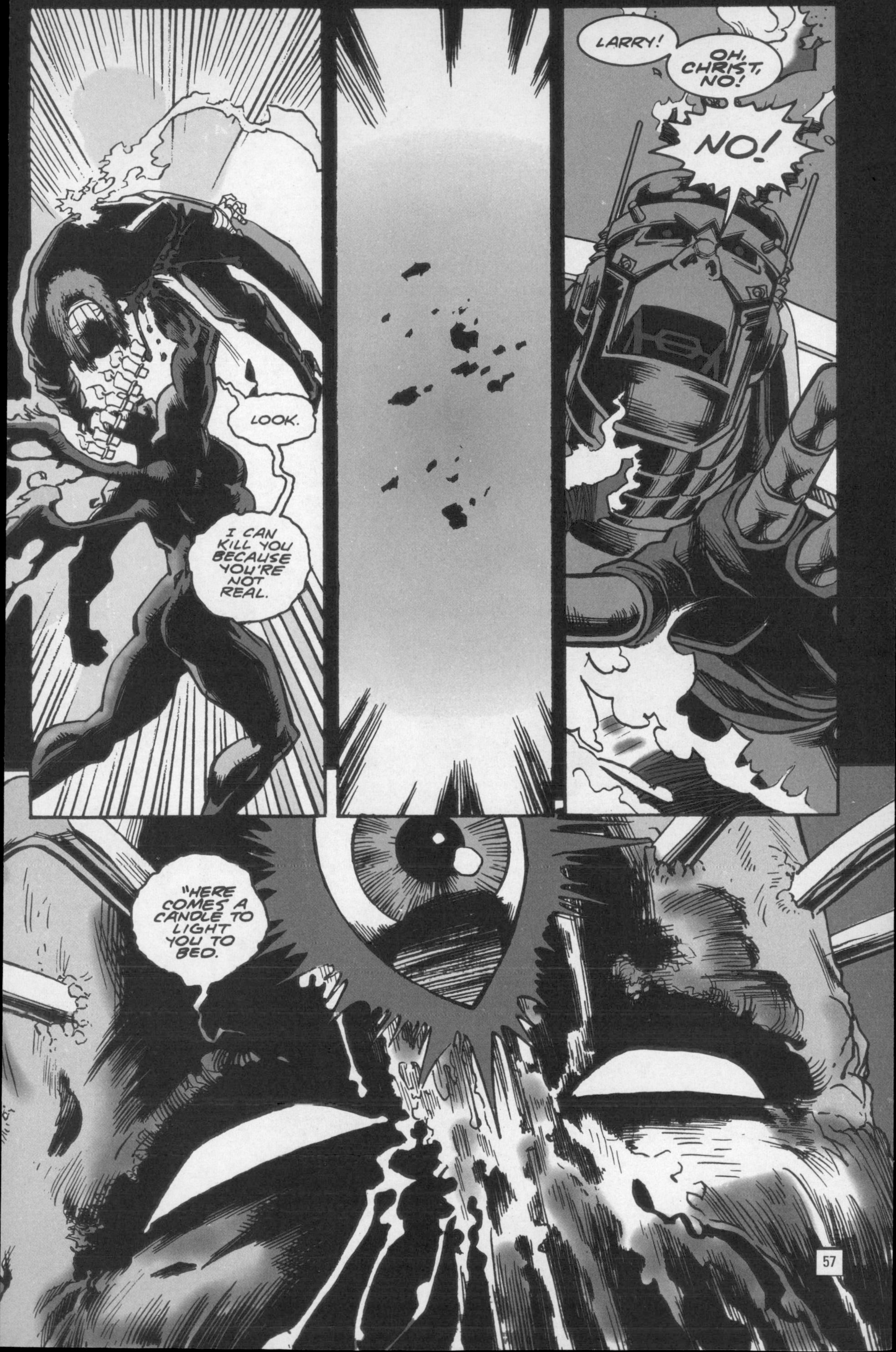
LOOK.
I CAN KILL YOU BECAUSE YOU'RE NOT REAL.
LARRY!
OH, CHRIST, NO!
NO!
"HERE COMES A CANDLE TO LIGHT YOU TO BED.

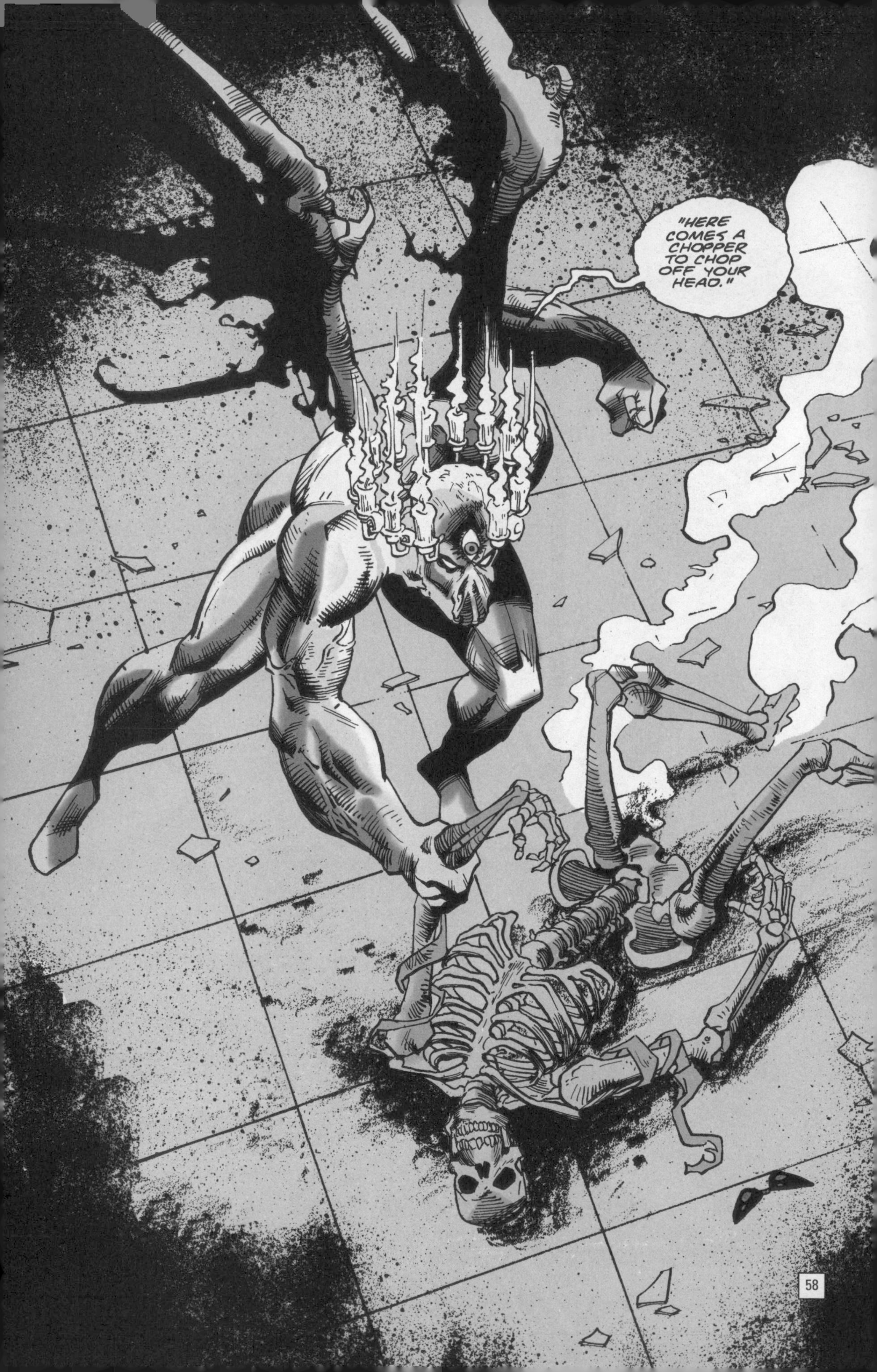
"HERE COMES A CHOPPER TO CHOP OFF YOUR HEAD."

"Listen.

If you want to destroy a people, first destroy its dreams."

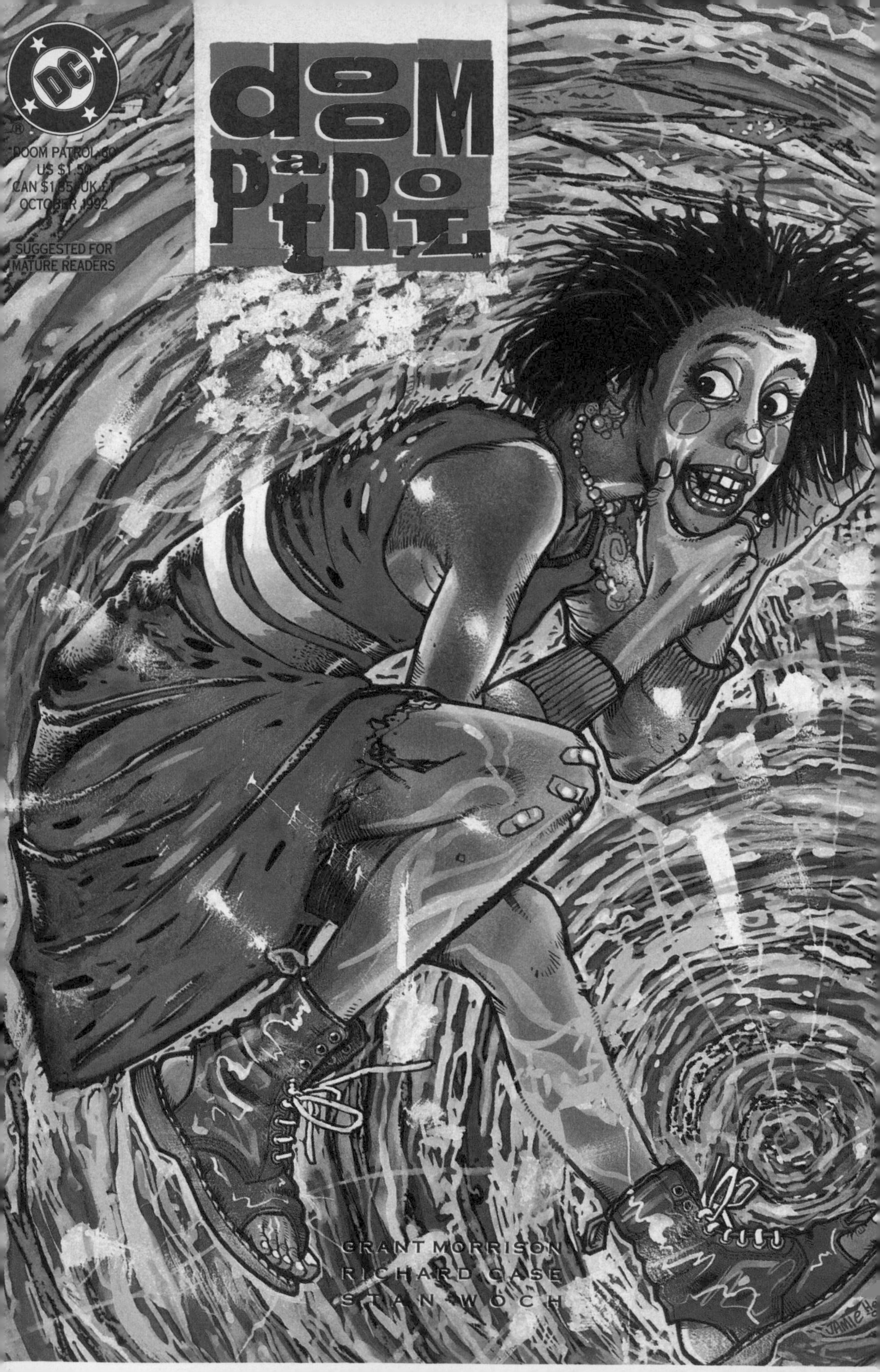
DC
DOOM PATROL 60
US $1.50
CAN $1.85 UK £1
OCTOBER 1992
doom patrol
SUGGESTED FOR MATURE READERS
GRANT MORRISON
RICHARD CASE
STAN WOCH
JAMIE H

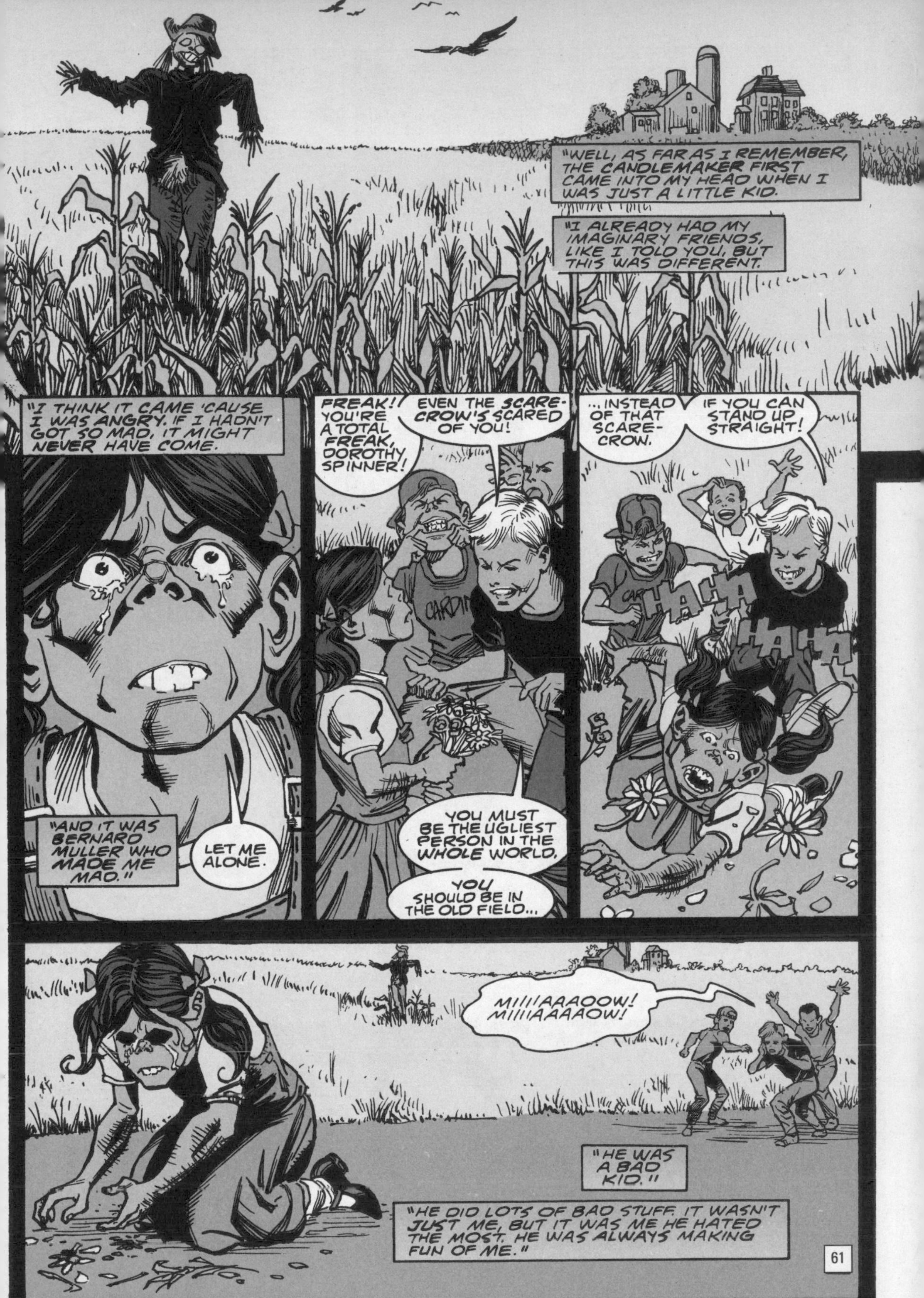
"WELL, AS FAR AS I REMEMBER, THE CANDLEMAKER FIRST CAME INTO MY HEAD WHEN I WAS JUST A LITTLE KID.
"I ALREADY HAD MY IMAGINARY FRIENDS, LIKE I TOLD YOU, BUT THIS WAS DIFFERENT.
"I THINK IT CAME 'CAUSE I WAS ANGRY. IF I HADN'T GOT SO MAD, IT MIGHT NEVER HAVE COME.
"AND IT WAS BERNARD MULLER WHO MADE ME MAD."
LET ME ALONE.
FREAK! YOU'RE A TOTAL FREAK, DOROTHY SPINNER!
EVEN THE SCARECROW'S SCARED OF YOU!
YOU MUST BE THE UGLIEST PERSON IN THE WHOLE WORLD.
YOU SHOULD BE IN THE OLD FIELD...
...INSTEAD OF THAT SCARECROW.
IF YOU CAN STAND UP STRAIGHT!
HA HA
HA HA
MIIIAAAOOW! MIIIAAAAOW!
"HE WAS A BAD KID."
"HE DID LOTS OF BAD STUFF. IT WASN'T JUST ME, BUT IT WAS ME HE HATED THE MOST. HE WAS ALWAYS MAKING FUN OF ME."

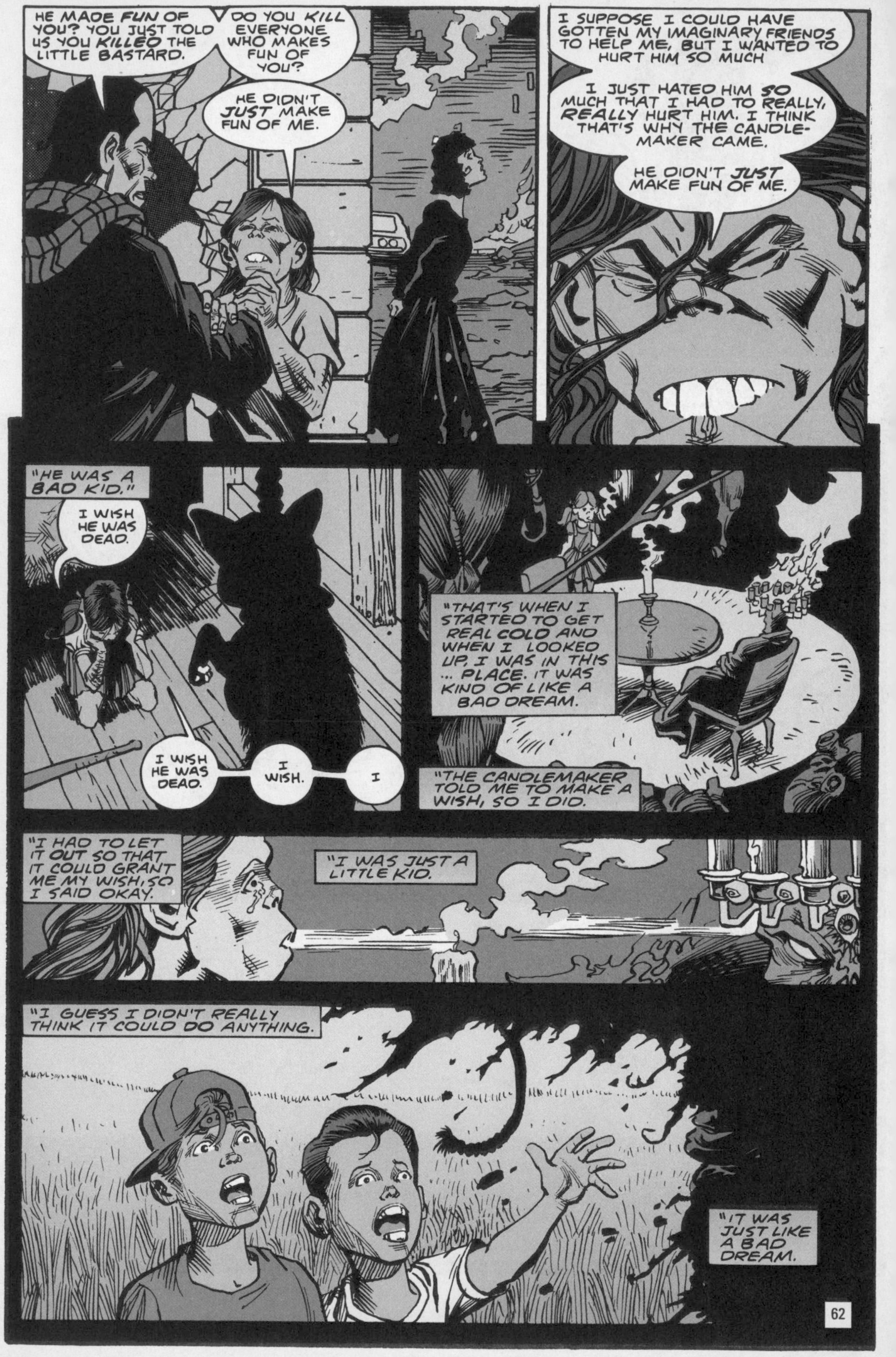

HE MADE FUN OF YOU? YOU JUST TOLD US YOU KILLED THE LITTLE BASTARD.
DO YOU KILL EVERYONE WHO MAKES FUN OF YOU?
HE DIDN'T JUST MAKE FUN OF ME.
I SUPPOSE I COULD HAVE GOTTEN MY IMAGINARY FRIENDS TO HELP ME, BUT I WANTED TO HURT HIM SO MUCH
I JUST HATED HIM SO MUCH THAT I HAD TO REALLY, REALLY HURT HIM. I THINK THAT'S WHY THE CANDLE-MAKER CAME.
HE DIDN'T JUST MAKE FUN OF ME.
"HE WAS A BAD KID."
I WISH HE WAS DEAD.
I WISH HE WAS DEAD.
I WISH.
I
"THAT'S WHEN I STARTED TO GET REAL COLD AND WHEN I LOOKED UP, I WAS IN THIS ... PLACE. IT WAS KIND OF LIKE A BAD DREAM.
"THE CANDLEMAKER TOLD ME TO MAKE A WISH, SO I DID.
"I HAD TO LET IT OUT SO THAT IT COULD GRANT ME MY WISH, SO I SAID OKAY.
"I WAS JUST A LITTLE KID.
"I GUESS I DIDN'T REALLY THINK IT COULD DO ANYTHING.
"IT WAS JUST LIKE A BAD DREAM.

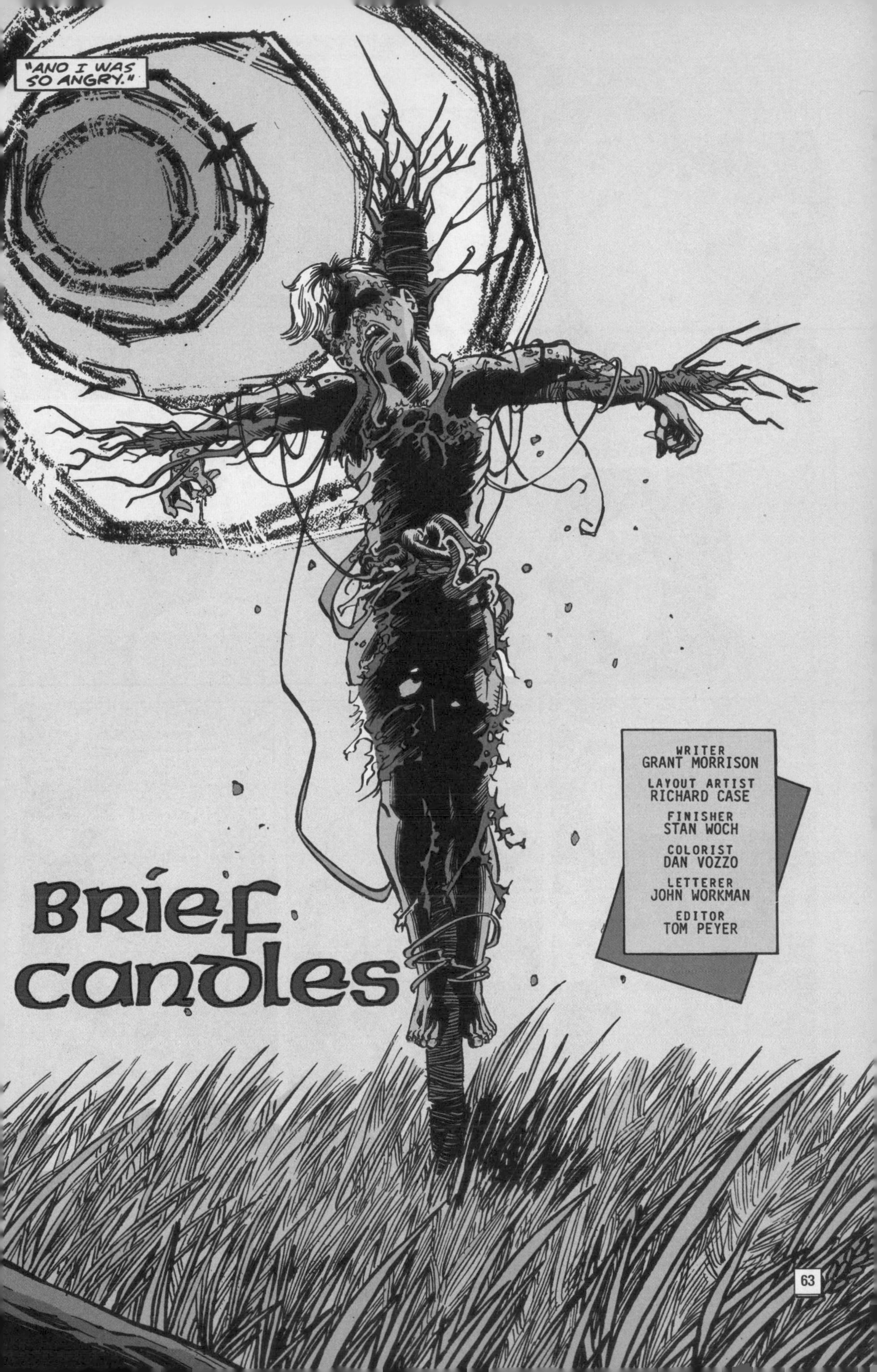
"AND I WAS SO ANGRY."
BRIEF CANDLES
WRITER GRANT MORRISON
LAYOUT ARTIST RICHARD CASE
FINISHER STAN WOCH
COLORIST DAN VOZZO
LETTERER JOHN WORKMAN
EDITOR TOM PEYER

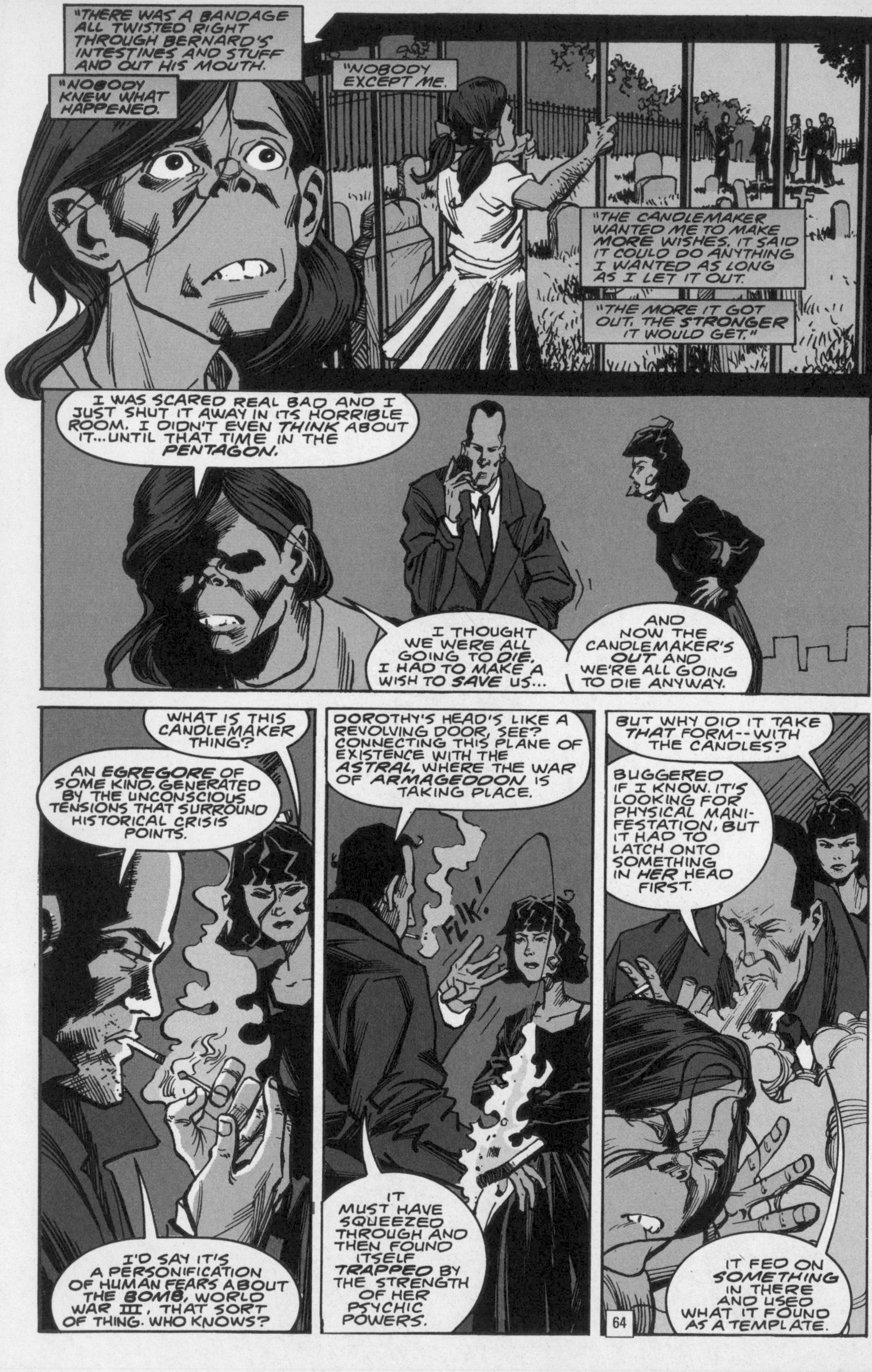
"THERE WAS A BANDAGE ALL TWISTED RIGHT THROUGH BERNARD'S INTESTINES AND STUFF AND OUT HIS MOUTH.
"NOBODY KNEW WHAT HAPPENED.
"NOBODY EXCEPT ME.
"THE CANDLEMAKER WANTED ME TO MAKE MORE WISHES. IT SAID IT COULD DO ANYTHING I WANTED AS LONG AS I LET IT OUT.
"THE MORE IT GOT OUT, THE STRONGER IT WOULD GET."
I WAS SCARED REAL BAD AND I JUST SHUT IT AWAY IN ITS HORRIBLE ROOM. I DIDN'T EVEN THINK ABOUT IT... UNTIL THAT TIME IN THE PENTAGON.
I THOUGHT WE WERE ALL GOING TO DIE. I HAD TO MAKE A WISH TO SAVE US...
AND NOW THE CANDLEMAKER'S OUT AND WE'RE ALL GOING TO DIE ANYWAY.
WHAT IS THIS CANDLEMAKER THING?
AN EGREGORE OF SOME KIND, GENERATED BY THE UNCONSCIOUS TENSIONS THAT SURROUND HISTORICAL CRISIS POINTS.
I'D SAY IT'S A PERSONIFICATION OF HUMAN FEARS ABOUT THE BOMB, WORLD WAR III, THAT SORT OF THING. WHO KNOWS?
DOROTHY'S HEAD'S LIKE A REVOLVING DOOR, SEE? CONNECTING THIS PLANE OF EXISTENCE WITH THE ASTRAL, WHERE THE WAR OF ARMAGEDDON IS TAKING PLACE.
FLIK!
IT MUST HAVE SQUEEZED THROUGH AND THEN FOUND ITSELF TRAPPED BY THE STRENGTH OF HER PSYCHIC POWERS.
BUT WHY DID IT TAKE THAT FORM-- WITH THE CANDLES?
BUGGERED IF I KNOW. IT'S LOOKING FOR PHYSICAL MANIFESTATION, BUT IT HAD TO LATCH ONTO SOMETHING IN HER HEAD FIRST.
IT FED ON SOMETHING IN THERE AND USED WHAT IT FOUND AS A TEMPLATE.

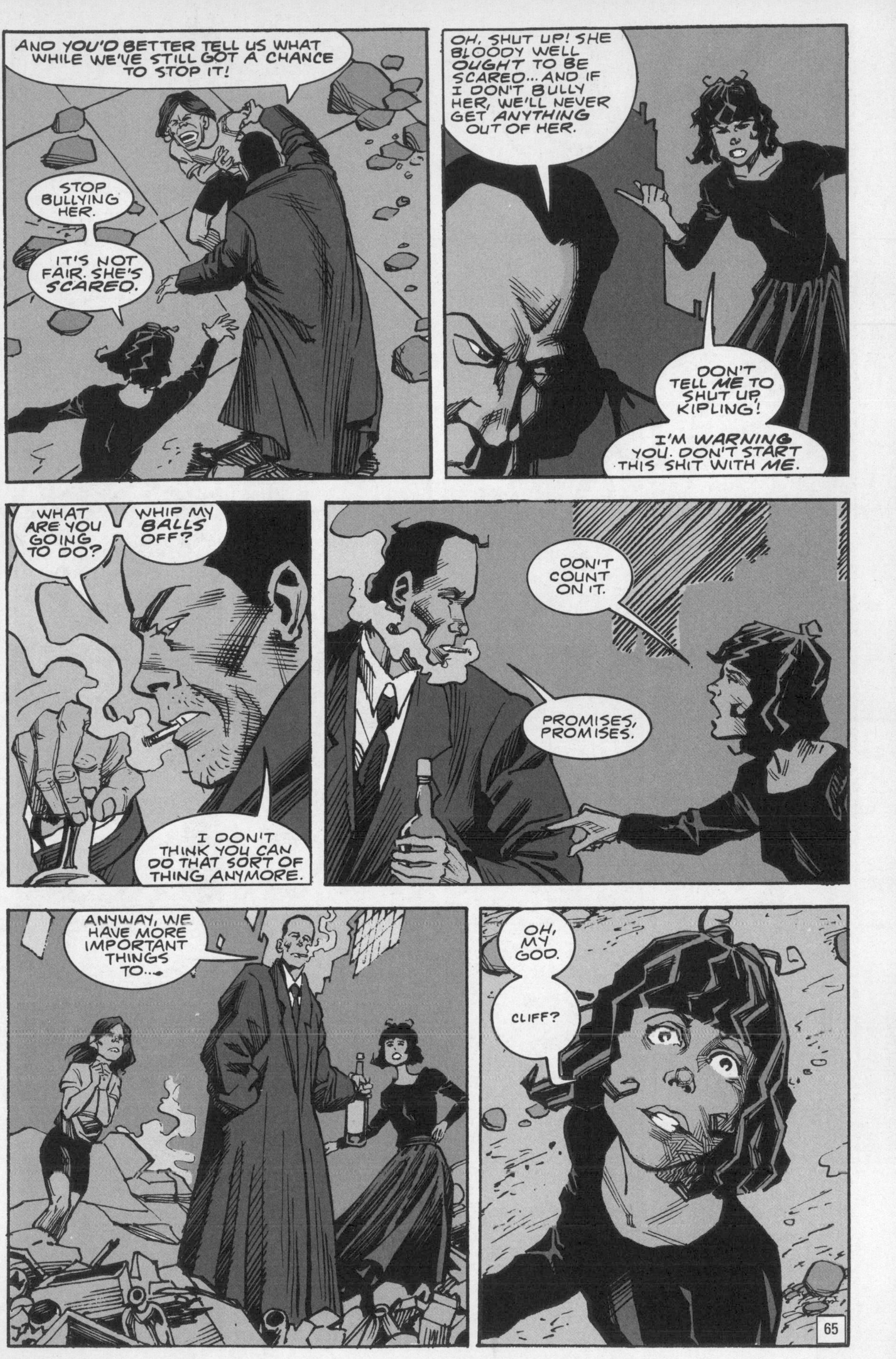
AND YOU'D BETTER TELL US WHAT WHILE WE'VE STILL GOT A CHANCE TO STOP IT!
STOP BULLYING HER.
IT'S NOT FAIR. SHE'S SCARED.
OH, SHUT UP! SHE BLOODY WELL OUGHT TO BE SCARED... AND IF I DON'T BULLY HER, WE'LL NEVER GET ANYTHING OUT OF HER.
DON'T TELL ME TO SHUT UP, KIPLING!
I'M WARNING YOU. DON'T START THIS SHIT WITH ME.
WHAT ARE YOU GOING TO DO?
WHIP MY BALLS OFF?
I DON'T THINK YOU CAN DO THAT SORT OF THING ANYMORE.
DON'T COUNT ON IT.
PROMISES, PROMISES.
ANYWAY, WE HAVE MORE IMPORTANT THINGS TO...
OH, MY GOD.
CLIFF?

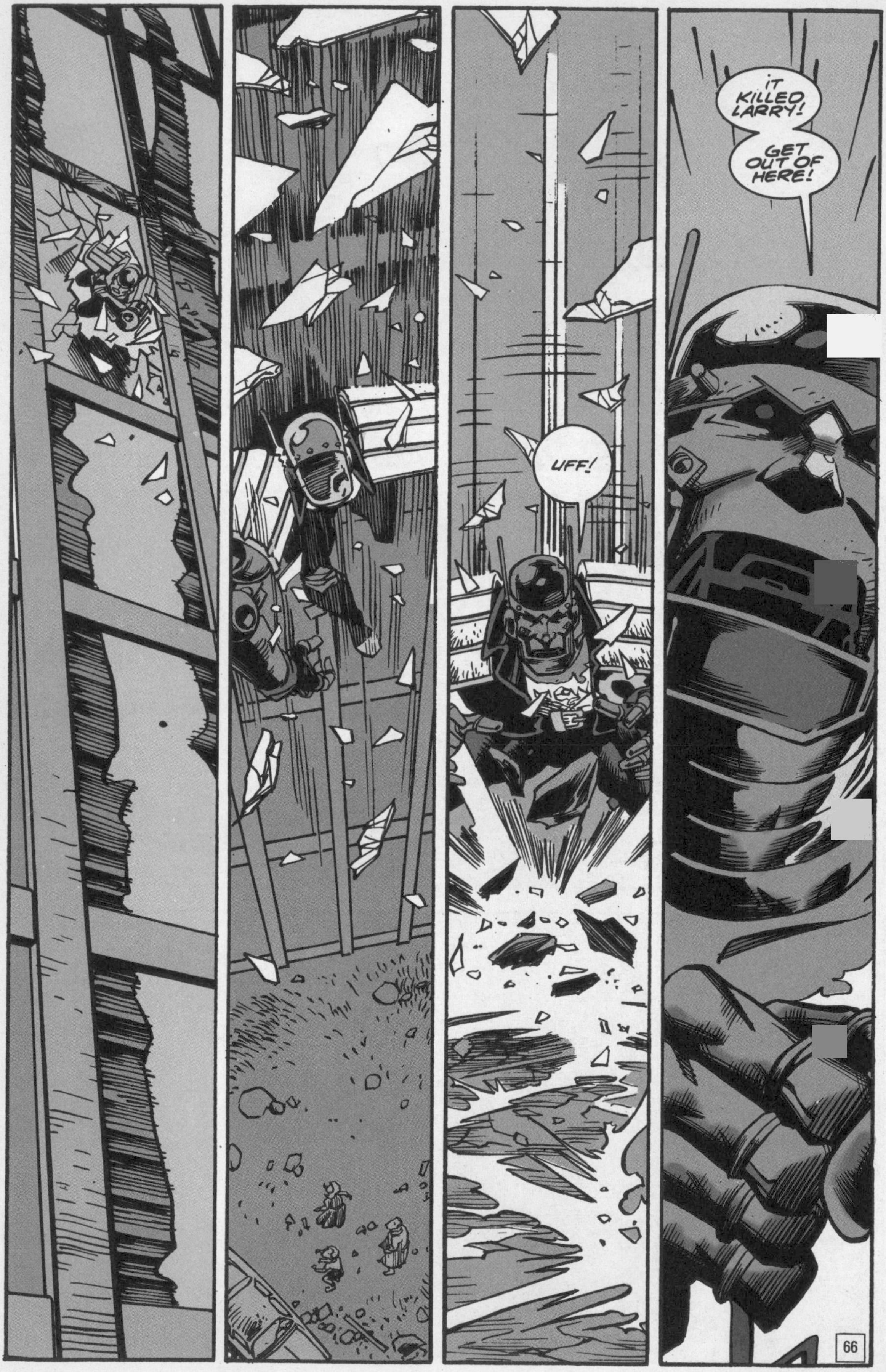
UFF!
IT KILLED LARRY!
GET OUT OF HERE!

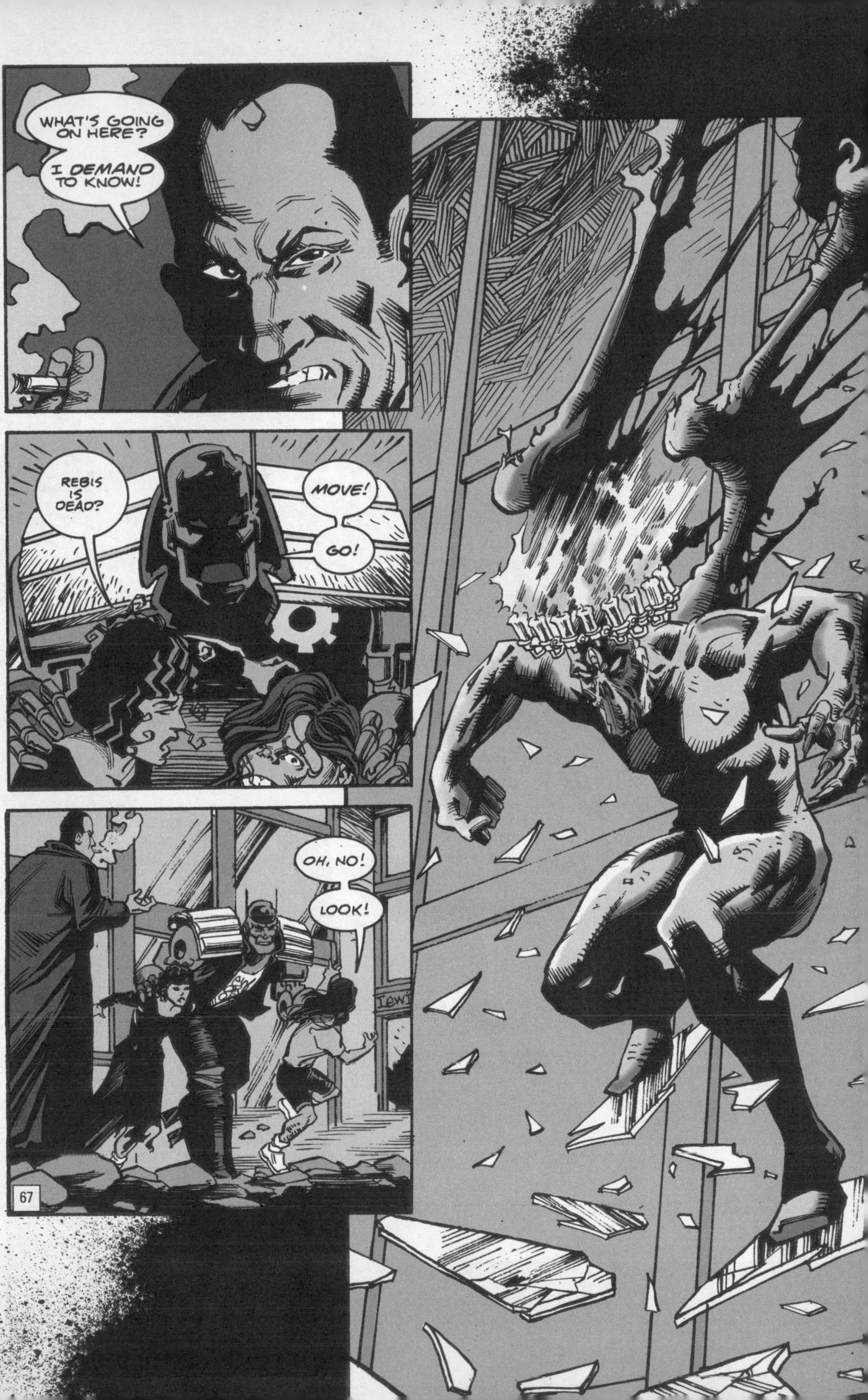
WHAT'S GOING ON HERE?
I DEMAND TO KNOW!
REBIS IS DEAD?
MOVE!
GO!
OH, NO!
LOOK!

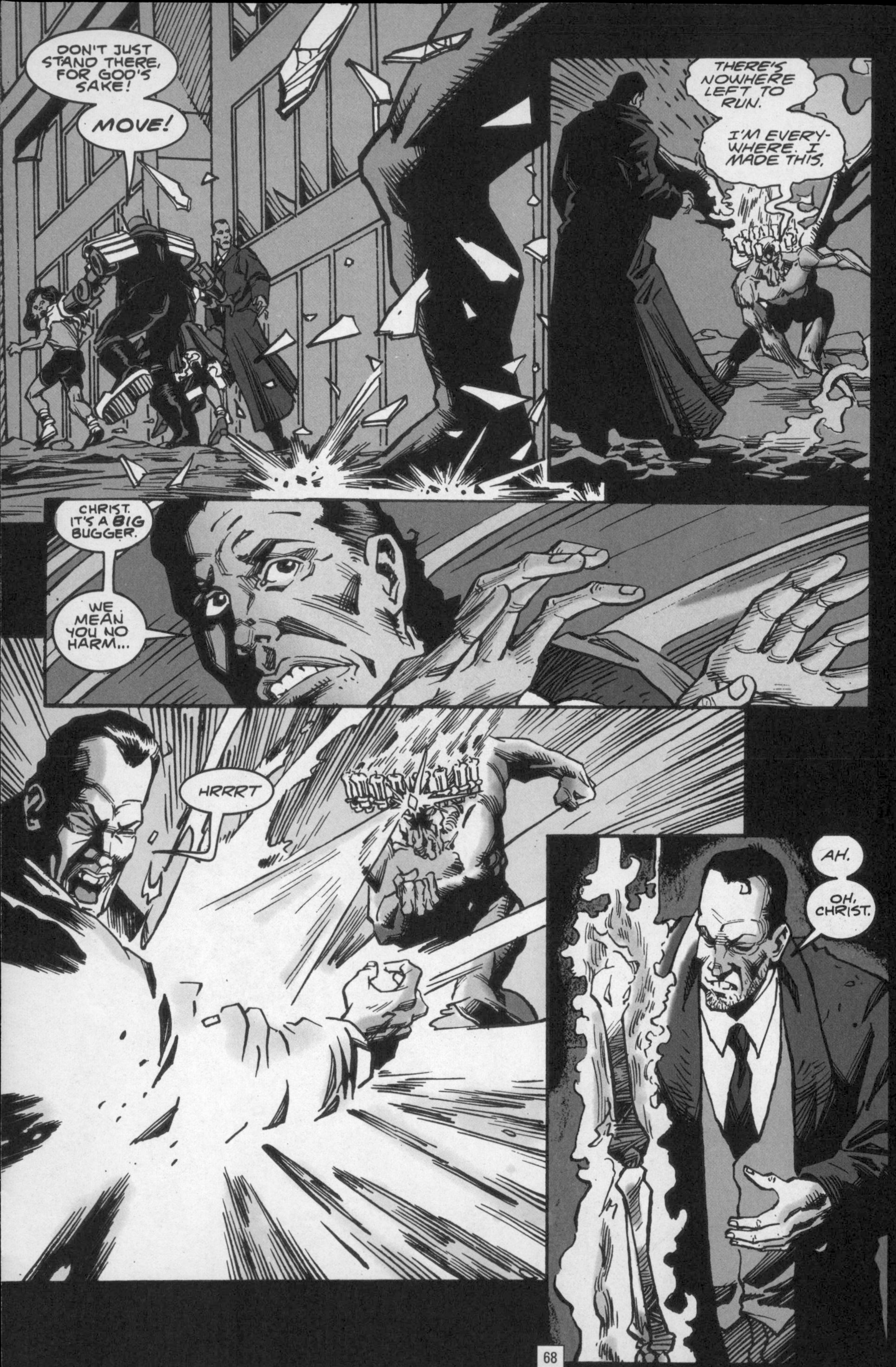
DON'T JUST STAND THERE, FOR GOD'S SAKE!
MOVE!
THERE'S NOWHERE LEFT TO RUN.
I'M EVERY-WHERE. I MADE THIS.
CHRIST. IT'S A BIG BUGGER.
WE MEAN YOU NO HARM...
HRRRT
AH.
OH, CHRIST.

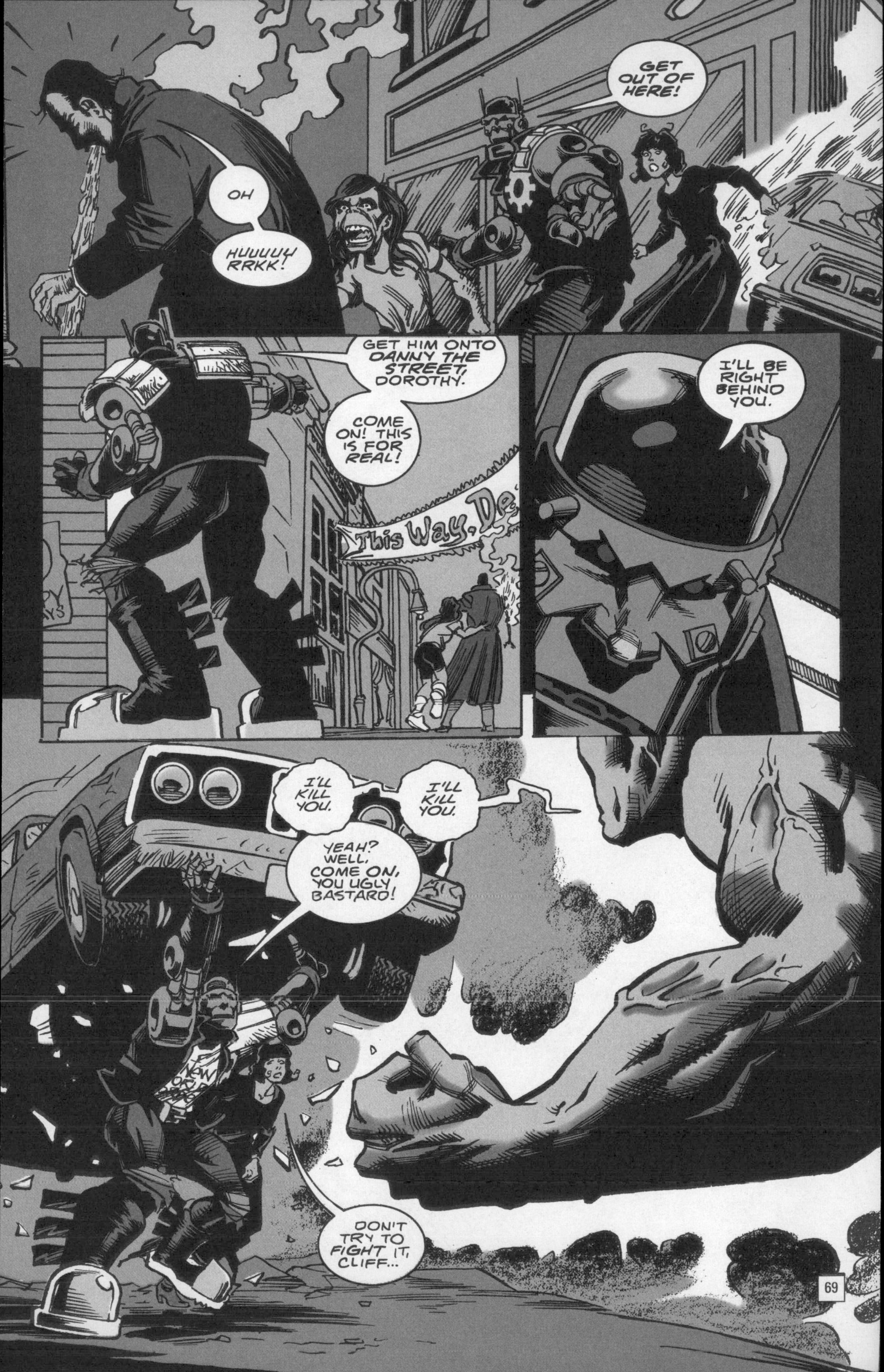

GET OUT OF HERE!
OH
HUUUUH RRKK!
GET HIM ONTO DANNY THE STREET, DOROTHY.
COME ON! THIS IS FOR REAL!
This Way, De
I'LL BE RIGHT BEHIND YOU.
I'LL KILL YOU.
I'LL KILL YOU.
YEAH? WELL, COME ON, YOU UGLY BASTARD!
DON'T TRY TO FIGHT IT, CLIFF...

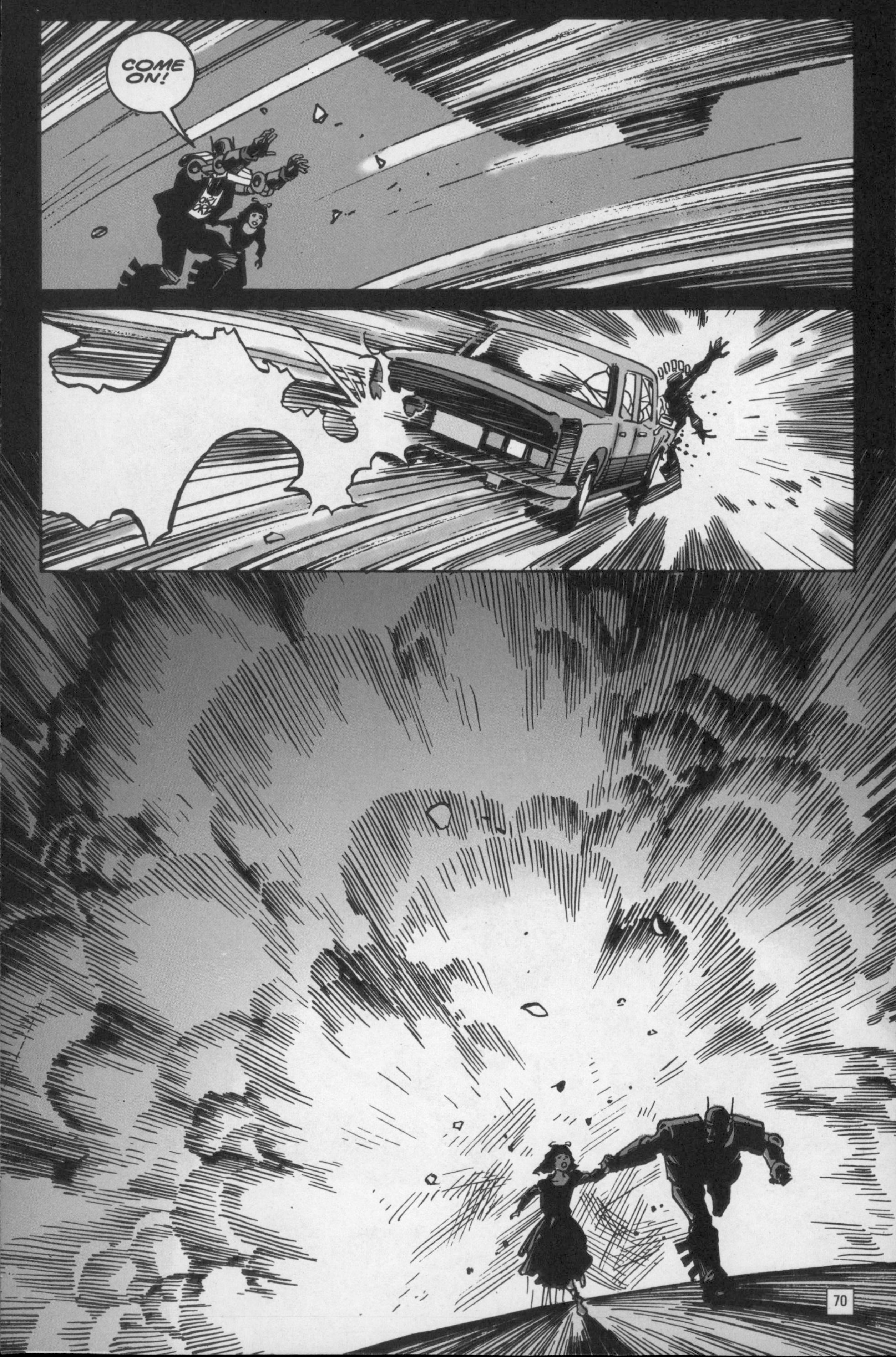
COME ON!

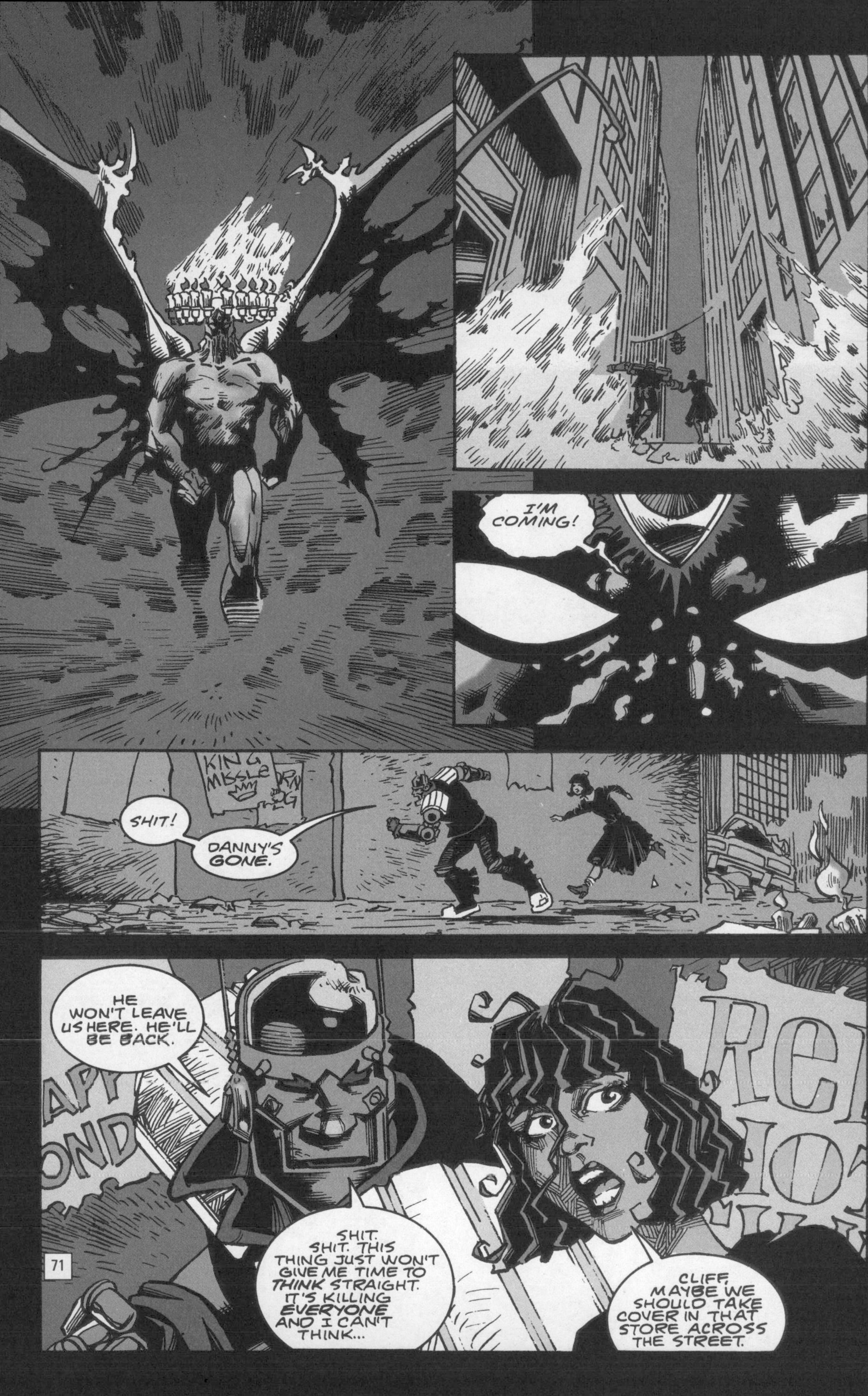
I'M COMING!
KING MISSLE
SHIT!
DANNY'S GONE.
HE WON'T LEAVE US HERE. HE'LL BE BACK.
SHIT. SHIT. THIS THING JUST WON'T GIVE ME TIME TO THINK STRAIGHT. IT'S KILLING EVERYONE AND I CAN'T THINK...
CLIFF, MAYBE WE SHOULD TAKE COVER IN THAT STORE ACROSS THE STREET.

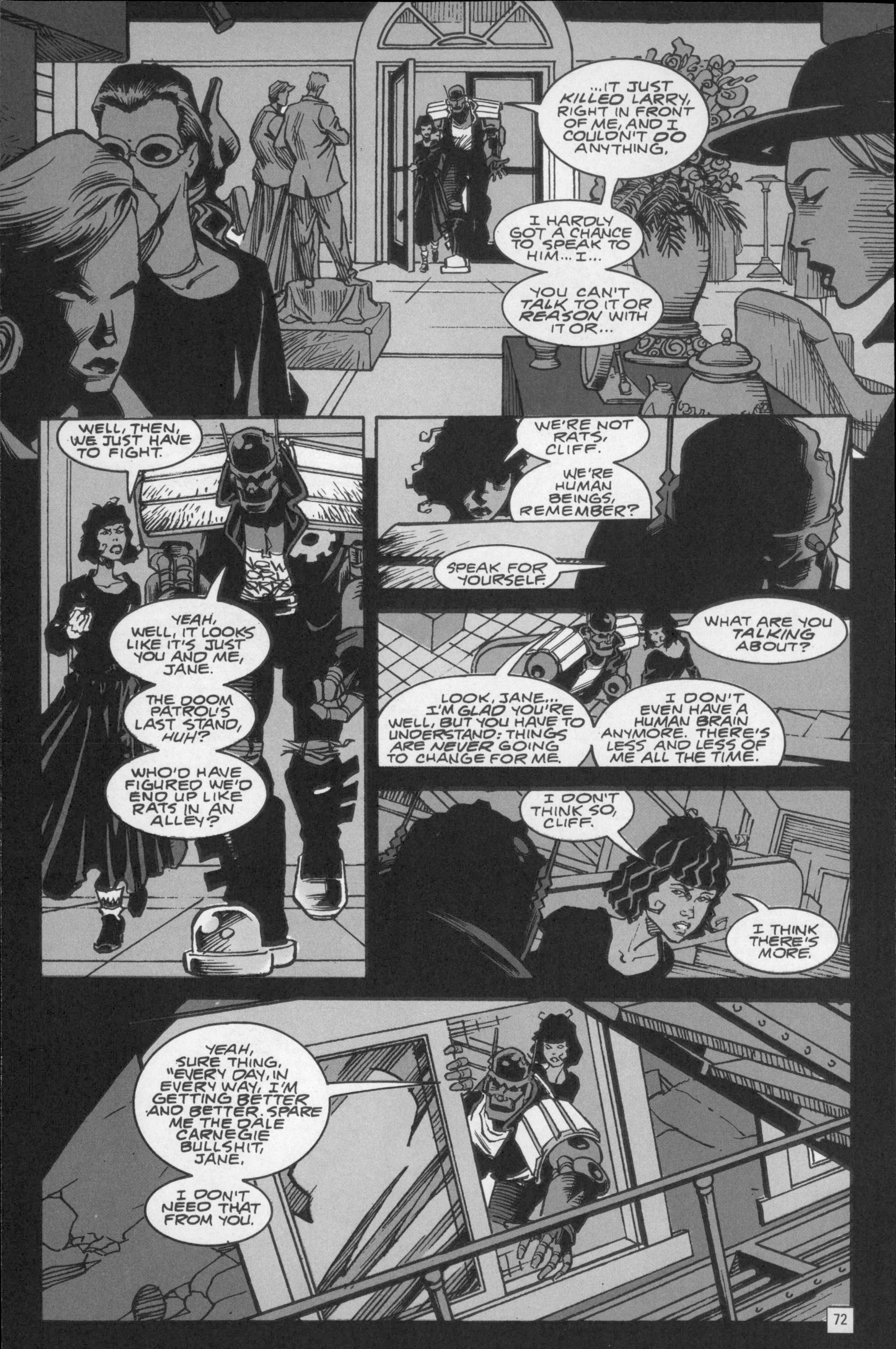
...IT JUST KILLED LARRY, RIGHT IN FRONT OF ME, AND I COULDN'T DO ANYTHING.
I HARDLY GOT A CHANCE TO SPEAK TO HIM... I...
YOU CAN'T TALK TO IT OR REASON WITH IT OR...
WELL, THEN, WE JUST HAVE TO FIGHT.
YEAH, WELL, IT LOOKS LIKE IT'S JUST YOU AND ME, JANE.
THE DOOM PATROL'S LAST STAND, HUH?
WHO'D HAVE FIGURED WE'D END UP LIKE RATS IN AN ALLEY?
WE'RE NOT RATS, CLIFF.
WE'RE HUMAN BEINGS, REMEMBER?
SPEAK FOR YOURSELF.
WHAT ARE YOU TALKING ABOUT?
LOOK, JANE... I'M GLAD YOU'RE WELL, BUT YOU HAVE TO UNDERSTAND: THINGS ARE NEVER GOING TO CHANGE FOR ME.
I DON'T EVEN HAVE A HUMAN BRAIN ANYMORE. THERE'S LESS AND LESS OF ME ALL THE TIME.
I DON'T THINK SO, CLIFF.
I THINK THERE'S MORE.
YEAH, SURE THING. "EVERY DAY, IN EVERY WAY, I'M GETTING BETTER AND BETTER. SPARE ME THE DALE CARNEGIE BULLSHIT, JANE.
I DON'T NEED THAT FROM YOU.

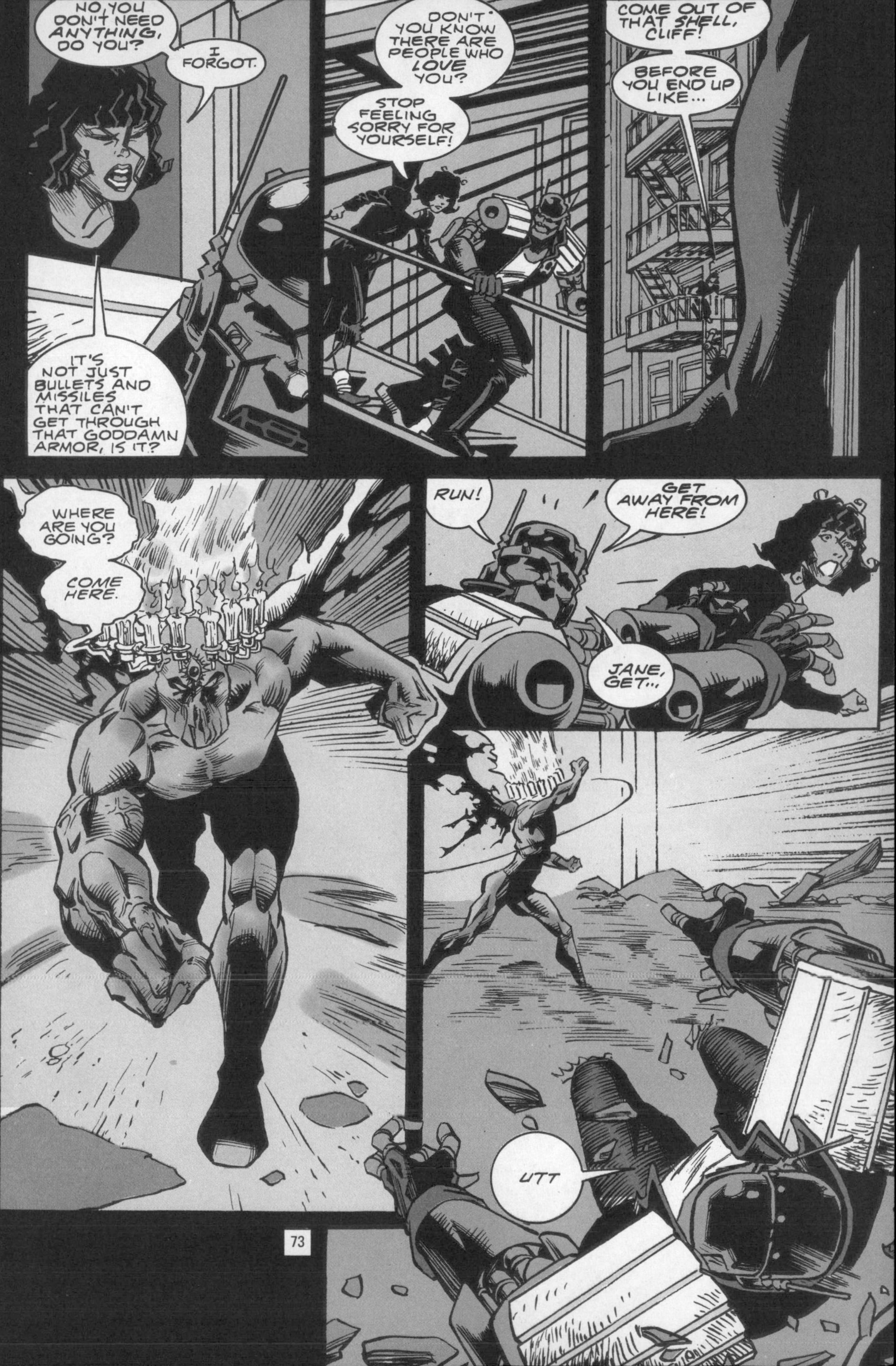
NO, YOU DON'T NEED ANYTHING, DO YOU?
I FORGOT.
IT'S NOT JUST BULLETS AND MISSILES THAT CAN'T GET THROUGH THAT GODDAMN ARMOR, IS IT?
DON'T YOU KNOW THERE ARE PEOPLE WHO LOVE YOU?
STOP FEELING SORRY FOR YOURSELF!
COME OUT OF THAT SHELL, CLIFF!
BEFORE YOU END UP LIKE...
WHERE ARE YOU GOING?
COME HERE.
RUN!
GET AWAY FROM HERE!
JANE, GET...
UTT

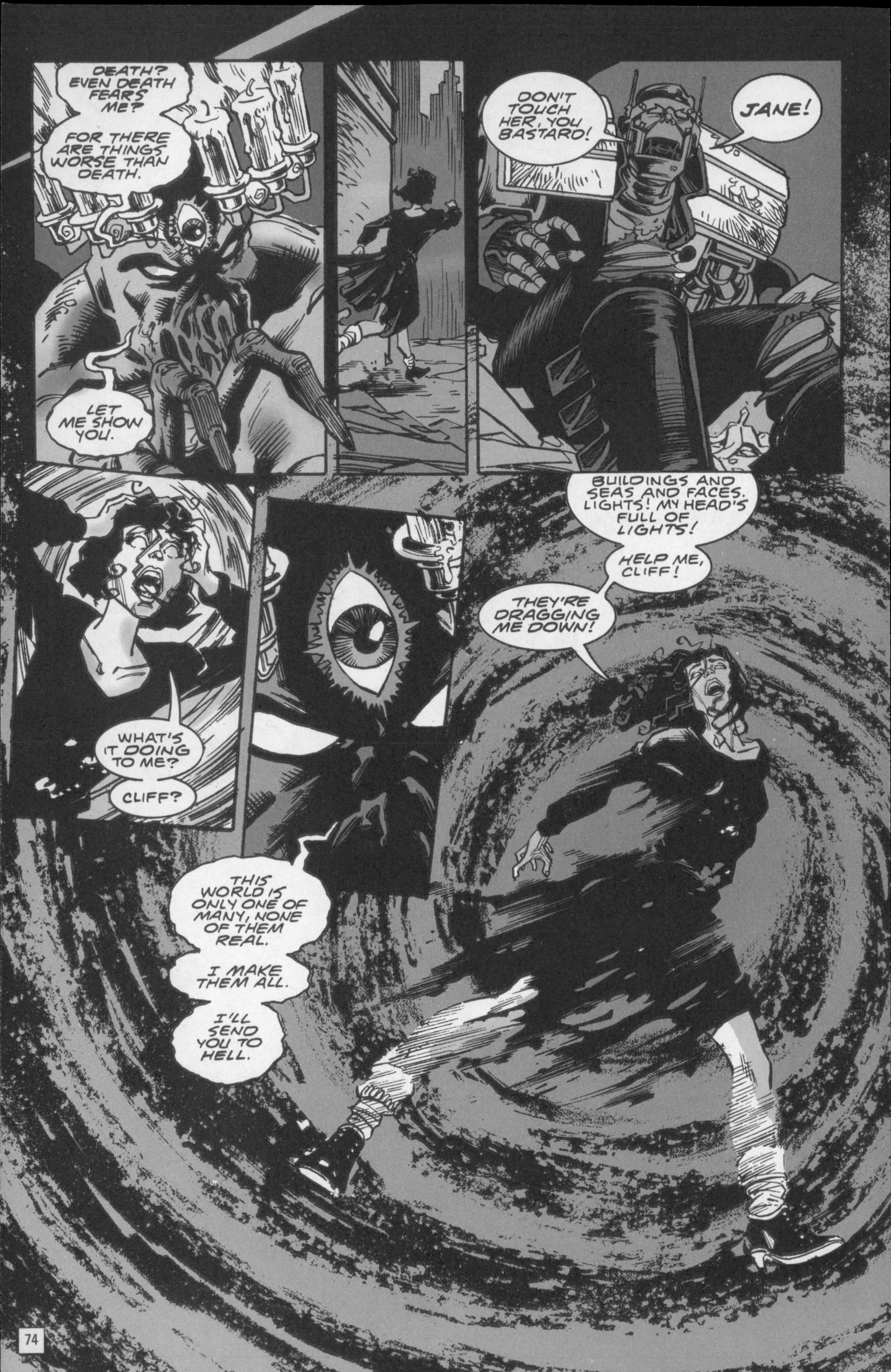
DEATH? EVEN DEATH FEARS ME?
FOR THERE ARE THINGS WORSE THAN DEATH.
LET ME SHOW YOU.
DON'T TOUCH HER, YOU BASTARD!
JANE!
WHAT'S IT DOING TO ME?
CLIFF?
BUILDINGS AND SEAS AND FACES. LIGHTS! MY HEAD'S FULL OF LIGHTS!
HELP ME, CLIFF!
THEY'RE DRAGGING ME DOWN!
THIS WORLD IS ONLY ONE OF MANY, NONE OF THEM REAL.
I MAKE THEM ALL.
I'LL SEND YOU TO HELL.

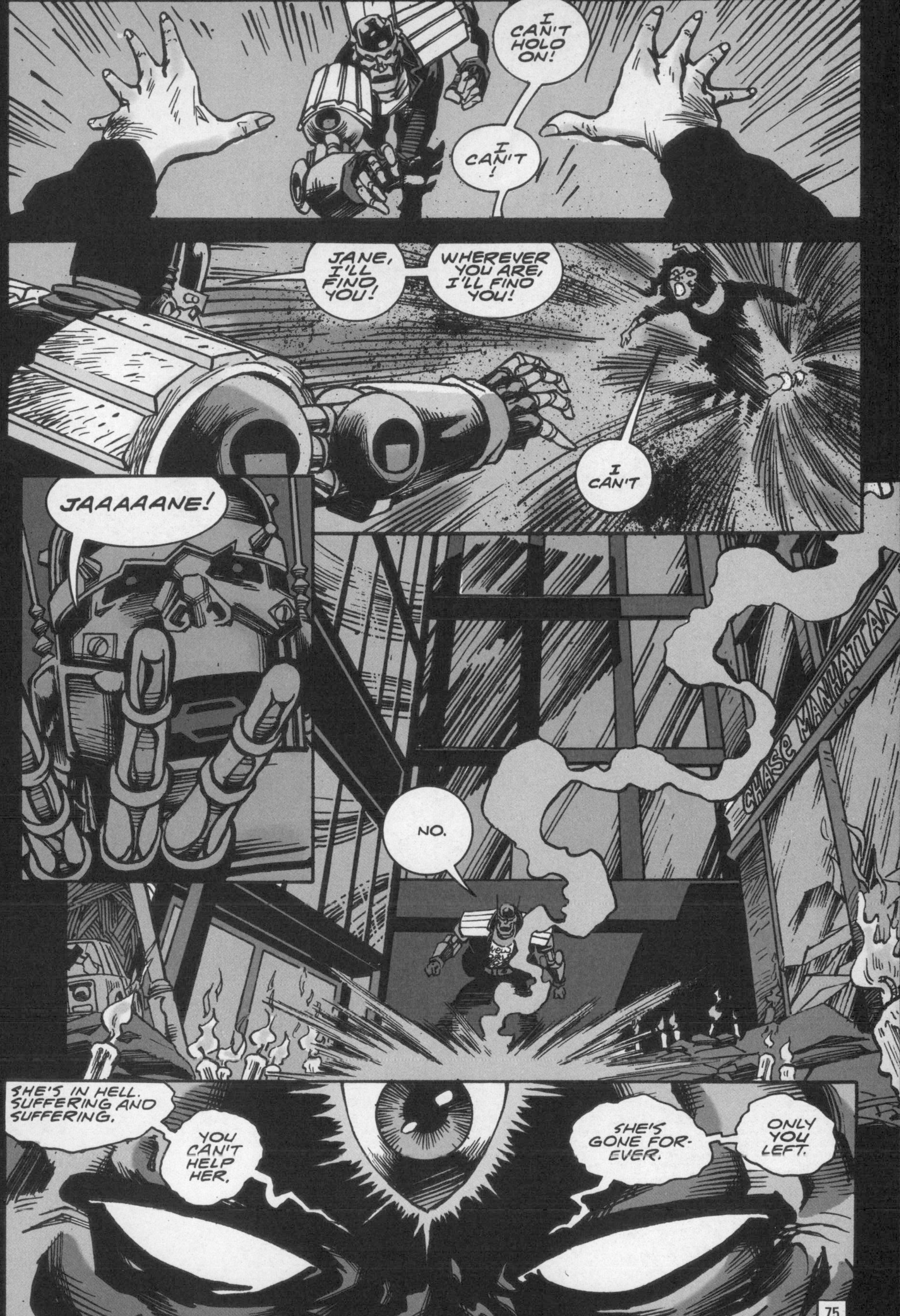

I CAN'T HOLD ON!
I CAN'T!
JANE, I'LL FIND YOU!
WHEREVER YOU ARE, I'LL FIND YOU!
I CAN'T
JAAAAANE!
CHASE MANHATTAN
NO.
SHE'S IN HELL. SUFFERING AND SUFFERING.
YOU CAN'T HELP HER.
SHE'S GONE FOREVER.
ONLY YOU LEFT.

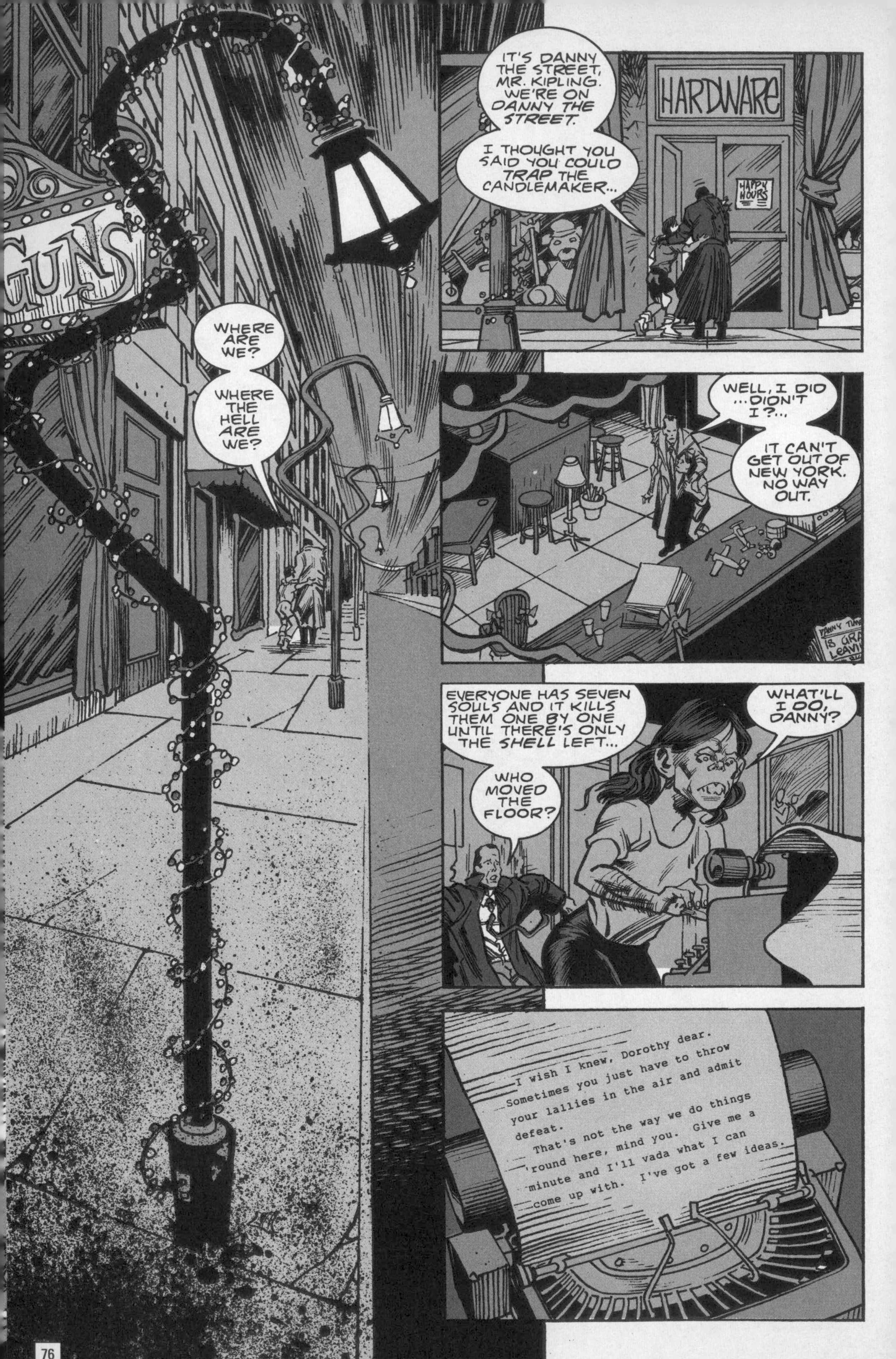

GUNS
WHERE ARE WE?
WHERE THE HELL ARE WE?
HARDWARE
HAPPY HOURS
IT'S DANNY THE STREET, MR. KIPLING. WE'RE ON DANNY THE STREET.
I THOUGHT YOU SAID YOU COULD TRAP THE CANDLEMAKER...
WELL, I DID ...DIDN'T I?...
IT CAN'T GET OUT OF NEW YORK. NO WAY OUT.
EVERYONE HAS SEVEN SOULS AND IT KILLS THEM ONE BY ONE UNTIL THERE'S ONLY THE SHELL LEFT...
WHAT'LL I DO, DANNY?
WHO MOVED THE FLOOR?
I wish I knew, Dorothy dear. Sometimes you just have to throw your lallies in the air and admit defeat.
That's not the way we do things 'round here, mind you. Give me a minute and I'll vada what I can come up with. I've got a few ideas.

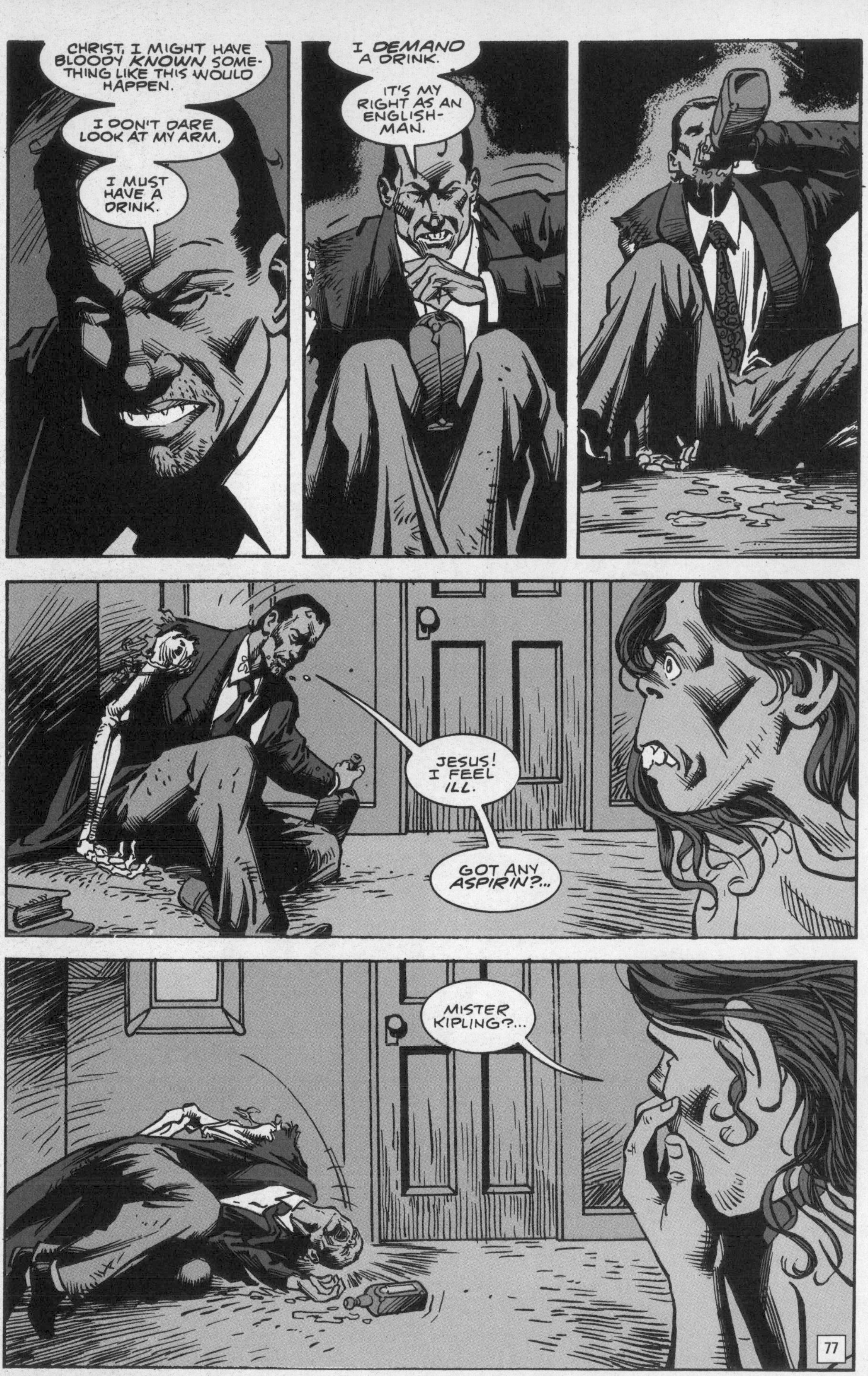
CHRIST, I MIGHT HAVE BLOODY KNOWN SOMETHING LIKE THIS WOULD HAPPEN.
I DON'T DARE LOOK AT MY ARM.
I MUST HAVE A DRINK.
I DEMAND A DRINK.
IT'S MY RIGHT AS AN ENGLISHMAN.
JESUS! I FEEL ILL.
GOT ANY ASPIRIN?...
MISTER KIPLING?...

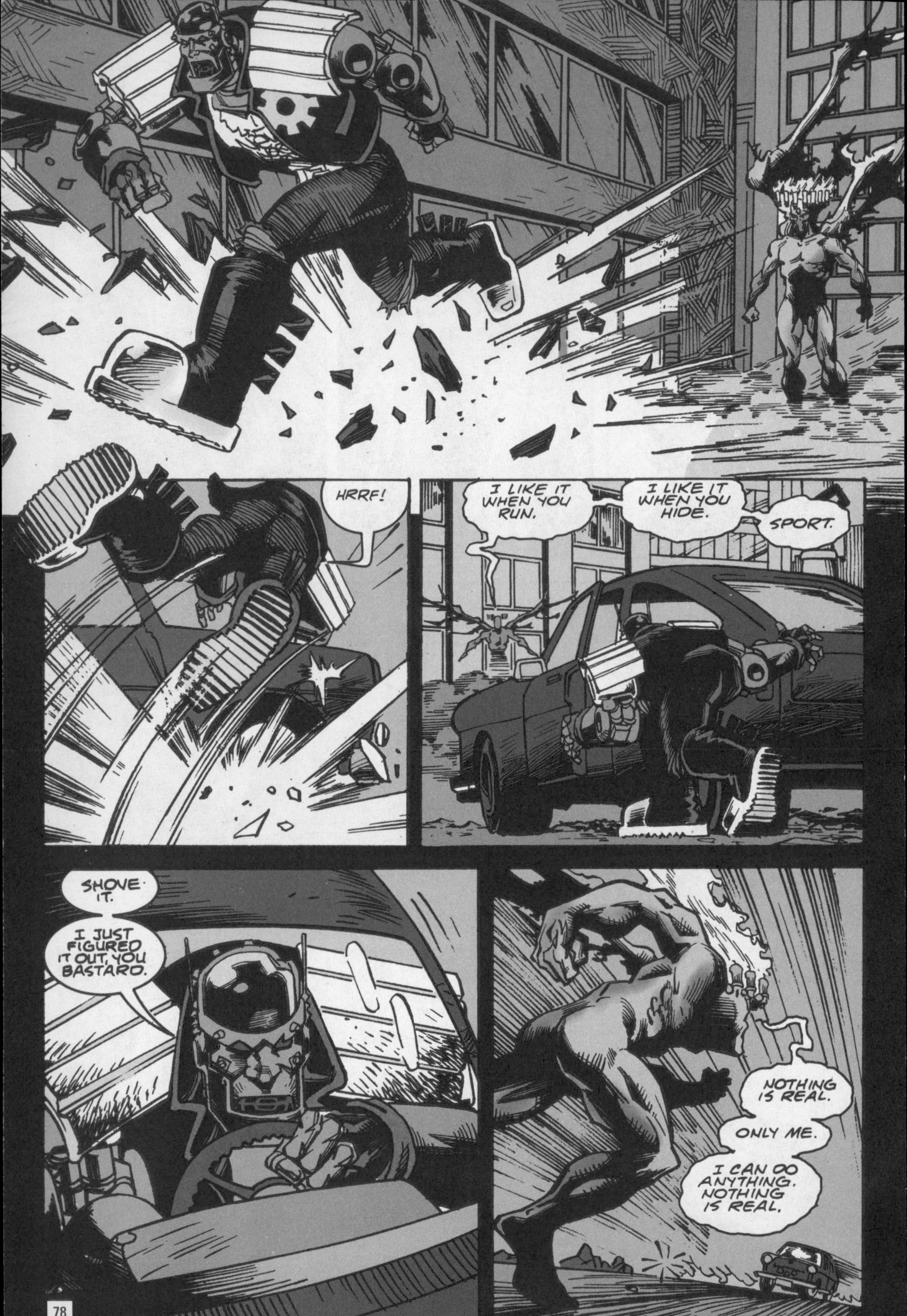
HRRF!
I LIKE IT WHEN YOU RUN.
I LIKE IT WHEN YOU HIDE.
SPORT.
SHOVE IT.
I JUST FIGURED IT OUT, YOU BASTARD.
NOTHING IS REAL.
ONLY ME.
I CAN DO ANYTHING. NOTHING IS REAL.

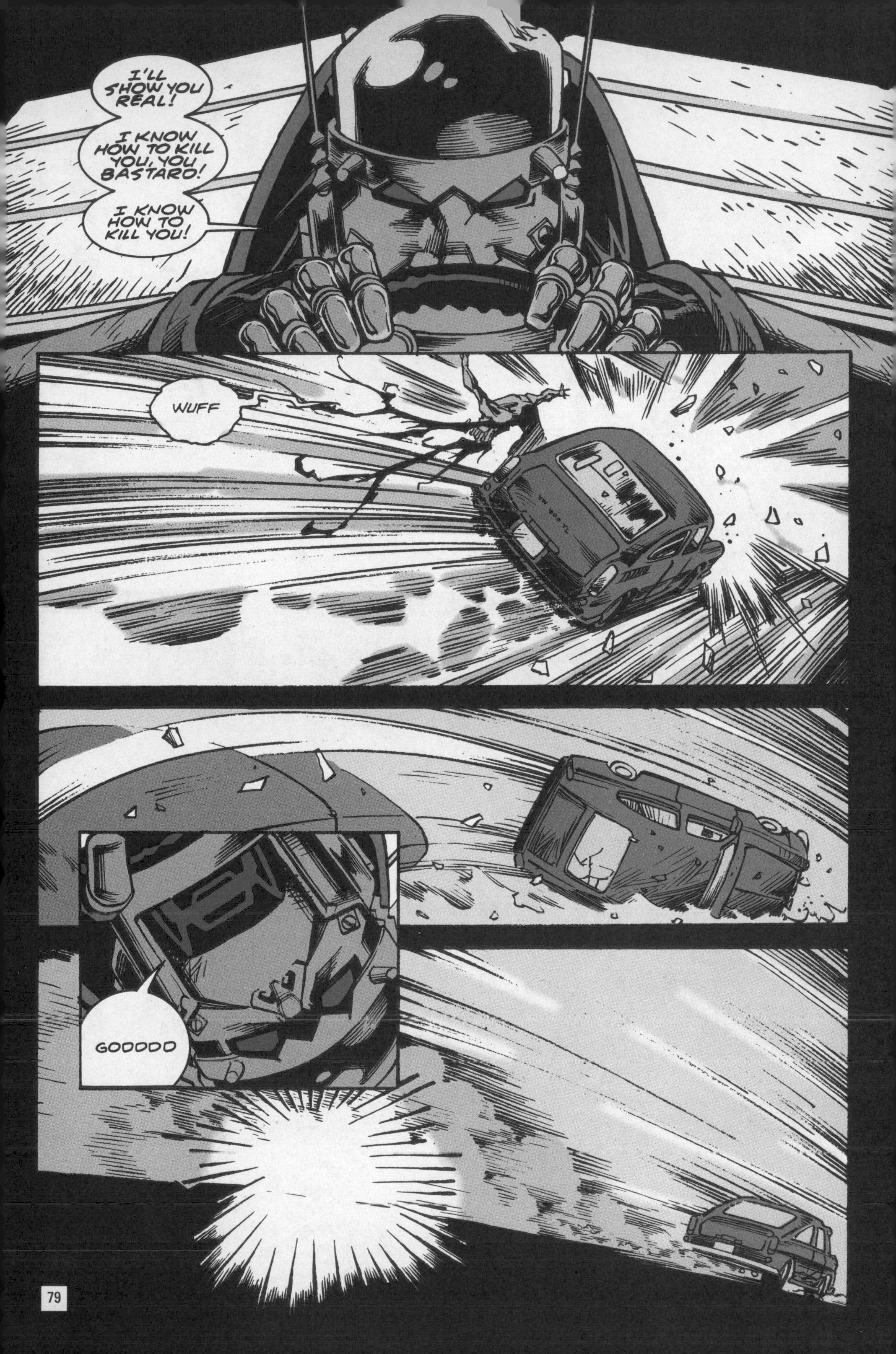
I'LL SHOW YOU REAL!
I KNOW HOW TO KILL YOU, YOU BASTARD!
I KNOW HOW TO KILL YOU!
WUFF
GOODDD

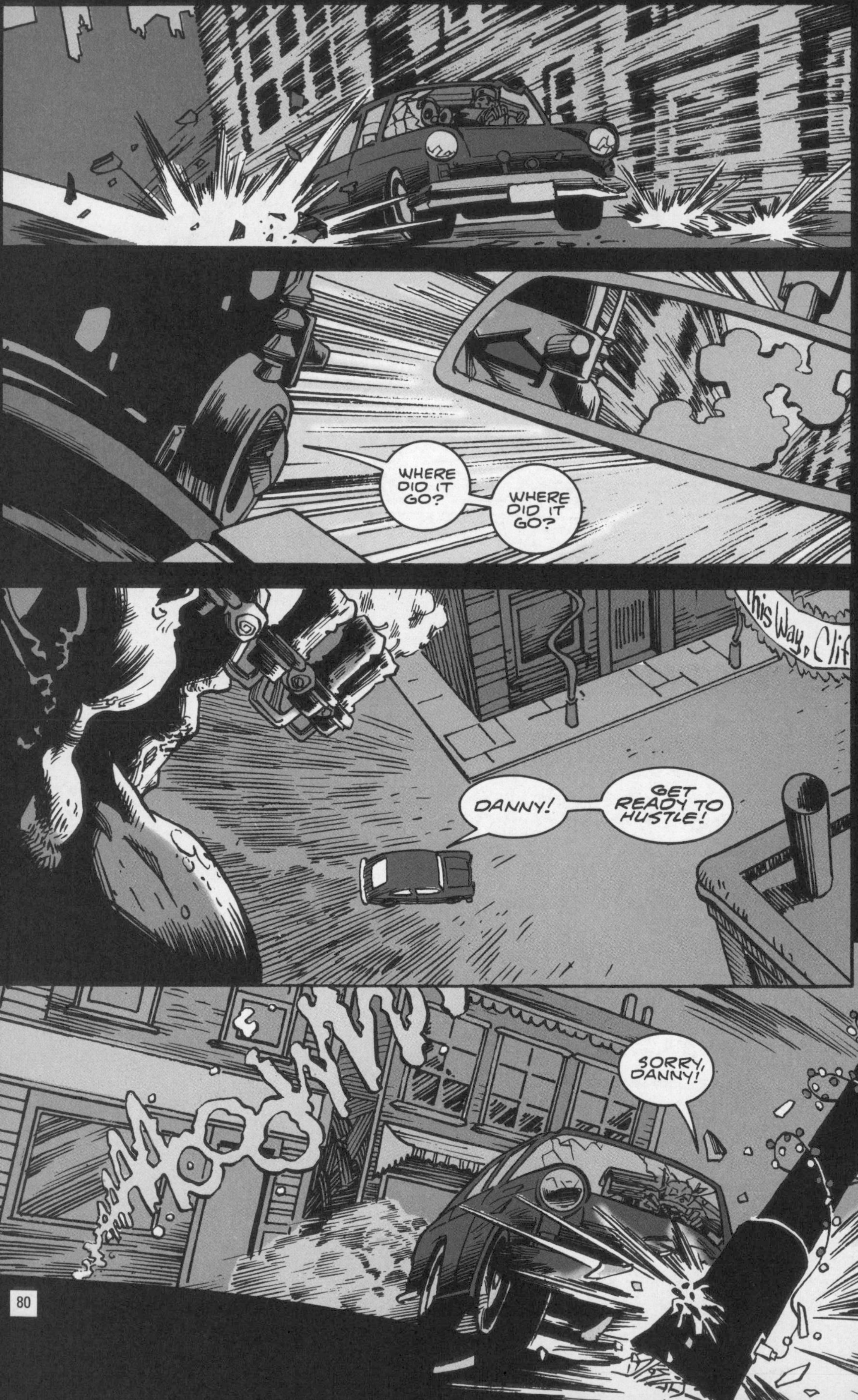
WHERE DID IT GO?
WHERE DID IT GO?
DANNY!
GET READY TO HUSTLE!
SORRY, DANNY!

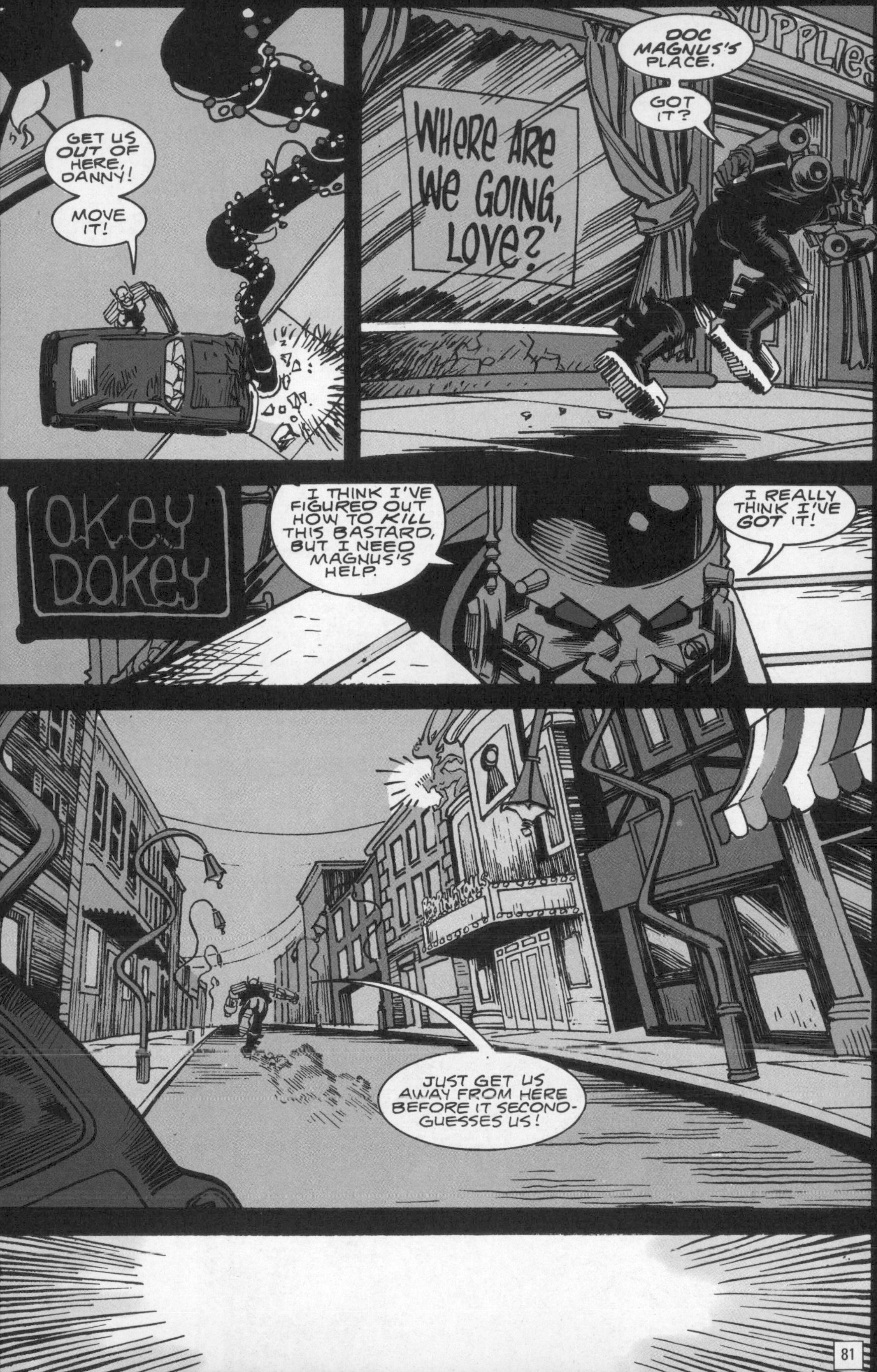
GET US OUT OF HERE, DANNY!
MOVE IT!
DOC MAGNUS'S PLACE.
GOT IT?
SUPPLIES
WHERE ARE WE GOING, LOVE?
OKEY DOKEY
I THINK I'VE FIGURED OUT HOW TO KILL THIS BASTARD, BUT I NEED MAGNUS'S HELP.
I REALLY THINK I'VE GOT IT!
JUST GET US AWAY FROM HERE BEFORE IT SECOND-GUESSES US!

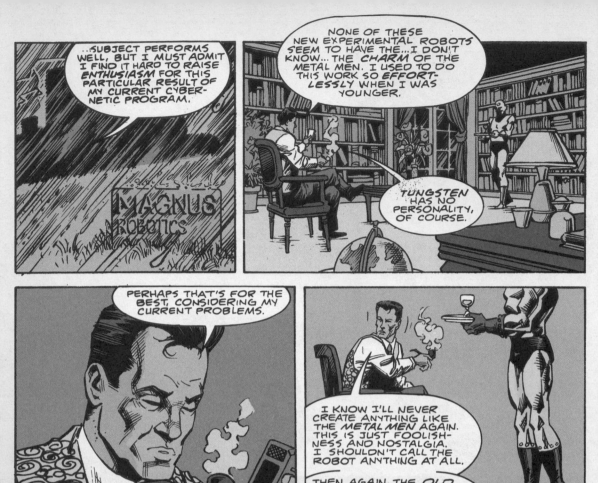

...SUBJECT PERFORMS WELL, BUT I MUST ADMIT I FIND IT HARD TO RAISE ENTHUSIASM FOR THIS PARTICULAR RESULT OF MY CURRENT CYBERNETIC PROGRAM.

NONE OF THESE NEW EXPERIMENTAL ROBOTS SEEM TO HAVE THE...I DON'T KNOW...THE *CHARM* OF THE METAL MEN. I USED TO DO THIS WORK SO EFFORTLESSLY WHEN I WAS YOUNGER.

TUNGSTEN HAS NO PERSONALITY, OF COURSE.

MAGNUS ROBOTICS

PERHAPS THAT'S FOR THE BEST, CONSIDERING MY CURRENT PROBLEMS.

I KNOW I'LL NEVER CREATE ANYTHING LIKE THE *METAL MEN* AGAIN. THIS IS JUST FOOLISHNESS AND NOSTALGIA. I SHOULDN'T CALL THE ROBOT ANYTHING AT ALL.

THEN AGAIN, THE *OLD* NAME FOR TUNGSTEN WAS *WOLFRAM*, WHICH IS A LITTLE MORE DRAMATIC AND MIGHT SUGGEST...

MAGNUS?

IS THAT...

CLIFF? IS THAT YOU?

82

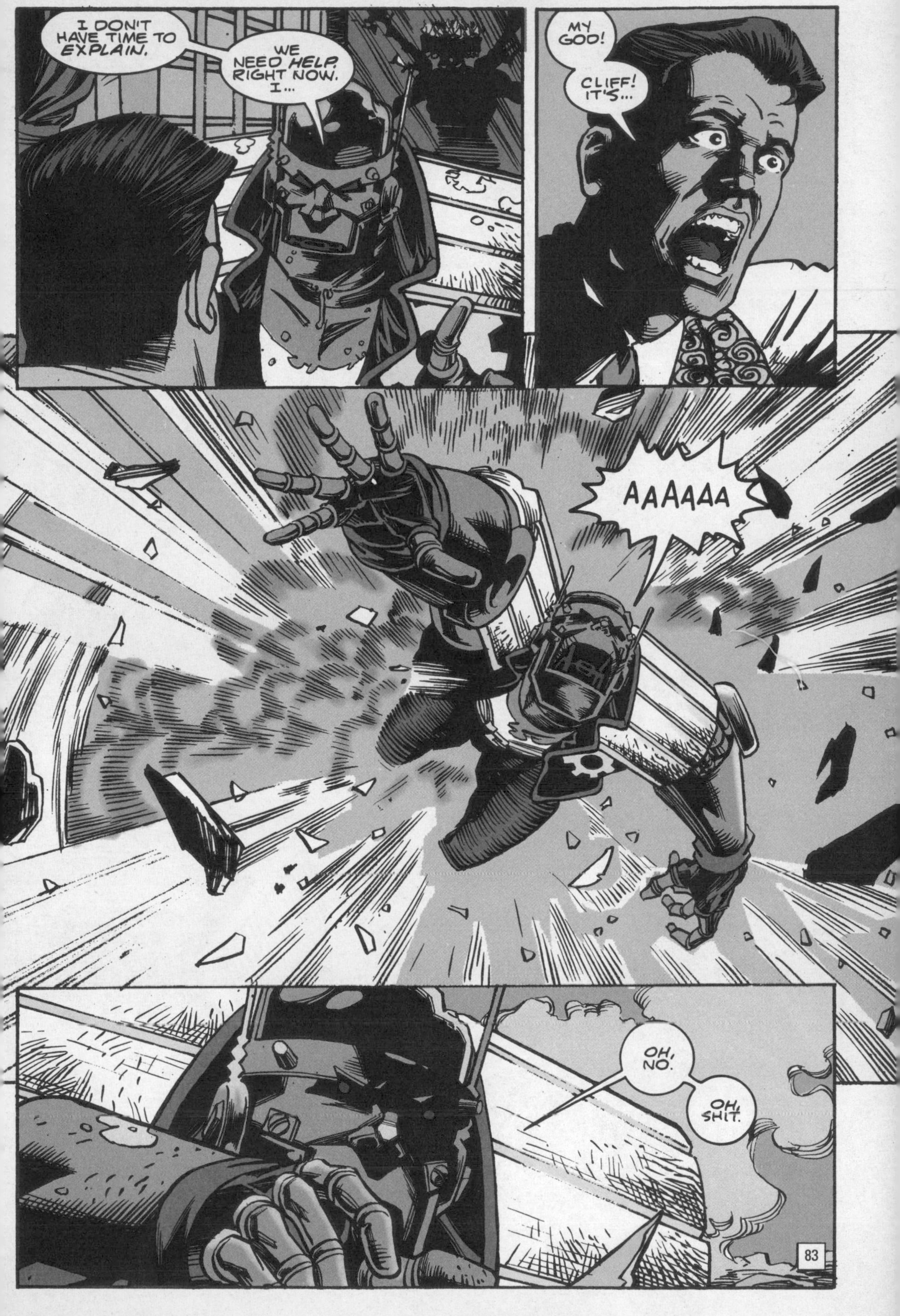

I DON'T HAVE TIME TO EXPLAIN.
WE NEED HELP. RIGHT NOW. I...
MY GOD!
CLIFF! IT'S...
AAAAAA
OH, NO.
OH, SHIT.

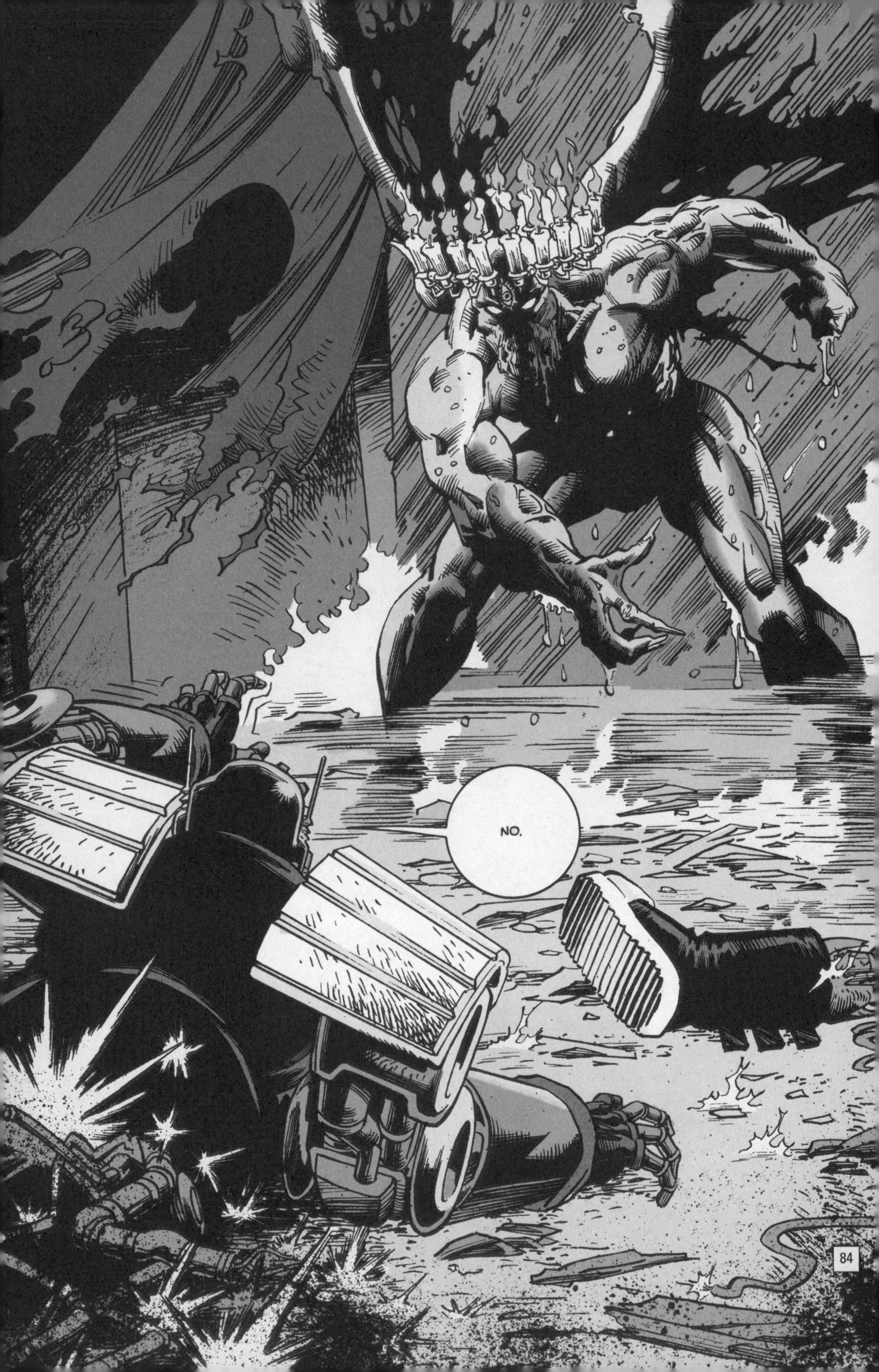
NO.

"You can't kill me. If you **kill** me, the world goes out like a candle."

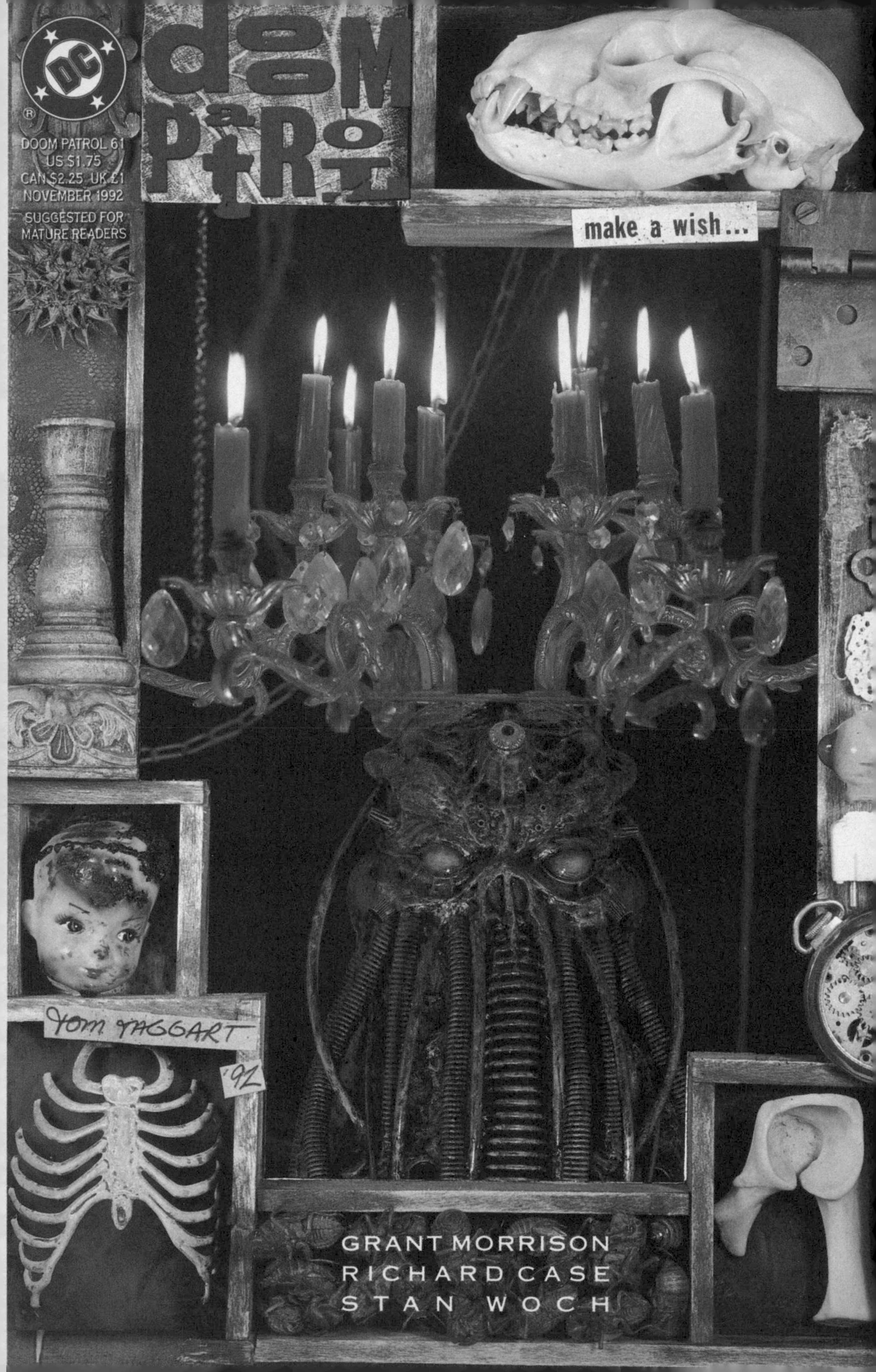
DC
doom Patrol
DOOM PATROL 61
US $1.75
CAN $2.25 UK £1
NOVEMBER 1992
SUGGESTED FOR MATURE READERS
make a wish...
Tom Taggart
'92
GRANT MORRISON
RICHARD CASE
STAN WOCH

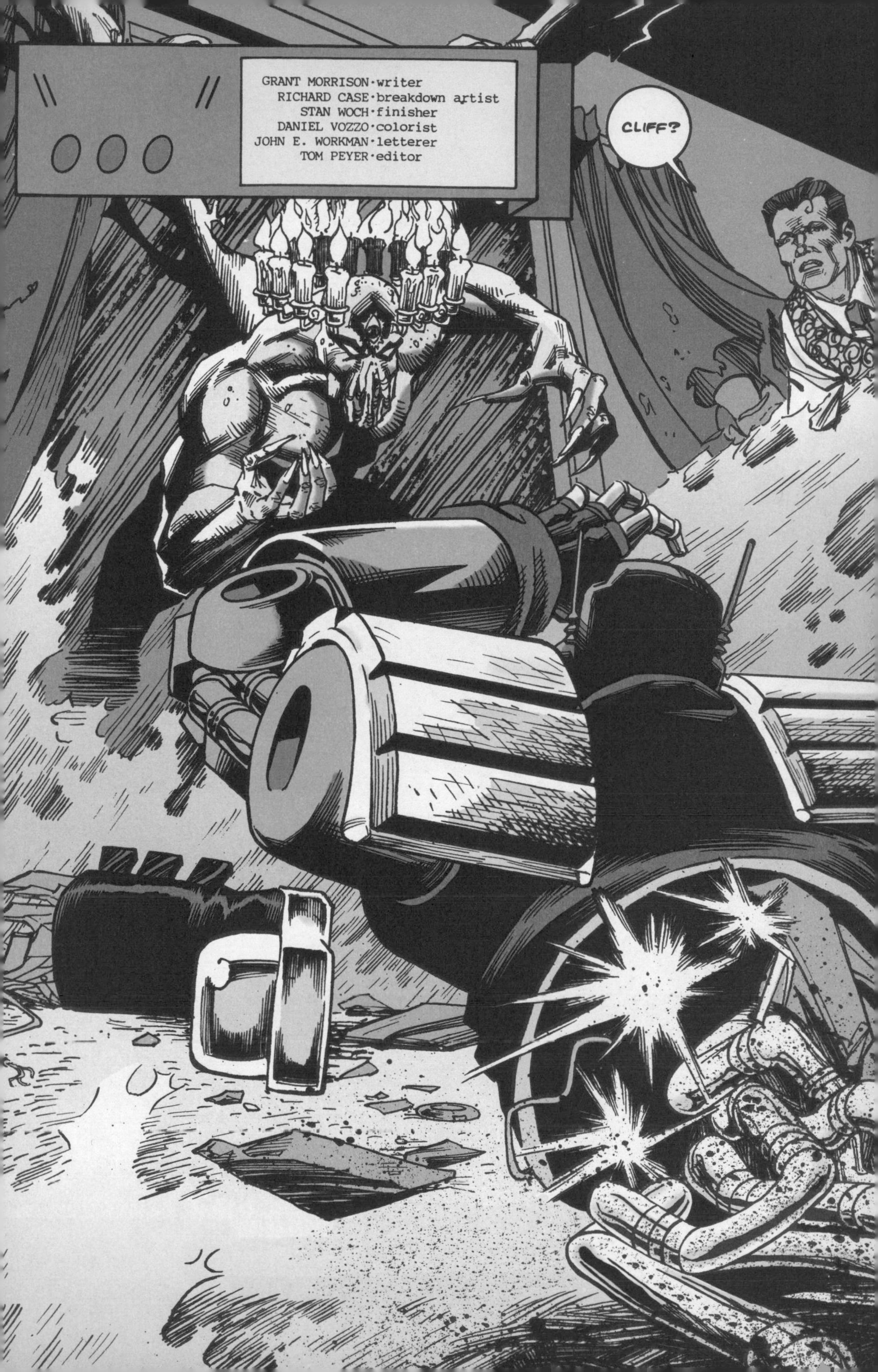
GRANT MORRISON·writer
RICHARD CASE·breakdown artist
STAN WOCH·finisher
DANIEL VOZZO·colorist
JOHN E. WORKMAN·letterer
TOM PEYER·editor
CLIFF?

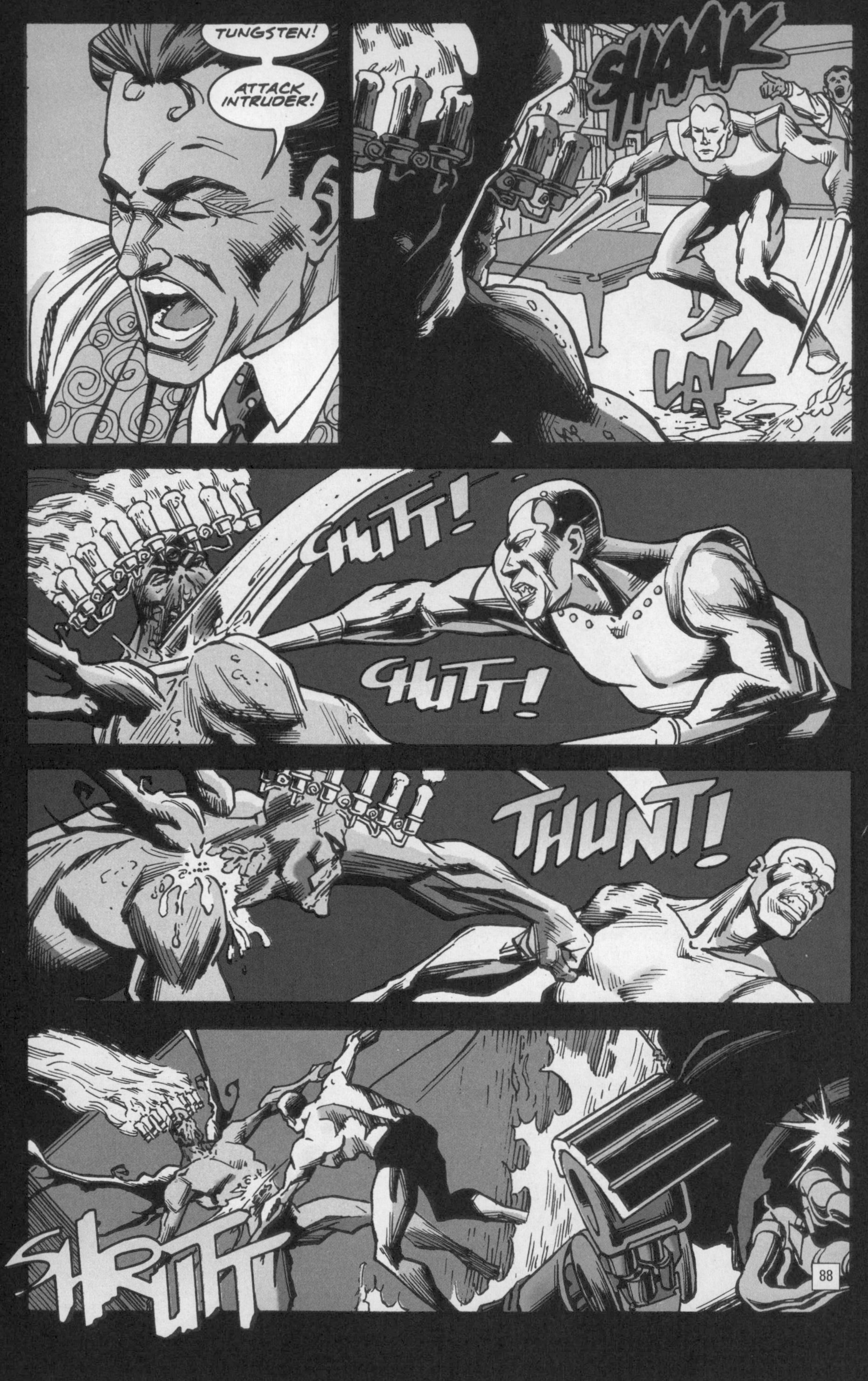
TUNGSTEN!
ATTACK INTRUDER!
SHAAK
LAK
CHUTT!
CHUTT!
THUNT!
SHRUTT

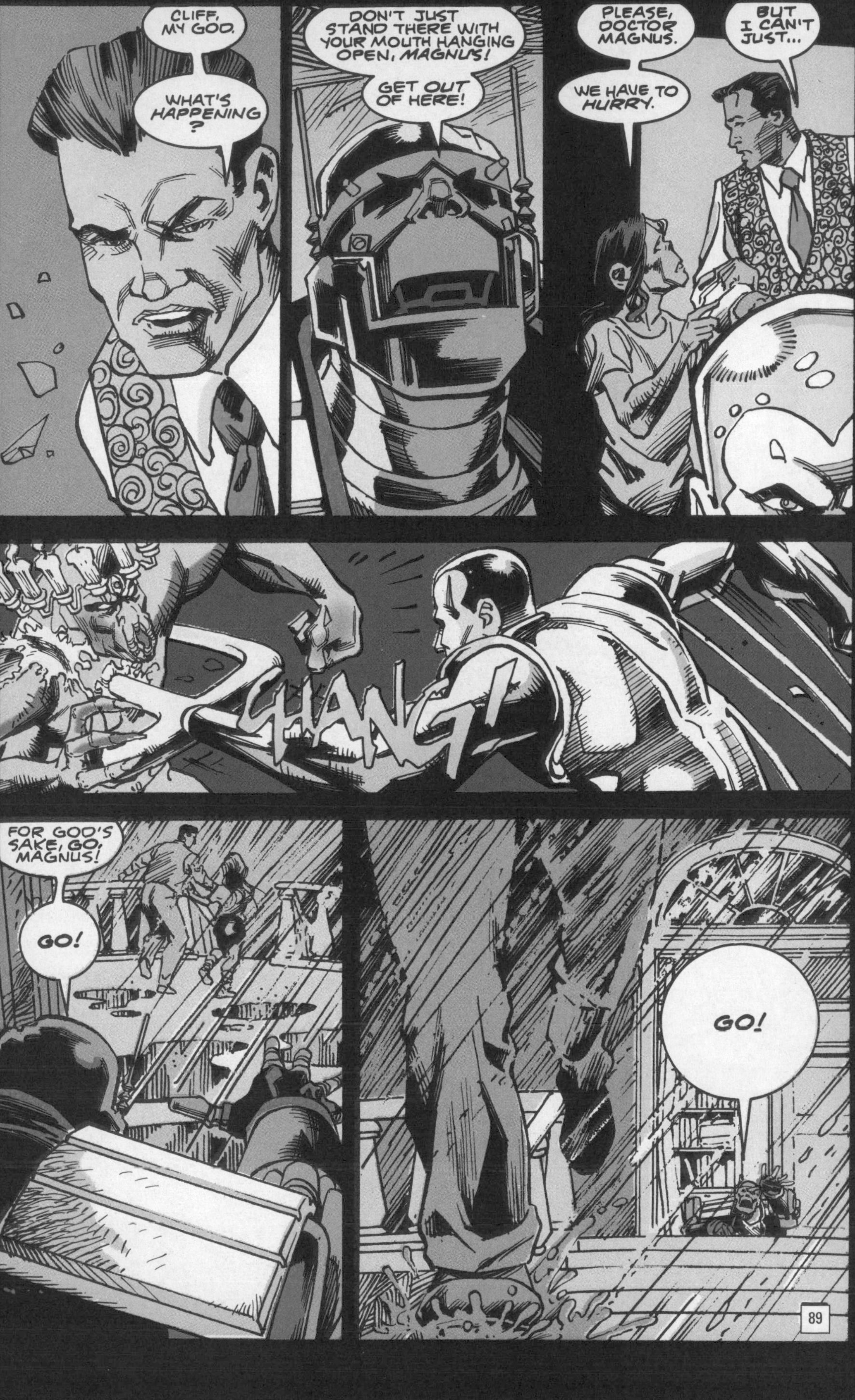
CLIFF, MY GOD.
WHAT'S HAPPENING?
DON'T JUST STAND THERE WITH YOUR MOUTH HANGING OPEN, MAGNUS!
GET OUT OF HERE!
PLEASE, DOCTOR MAGNUS.
WE HAVE TO HURRY.
BUT I CAN'T JUST...
CHANG!
FOR GOD'S SAKE, GO, MAGNUS!
GO!
GO!

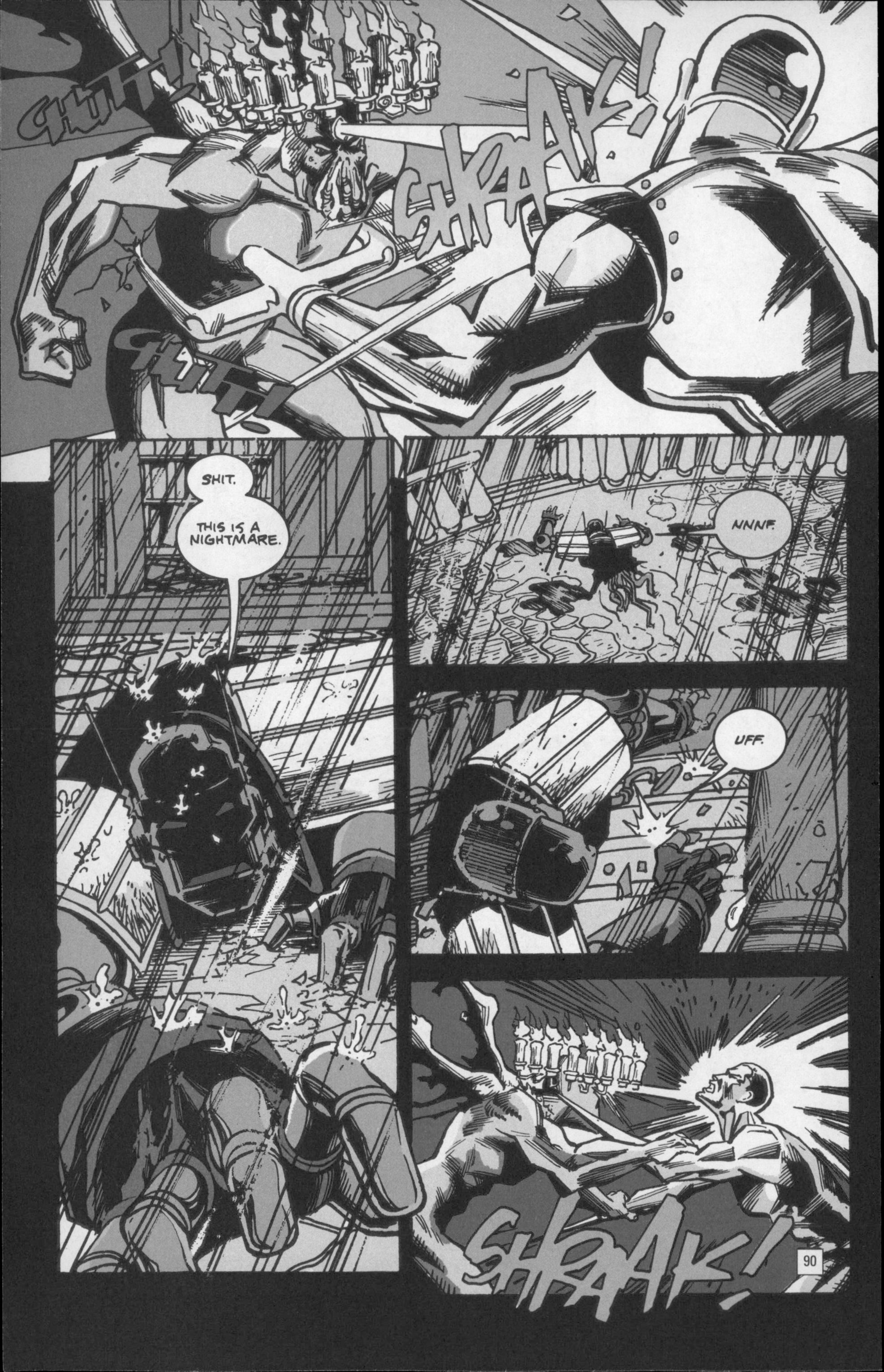
CHUTT!
SHAAK!
CHUTT!
SHIT.
THIS IS A NIGHTMARE.
NNNF.
UFF.
SHAAK!

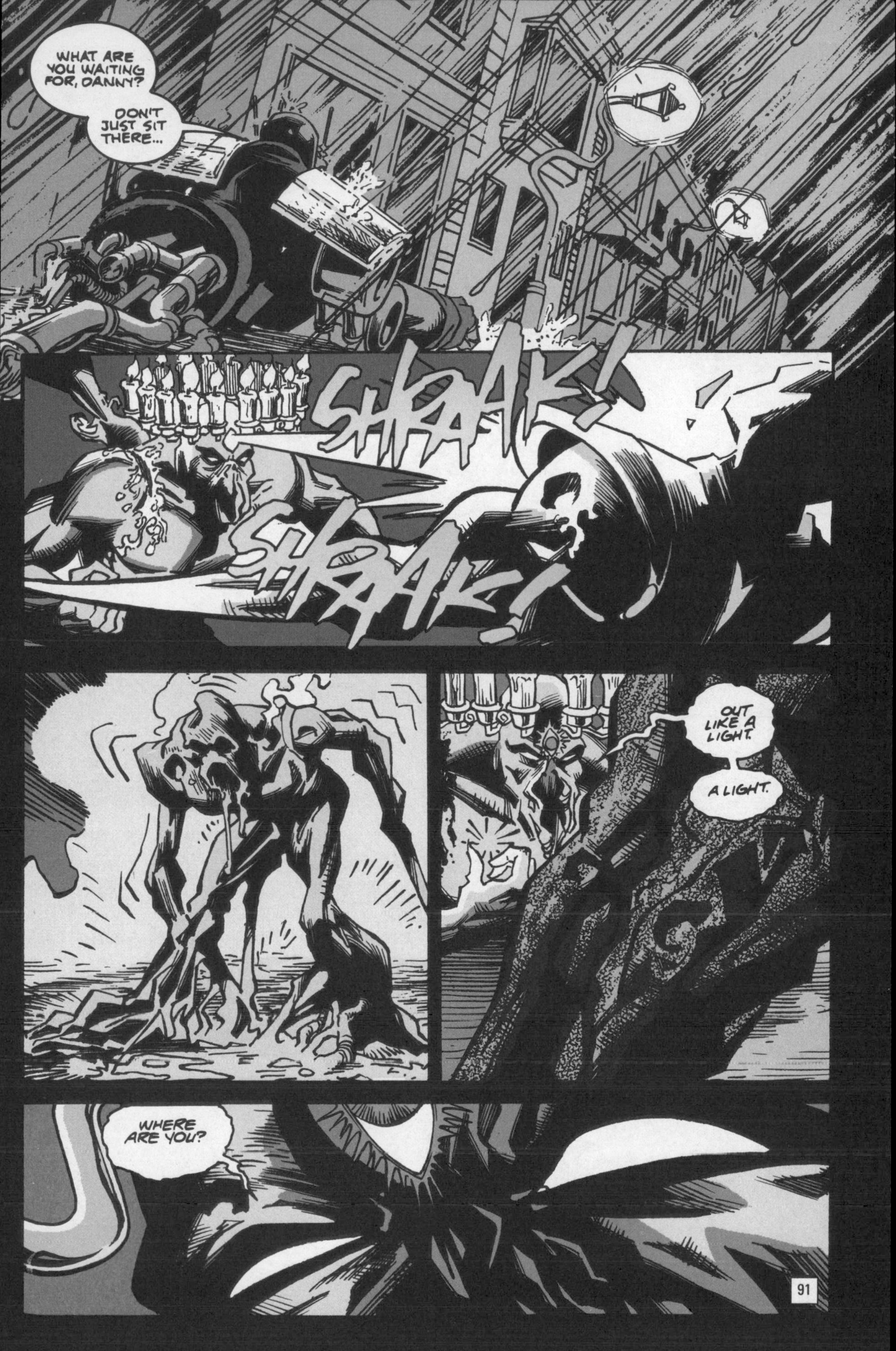
WHAT ARE YOU WAITING FOR, DANNY?
DON'T JUST SIT THERE...
SHRAAK!
SHRAAK!
OUT LIKE A LIGHT.
A LIGHT.
WHERE ARE YOU?

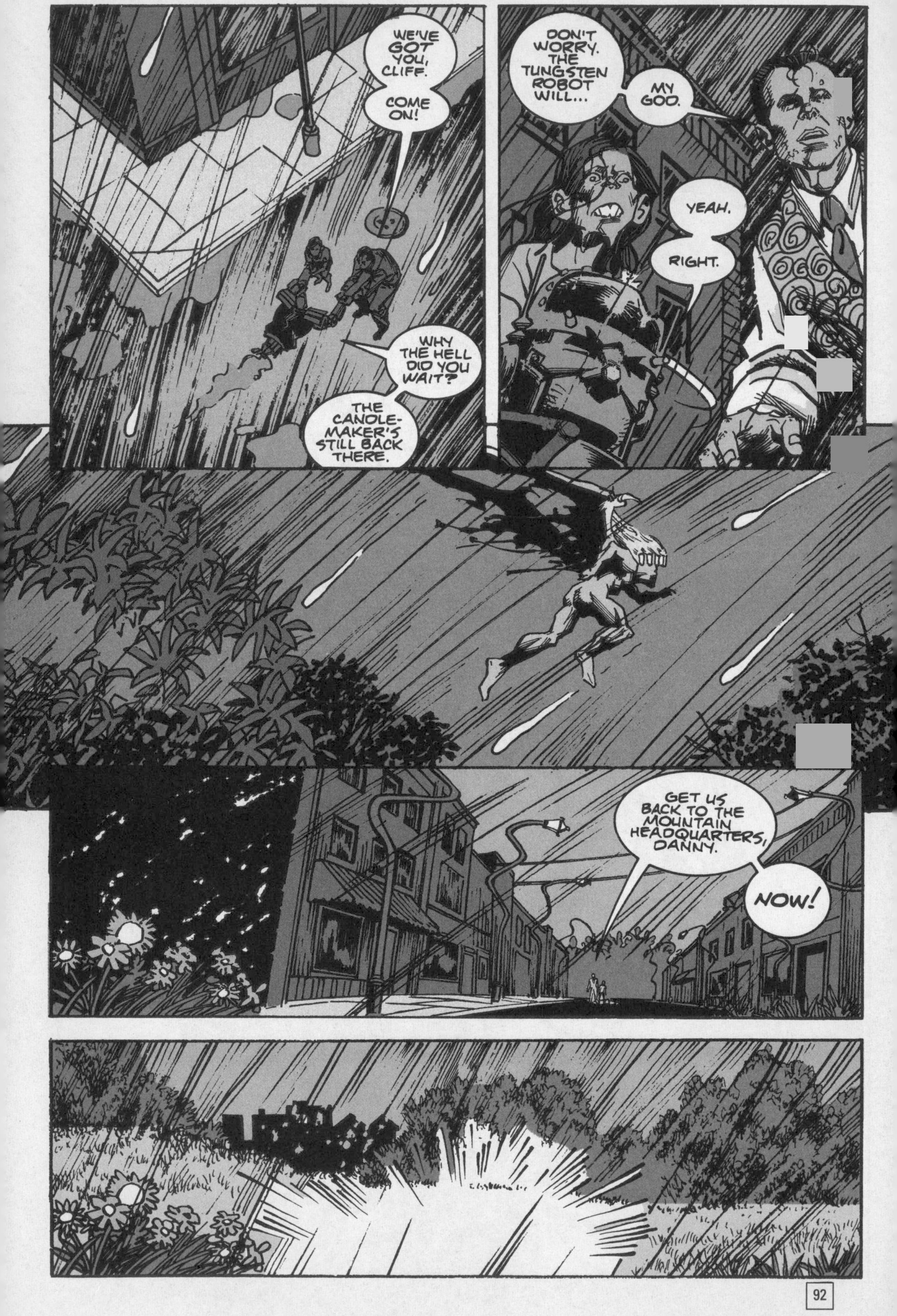
WE'VE GOT YOU, CLIFF.
COME ON!
WHY THE HELL DID YOU WAIT?
THE CANDLE-MAKER'S STILL BACK THERE.
DON'T WORRY. THE TUNGSTEN ROBOT WILL...
MY GOD.
YEAH.
RIGHT.
GET US BACK TO THE MOUNTAIN HEADQUARTERS, DANNY.
NOW!

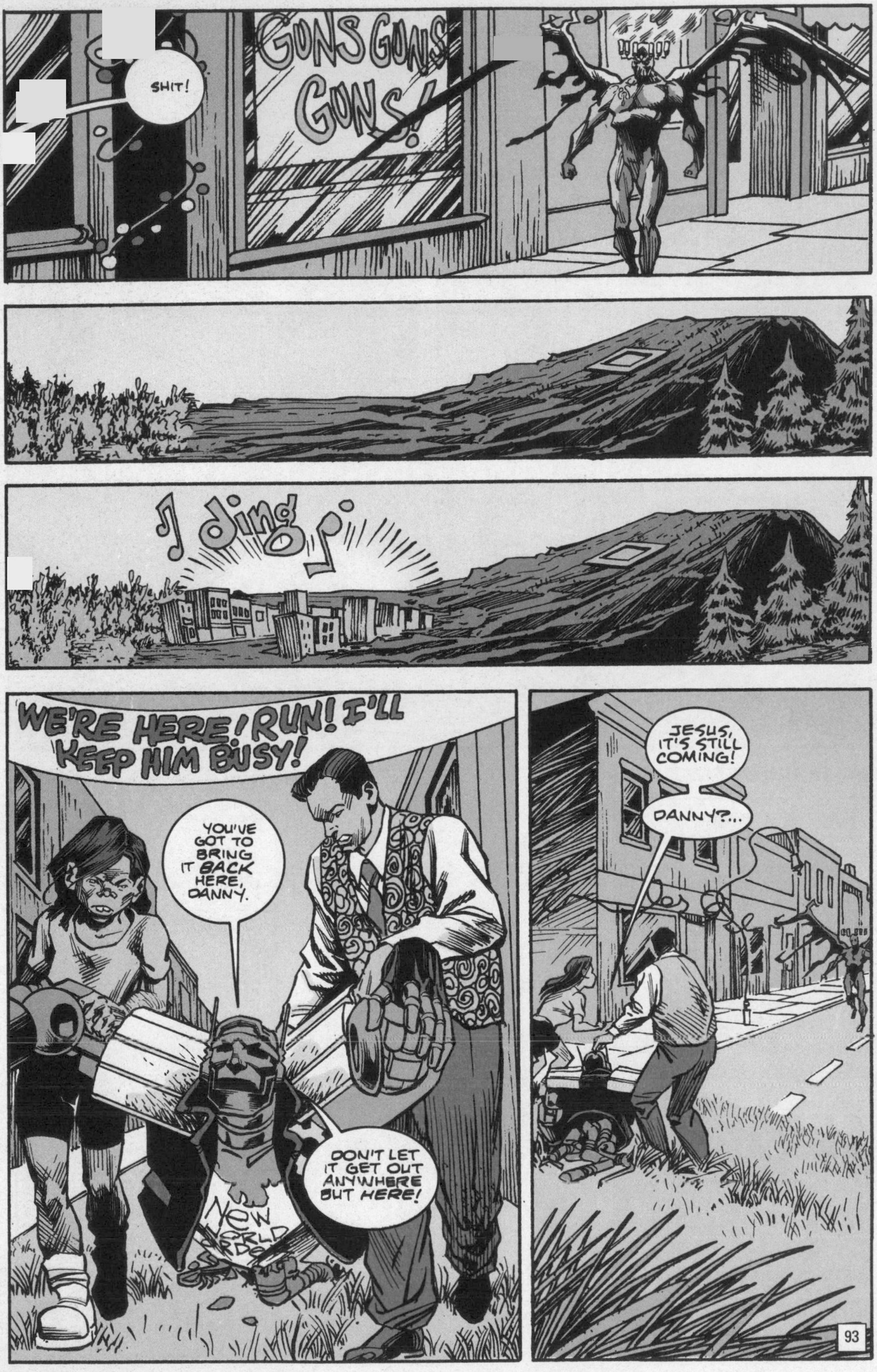

SHIT!
GUNS GUNS GUNS!
ding
WE'RE HERE! RUN! I'LL KEEP HIM BUSY!
YOU'VE GOT TO BRING IT BACK HERE, DANNY.
DON'T LET IT GET OUT ANYWHERE BUT HERE!
NEW WORLD ORDE
JESUS, IT'S STILL COMING!
DANNY?...

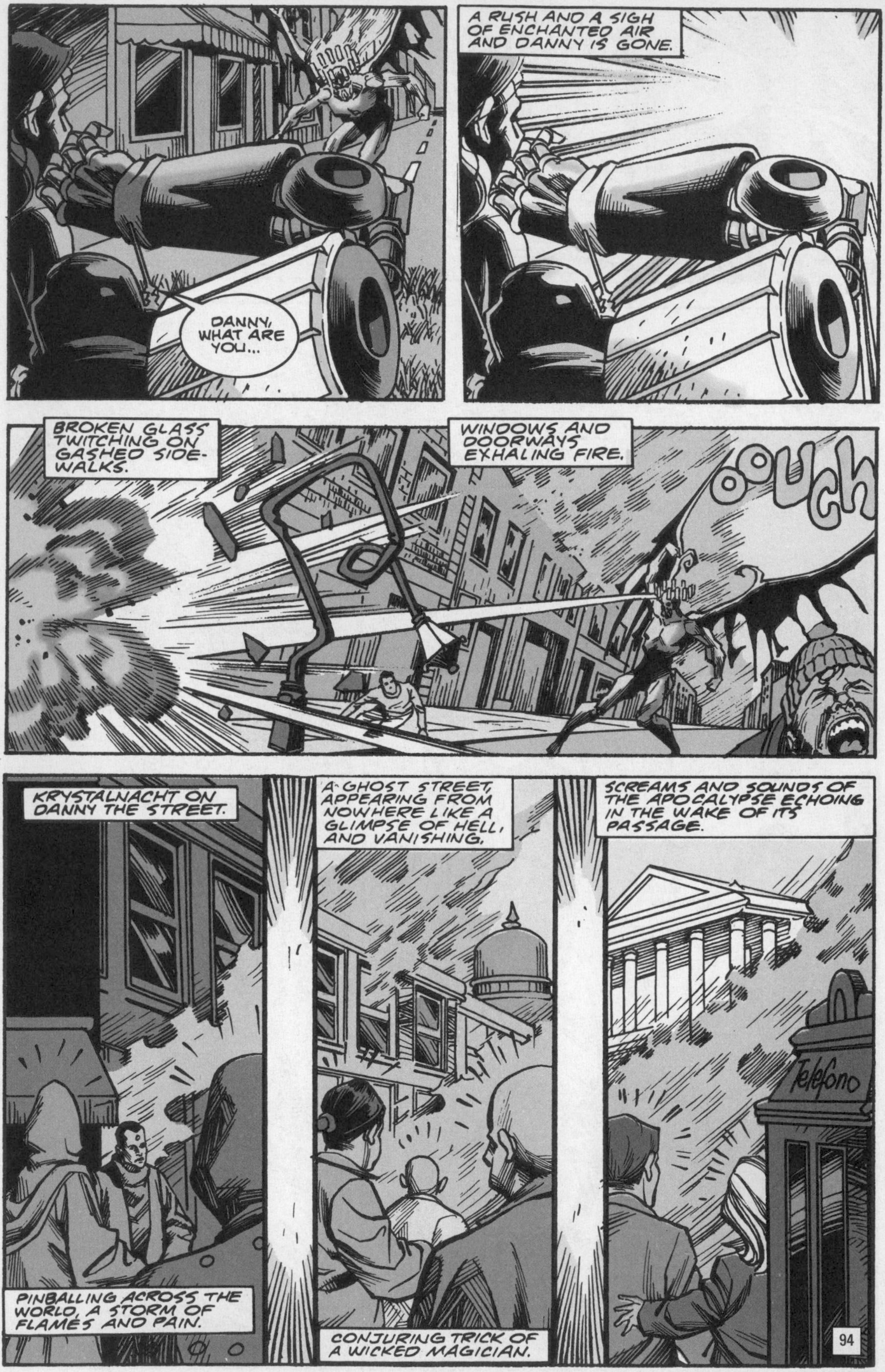
DANNY, WHAT ARE YOU...
A RUSH AND A SIGH OF ENCHANTED AIR AND DANNY IS GONE.
BROKEN GLASS TWITCHING ON GASHED SIDE-WALKS.
WINDOWS AND DOORWAYS EXHALING FIRE.
OOUCH
KRYSTALNACHT ON DANNY THE STREET.
PINBALLING ACROSS THE WORLD, A STORM OF FLAMES AND PAIN.
A GHOST STREET, APPEARING FROM NOWHERE LIKE A GLIMPSE OF HELL, AND VANISHING.
CONJURING TRICK OF A WICKED MAGICIAN.
SCREAMS AND SOUNDS OF THE APOCALYPSE ECHOING IN THE WAKE OF ITS PASSAGE.
Telefono

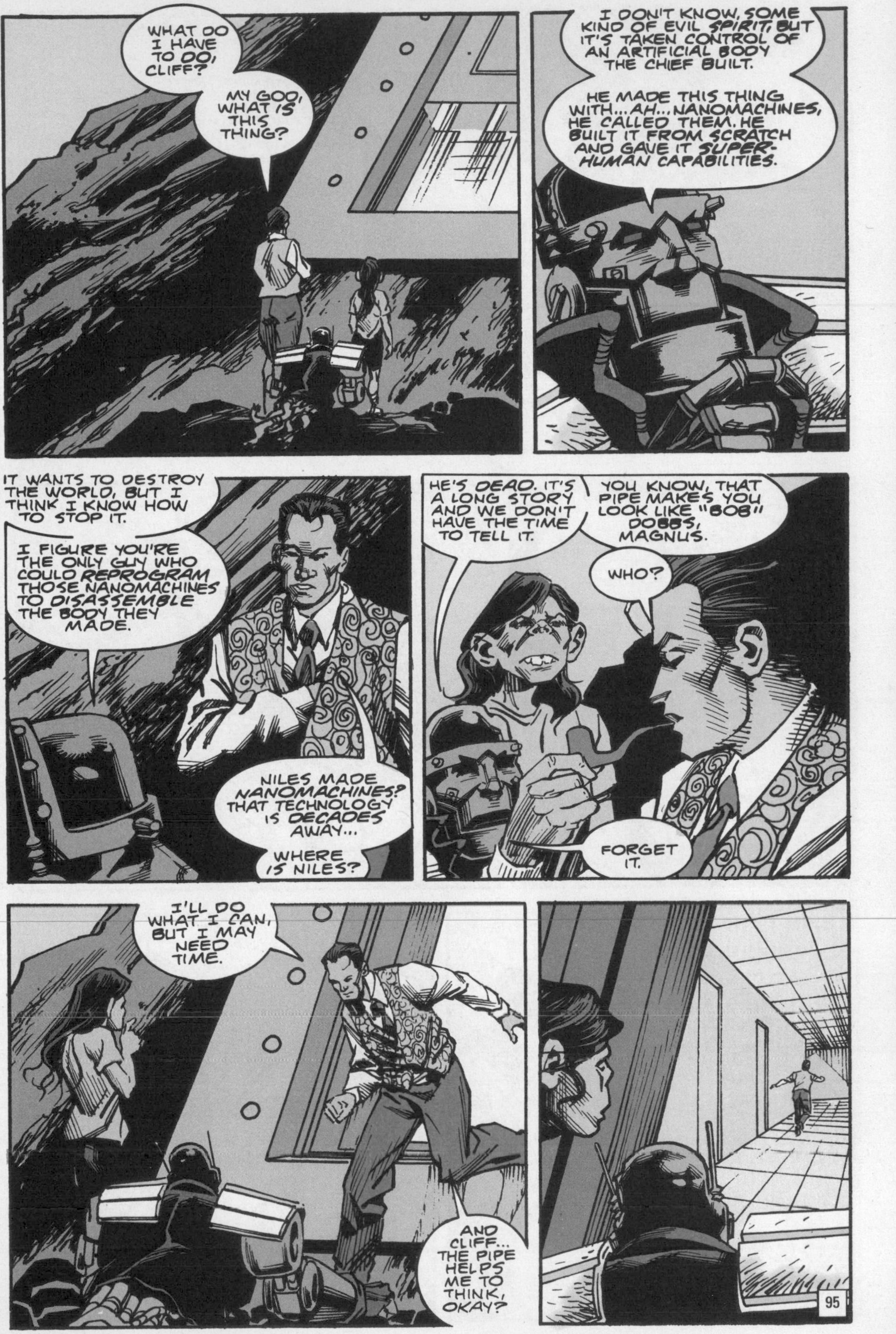
WHAT DO I HAVE TO DO, CLIFF?
MY GOD, WHAT IS THIS THING?
I DON'T KNOW, SOME KIND OF EVIL SPIRIT, BUT IT'S TAKEN CONTROL OF AN ARTIFICIAL BODY THE CHIEF BUILT.
HE MADE THIS THING WITH... AH... NANOMACHINES, HE CALLED THEM. HE BUILT IT FROM SCRATCH AND GAVE IT SUPER-HUMAN CAPABILITIES.
IT WANTS TO DESTROY THE WORLD, BUT I THINK I KNOW HOW TO STOP IT.
I FIGURE YOU'RE THE ONLY GUY WHO COULD REPROGRAM THOSE NANOMACHINES TO DISASSEMBLE THE BODY THEY MADE.
NILES MADE NANOMACHINES? THAT TECHNOLOGY IS DECADES AWAY...
WHERE IS NILES?
HE'S DEAD. IT'S A LONG STORY AND WE DON'T HAVE THE TIME TO TELL IT.
YOU KNOW, THAT PIPE MAKES YOU LOOK LIKE "BOB" DOBBS, MAGNUS.
WHO?
FORGET IT.
I'LL DO WHAT I CAN, BUT I MAY NEED TIME.
AND CLIFF... THE PIPE HELPS ME TO THINK, OKAY?

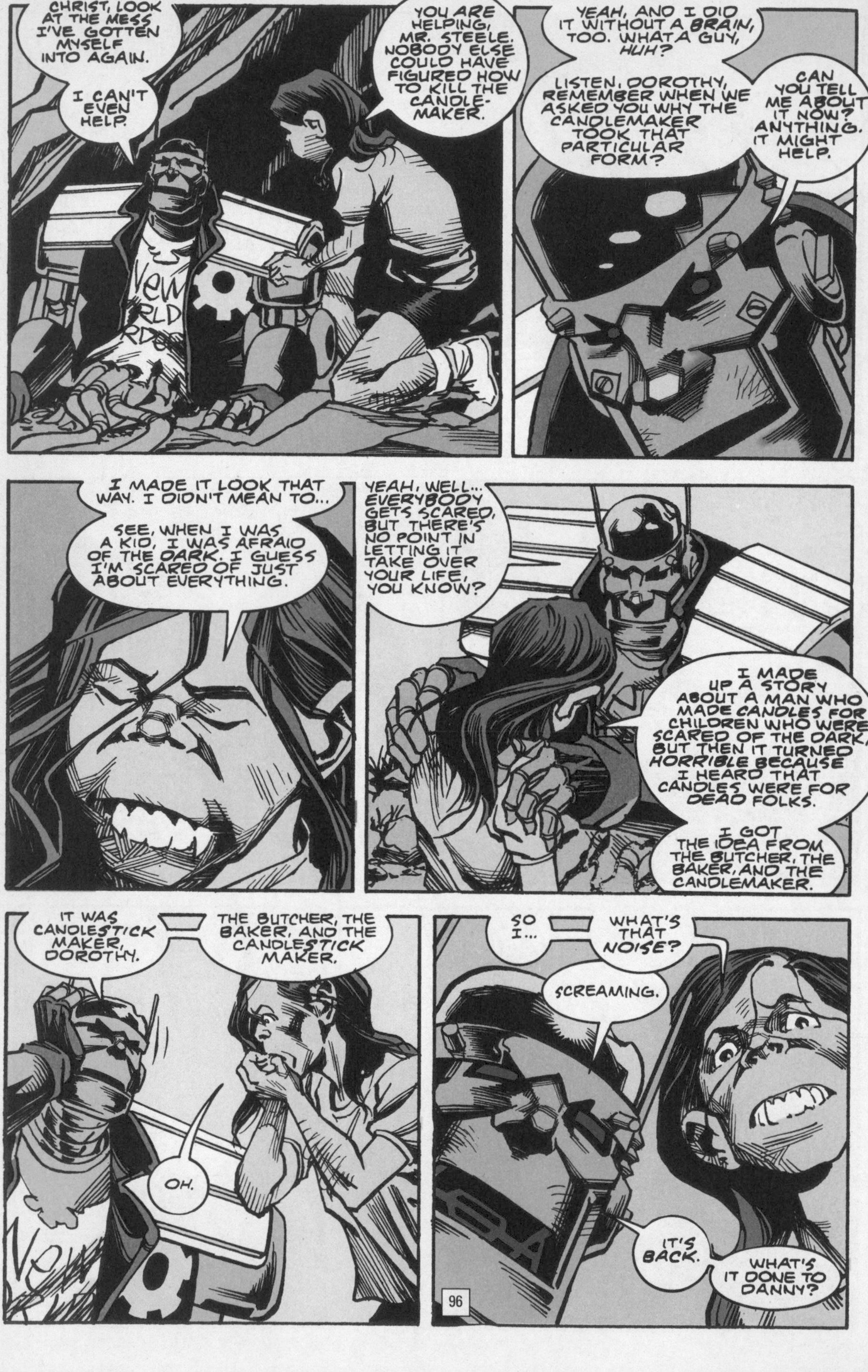
CHRIST, LOOK AT THE MESS I'VE GOTTEN MYSELF INTO AGAIN.
I CAN'T EVEN HELP.
YOU ARE HELPING, MR. STEELE. NOBODY ELSE COULD HAVE FIGURED HOW TO KILL THE CANDLE-MAKER.
YEAH, AND I DID IT WITHOUT A BRAIN, TOO. WHAT A GUY, HUH?
LISTEN, DOROTHY, REMEMBER WHEN WE ASKED YOU WHY THE CANDLEMAKER TOOK THAT PARTICULAR FORM?
CAN YOU TELL ME ABOUT IT NOW? ANYTHING. IT MIGHT HELP.
I MADE IT LOOK THAT WAY. I DIDN'T MEAN TO...
SEE, WHEN I WAS A KID, I WAS AFRAID OF THE DARK. I GUESS I'M SCARED OF JUST ABOUT EVERYTHING.
YEAH, WELL... EVERYBODY GETS SCARED, BUT THERE'S NO POINT IN LETTING IT TAKE OVER YOUR LIFE, YOU KNOW?
I MADE UP A STORY ABOUT A MAN WHO MADE CANDLES FOR CHILDREN WHO WERE SCARED OF THE DARK, BUT THEN IT TURNED HORRIBLE BECAUSE I HEARD THAT CANDLES WERE FOR DEAD FOLKS.
I GOT THE IDEA FROM THE BUTCHER, THE BAKER, AND THE CANDLEMAKER.
IT WAS CANDLESTICK MAKER, DOROTHY.
THE BUTCHER, THE BAKER, AND THE CANDLESTICK MAKER.
OH.
SO I...
WHAT'S THAT NOISE?
SCREAMING.
IT'S BACK.
WHAT'S IT DONE TO DANNY?

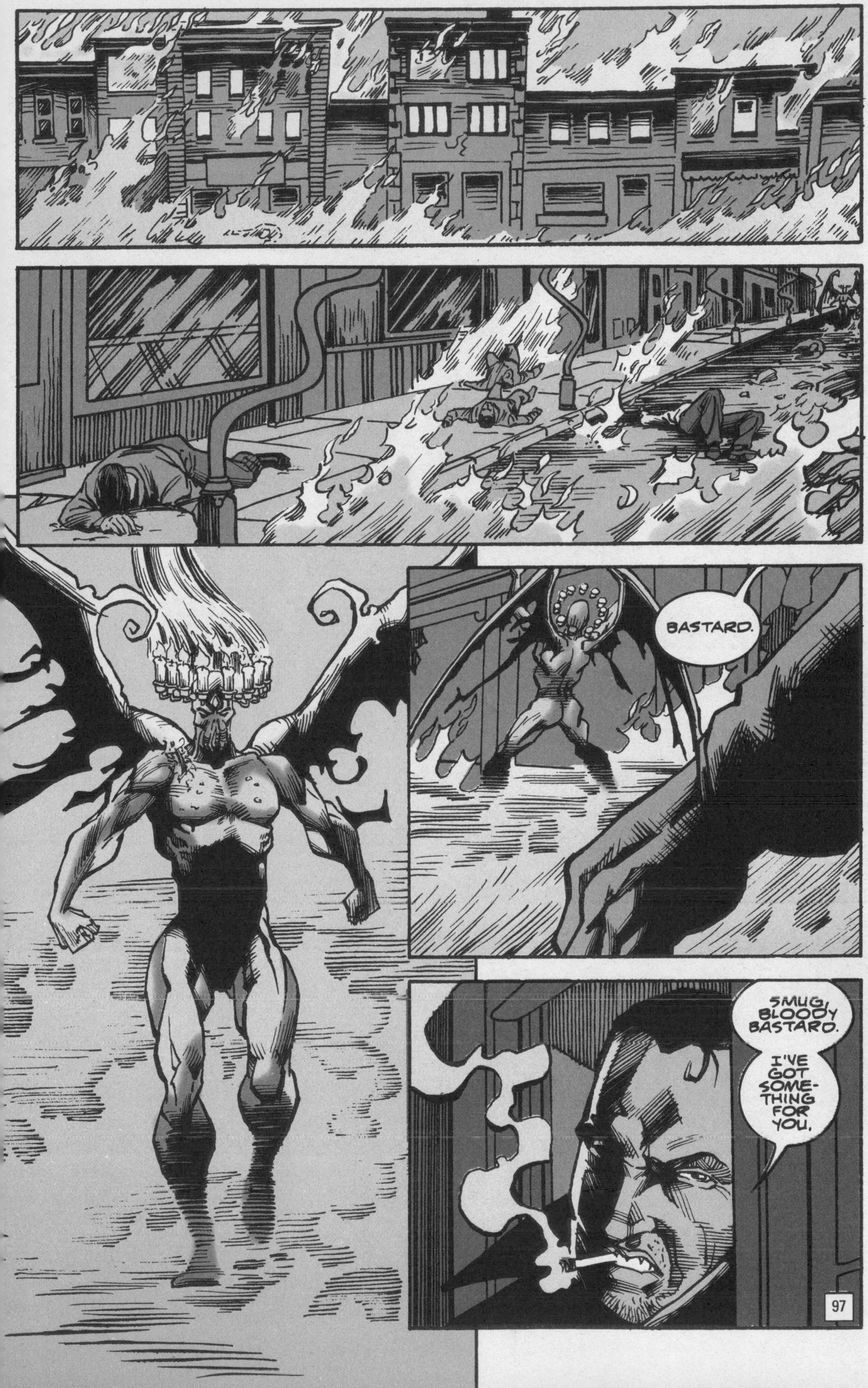
BASTARD.
SMUG, BLOODY BASTARD.
I'VE GOT SOME-THING FOR YOU.

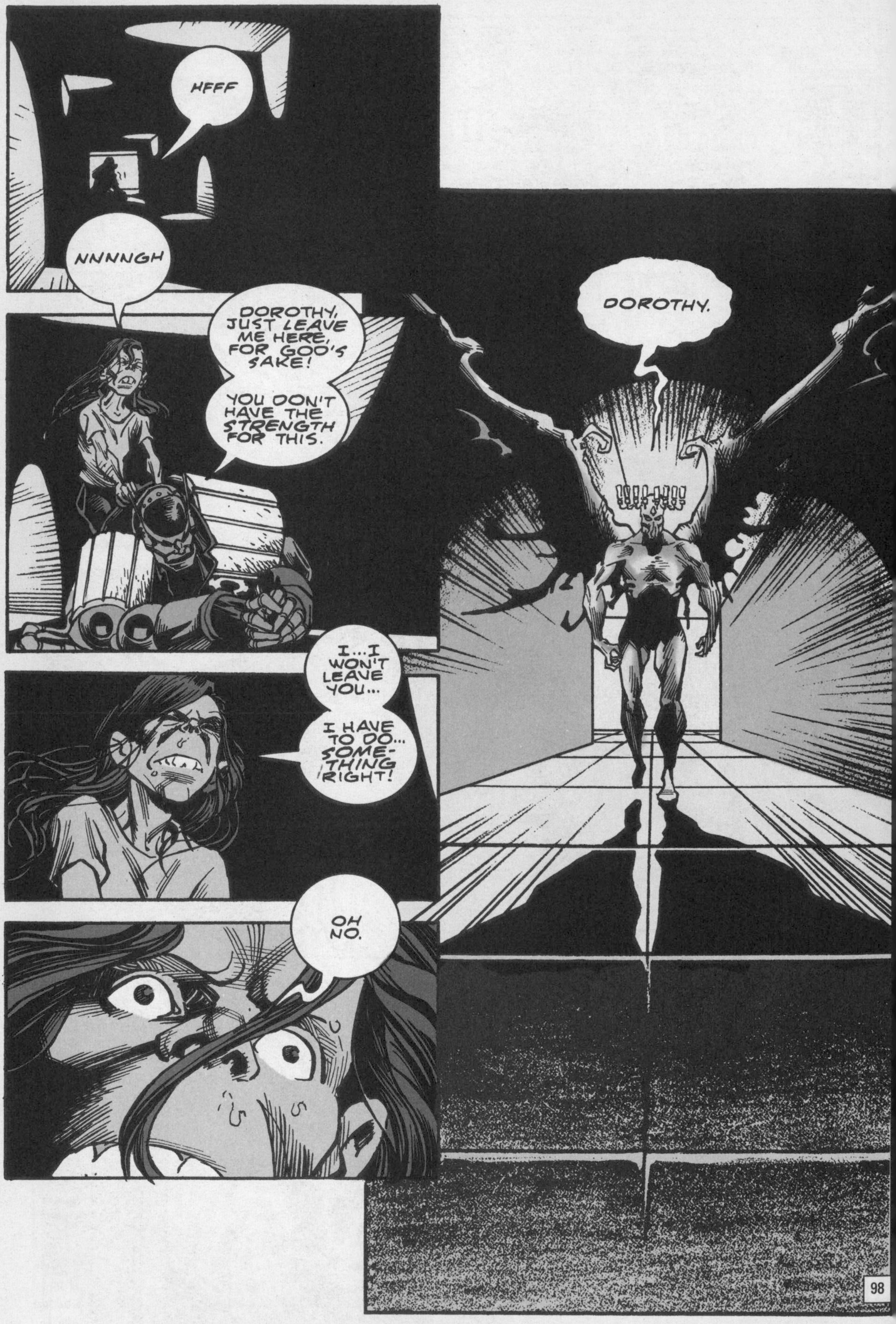
HFFF
NNNNGH
DOROTHY, JUST LEAVE ME HERE, FOR GOD'S SAKE!
YOU DON'T HAVE THE STRENGTH FOR THIS.
DOROTHY.
I...I WON'T LEAVE YOU...
I HAVE TO DO... SOME-THING RIGHT!
OH NO.

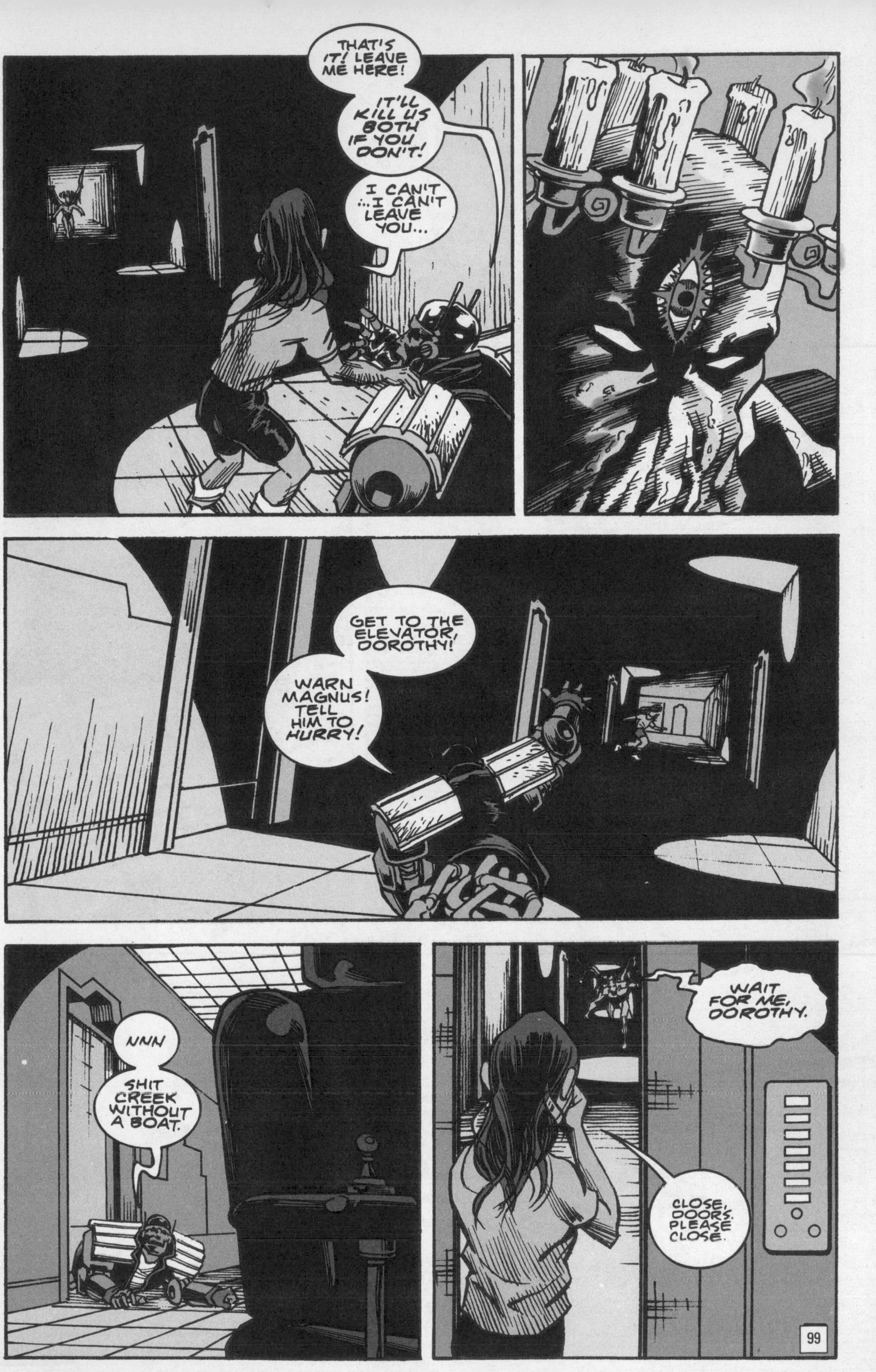
THAT'S IT! LEAVE ME HERE!
IT'LL KILL US BOTH IF YOU DON'T!
I CAN'T ...I CAN'T LEAVE YOU...
GET TO THE ELEVATOR, DOROTHY!
WARN MAGNUS! TELL HIM TO HURRY!
NNN
SHIT CREEK WITHOUT A BOAT.
WAIT FOR ME, DOROTHY.
CLOSE, DOORS. PLEASE CLOSE.

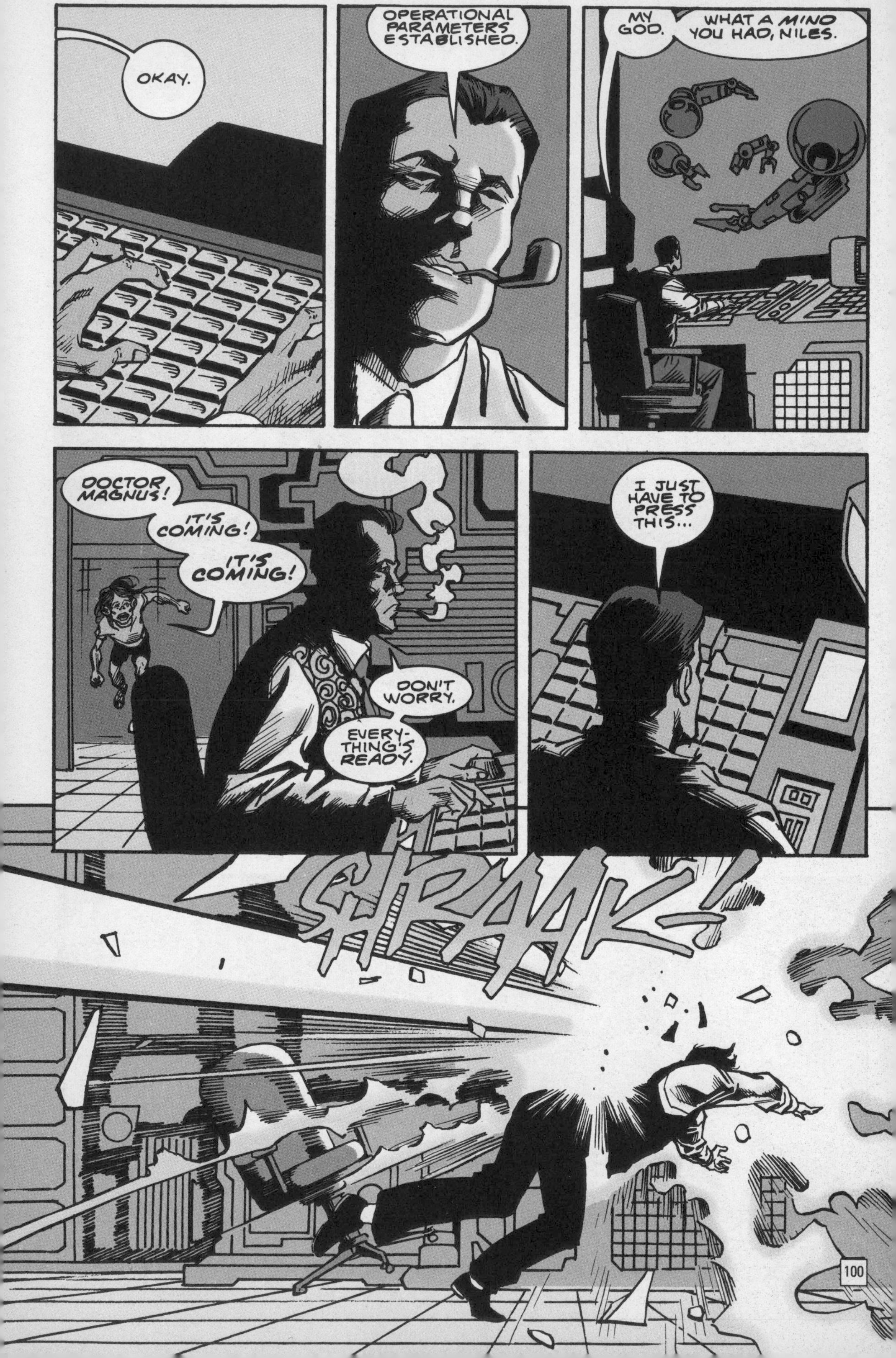
OKAY.
OPERATIONAL PARAMETERS ESTABLISHED.
MY GOD.
WHAT A MIND YOU HAD, NILES.
DOCTOR MAGNUS!
IT'S COMING!
IT'S COMING!
DON'T WORRY.
EVERY-THING'S READY.
I JUST HAVE TO PRESS THIS...
SKRAAK!

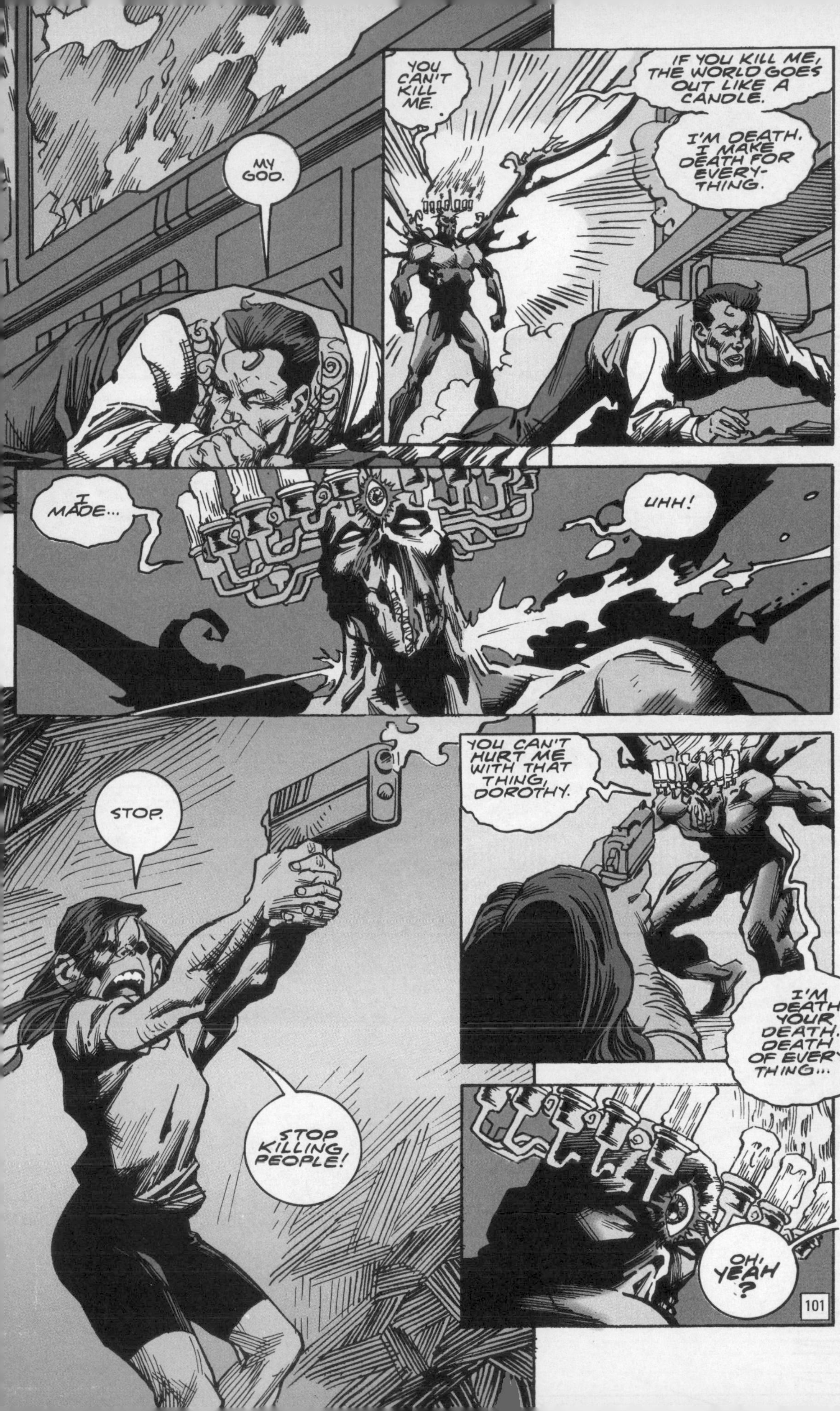

MY GOD.
YOU CAN'T KILL ME.
IF YOU KILL ME, THE WORLD GOES OUT LIKE A CANDLE.
I'M DEATH. I MAKE DEATH FOR EVERY-THING.
I MADE...
UHH!
STOP.
STOP KILLING PEOPLE!
YOU CAN'T HURT ME WITH THAT THING, DOROTHY.
I'M DEATH. YOUR DEATH. DEATH OF EVERY-THING...
OH, YEAH?

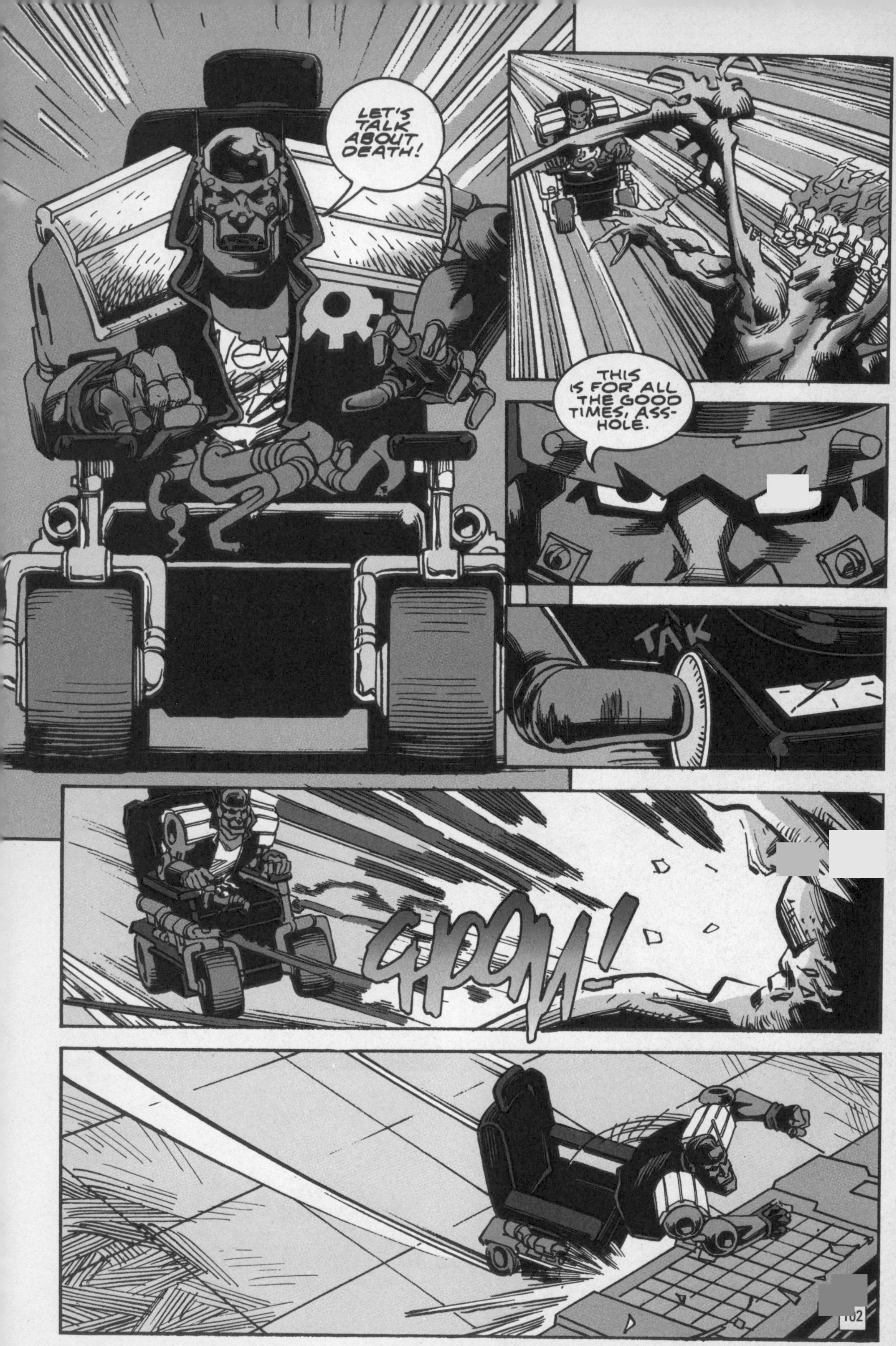
LET'S TALK ABOUT DEATH!
THIS IS FOR ALL THE GOOD TIMES, ASS-HOLE.
TAK
GRONK!

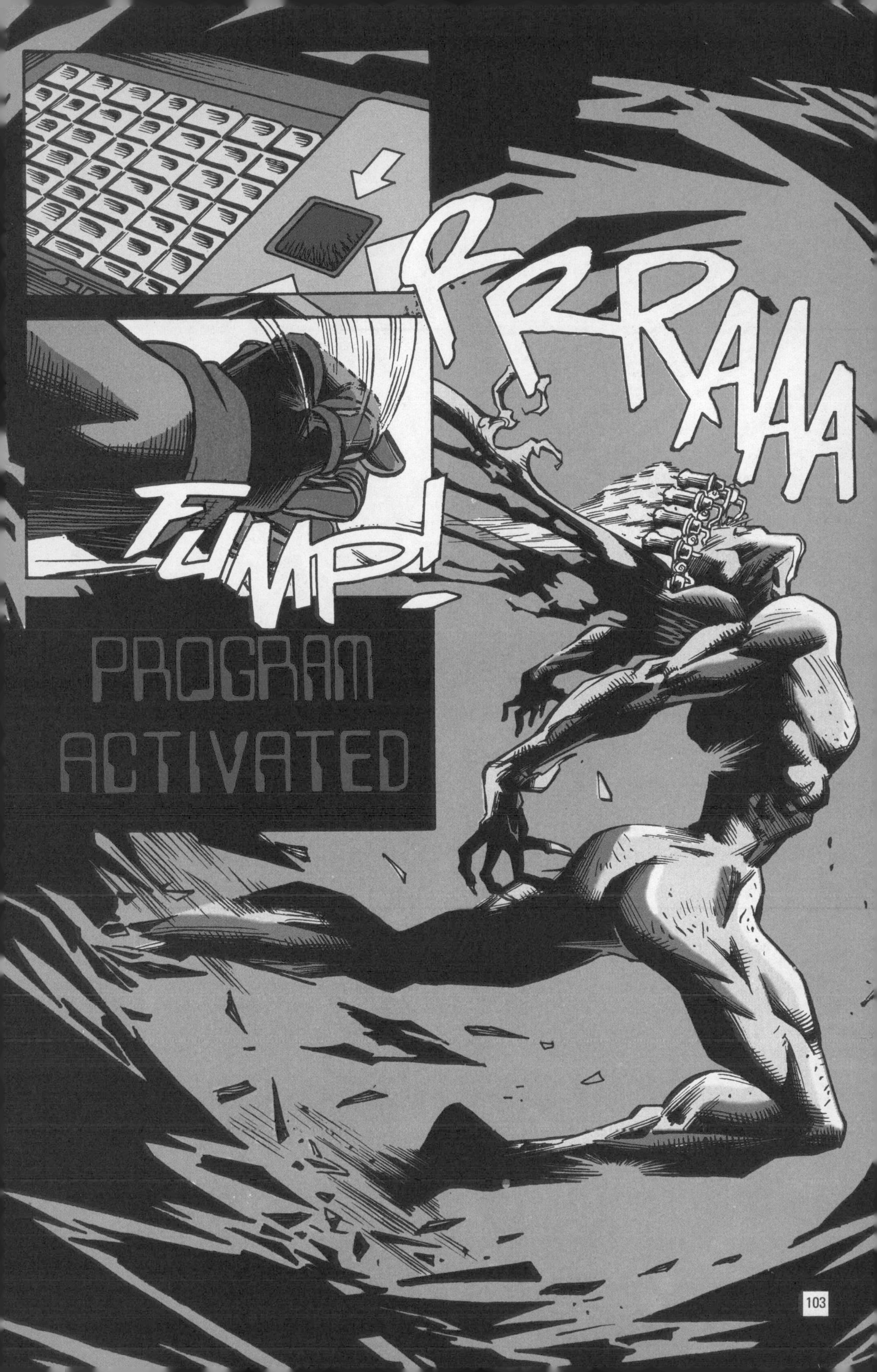
RRRAAAA
FUMP!
PROGRAM ACTIVATED

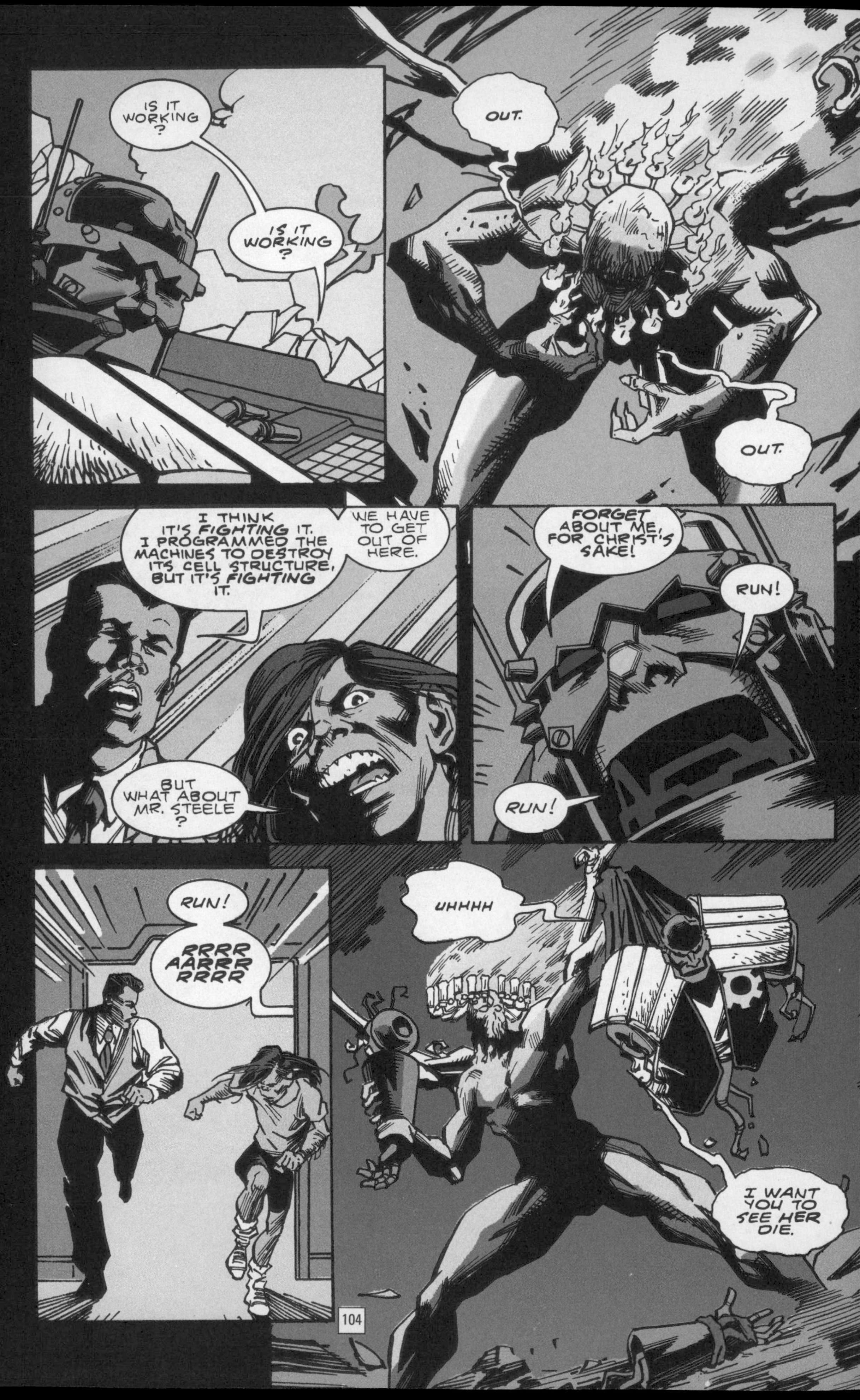

IS IT WORKING ?
OUT.
IS IT WORKING ?
OUT.
I THINK IT'S *FIGHTING* IT. I PROGRAMMED THE MACHINES TO DESTROY ITS CELL STRUCTURE, BUT IT'S *FIGHTING* IT.
WE HAVE TO GET OUT OF HERE.
BUT WHAT ABOUT MR. STEELE ?
FORGET ABOUT ME, FOR CHRIST'S SAKE!
RUN!
RUN!
RUN!
RRRR AARRR RRRR
UHHHH
I WANT YOU TO SEE HER DIE.

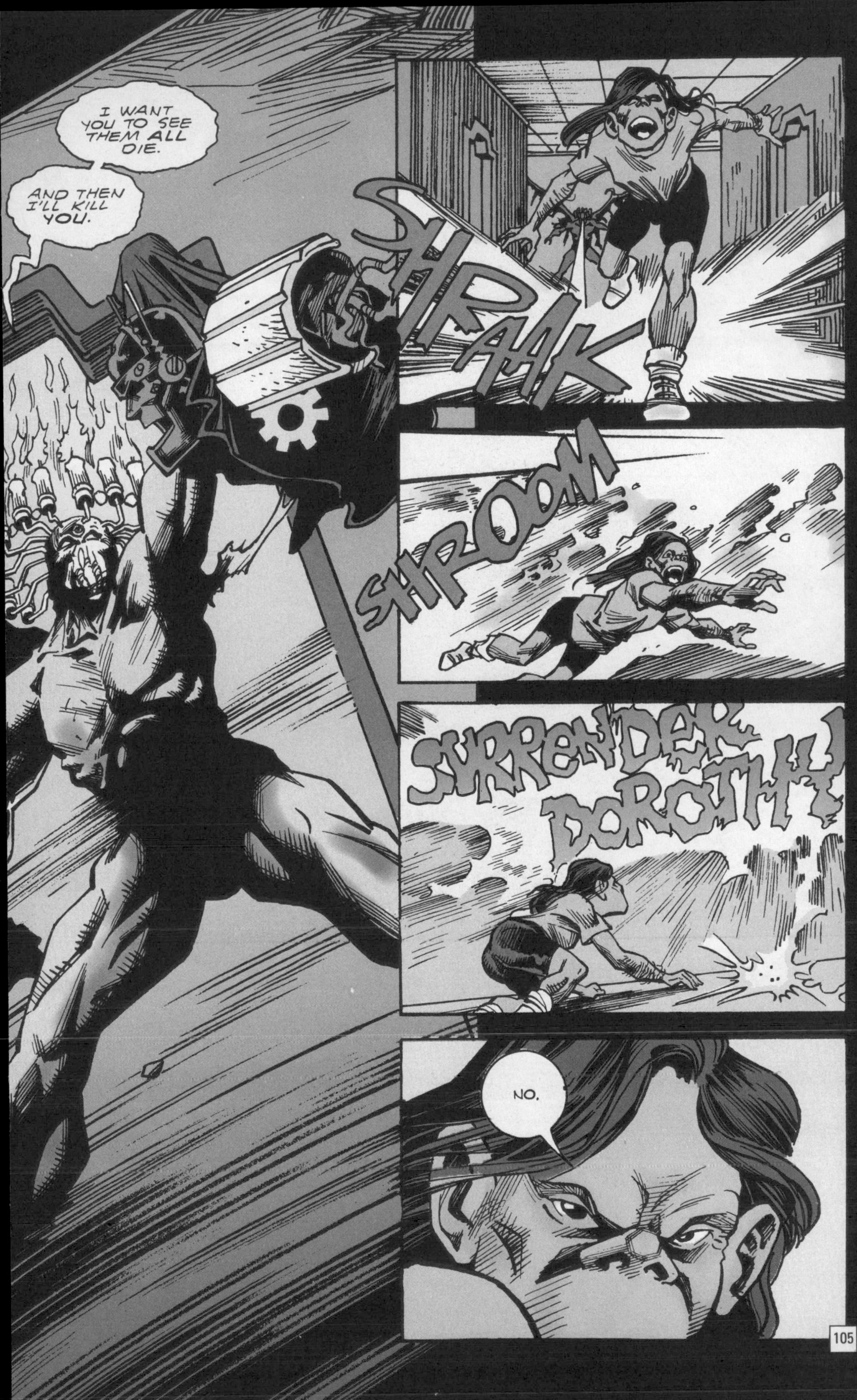

I WANT YOU TO SEE THEM ALL DIE.
AND THEN I'LL KILL YOU.
SHRAAK
SHROOM
SURRENDER DOROTHY!
NO.

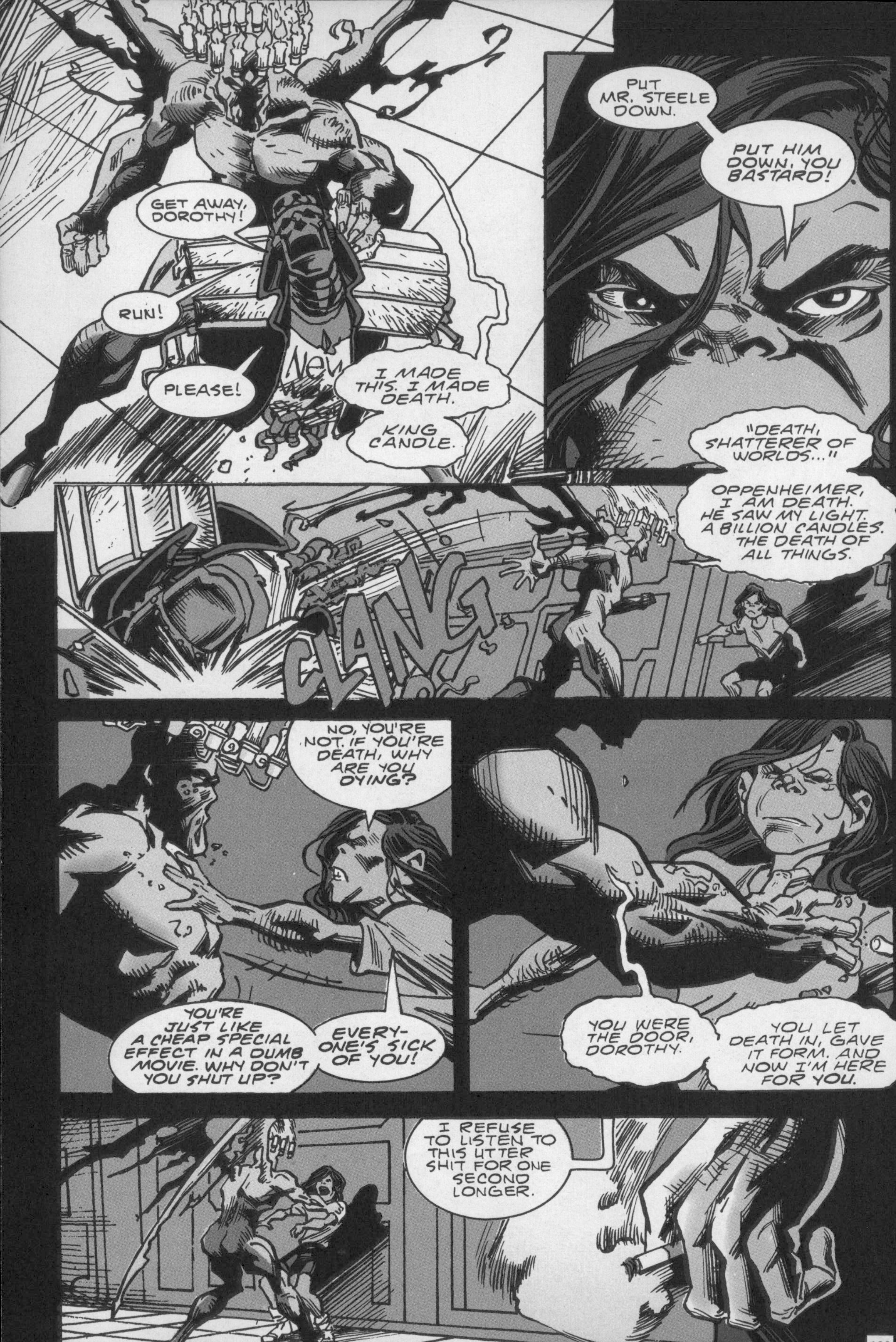
GET AWAY, DOROTHY!
RUN!
PLEASE!
I MADE THIS. I MADE DEATH.
KING CANDLE.
PUT MR. STEELE DOWN.
PUT HIM DOWN, YOU BASTARD!
"DEATH, SHATTERER OF WORLDS..."
OPPENHEIMER, I AM DEATH. HE SAW MY LIGHT. A BILLION CANDLES. THE DEATH OF ALL THINGS.
CLANG
NO, YOU'RE NOT. IF YOU'RE DEATH, WHY ARE YOU DYING?
YOU'RE JUST LIKE A CHEAP SPECIAL EFFECT IN A DUMB MOVIE. WHY DON'T YOU SHUT UP?
EVERY-ONE'S SICK OF YOU!
YOU WERE THE DOOR, DOROTHY.
YOU LET DEATH IN, GAVE IT FORM. AND NOW I'M HERE FOR YOU.
I REFUSE TO LISTEN TO THIS UTTER SHIT FOR ONE SECOND LONGER.

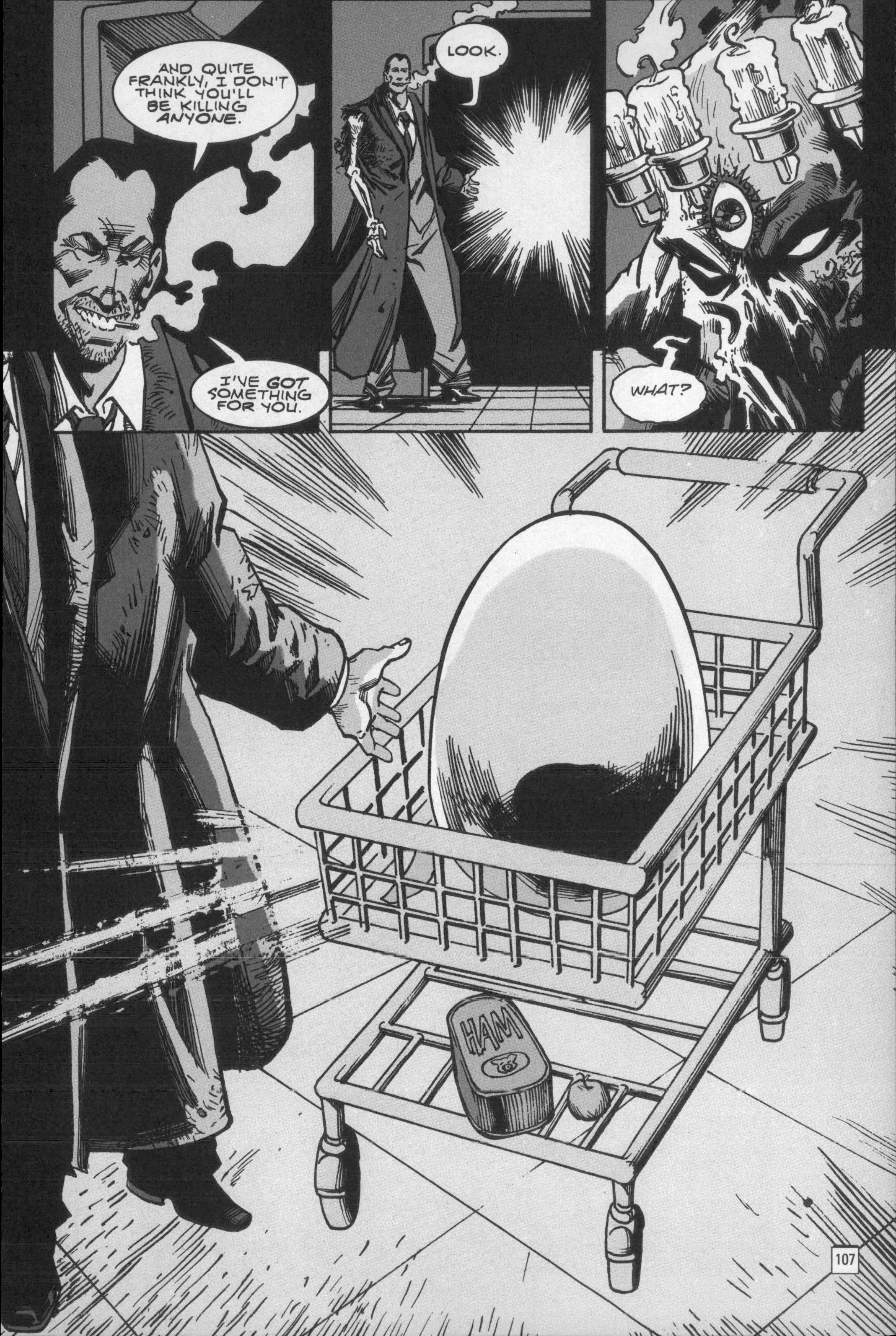
AND QUITE FRANKLY, I DON'T THINK YOU'LL BE KILLING ANYONE.
I'VE GOT SOMETHING FOR YOU.
LOOK.
WHAT?
HAM

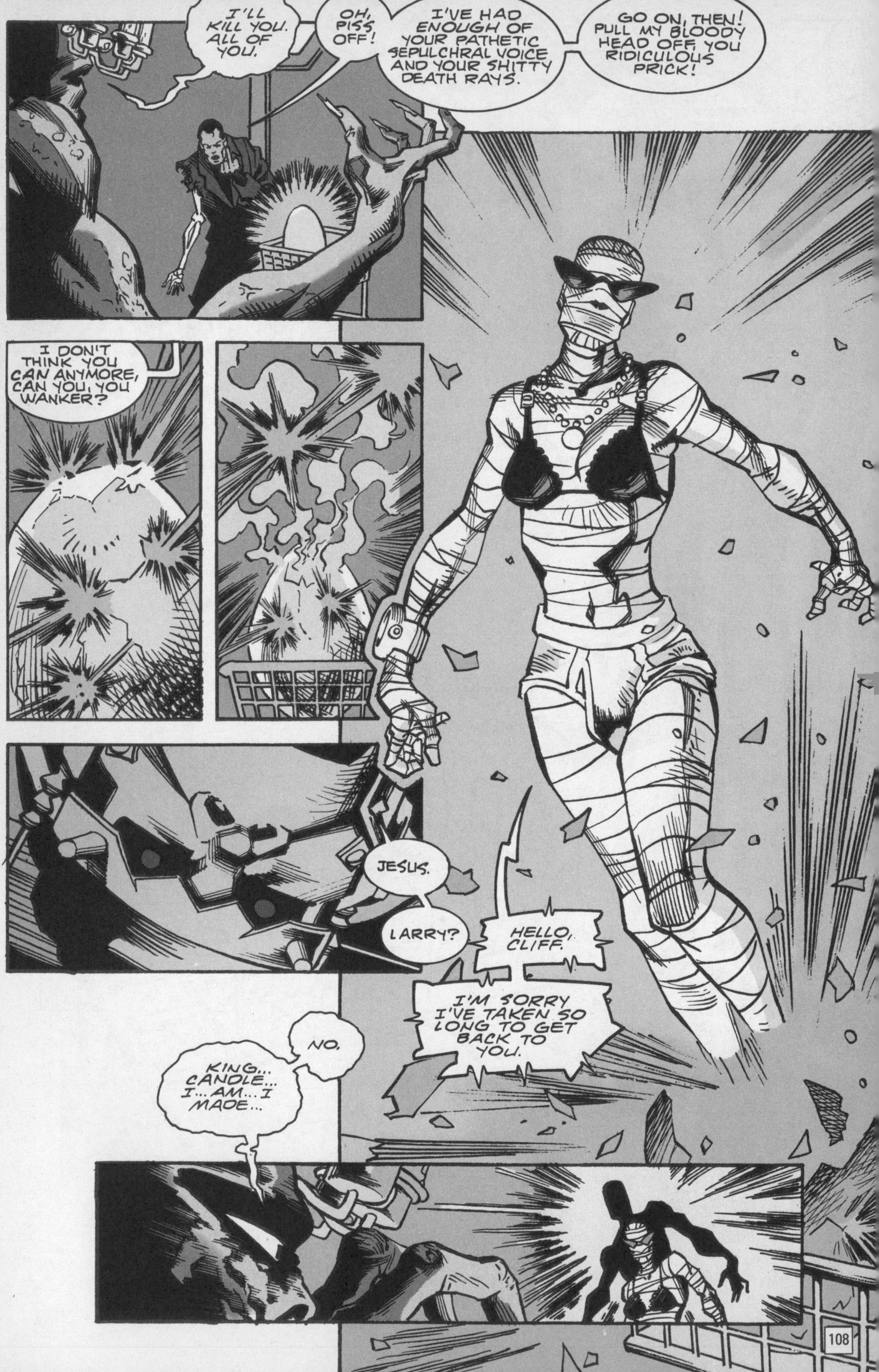

I'LL KILL YOU. ALL OF YOU.
OH, PISS OFF!
I'VE HAD ENOUGH OF YOUR PATHETIC SEPULCHRAL VOICE AND YOUR SHITTY DEATH RAYS.
GO ON, THEN! PULL MY BLOODY HEAD OFF, YOU RIDICULOUS PRICK!
I DON'T THINK YOU CAN ANYMORE, CAN YOU, YOU WANKER?
JESUS.
LARRY?
HELLO, CLIFF.
I'M SORRY I'VE TAKEN SO LONG TO GET BACK TO YOU.
NO.
KING... CANDLE... I... AM... I MADE...

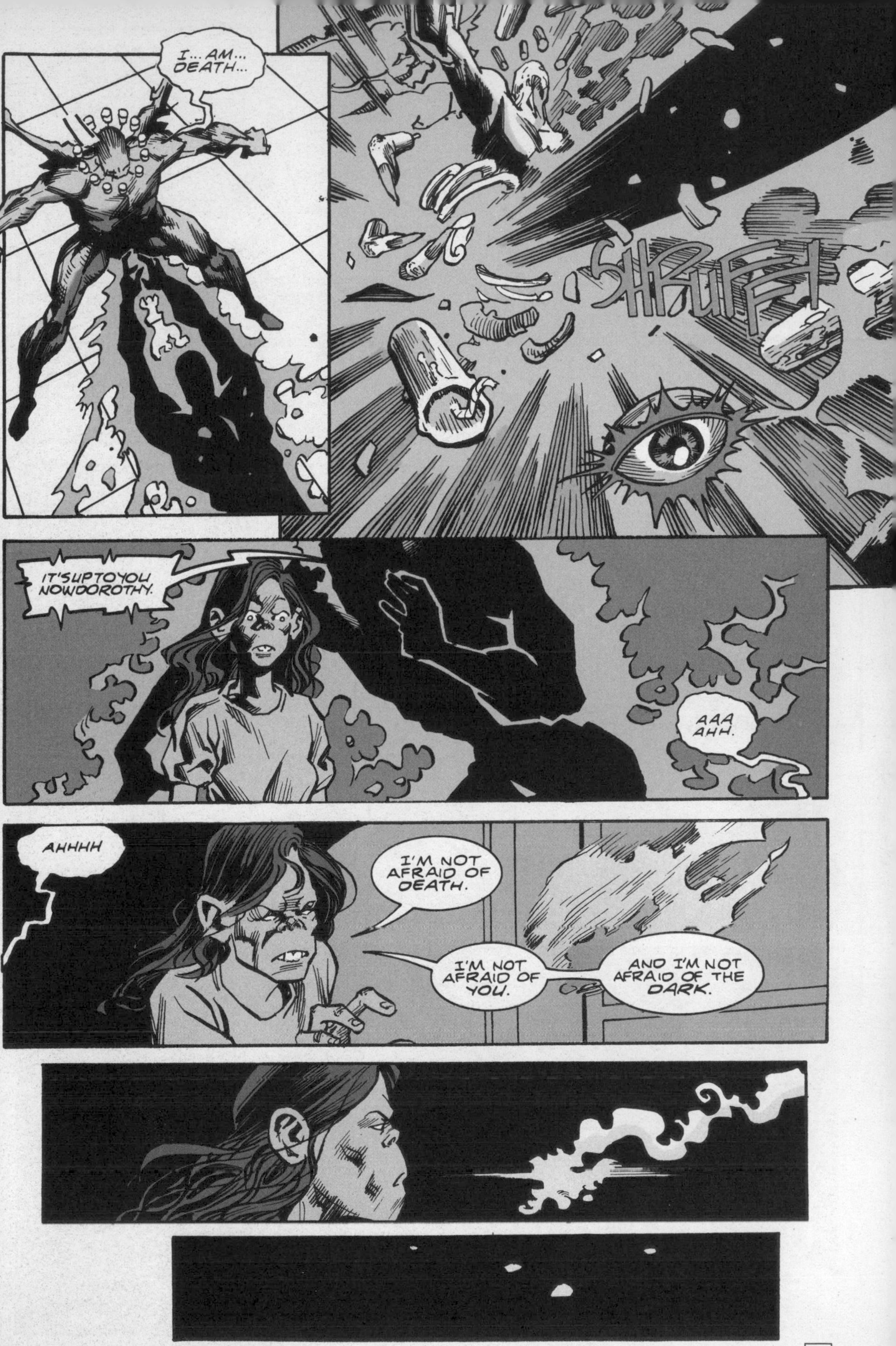
I... AM... DEATH...
SHRUFF!
IT'SUPTOYOU NOWDOROTHY.
AAA AHH.
AHHHH
I'M NOT AFRAID OF DEATH.
I'M NOT AFRAID OF YOU.
AND I'M NOT AFRAID OF THE DARK.

PROFESSOR CAULDER WAS WORKING ON SOME VERY UNUSUAL EXPERIMENTS, DOCTOR MAGNUS.

I JUST WONDERED IF THEY HAD COME TO FRUITION.

THERE'S SOMETHING...

MY GOD, IF THIS IS RIGHT...

I ONLY USED *SOME* OF THE NANOMACHINES. THERE ARE THOUSANDS OF OTHERS. NILES MUST HAVE PROGRAMMED THEM BEFORE HE DIED.

IT...IT LOOKS LIKE SOME KIND OF CATASTROPHE PROGRAM. I CAN'T UNDERSTAND IT...

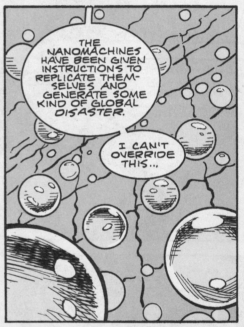

THE NANOMACHINES HAVE BEEN GIVEN INSTRUCTIONS TO REPLICATE THEM-SELVES AND GENERATE SOME KIND OF GLOBAL DISASTER.

I CAN'T OVERRIDE THIS...

WE HAVE... *HOURS* LEFT BEFORE THEY SWARM OVER THE WHOLE WORLD.

HOURS.

NILES, WHAT HAVE YOU DONE?

"I can't believe it's the end of the world and I don't have any bloody *booze*."

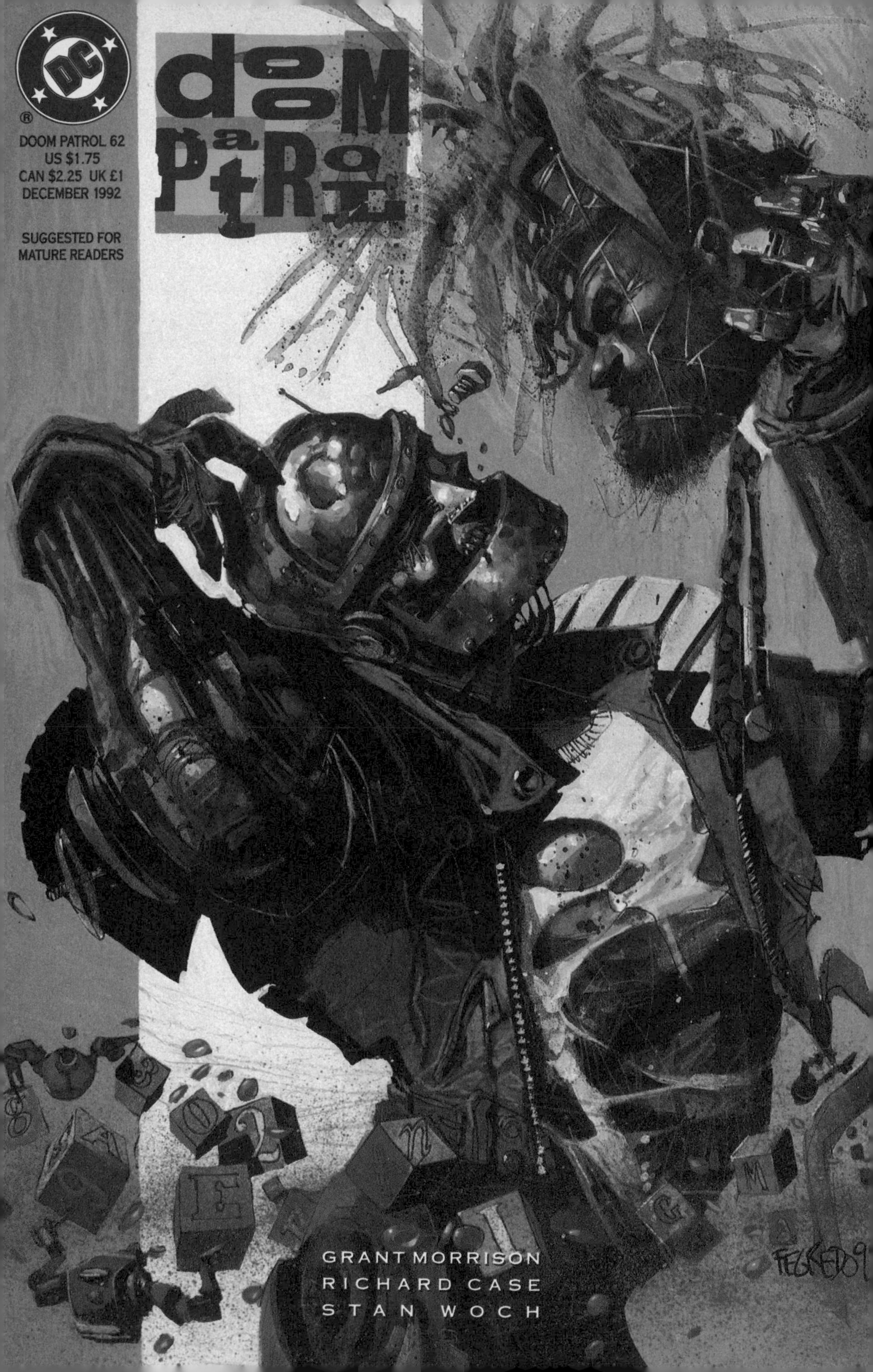
DC
DOOM PATROL
DOOM PATROL 62
US $1.75
CAN $2.25 UK £1
DECEMBER 1992
SUGGESTED FOR MATURE READERS
GRANT MORRISON
RICHARD CASE
STAN WOCH
FEGREDO 9

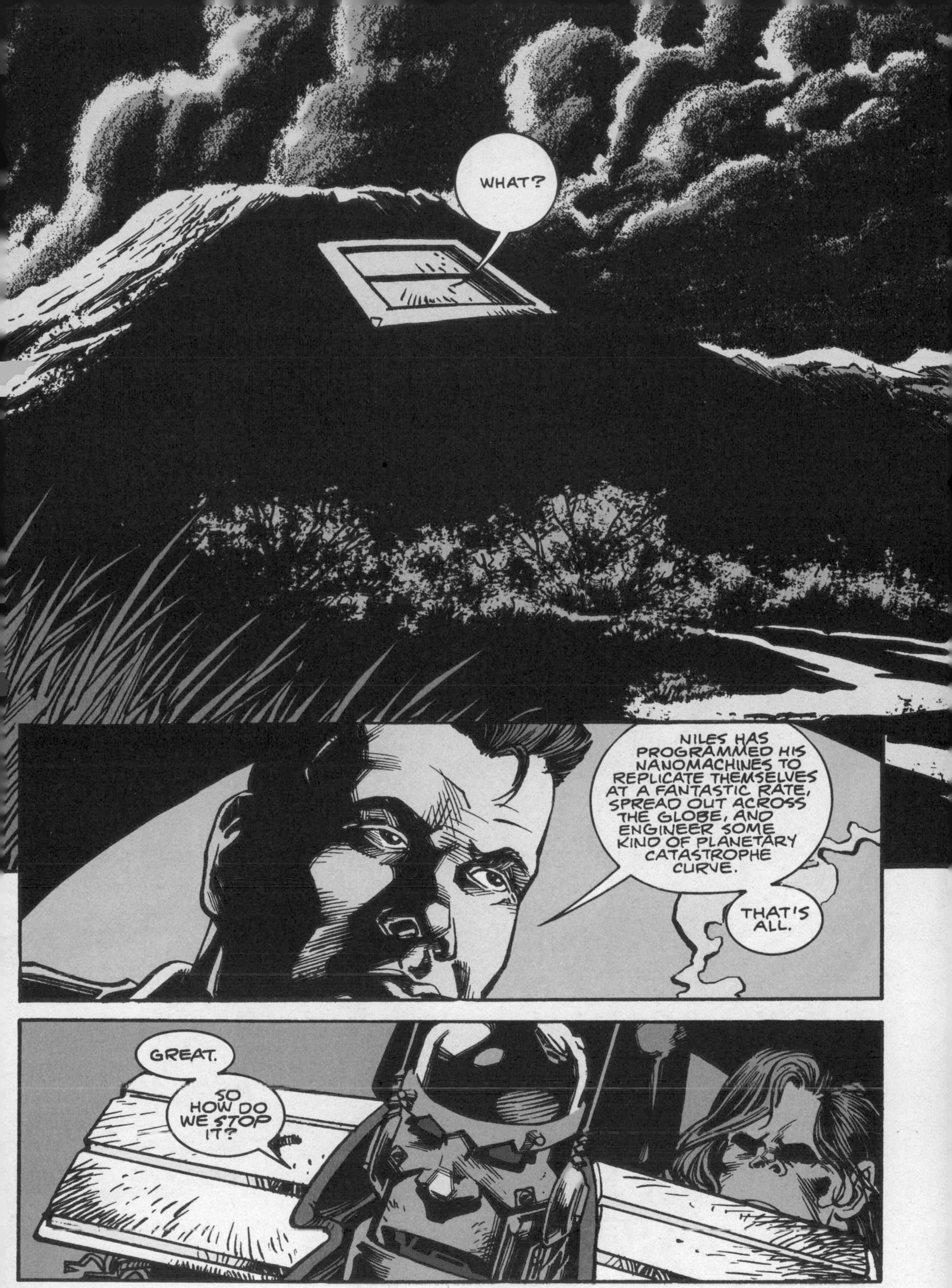
WHAT?
NILES HAS PROGRAMMED HIS NANOMACHINES TO REPLICATE THEMSELVES AT A FANTASTIC RATE, SPREAD OUT ACROSS THE GLOBE, AND ENGINEER SOME KIND OF PLANETARY CATASTROPHE CURVE.
THAT'S ALL.
GREAT.
SO HOW DO WE STOP IT?

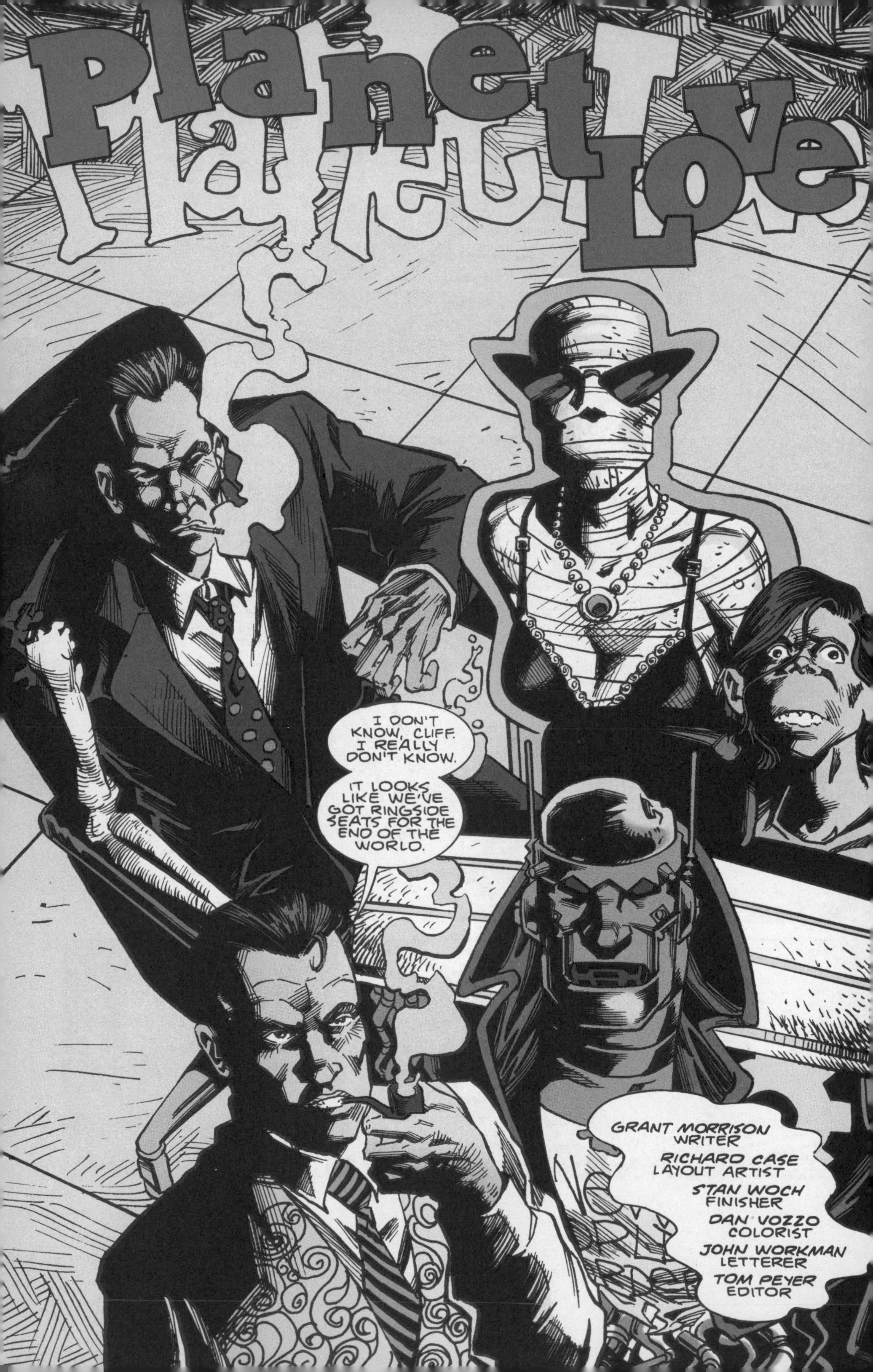
Planet Love
I DON'T KNOW, CLIFF. I REALLY DON'T KNOW.
IT LOOKS LIKE WE'VE GOT RINGSIDE SEATS FOR THE END OF THE WORLD.
GRANT MORRISON WRITER
RICHARD CASE LAYOUT ARTIST
STAN WOCH FINISHER
DAN VOZZO COLORIST
JOHN WORKMAN LETTERER
TOM PEYER EDITOR

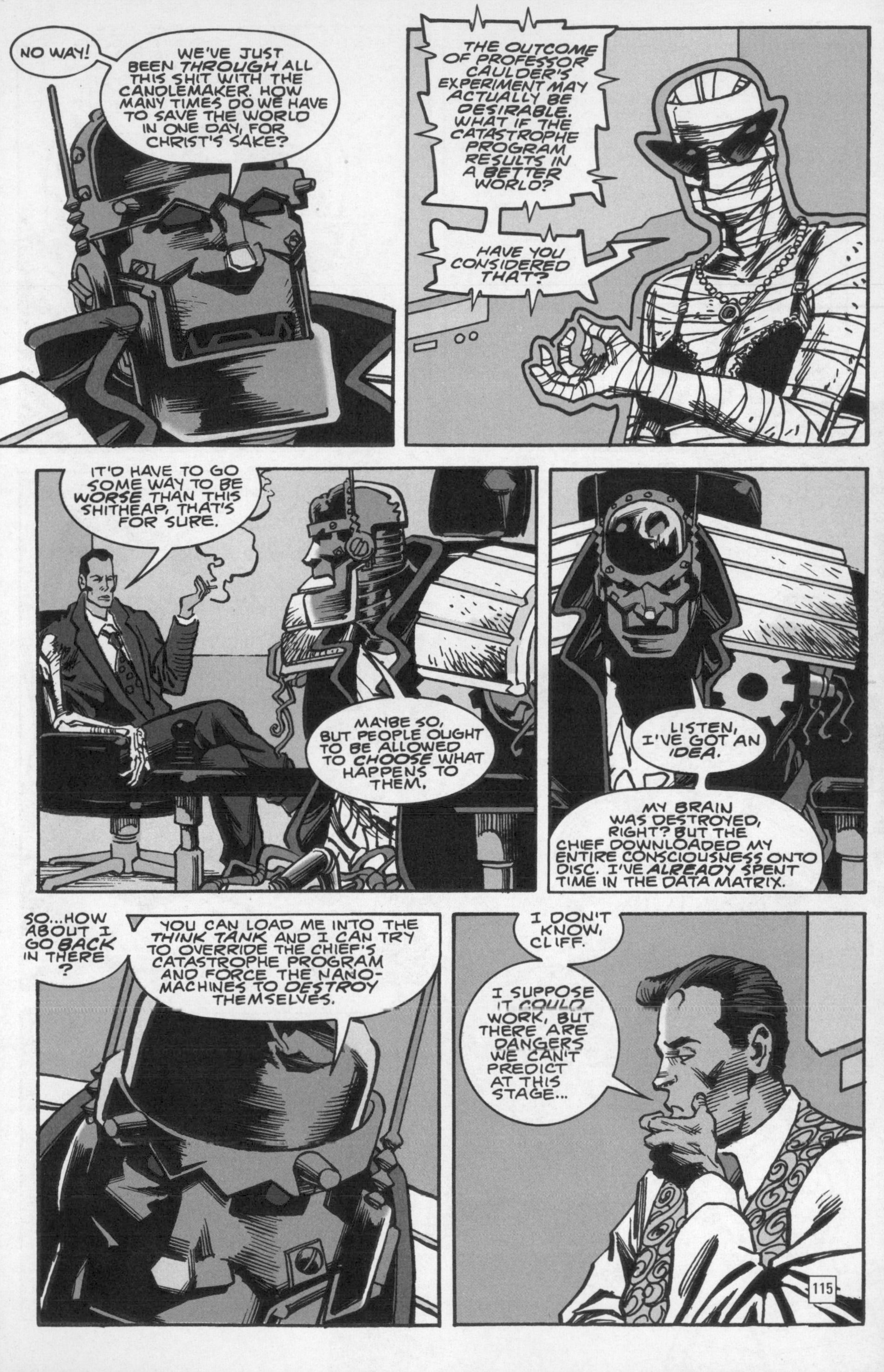
NO WAY!
WE'VE JUST BEEN THROUGH ALL THIS SHIT WITH THE CANDLEMAKER. HOW MANY TIMES DO WE HAVE TO SAVE THE WORLD IN ONE DAY, FOR CHRIST'S SAKE?
THE OUTCOME OF PROFESSOR CAULDER'S EXPERIMENT MAY ACTUALLY BE DESIRABLE. WHAT IF THE CATASTROPHE PROGRAM RESULTS IN A BETTER WORLD?
HAVE YOU CONSIDERED THAT?
IT'D HAVE TO GO SOME WAY TO BE WORSE THAN THIS SHITHEAP, THAT'S FOR SURE.
MAYBE SO, BUT PEOPLE OUGHT TO BE ALLOWED TO CHOOSE WHAT HAPPENS TO THEM.
LISTEN, I'VE GOT AN IDEA.
MY BRAIN WAS DESTROYED, RIGHT? BUT THE CHIEF DOWNLOADED MY ENTIRE CONSCIOUSNESS ONTO DISC. I'VE ALREADY SPENT TIME IN THE DATA MATRIX.
SO...HOW ABOUT I GO BACK IN THERE?
YOU CAN LOAD ME INTO THE THINK TANK AND I CAN TRY TO OVERRIDE THE CHIEF'S CATASTROPHE PROGRAM AND FORCE THE NANO-MACHINES TO DESTROY THEMSELVES.
I DON'T KNOW, CLIFF.
I SUPPOSE IT COULD WORK, BUT THERE ARE DANGERS WE CAN'T PREDICT AT THIS STAGE...

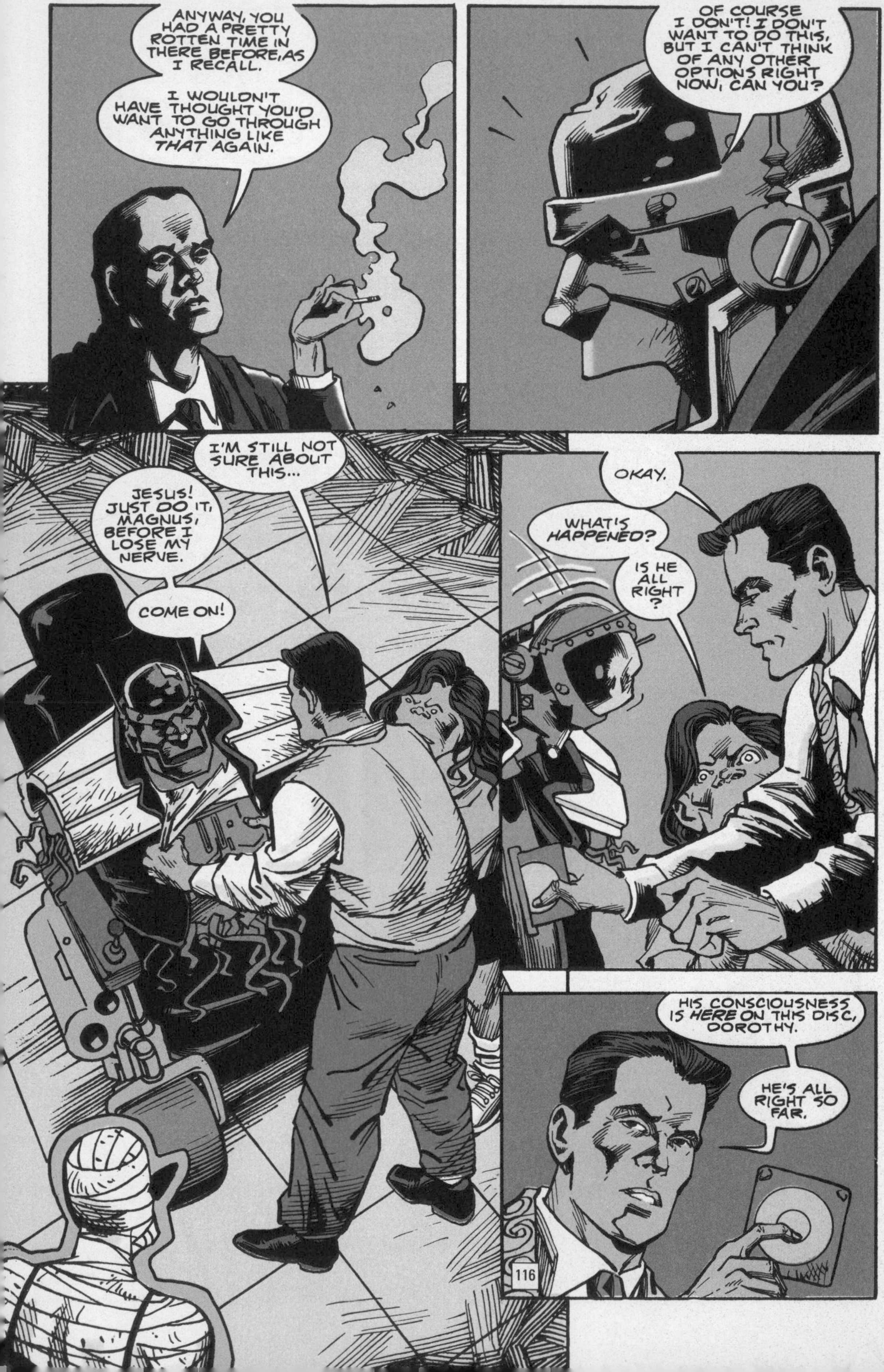
ANYWAY, YOU HAD A PRETTY ROTTEN TIME IN THERE BEFORE, AS I RECALL.
I WOULDN'T HAVE THOUGHT YOU'D WANT TO GO THROUGH ANYTHING LIKE *THAT* AGAIN.
OF COURSE I DON'T! I DON'T WANT TO DO THIS, BUT I CAN'T THINK OF ANY OTHER OPTIONS RIGHT NOW, CAN YOU?
I'M STILL NOT SURE ABOUT THIS...
JESUS! JUST *DO* IT, MAGNUS, BEFORE I LOSE MY NERVE.
COME ON!
OKAY.
WHAT'S *HAPPENED*?
IS HE ALL RIGHT?
HIS CONSCIOUSNESS IS *HERE* ON THIS DISC, DOROTHY.
HE'S ALL RIGHT SO FAR.

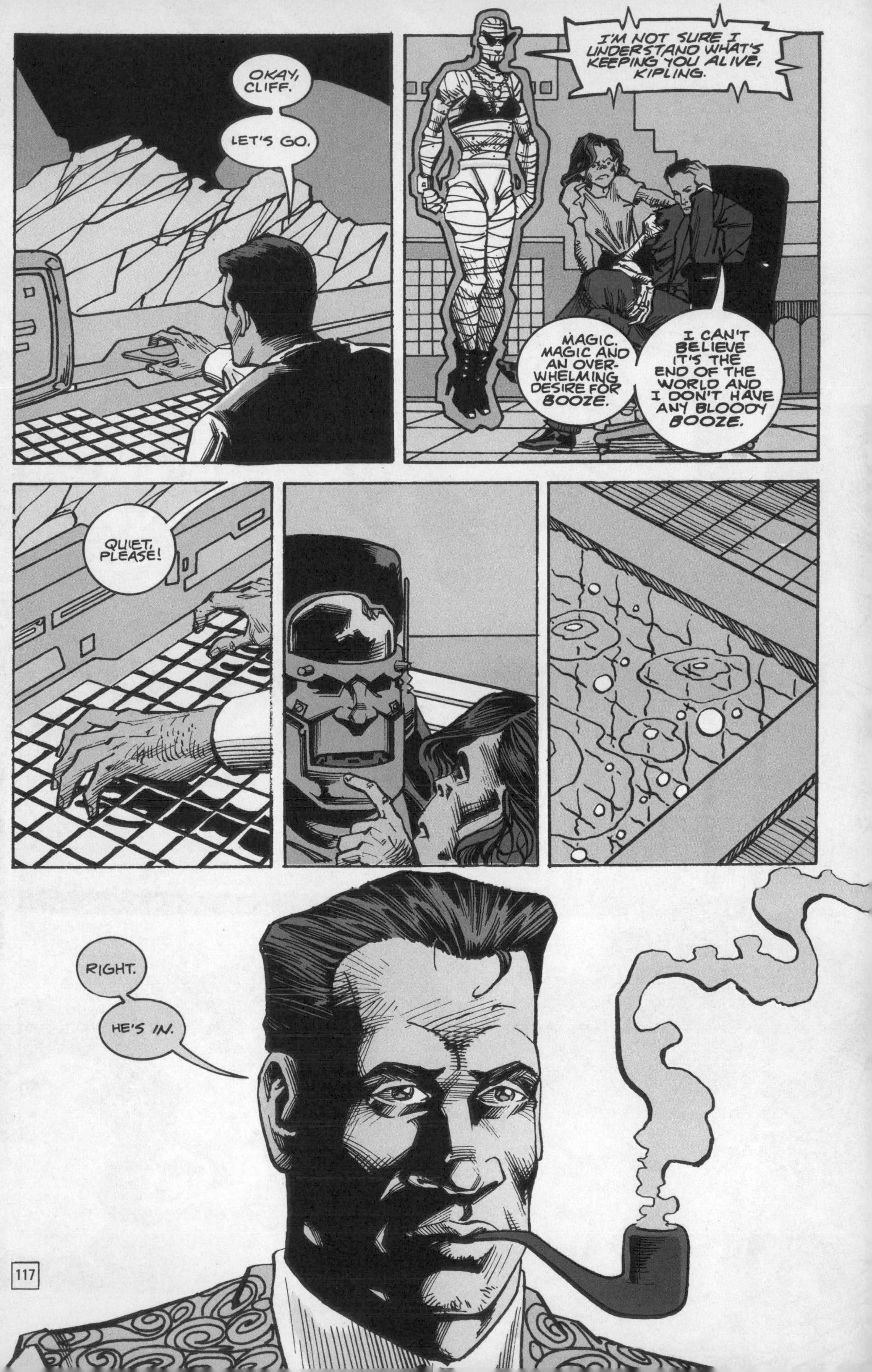
OKAY, CLIFF.
LET'S GO.
I'M NOT SURE I UNDERSTAND WHAT'S KEEPING YOU ALIVE, KIPLING.
MAGIC. MAGIC AND AN OVER-WHELMING DESIRE FOR BOOZE.
I CAN'T BELIEVE IT'S THE END OF THE WORLD AND I DON'T HAVE ANY BLOODY BOOZE.
QUIET, PLEASE!
RIGHT.
HE'S IN.

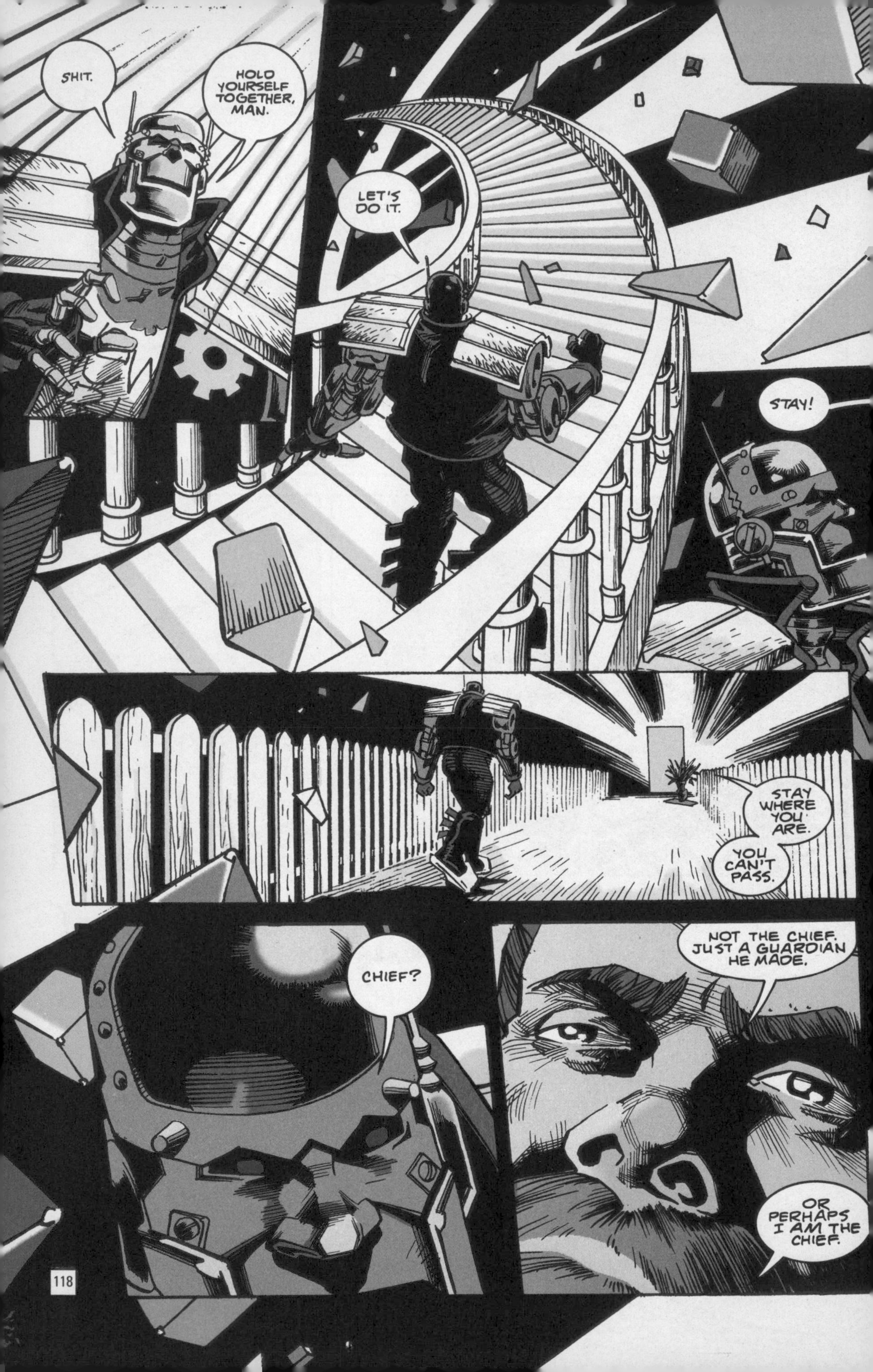
SHIT.
HOLD YOURSELF TOGETHER, MAN.
LET'S DO IT.
STAY!
STAY WHERE YOU ARE.
YOU CAN'T PASS.
CHIEF?
NOT THE CHIEF. JUST A GUARDIAN HE MADE.
OR PERHAPS I AM THE CHIEF.

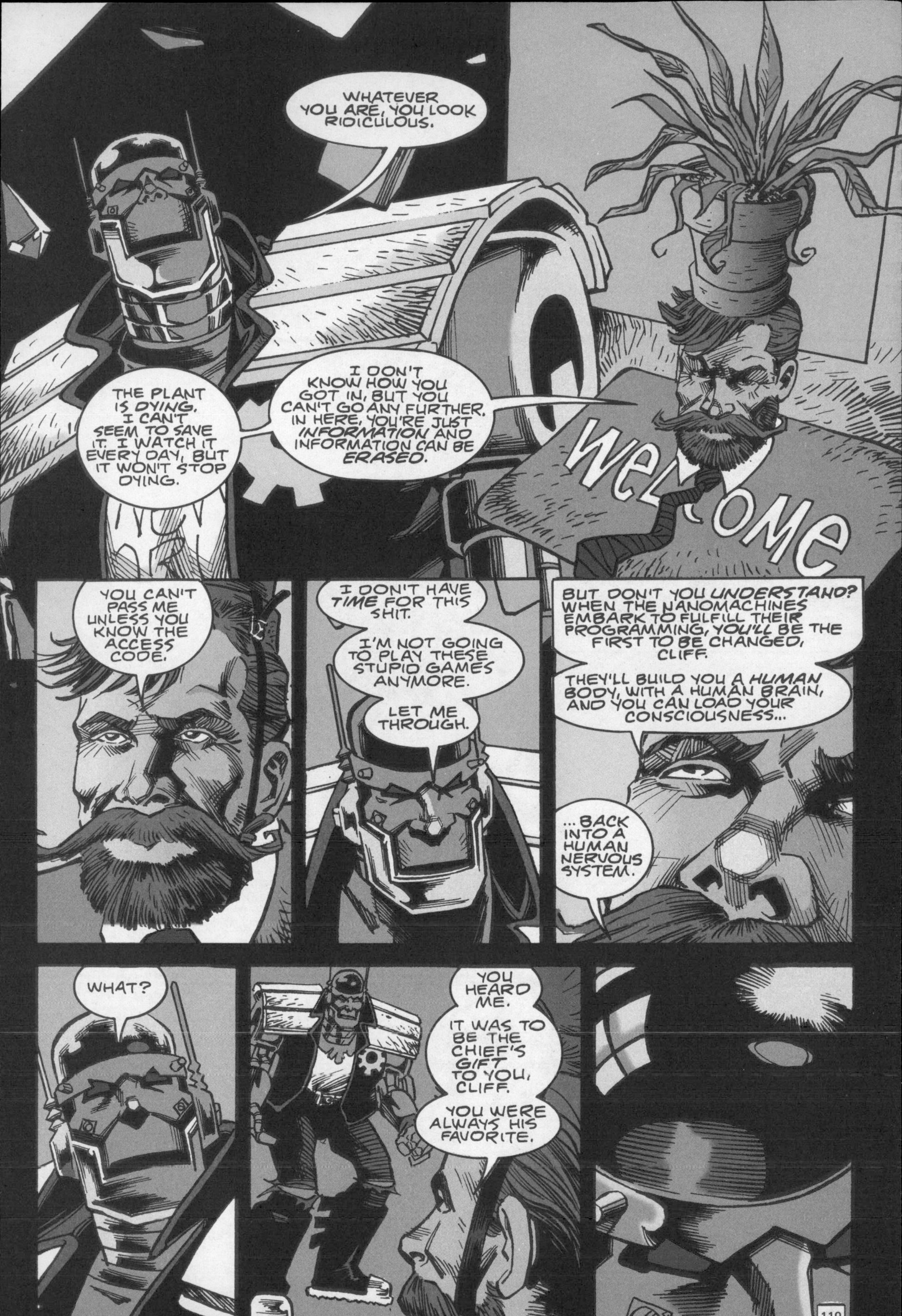
WHATEVER YOU ARE, YOU LOOK RIDICULOUS.
THE PLANT IS DYING. I CAN'T SEEM TO SAVE IT. I WATCH IT EVERY DAY, BUT IT WON'T STOP DYING.
I DON'T KNOW HOW YOU GOT IN, BUT YOU CAN'T GO ANY FURTHER. IN HERE, YOU'RE JUST INFORMATION AND INFORMATION CAN BE ERASED.
WELCOME
YOU CAN'T PASS ME UNLESS YOU KNOW THE ACCESS CODE.
I DON'T HAVE TIME FOR THIS SHIT.
I'M NOT GOING TO PLAY THESE STUPID GAMES ANYMORE.
LET ME THROUGH.
BUT DON'T YOU UNDERSTAND? WHEN THE NANOMACHINES EMBARK TO FULFILL THEIR PROGRAMMING, YOU'LL BE THE FIRST TO BE CHANGED, CLIFF.
THEY'LL BUILD YOU A HUMAN BODY, WITH A HUMAN BRAIN, AND YOU CAN LOAD YOUR CONSCIOUSNESS...
...BACK INTO A HUMAN NERVOUS SYSTEM.
WHAT?
YOU HEARD ME.
IT WAS TO BE THE CHIEF'S GIFT TO YOU, CLIFF.
YOU WERE ALWAYS HIS FAVORITE.

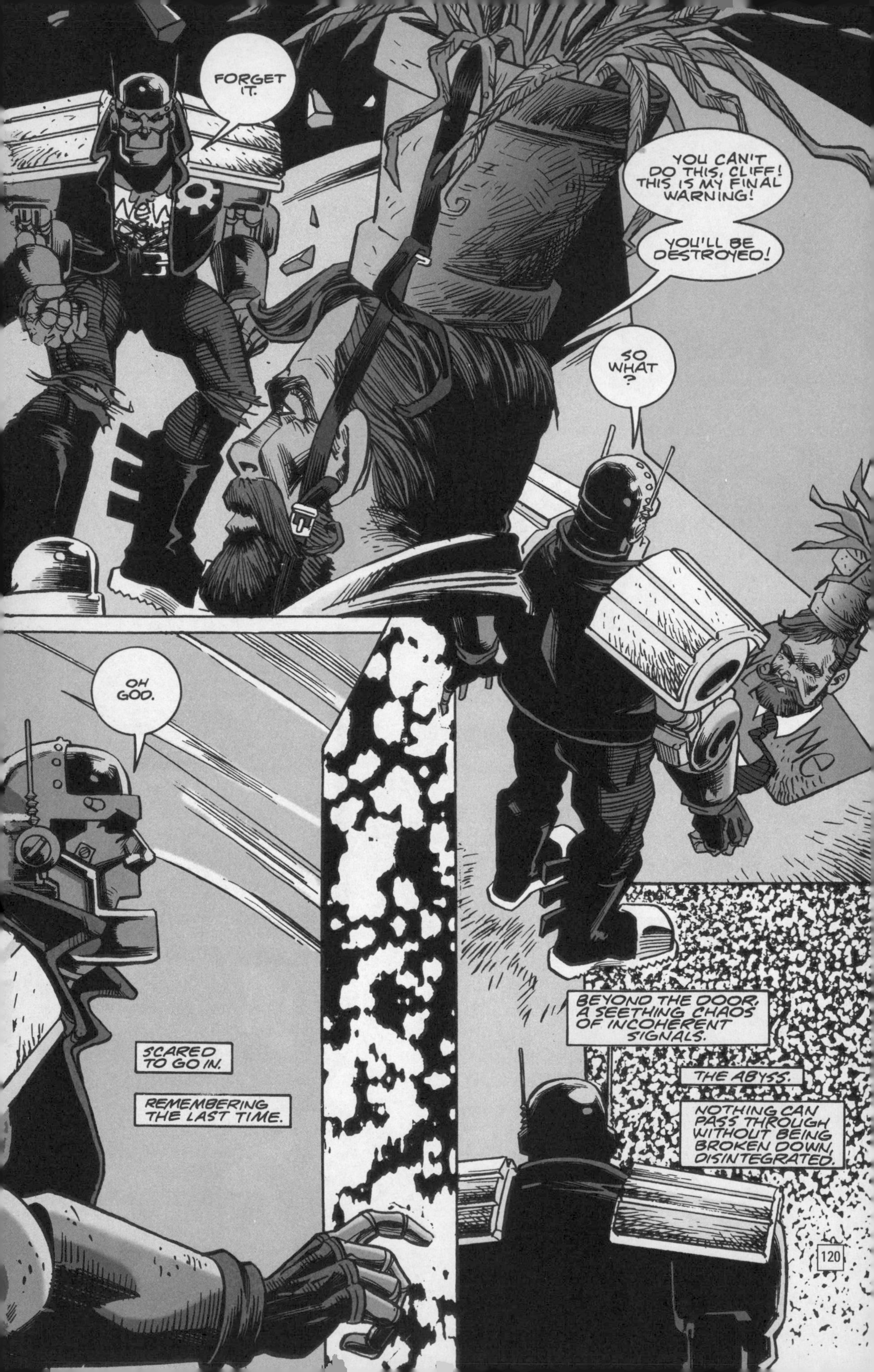

FORGET IT.
YOU CAN'T DO THIS, CLIFF! THIS IS MY FINAL WARNING!
YOU'LL BE DESTROYED!
SO WHAT?
OH GOD.
SCARED TO GO IN.
REMEMBERING THE LAST TIME.
BEYOND THE DOOR, A SEETHING CHAOS OF INCOHERENT SIGNALS.
THE ABYSS.
NOTHING CAN PASS THROUGH WITHOUT BEING BROKEN DOWN, DISINTEGRATED.

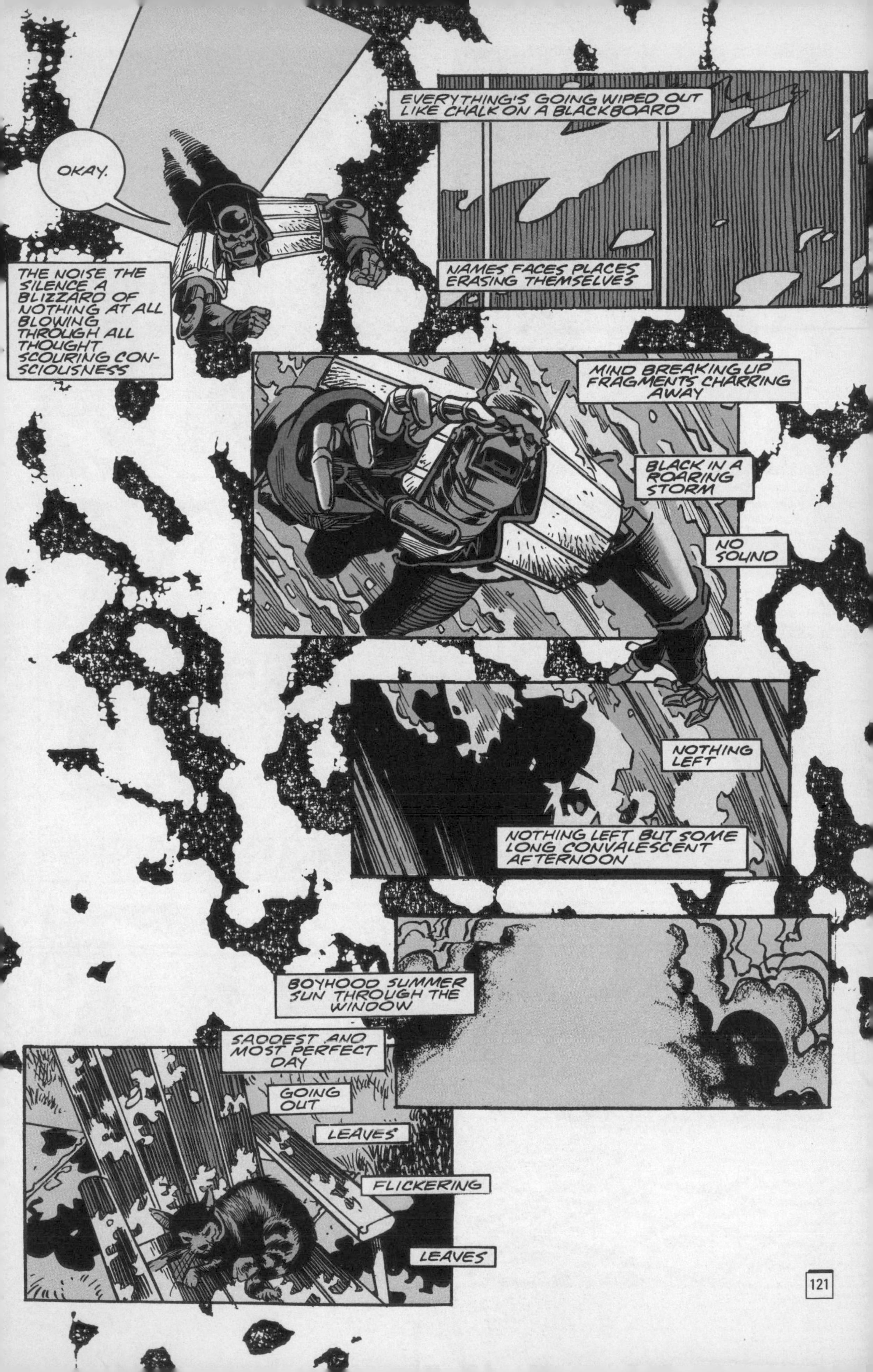
OKAY.
THE NOISE THE SILENCE A BLIZZARD OF NOTHING AT ALL BLOWING THROUGH ALL THOUGHT SCOURING CON-SCIOUSNESS
EVERYTHING'S GOING WIPED OUT LIKE CHALK ON A BLACKBOARD
NAMES FACES PLACES ERASING THEMSELVES
MIND BREAKING UP FRAGMENTS CHARRING AWAY
BLACK IN A ROARING STORM
NO SOUND
NOTHING LEFT
NOTHING LEFT BUT SOME LONG CONVALESCENT AFTERNOON
BOYHOOD SUMMER SUN THROUGH THE WINDOW
SADDEST AND MOST PERFECT DAY
GOING OUT
LEAVES
FLICKERING
LEAVES

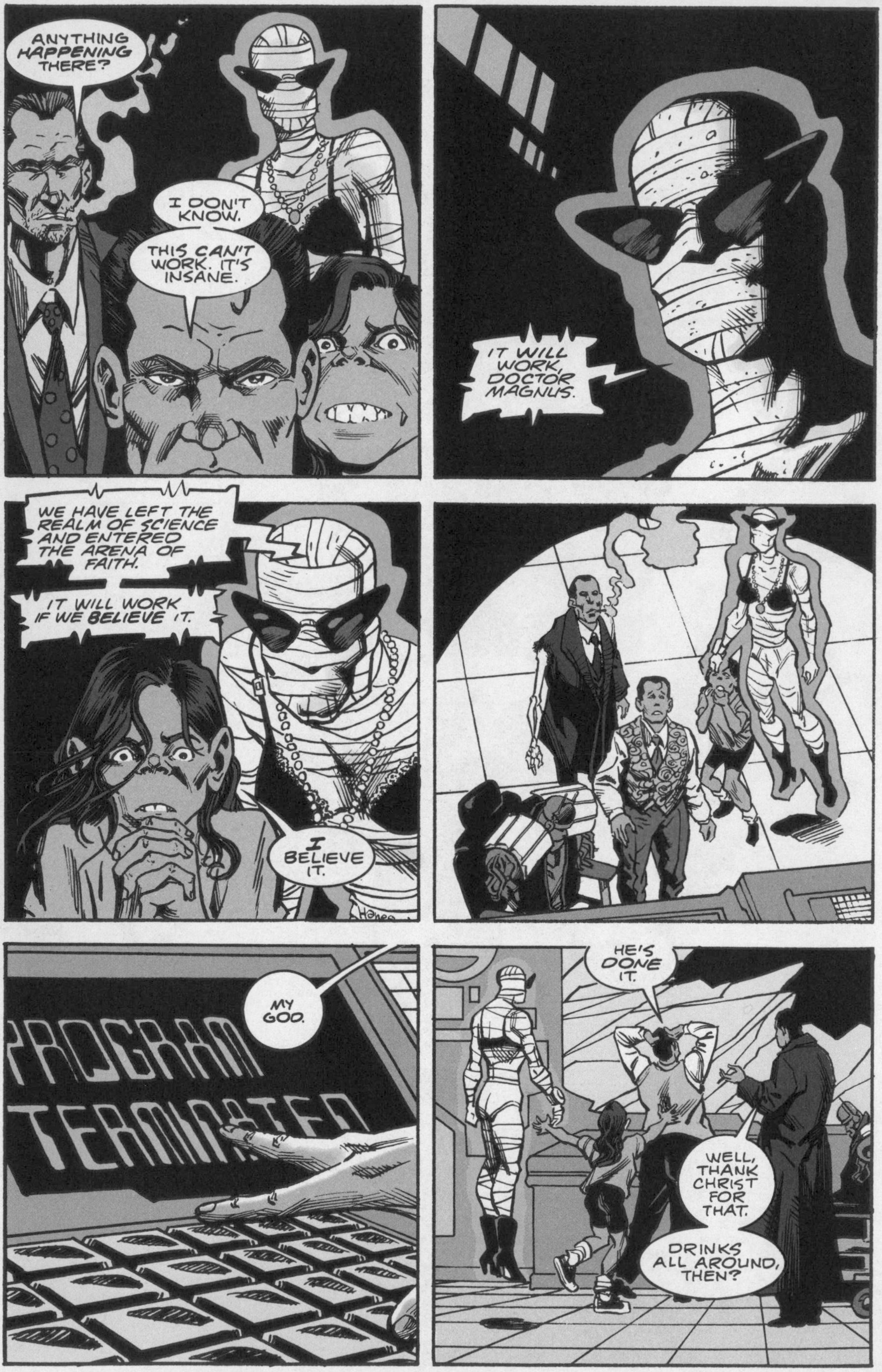
ANYTHING HAPPENING THERE?
I DON'T KNOW.
THIS CAN'T WORK. IT'S INSANE.
IT WILL WORK, DOCTOR MAGNUS.
WE HAVE LEFT THE REALM OF SCIENCE AND ENTERED THE ARENA OF FAITH.
IT WILL WORK IF WE BELIEVE IT.
I BELIEVE IT.
PROGRAM TERMINATED
MY GOD.
HE'S DONE IT.
WELL, THANK CHRIST FOR THAT.
DRINKS ALL AROUND, THEN?

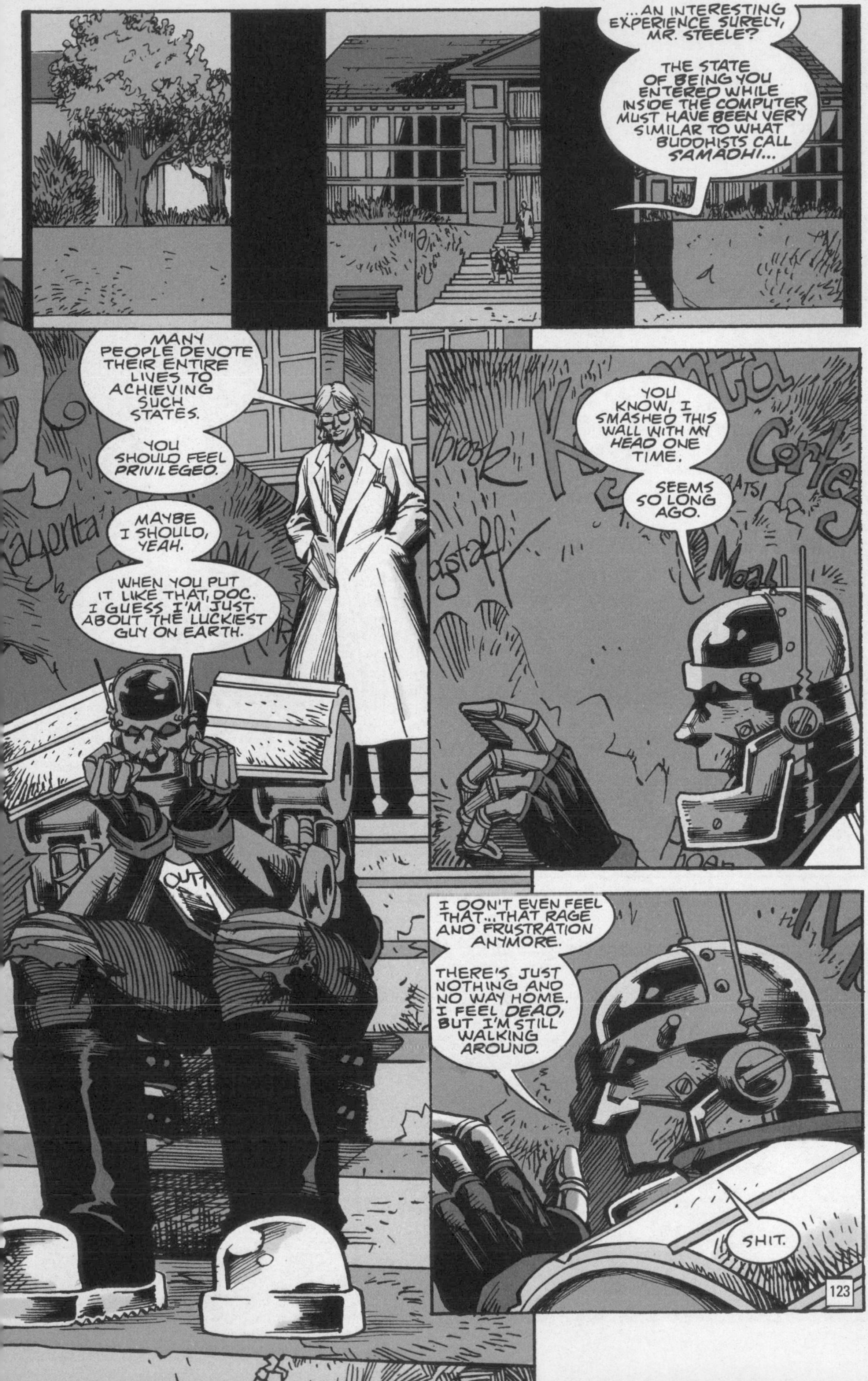
...AN INTERESTING EXPERIENCE SURELY, MR. STEELE?
THE STATE OF BEING YOU ENTERED WHILE INSIDE THE COMPUTER MUST HAVE BEEN VERY SIMILAR TO WHAT BUDDHISTS CALL SAMADHI...
MANY PEOPLE DEVOTE THEIR ENTIRE LIVES TO ACHIEVING SUCH STATES.
YOU SHOULD FEEL PRIVILEGED.
MAYBE I SHOULD, YEAH.
WHEN YOU PUT IT LIKE THAT, DOC. I GUESS I'M JUST ABOUT THE LUCKIEST GUY ON EARTH.
YOU KNOW, I SMASHED THIS WALL WITH MY HEAD ONE TIME.
SEEMS SO LONG AGO.
I DON'T EVEN FEEL THAT...THAT RAGE AND FRUSTRATION ANYMORE.
THERE'S JUST NOTHING AND NO WAY HOME. I FEEL DEAD, BUT I'M STILL WALKING AROUND.
SHIT.

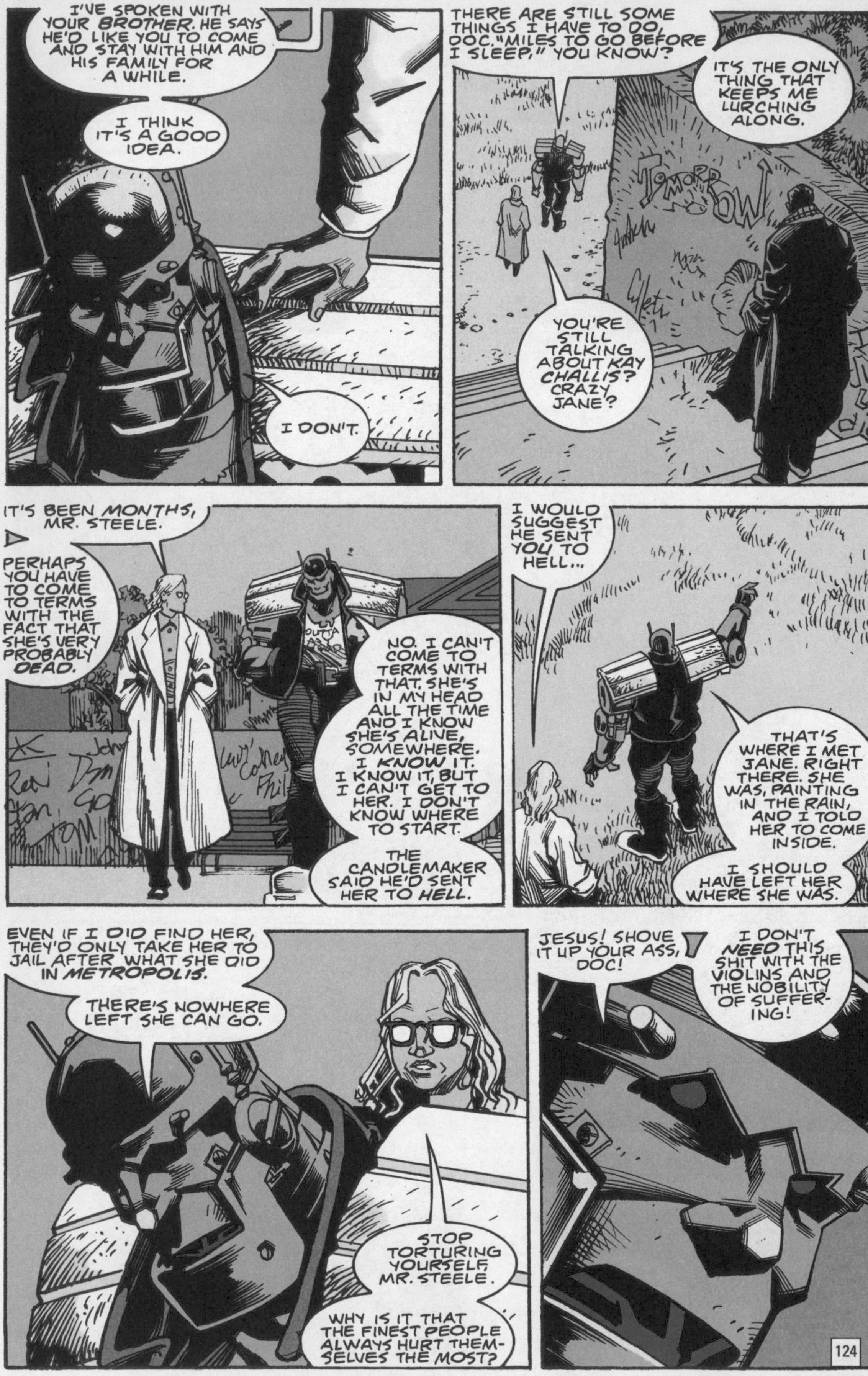
I'VE SPOKEN WITH YOUR BROTHER. HE SAYS HE'D LIKE YOU TO COME AND STAY WITH HIM AND HIS FAMILY FOR A WHILE.
I THINK IT'S A GOOD IDEA.
I DON'T.
THERE ARE STILL SOME THINGS I HAVE TO DO, DOC. "MILES TO GO BEFORE I SLEEP," YOU KNOW?
IT'S THE ONLY THING THAT KEEPS ME LURCHING ALONG.
TOMORROW
YOU'RE STILL TALKING ABOUT KAY CHALLIS? CRAZY JANE?
IT'S BEEN MONTHS, MR. STEELE.
PERHAPS YOU HAVE TO COME TO TERMS WITH THE FACT THAT SHE'S VERY PROBABLY DEAD.
NO. I CAN'T COME TO TERMS WITH THAT. SHE'S IN MY HEAD ALL THE TIME AND I KNOW SHE'S ALIVE, SOMEWHERE. I KNOW IT. I KNOW IT, BUT I CAN'T GET TO HER. I DON'T KNOW WHERE TO START.
THE CANDLEMAKER SAID HE'D SENT HER TO HELL.
I WOULD SUGGEST HE SENT YOU TO HELL...
THAT'S WHERE I MET JANE. RIGHT THERE. SHE WAS, PAINTING IN THE RAIN, AND I TOLD HER TO COME INSIDE.
I SHOULD HAVE LEFT HER WHERE SHE WAS.
EVEN IF I DID FIND HER, THEY'D ONLY TAKE HER TO JAIL AFTER WHAT SHE DID IN METROPOLIS.
THERE'S NOWHERE LEFT SHE CAN GO.
STOP TORTURING YOURSELF, MR. STEELE.
WHY IS IT THAT THE FINEST PEOPLE ALWAYS HURT THEMSELVES THE MOST?
JESUS! SHOVE IT UP YOUR ASS, DOC!
I DON'T NEED THIS SHIT WITH THE VIOLINS AND THE NOBILITY OF SUFFERING!

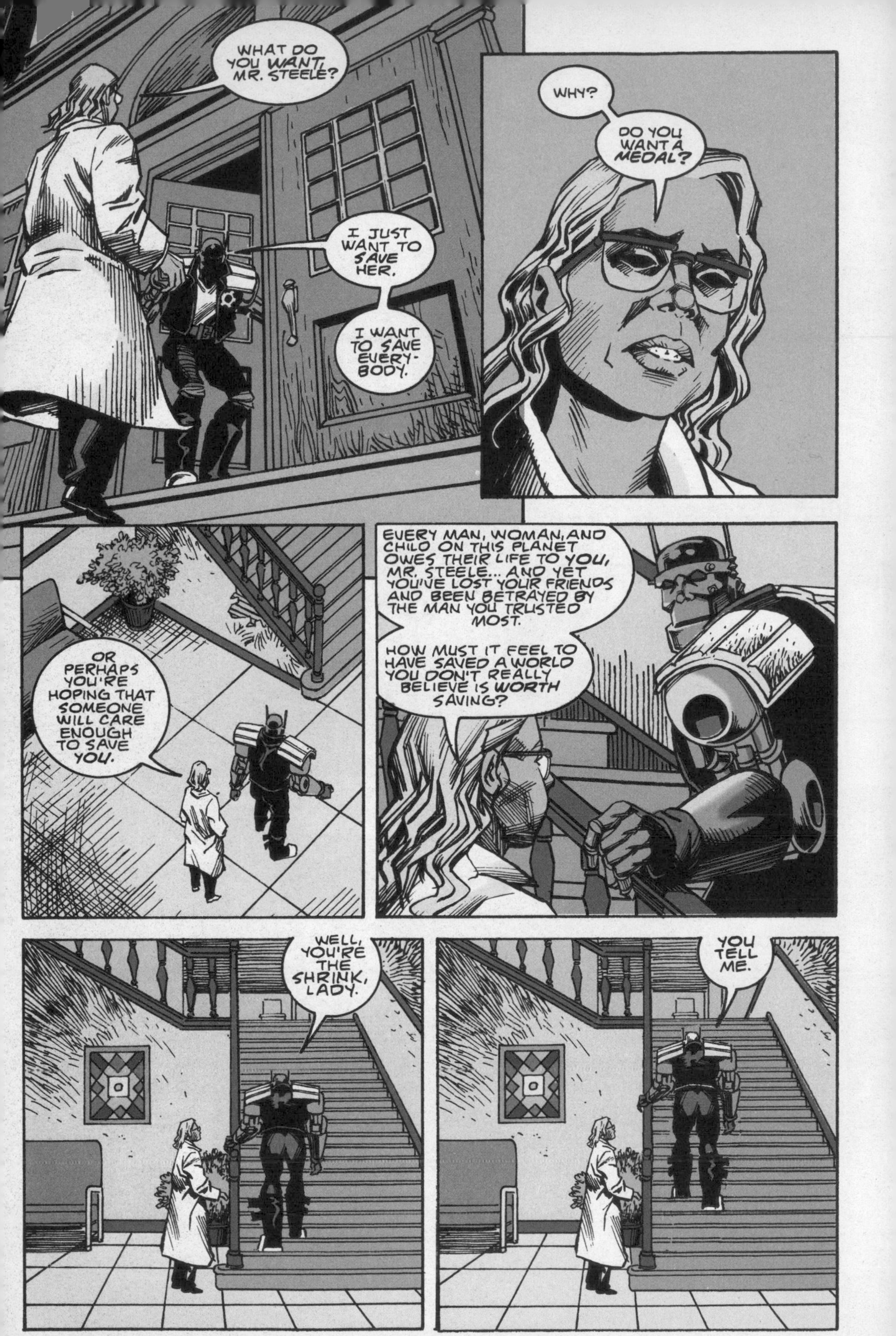
WHAT DO YOU WANT, MR. STEELE?
WHY?
DO YOU WANT A MEDAL?
I JUST WANT TO SAVE HER.
I WANT TO SAVE EVERY-BODY.
OR PERHAPS YOU'RE HOPING THAT SOMEONE WILL CARE ENOUGH TO SAVE YOU.
EVERY MAN, WOMAN, AND CHILD ON THIS PLANET OWES THEIR LIFE TO YOU, MR. STEELE... AND YET YOU'VE LOST YOUR FRIENDS AND BEEN BETRAYED BY THE MAN YOU TRUSTED MOST.
HOW MUST IT FEEL TO HAVE SAVED A WORLD YOU DON'T REALLY BELIEVE IS WORTH SAVING?
WELL, YOU'RE THE SHRINK, LADY.
YOU TELL ME.

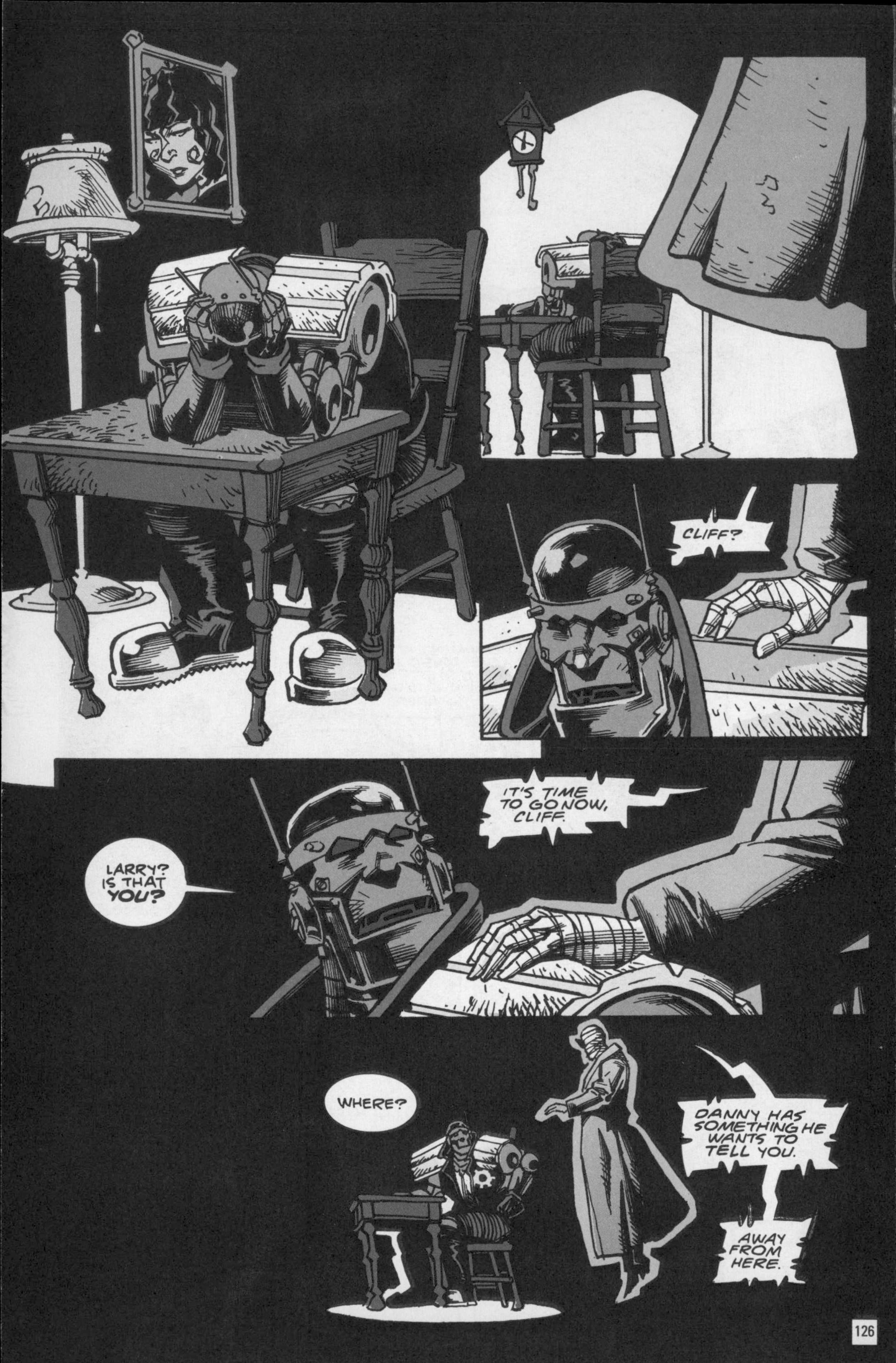
CLIFF?
IT'S TIME TO GO NOW, CLIFF.
LARRY? IS THAT YOU?
WHERE?
DANNY HAS SOMETHING HE WANTS TO TELL YOU.
AWAY FROM HERE.

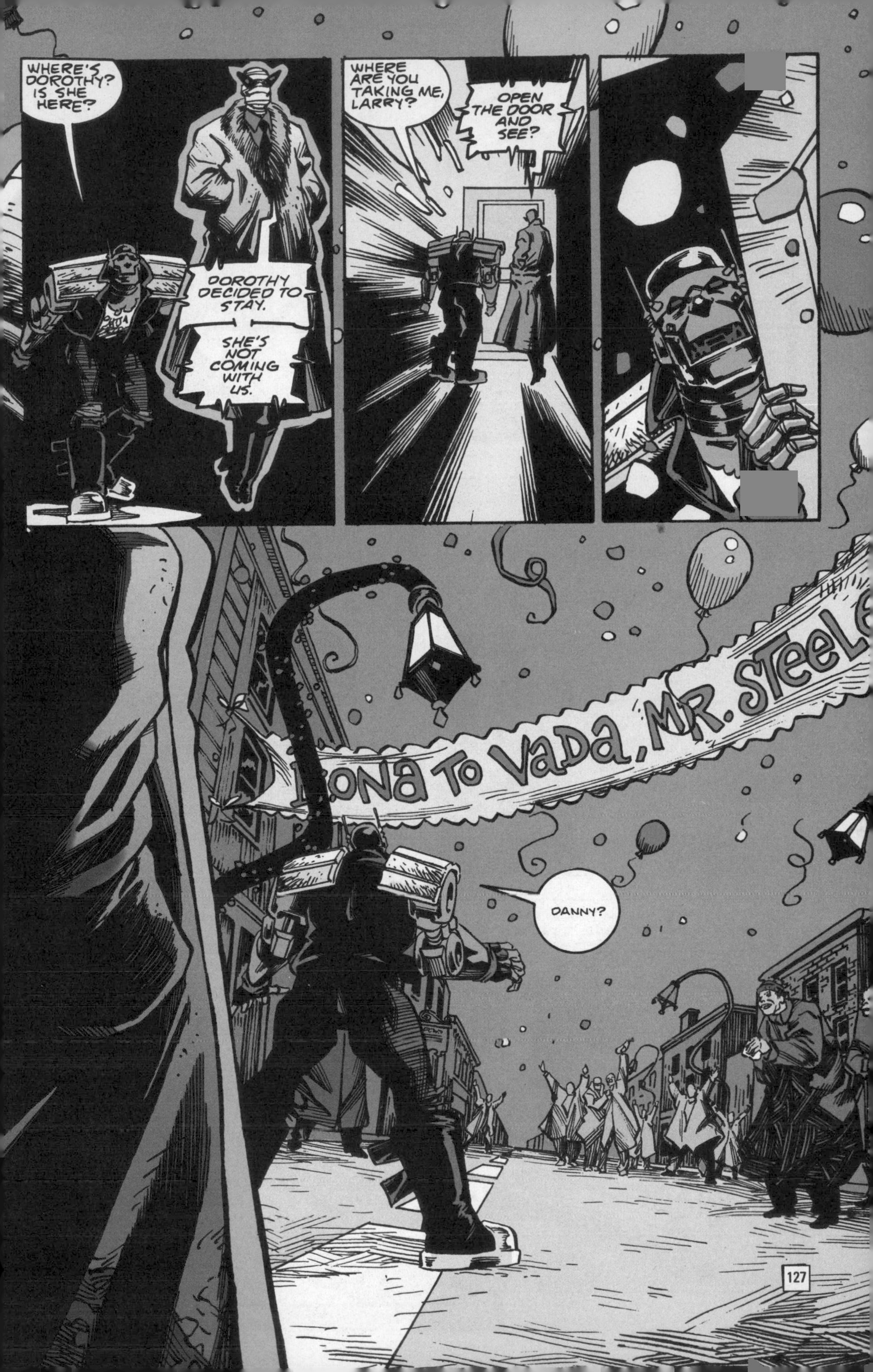
WHERE'S DOROTHY? IS SHE HERE?
DOROTHY DECIDED TO STAY.
SHE'S NOT COMING WITH US.
WHERE ARE YOU TAKING ME, LARRY?
OPEN THE DOOR AND SEE?
ONA TO VADA, MR. STEEL
DANNY?

NICE TA HAVE YA BACK AGAIN, BIG FELLA!

AH, YER A FINE MAN, MR. STEELE, A FINE MAN!

IN HERE, CLIFF.

DANNY HAS SOMETHING HE WANTS TO TELL YOU.

HI, DANNY. IT'S GOOD TO SEE YOU.

I THOUGHT THE CANDLE-MAKER HAD DESTROYED YOU.

Takes more than that to shut me up, love. Us old queens are hard as nails. Sorry I took so long to collect you. You must have been sick to the gills in that horrible place.

Anyway, I wanted to make sure you were here to vada the big event.

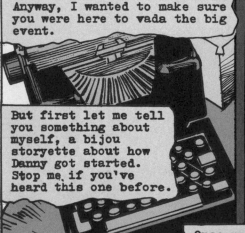

But first let me tell you something about myself, a bijou storyette about how Danny got started. Stop me if you've heard this one before.

Once upon a time...

There was a world like this one but better. Ever so dolly.

A world where everything was marvelous or frightening or strange. A world where everything was alive and significant.

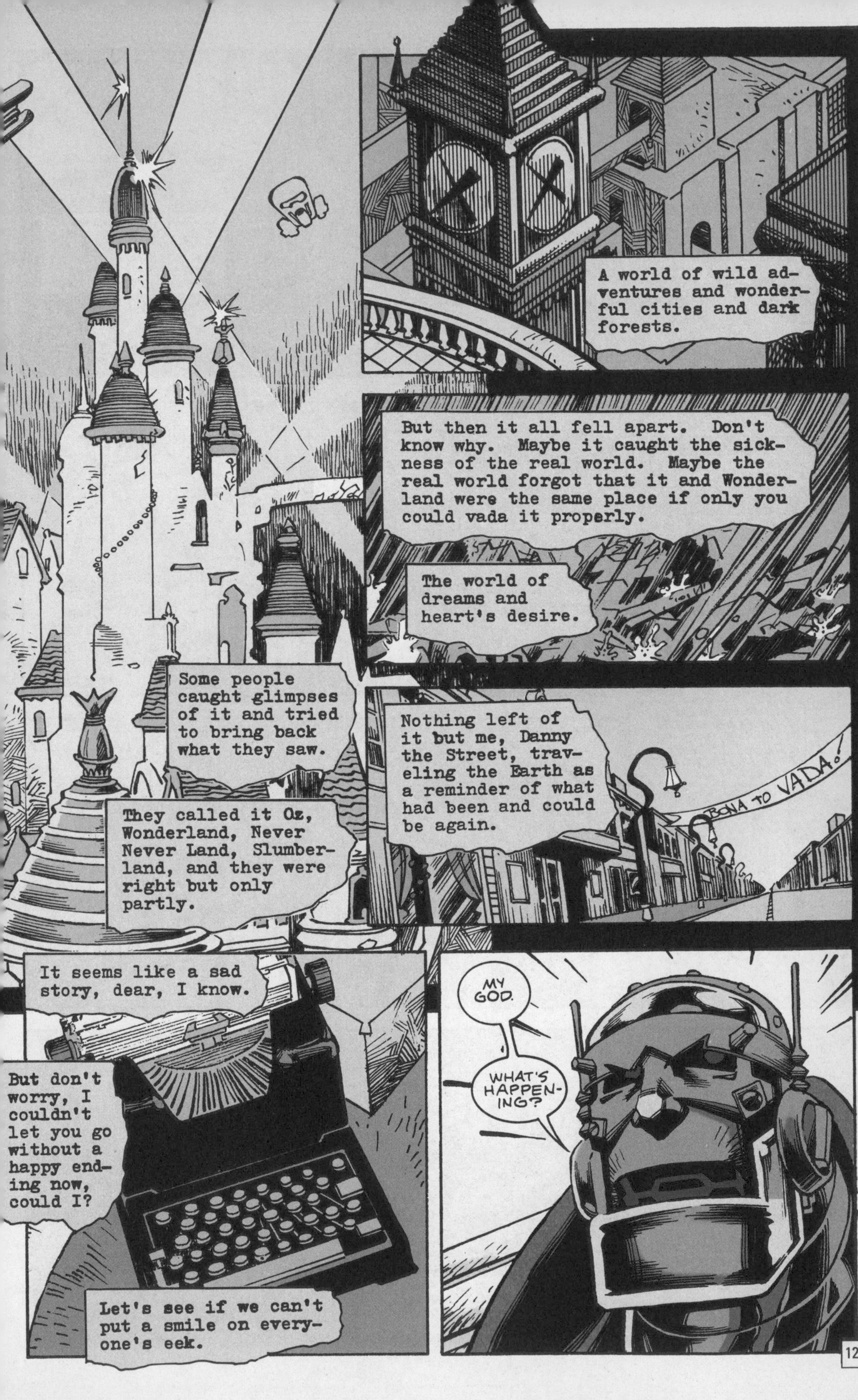
A world of wild adventures and wonderful cities and dark forests.
Some people caught glimpses of it and tried to bring back what they saw.
They called it Oz, Wonderland, Never Never Land, Slumberland, and they were right but only partly.
But then it all fell apart. Don't know why. Maybe it caught the sickness of the real world. Maybe the real world forgot that it and Wonderland were the same place if only you could vada it properly.
The world of dreams and heart's desire.
Nothing left of it but me, Danny the Street, traveling the Earth as a reminder of what had been and could be again.
BONA TO VADA!
It seems like a sad story, dear, I know.
But don't worry, I couldn't let you go without a happy ending now, could I?
Let's see if we can't put a smile on everyone's eek.
MY GOD.
WHAT'S HAPPENING?

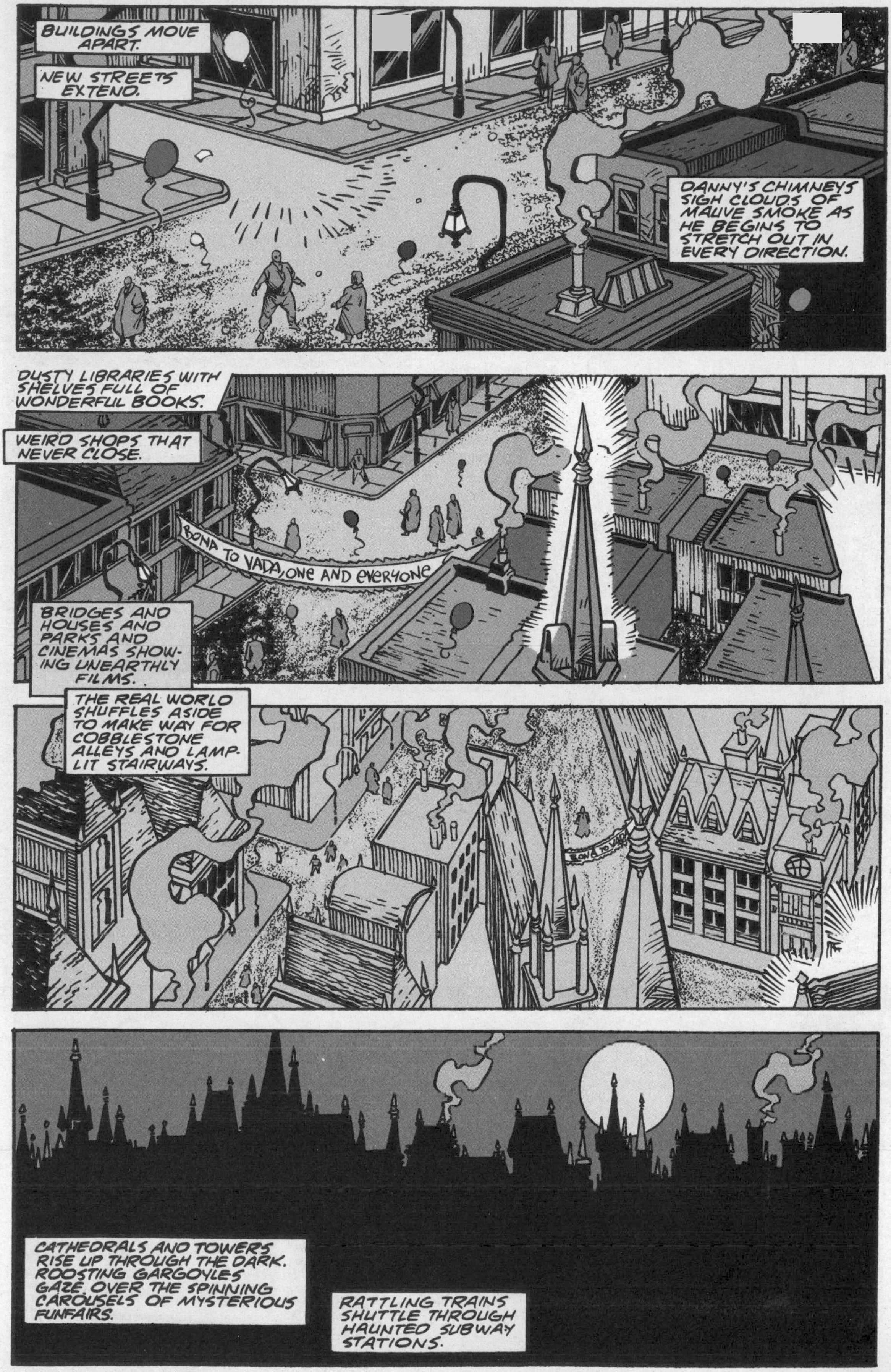
BUILDINGS MOVE APART.
NEW STREETS EXTEND.
DANNY'S CHIMNEYS SIGH CLOUDS OF MAUVE SMOKE AS HE BEGINS TO STRETCH OUT IN EVERY DIRECTION.
DUSTY LIBRARIES WITH SHELVES FULL OF WONDERFUL BOOKS.
WEIRD SHOPS THAT NEVER CLOSE.
BONA TO VADA, ONE AND EVERYONE
BRIDGES AND HOUSES AND PARKS AND CINEMAS SHOWING UNEARTHLY FILMS.
THE REAL WORLD SHUFFLES ASIDE TO MAKE WAY FOR COBBLESTONE ALLEYS AND LAMP-LIT STAIRWAYS.
BONA TO VADA
CATHEDRALS AND TOWERS RISE UP THROUGH THE DARK. ROOSTING GARGOYLES GAZE OVER THE SPINNING CAROUSELS OF MYSTERIOUS FUNFAIRS.
RATTLING TRAINS SHUTTLE THROUGH HAUNTED SUBWAY STATIONS.

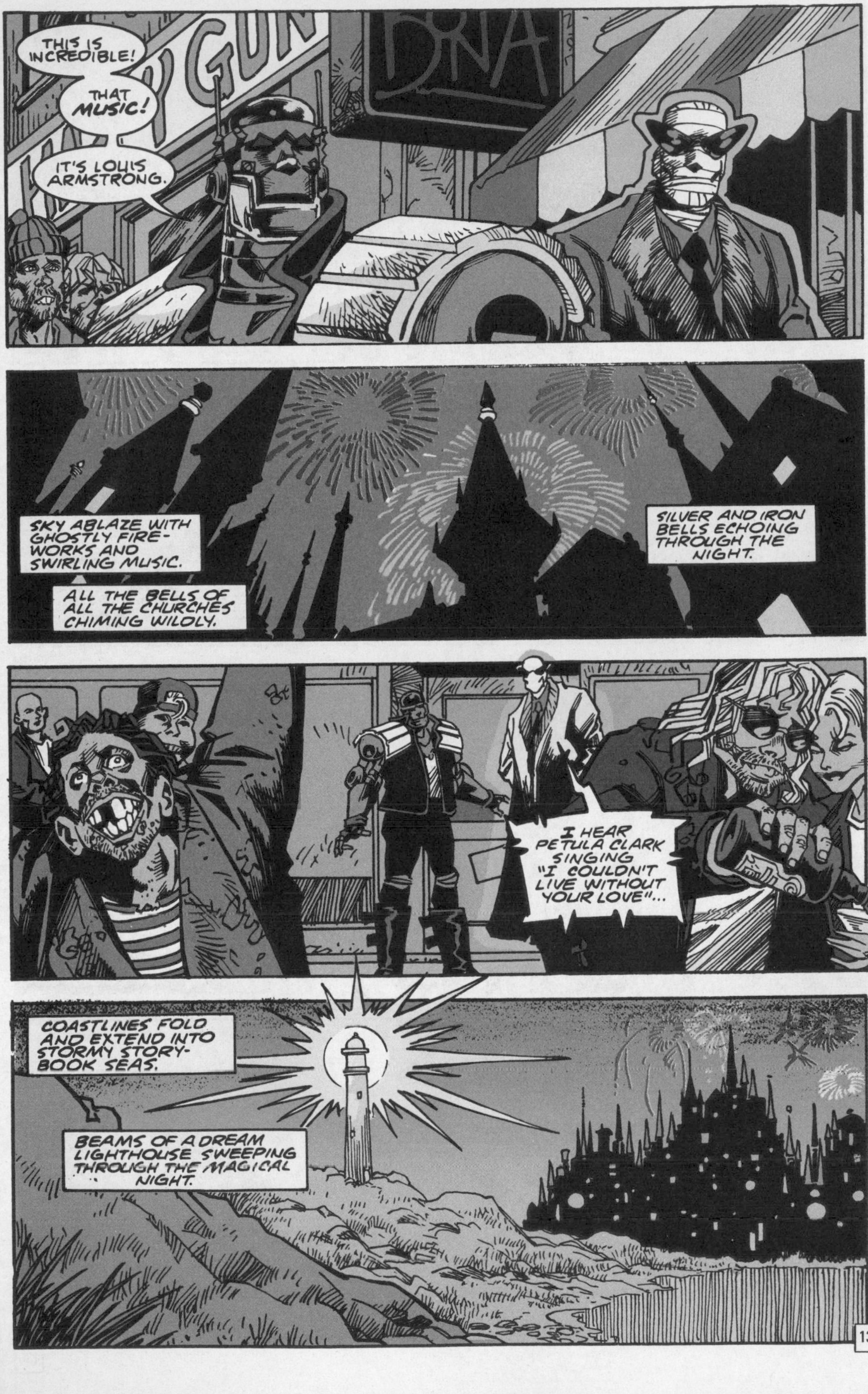

GUN
DNA
THIS IS INCREDIBLE!
THAT MUSIC!
IT'S LOUIS ARMSTRONG.
SKY ABLAZE WITH GHOSTLY FIRE-WORKS AND SWIRLING MUSIC.
ALL THE BELLS OF ALL THE CHURCHES CHIMING WILDLY.
SILVER AND IRON BELLS ECHOING THROUGH THE NIGHT.
I HEAR PETULA CLARK SINGING "I COULDN'T LIVE WITHOUT YOUR LOVE"...
COASTLINES FOLD AND EXTEND INTO STORMY STORY-BOOK SEAS.
BEAMS OF A DREAM LIGHTHOUSE SWEEPING THROUGH THE MAGICAL NIGHT.

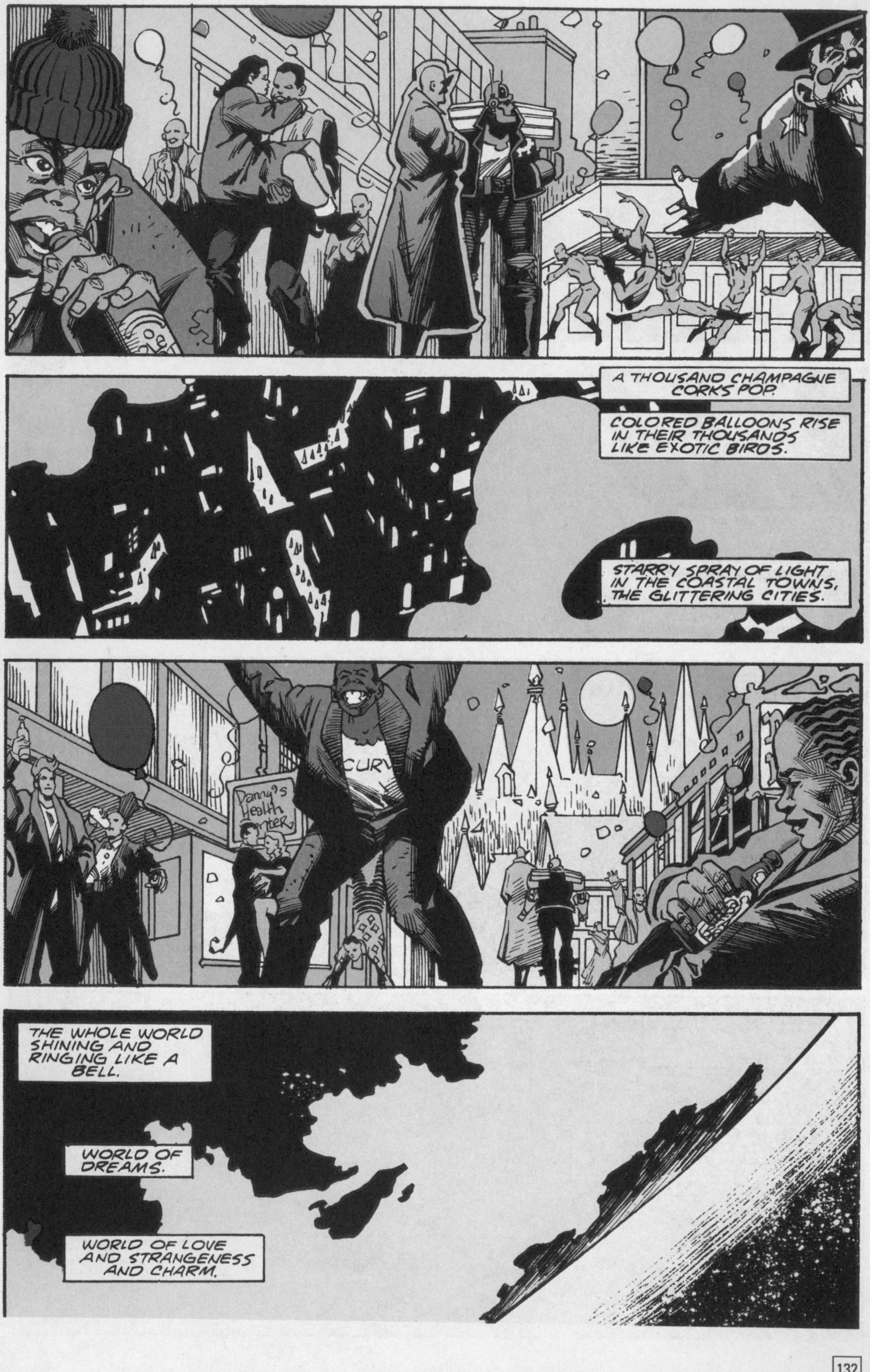
A THOUSAND CHAMPAGNE CORKS POP.
COLORED BALLOONS RISE IN THEIR THOUSANDS LIKE EXOTIC BIRDS.
STARRY SPRAY OF LIGHT IN THE COASTAL TOWNS, THE GLITTERING CITIES.
Danny's Health Center
THE WHOLE WORLD SHINING AND RINGING LIKE A BELL.
WORLD OF DREAMS.
WORLD OF LOVE AND STRANGENESS AND CHARM.

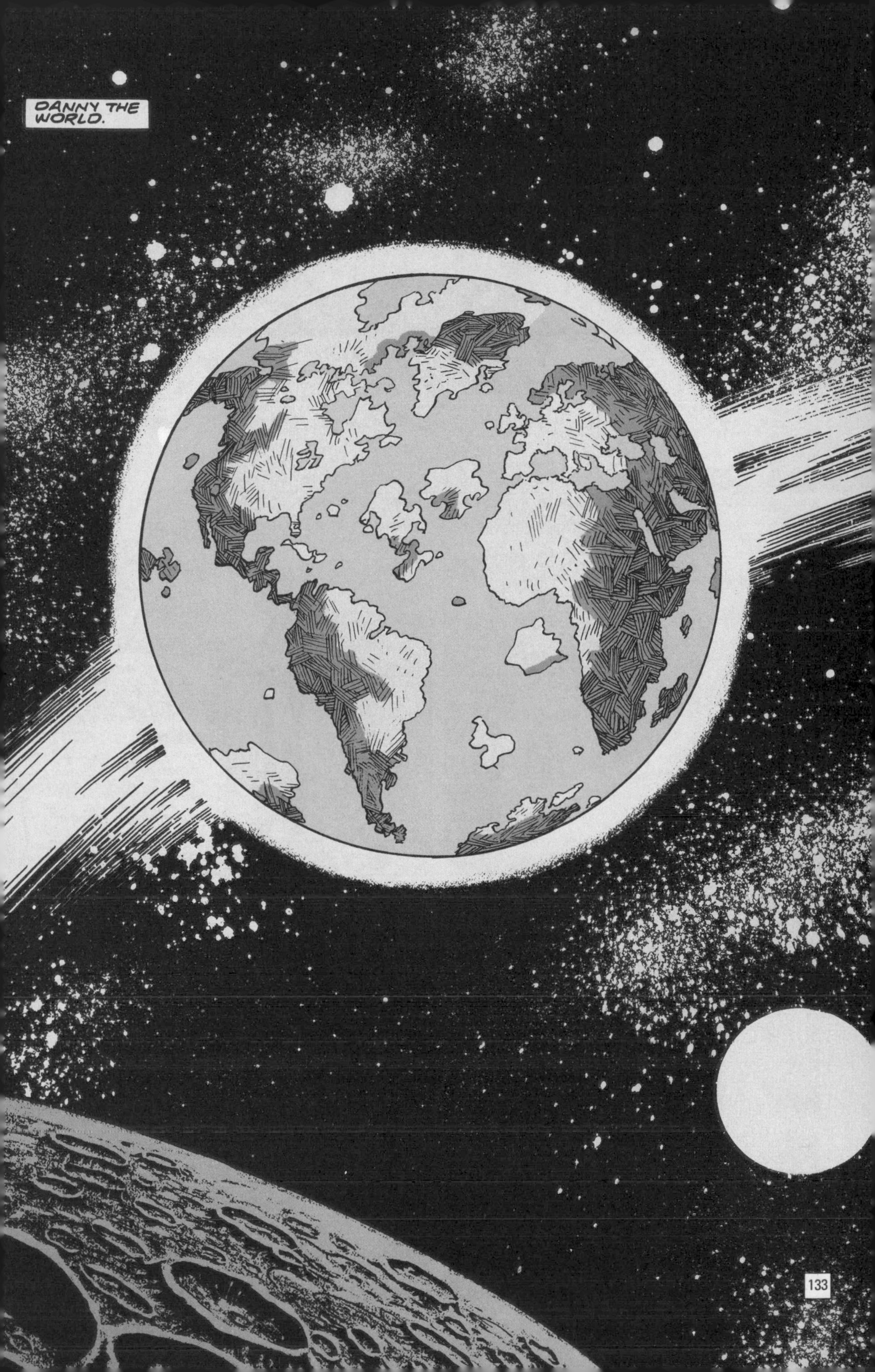
DANNY THE WORLD.

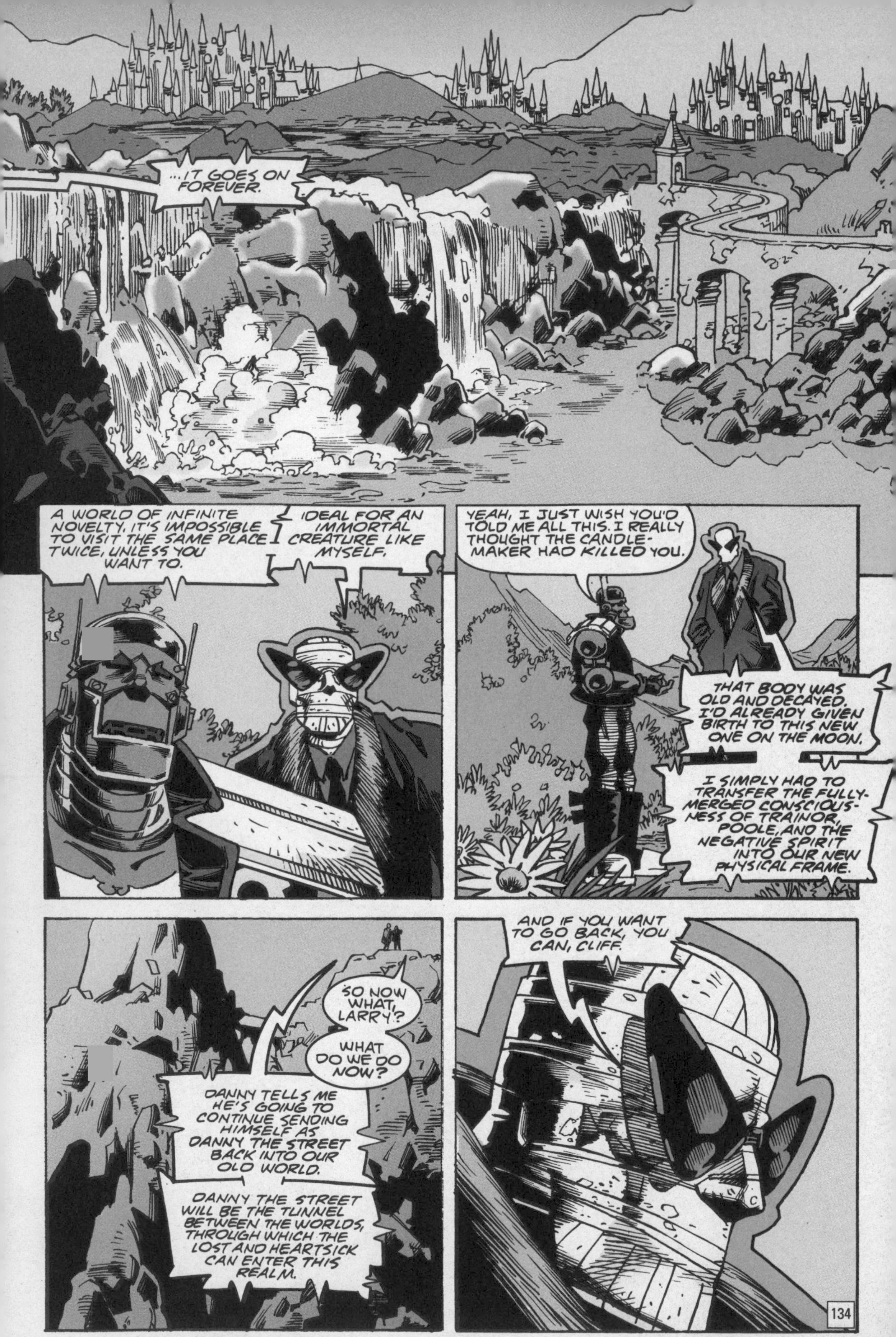

...IT GOES ON FOREVER.
A WORLD OF INFINITE NOVELTY. IT'S IMPOSSIBLE TO VISIT THE SAME PLACE TWICE, UNLESS YOU WANT TO.
IDEAL FOR AN IMMORTAL CREATURE LIKE MYSELF.
YEAH, I JUST WISH YOU'D TOLD ME ALL THIS. I REALLY THOUGHT THE CANDLE-MAKER HAD KILLED YOU.
THAT BODY WAS OLD AND DECAYED. I'D ALREADY GIVEN BIRTH TO THIS NEW ONE ON THE MOON.
I SIMPLY HAD TO TRANSFER THE FULLY-MERGED CONSCIOUS-NESS OF TRAINOR, POOLE, AND THE NEGATIVE SPIRIT INTO OUR NEW PHYSICAL FRAME.
SO NOW WHAT, LARRY?
WHAT DO WE DO NOW?
DANNY TELLS ME HE'S GOING TO CONTINUE SENDING HIMSELF AS DANNY THE STREET BACK INTO OUR OLD WORLD.
DANNY THE STREET WILL BE THE TUNNEL BETWEEN THE WORLDS, THROUGH WHICH THE LOST AND HEARTSICK CAN ENTER THIS REALM.
AND IF YOU WANT TO GO BACK, YOU CAN, CLIFF.

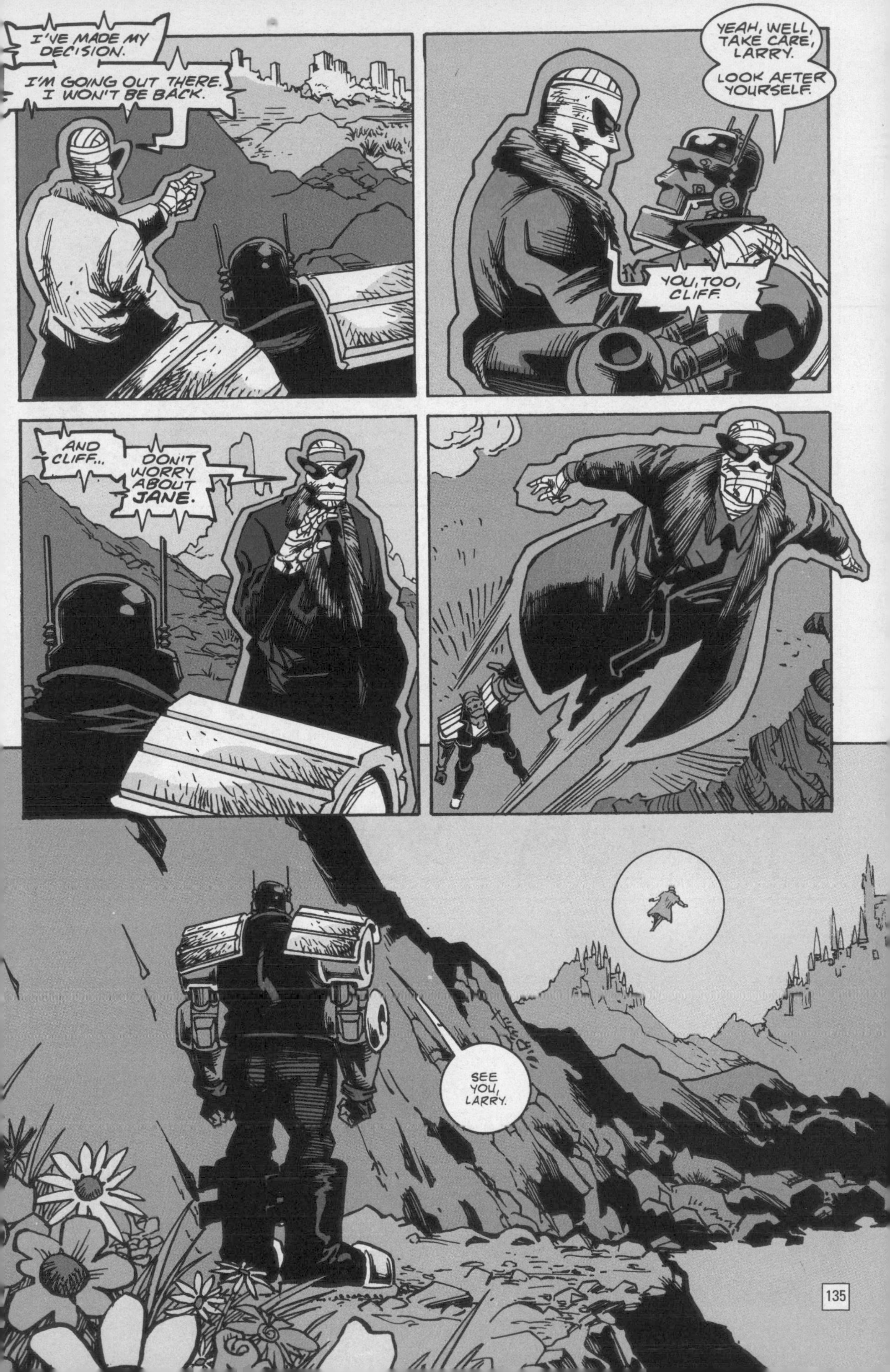
I'VE MADE MY DECISION.
I'M GOING OUT THERE. I WON'T BE BACK.
YEAH, WELL, TAKE CARE, LARRY.
LOOK AFTER YOURSELF.
YOU, TOO, CLIFF.
AND CLIFF...
DON'T WORRY ABOUT JANE.
SEE YOU, LARRY.

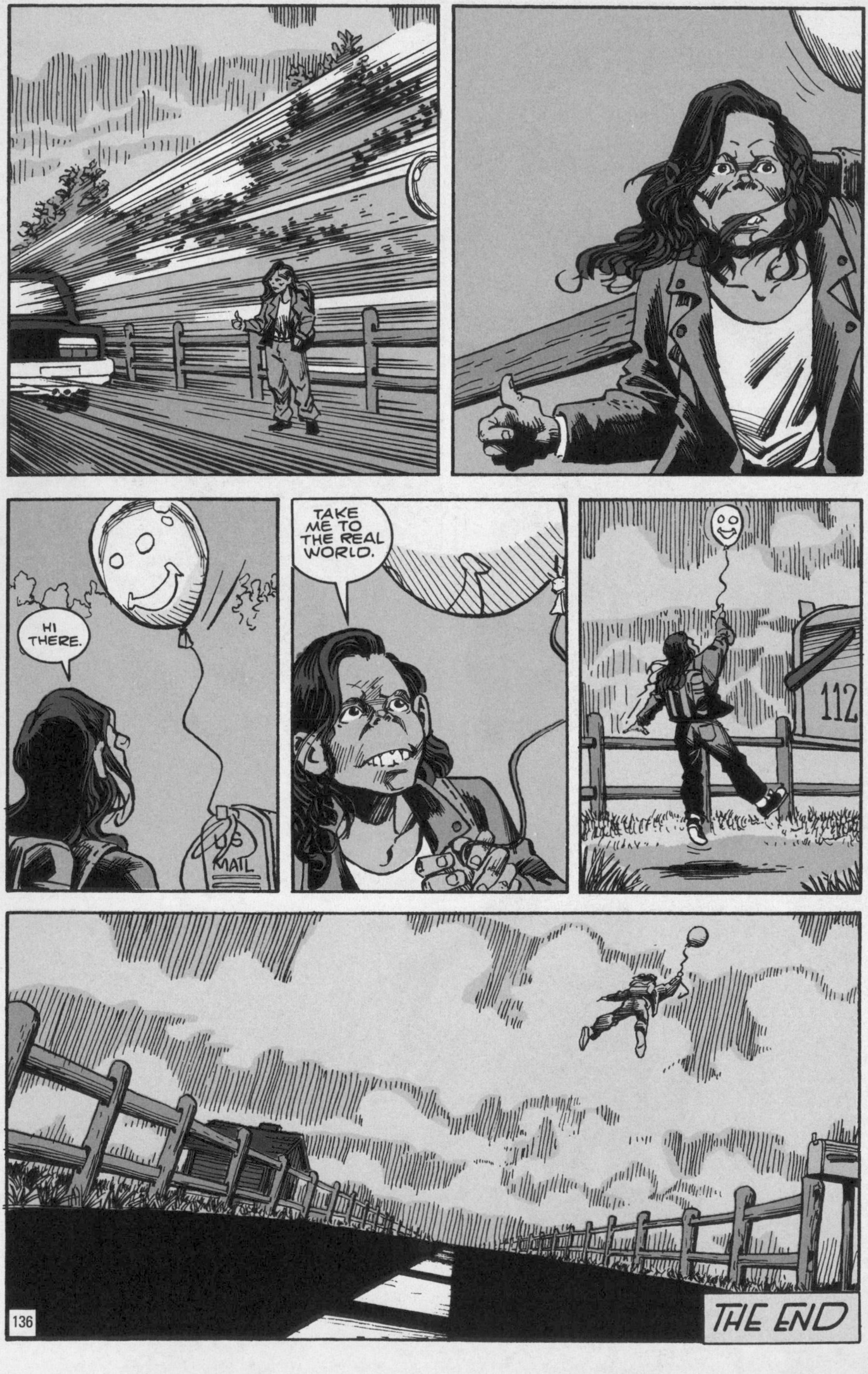
HI THERE.
US MAIL
TAKE ME TO THE REAL WORLD.
112
THE END

"There is another world.   There is a better world."

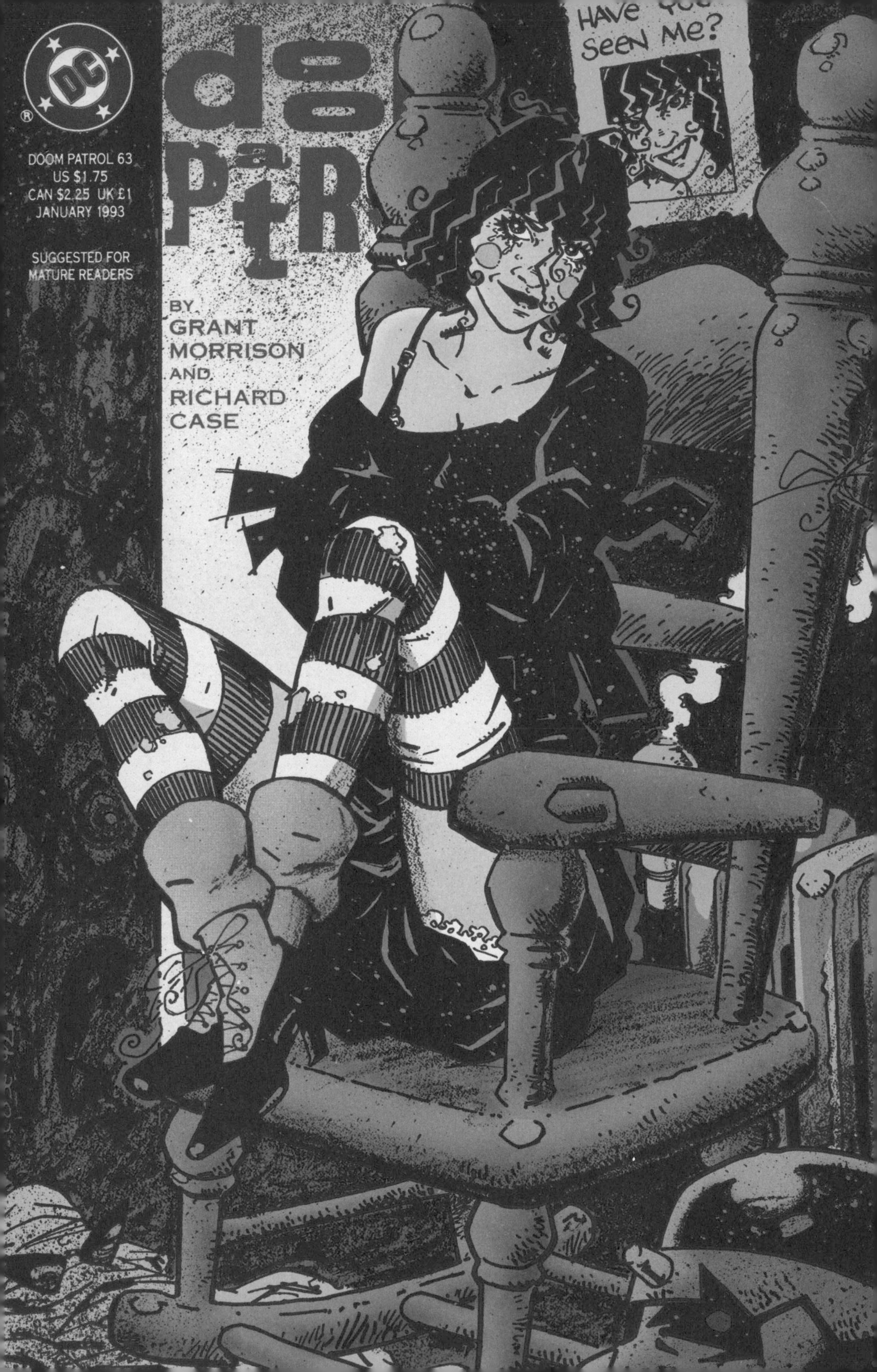

DOOM PATROL 63
US $1.75
CAN $2.25 UK £1
JANUARY 1993
SUGGESTED FOR MATURE READERS
BY GRANT MORRISON AND RICHARD CASE
HAVE YOU SEEN ME?

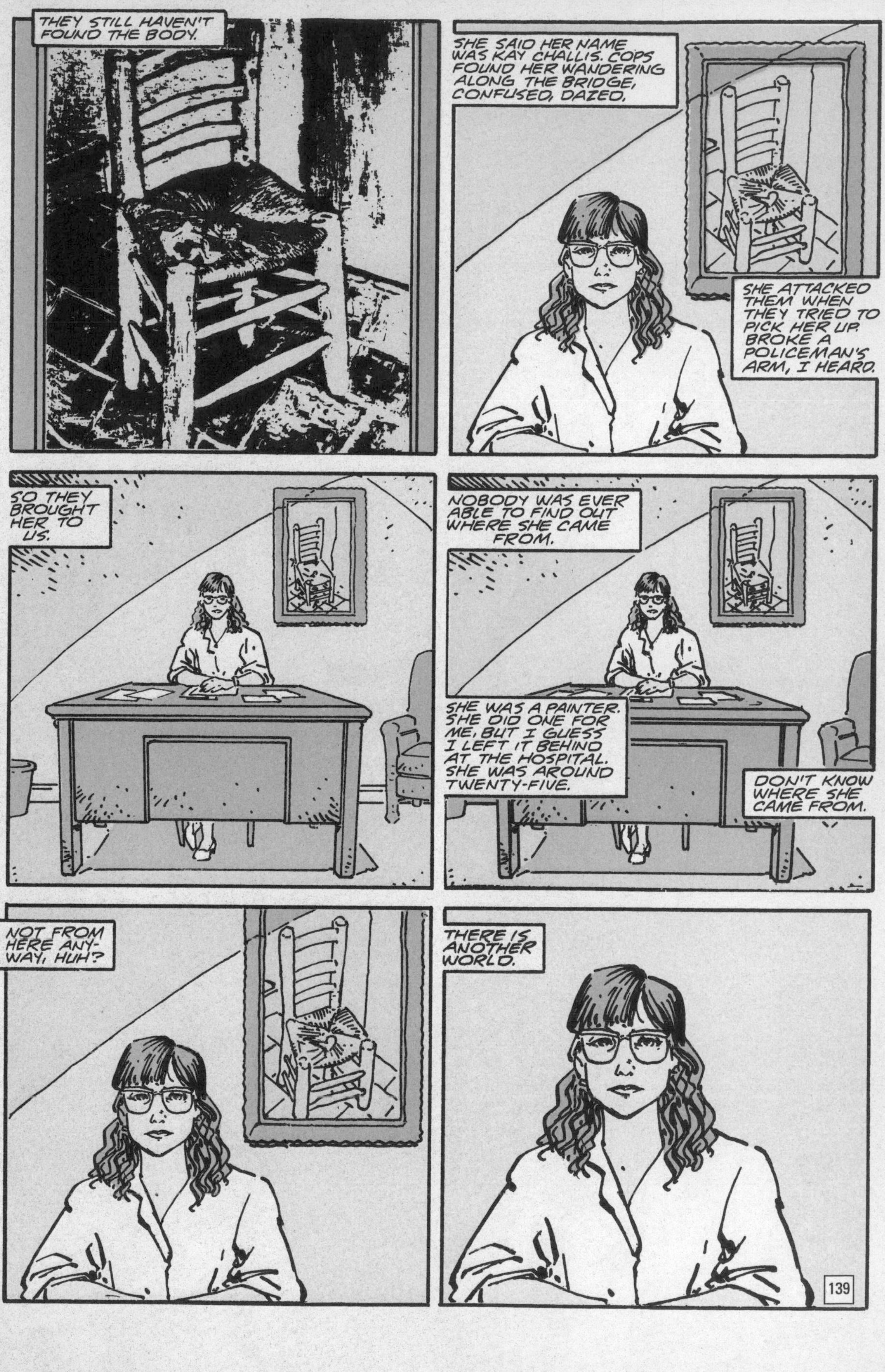
THEY STILL HAVEN'T FOUND THE BODY.
SHE SAID HER NAME WAS KAY CHALLIS. COPS FOUND HER WANDERING ALONG THE BRIDGE, CONFUSED, DAZED.
SHE ATTACKED THEM WHEN THEY TRIED TO PICK HER UP. BROKE A POLICEMAN'S ARM, I HEARD.
SO THEY BROUGHT HER TO US.
NOBODY WAS EVER ABLE TO FIND OUT WHERE SHE CAME FROM.
SHE WAS A PAINTER. SHE DID ONE FOR ME, BUT I GUESS I LEFT IT BEHIND AT THE HOSPITAL. SHE WAS AROUND TWENTY-FIVE.
DON'T KNOW WHERE SHE CAME FROM.
NOT FROM HERE ANY-WAY, HUH?
THERE IS ANOTHER WORLD.

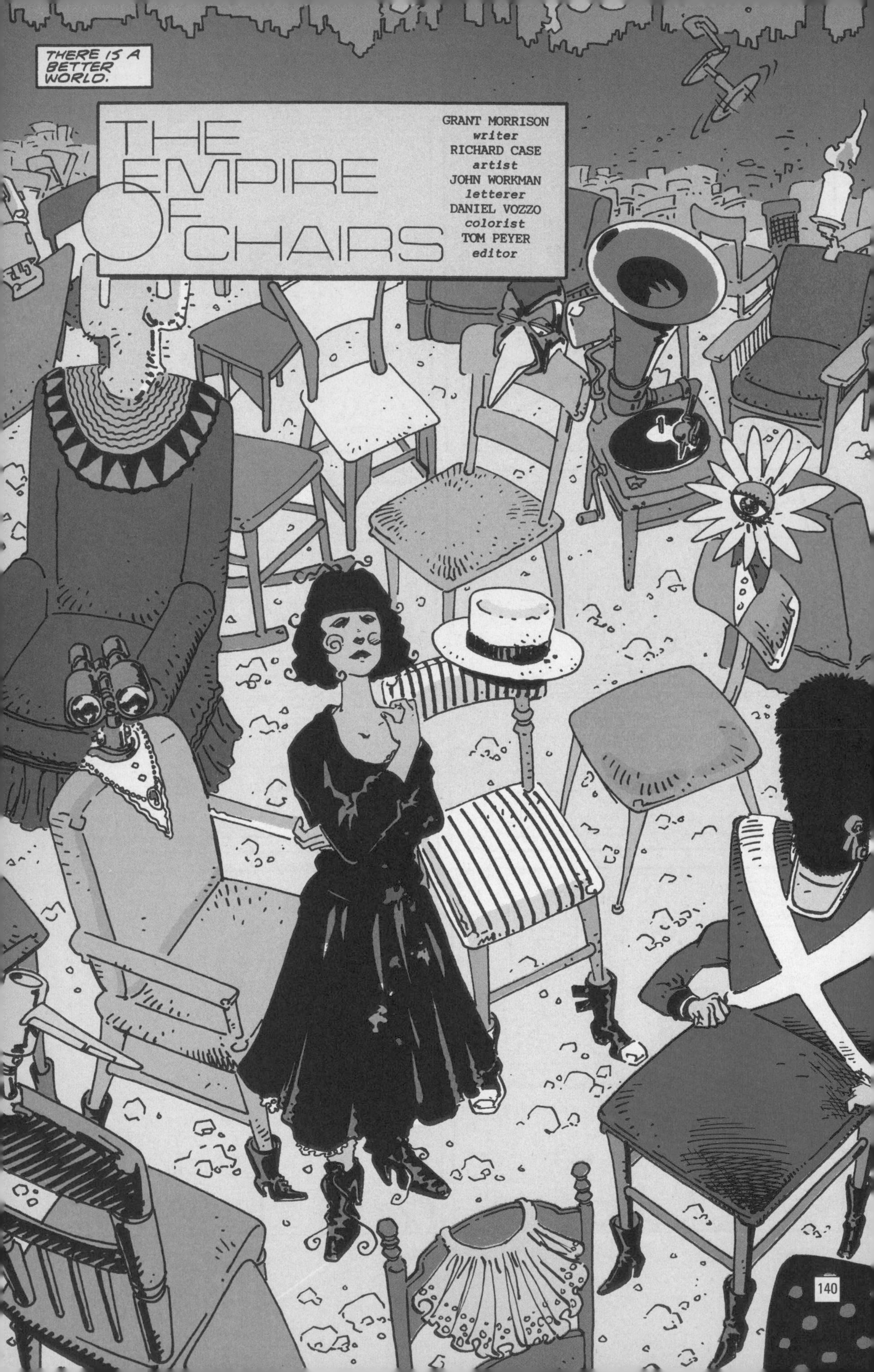

THERE IS A BETTER WORLD.
THE EMPIRE OF CHAIRS
GRANT MORRISON writer
RICHARD CASE artist
JOHN WORKMAN letterer
DANIEL VOZZO colorist
TOM PEYER editor

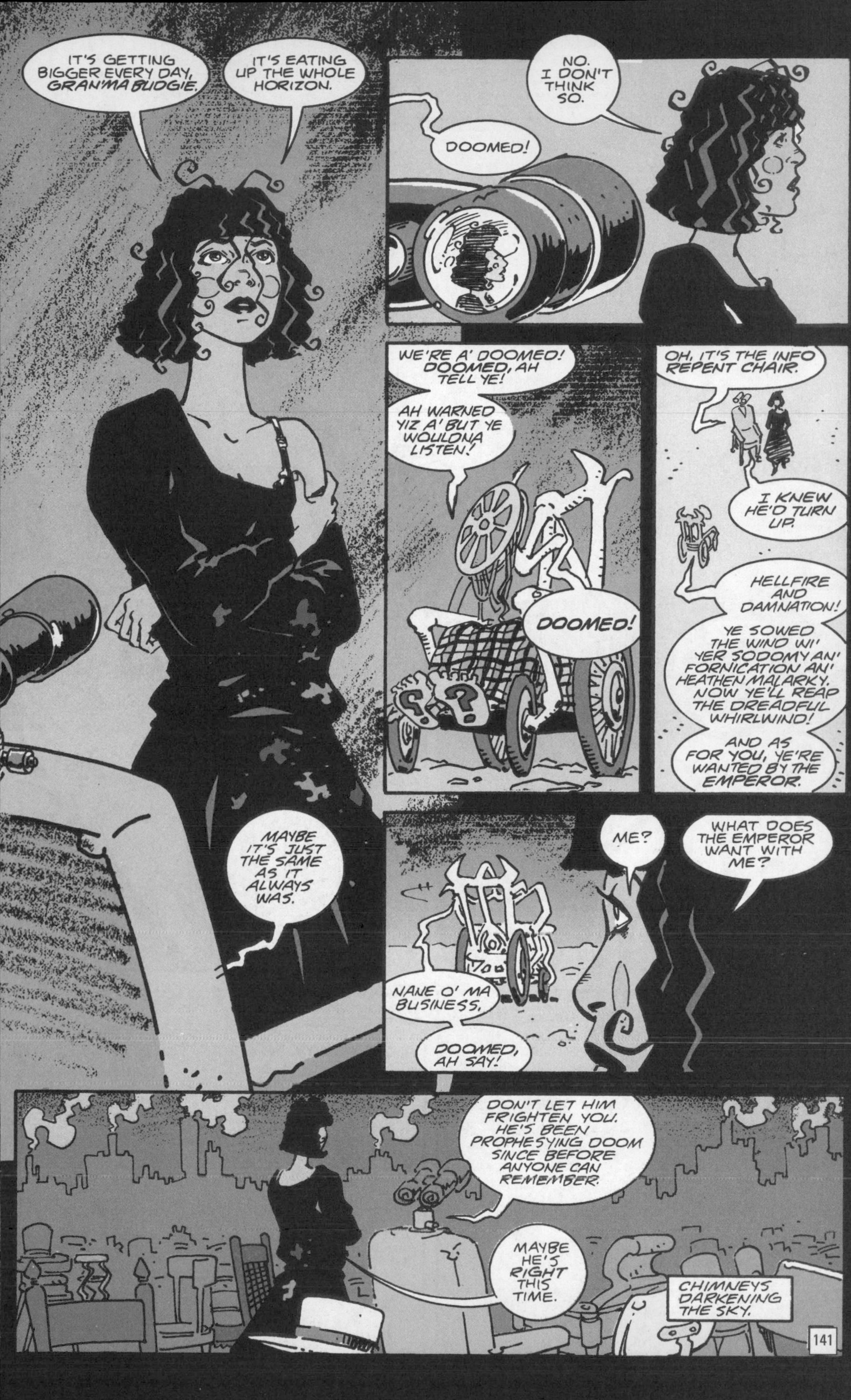
IT'S GETTING BIGGER EVERY DAY, GRAN'MA BUDGIE.
IT'S EATING UP THE WHOLE HORIZON.
DOOMED!
NO. I DON'T THINK SO.
WE'RE A' DOOMED! DOOMED, AH TELL YE!
AH WARNED YIZ A' BUT YE WOULDNA LISTEN!
DOOMED!
OH, IT'S THE INFO REPENT CHAIR.
I KNEW HE'D TURN UP.
HELLFIRE AND DAMNATION!
YE SOWED THE WIND WI' YER SODOMY AN' FORNICATION AN' HEATHEN MALARKY. NOW YE'LL REAP THE DREADFUL WHIRLWIND!
AND AS FOR YOU, YE'RE WANTED BY THE EMPEROR.
MAYBE IT'S JUST THE SAME AS IT ALWAYS WAS.
ME?
WHAT DOES THE EMPEROR WANT WITH ME?
NANE O' MA BUSINESS.
DOOMED, AH SAY!
DON'T LET HIM FRIGHTEN YOU. HE'S BEEN PROPHESYING DOOM SINCE BEFORE ANYONE CAN REMEMBER.
MAYBE HE'S RIGHT THIS TIME.
CHIMNEYS DARKENING THE SKY.

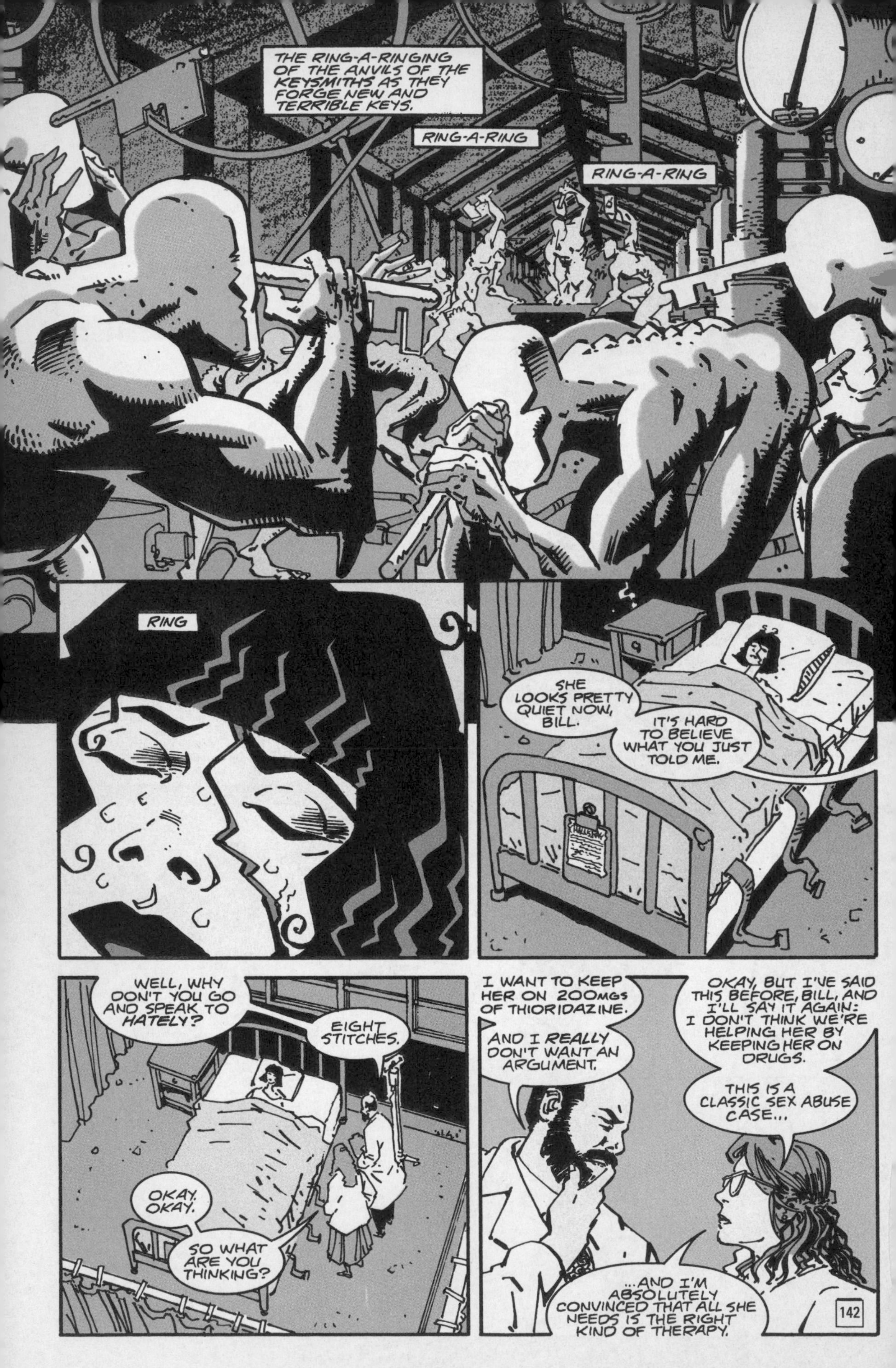

THE RING-A-RINGING OF THE ANVILS OF THE KEYSMITHS AS THEY FORGE NEW AND TERRIBLE KEYS.
RING-A-RING
RING-A-RING
RING
SHE LOOKS PRETTY QUIET NOW, BILL.
IT'S HARD TO BELIEVE WHAT YOU JUST TOLD ME.
WELL, WHY DON'T YOU GO AND SPEAK TO HATELY?
EIGHT STITCHES.
OKAY. OKAY.
SO WHAT ARE YOU THINKING?
I WANT TO KEEP HER ON 200MGS OF THIORIDAZINE.
AND I REALLY DON'T WANT AN ARGUMENT.
OKAY, BUT I'VE SAID THIS BEFORE, BILL, AND I'LL SAY IT AGAIN: I DON'T THINK WE'RE HELPING HER BY KEEPING HER ON DRUGS.
THIS IS A CLASSIC SEX ABUSE CASE...
...AND I'M ABSOLUTELY CONVINCED THAT ALL SHE NEEDS IS THE RIGHT KIND OF THERAPY.

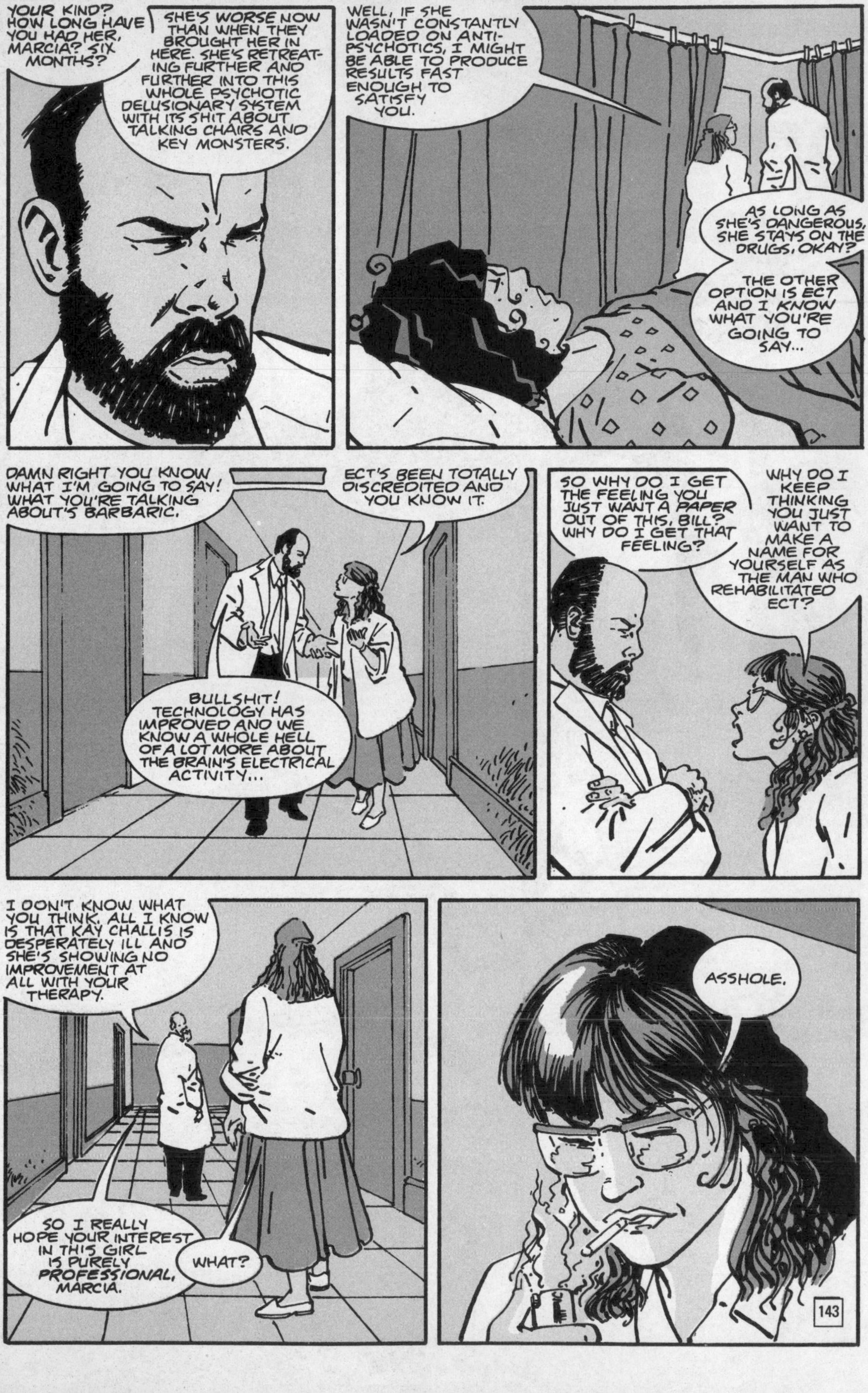
YOUR KIND? HOW LONG HAVE YOU HAD HER, MARCIA? SIX MONTHS?
SHE'S WORSE NOW THAN WHEN THEY BROUGHT HER IN HERE. SHE'S RETREATING FURTHER AND FURTHER INTO THIS WHOLE PSYCHOTIC DELUSIONARY SYSTEM WITH ITS SHIT ABOUT TALKING CHAIRS AND KEY MONSTERS.
WELL, IF SHE WASN'T CONSTANTLY LOADED ON ANTI-PSYCHOTICS, I MIGHT BE ABLE TO PRODUCE RESULTS FAST ENOUGH TO SATISFY YOU.
AS LONG AS SHE'S DANGEROUS, SHE STAYS ON THE DRUGS, OKAY?
THE OTHER OPTION IS ECT AND I KNOW WHAT YOU'RE GOING TO SAY...
DAMN RIGHT YOU KNOW WHAT I'M GOING TO SAY! WHAT YOU'RE TALKING ABOUT'S BARBARIC.
ECT'S BEEN TOTALLY DISCREDITED AND YOU KNOW IT.
BULLSHIT! TECHNOLOGY HAS IMPROVED AND WE KNOW A WHOLE HELL OF A LOT MORE ABOUT THE BRAIN'S ELECTRICAL ACTIVITY...
SO WHY DO I GET THE FEELING YOU JUST WANT A PAPER OUT OF THIS, BILL? WHY DO I GET THAT FEELING?
WHY DO I KEEP THINKING YOU JUST WANT TO MAKE A NAME FOR YOURSELF AS THE MAN WHO REHABILITATED ECT?
I DON'T KNOW WHAT YOU THINK. ALL I KNOW IS THAT KAY CHALLIS IS DESPERATELY ILL AND SHE'S SHOWING NO IMPROVEMENT AT ALL WITH YOUR THERAPY.
SO I REALLY HOPE YOUR INTEREST IN THIS GIRL IS PURELY PROFESSIONAL, MARCIA.
WHAT?
ASSHOLE.

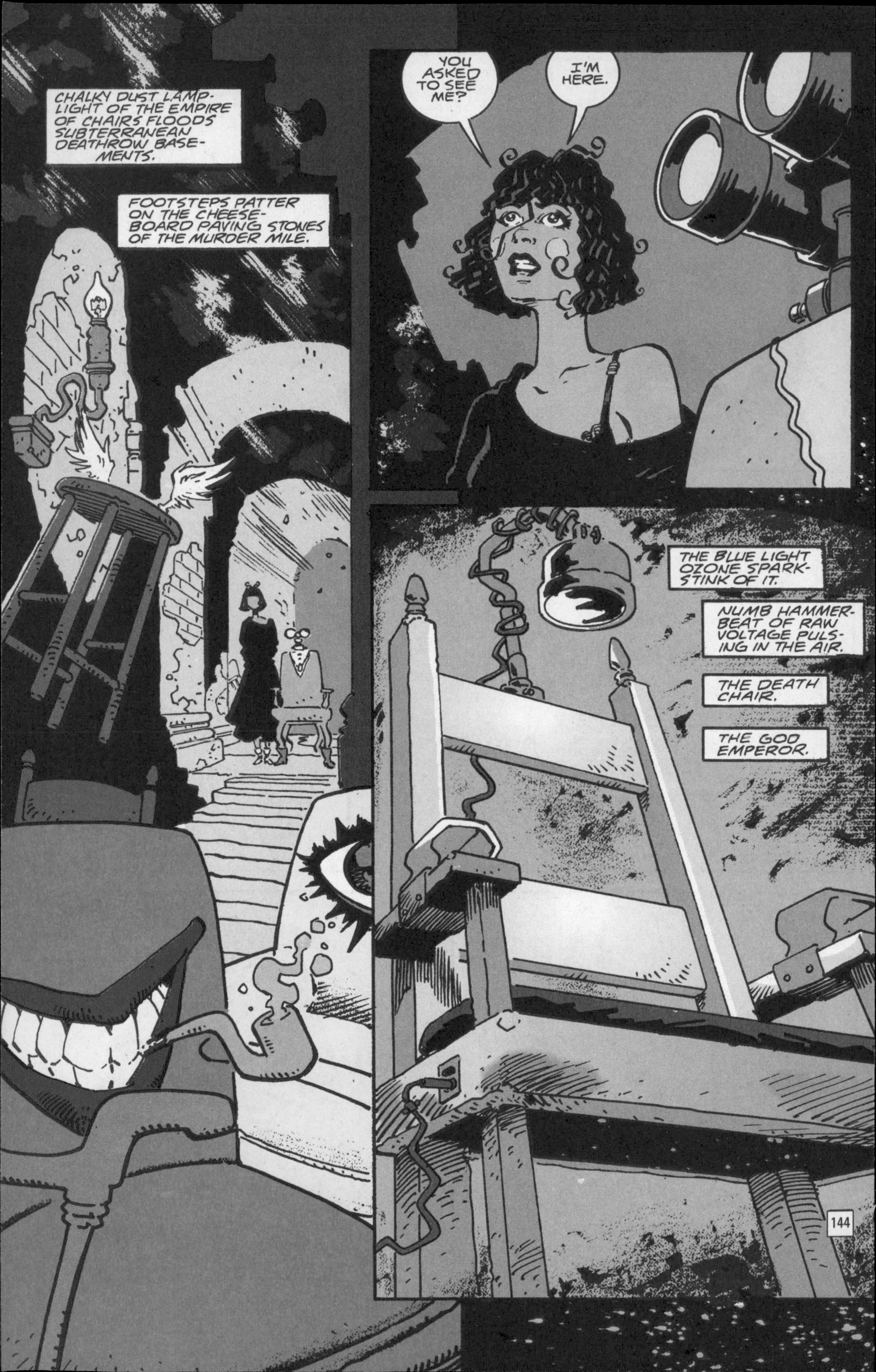
CHALKY DUST LAMP-LIGHT OF THE EMPIRE OF CHAIRS FLOODS SUBTERRANEAN DEATHROW BASEMENTS.
FOOTSTEPS PATTER ON THE CHEESE-BOARD PAVING STONES OF THE MURDER MILE.
YOU ASKED TO SEE ME?
I'M HERE.
THE BLUE LIGHT OZONE SPARK-STINK OF IT.
NUMB HAMMER-BEAT OF RAW VOLTAGE PULSING IN THE AIR.
THE DEATH CHAIR.
THE GOD EMPEROR.
144

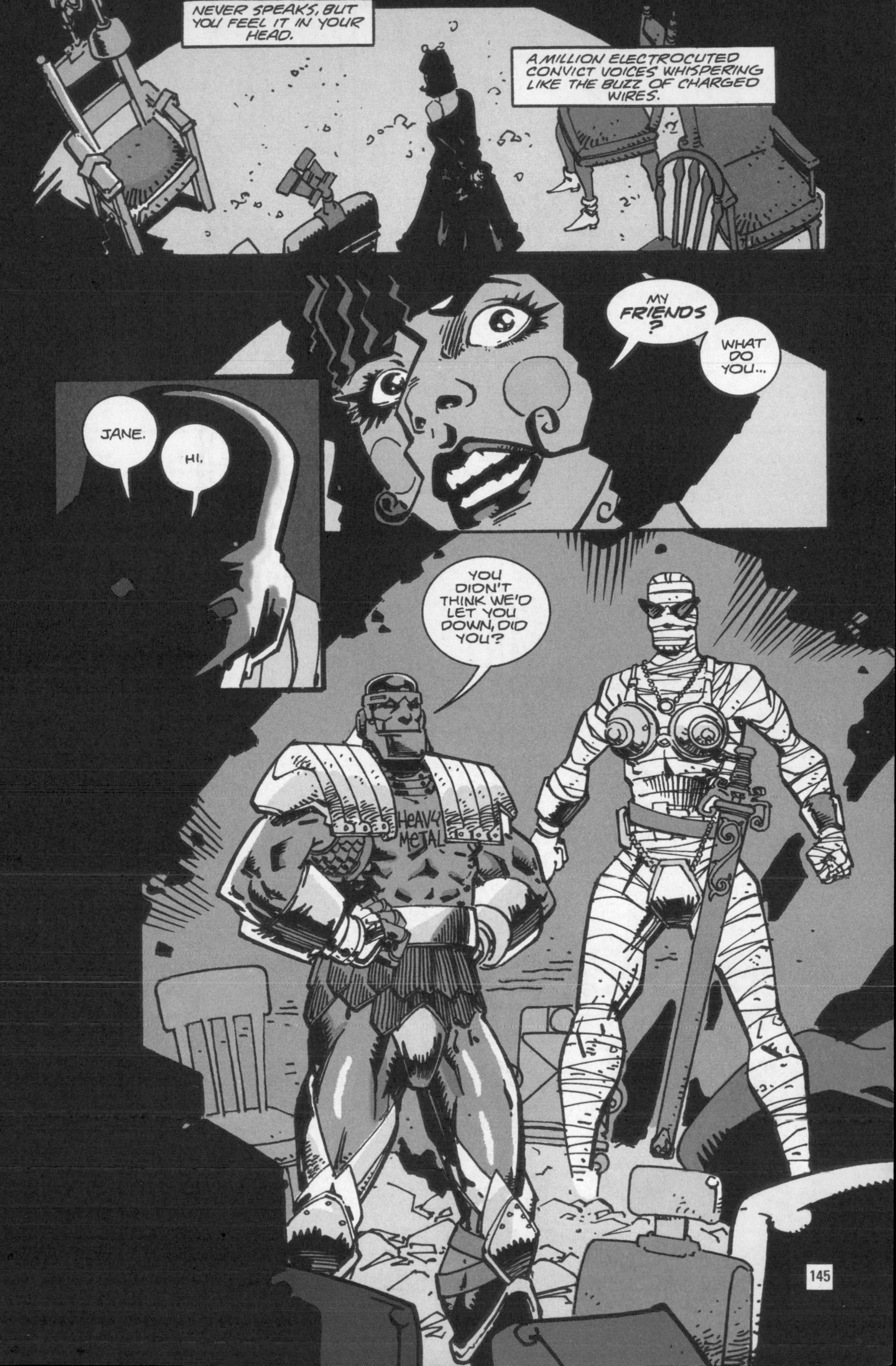

NEVER SPEAKS, BUT YOU FEEL IT IN YOUR HEAD.
A MILLION ELECTROCUTED CONVICT VOICES WHISPERING LIKE THE BUZZ OF CHARGED WIRES.
MY FRIENDS?
WHAT DO YOU...
JANE.
HI.
YOU DIDN'T THINK WE'D LET YOU DOWN, DID YOU?
HEAVY METAL

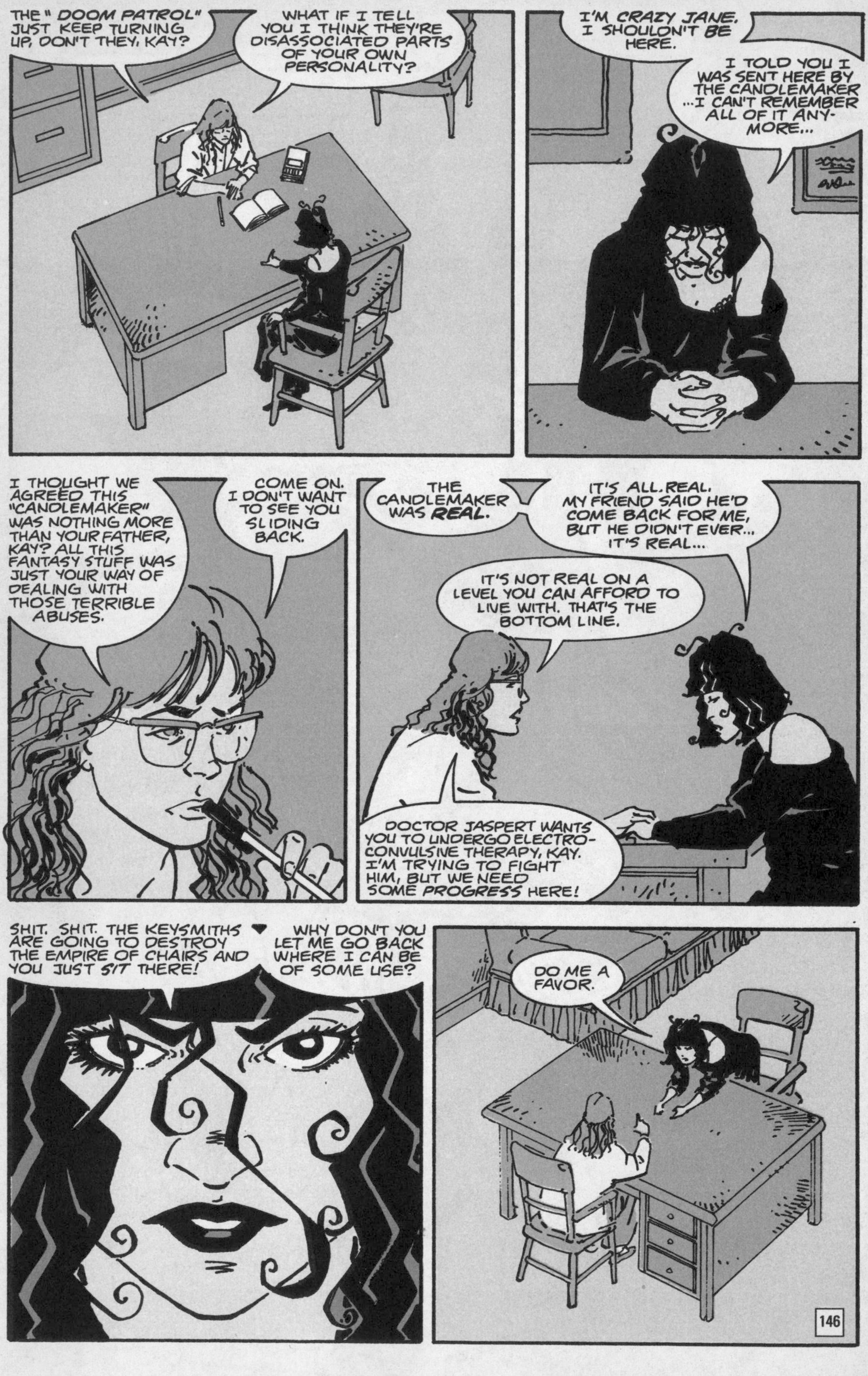
THE "DOOM PATROL" JUST KEEP TURNING UP, DON'T THEY, KAY?
WHAT IF I TELL YOU I THINK THEY'RE DISASSOCIATED PARTS OF YOUR OWN PERSONALITY?
I'M CRAZY JANE. I SHOULDN'T BE HERE.
I TOLD YOU I WAS SENT HERE BY THE CANDLEMAKER ...I CAN'T REMEMBER ALL OF IT ANY-MORE...
I THOUGHT WE AGREED THIS "CANDLEMAKER" WAS NOTHING MORE THAN YOUR FATHER, KAY? ALL THIS FANTASY STUFF WAS JUST YOUR WAY OF DEALING WITH THOSE TERRIBLE ABUSES.
COME ON. I DON'T WANT TO SEE YOU SLIDING BACK.
THE CANDLEMAKER WAS REAL.
IT'S ALL. REAL. MY FRIEND SAID HE'D COME BACK FOR ME, BUT HE DIDN'T EVER... IT'S REAL...
IT'S NOT REAL ON A LEVEL YOU CAN AFFORD TO LIVE WITH. THAT'S THE BOTTOM LINE.
DOCTOR JASPERT WANTS YOU TO UNDERGO ELECTRO-CONVULSIVE THERAPY, KAY. I'M TRYING TO FIGHT HIM, BUT WE NEED SOME PROGRESS HERE!
SHIT. SHIT. THE KEYSMITHS ARE GOING TO DESTROY THE EMPIRE OF CHAIRS AND YOU JUST SIT THERE!
WHY DON'T YOU LET ME GO BACK WHERE I CAN BE OF SOME USE?
DO ME A FAVOR.

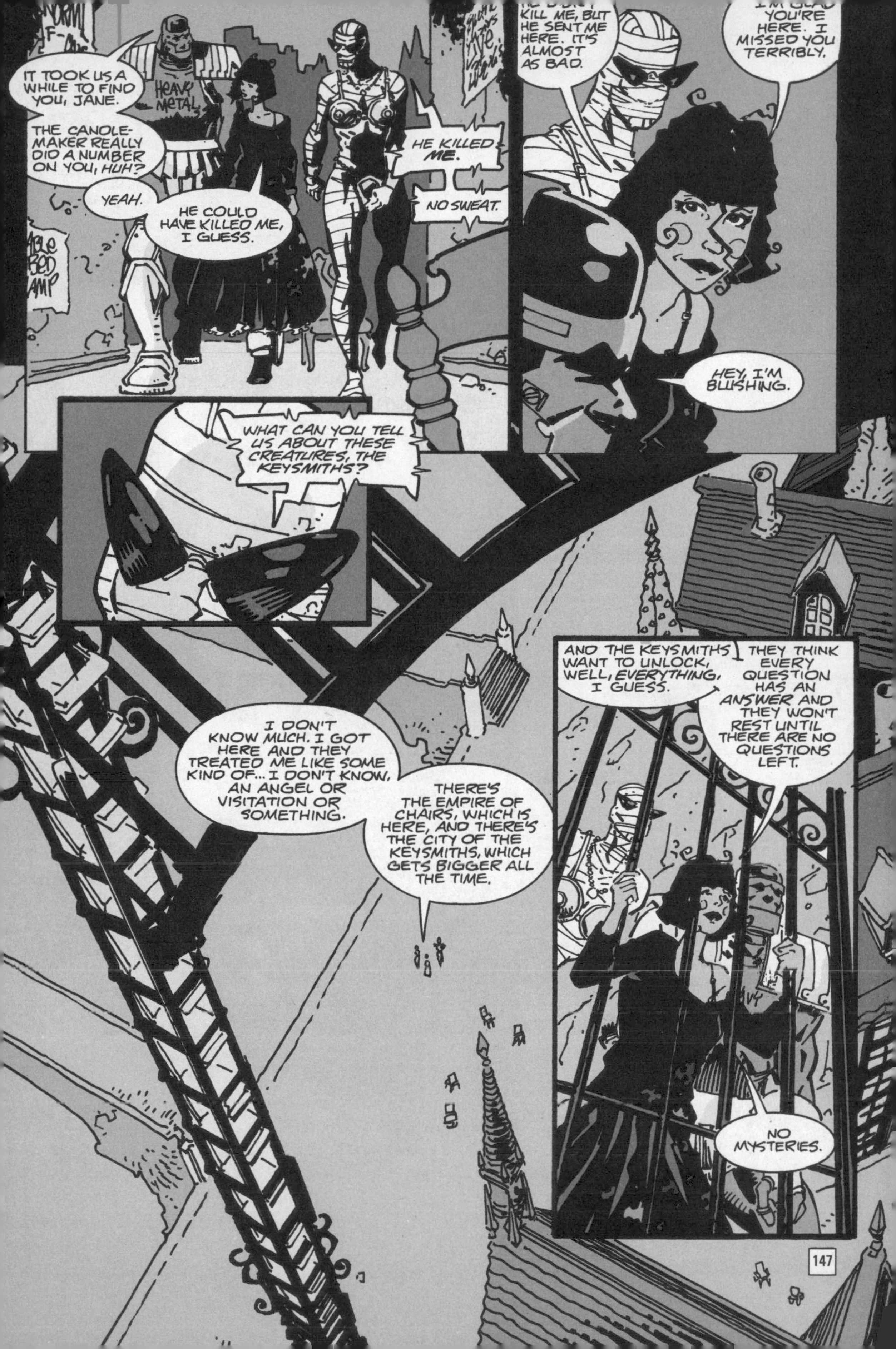
IT TOOK US A WHILE TO FIND YOU, JANE.
THE CANDLE-MAKER REALLY DID A NUMBER ON YOU, HUH?
YEAH.
HE COULD HAVE KILLED ME, I GUESS.
HE KILLED ME.
NO SWEAT.
KILL ME, BUT HE SENT ME HERE. IT'S ALMOST AS BAD.
YOU'RE HERE. I MISSED YOU TERRIBLY.
HEY, I'M BLUSHING.
WHAT CAN YOU TELL US ABOUT THESE CREATURES, THE KEYSMITHS?
I DON'T KNOW MUCH. I GOT HERE AND THEY TREATED ME LIKE SOME KIND OF... I DON'T KNOW. AN ANGEL OR VISITATION OR SOMETHING.
THERE'S THE EMPIRE OF CHAIRS, WHICH IS HERE, AND THERE'S THE CITY OF THE KEYSMITHS, WHICH GETS BIGGER ALL THE TIME.
AND THE KEYSMITHS WANT TO UNLOCK, WELL, EVERYTHING, I GUESS.
THEY THINK EVERY QUESTION HAS AN ANSWER AND THEY WON'T REST UNTIL THERE ARE NO QUESTIONS LEFT.
NO MYSTERIES.

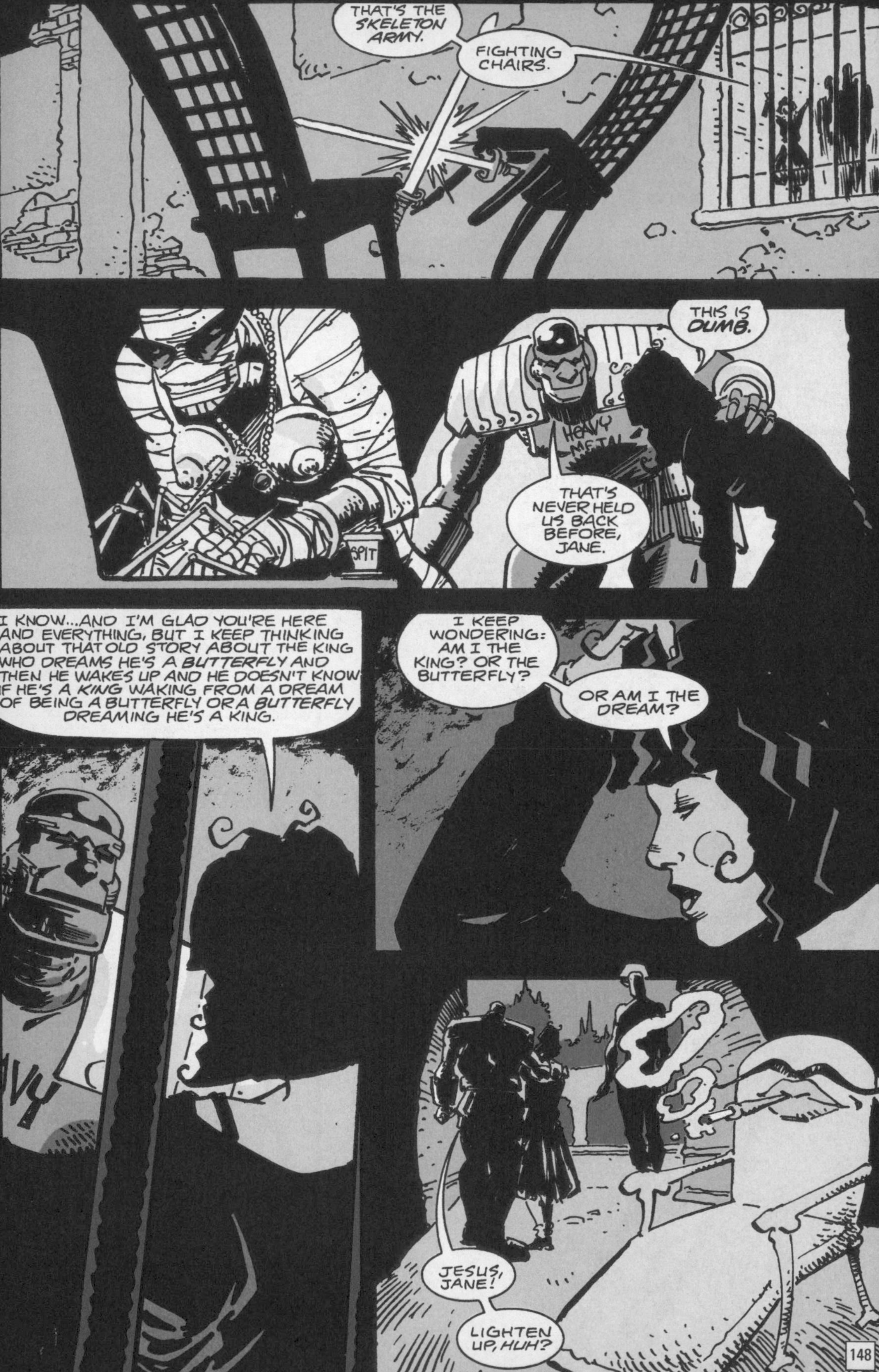
THAT'S THE SKELETON ARMY.
FIGHTING CHAIRS.
THIS IS DUMB.
HEAVY METAL
THAT'S NEVER HELD US BACK BEFORE, JANE.
SPIT
I KNOW...AND I'M GLAD YOU'RE HERE AND EVERYTHING, BUT I KEEP THINKING ABOUT THAT OLD STORY ABOUT THE KING WHO DREAMS HE'S A BUTTERFLY AND THEN HE WAKES UP AND HE DOESN'T KNOW IF HE'S A KING WAKING FROM A DREAM OF BEING A BUTTERFLY OR A BUTTERFLY DREAMING HE'S A KING.
I KEEP WONDERING: AM I THE KING? OR THE BUTTERFLY?
OR AM I THE DREAM?
JESUS, JANE!
LIGHTEN UP, HUH?

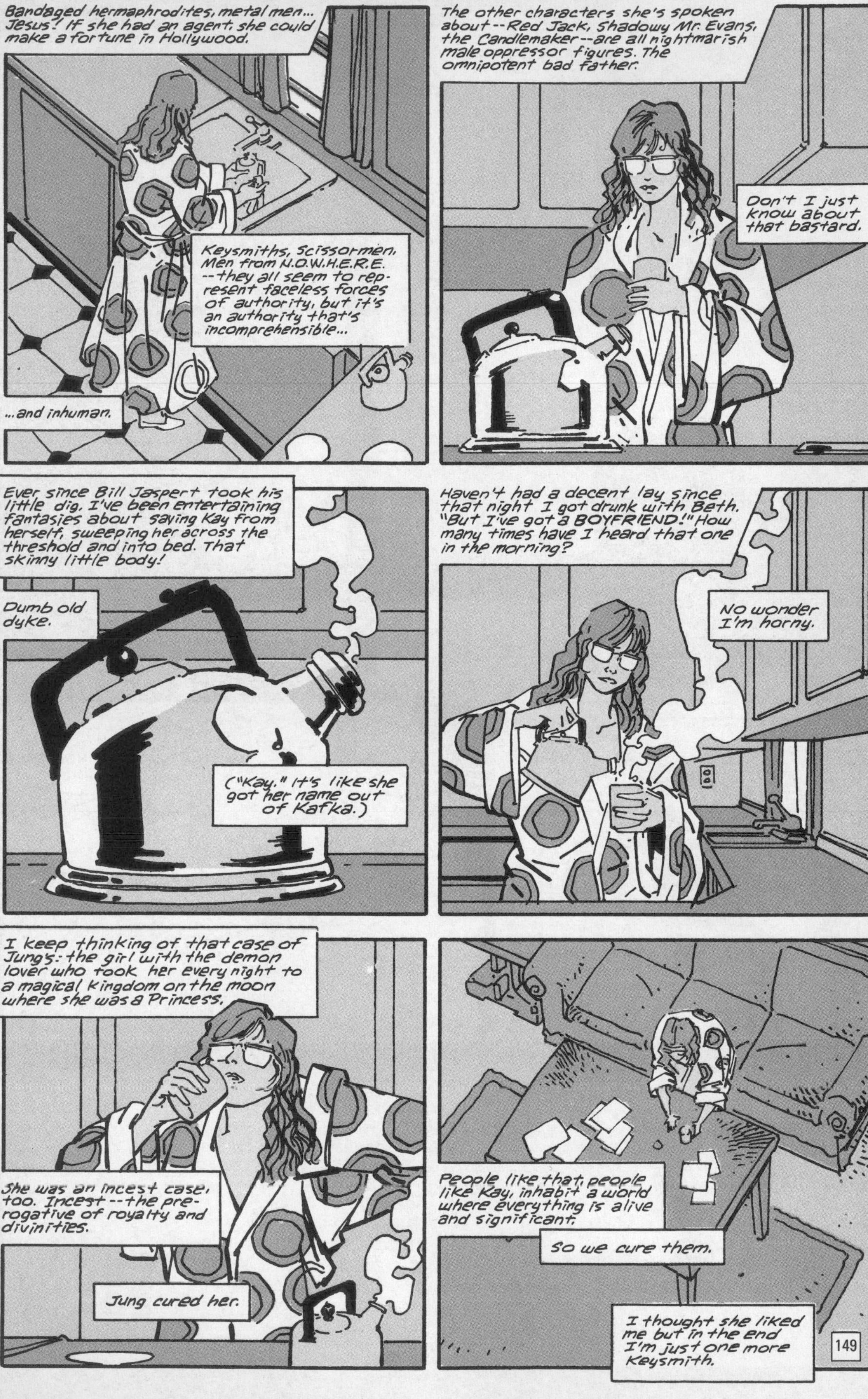
Bandaged hermaphrodites, metal men... Jesus! If she had an agent, she could make a fortune in Hollywood.
Keysmiths, Scissormen, Men from N.O.W.H.E.R.E. --they all seem to represent faceless forces of authority, but it's an authority that's incomprehensible...
...and inhuman.
The other characters she's spoken about--Red Jack, Shadowy Mr. Evans, the Candlemaker--are all nightmarish male oppressor figures. The omnipotent bad father.
Don't I just know about that bastard.
Ever since Bill Jaspert took his little dig, I've been entertaining fantasies about saving Kay from herself, sweeping her across the threshold and into bed. That skinny little body!
Dumb old dyke.
("Kay." It's like she got her name out of Kafka.)
Haven't had a decent lay since that night I got drunk with Beth. "But I've got a BOYFRIEND!" How many times have I heard that one in the morning?
No wonder I'm horny.
I keep thinking of that case of Jung's: the girl with the demon lover who took her every night to a magical kingdom on the moon where she was a Princess.
She was an incest case, too. Incest--the prerogative of royalty and divinities.
Jung cured her.
People like that, people like Kay, inhabit a world where everything is alive and significant.
So we cure them.
I thought she liked me but in the end I'm just one more Keysmith.

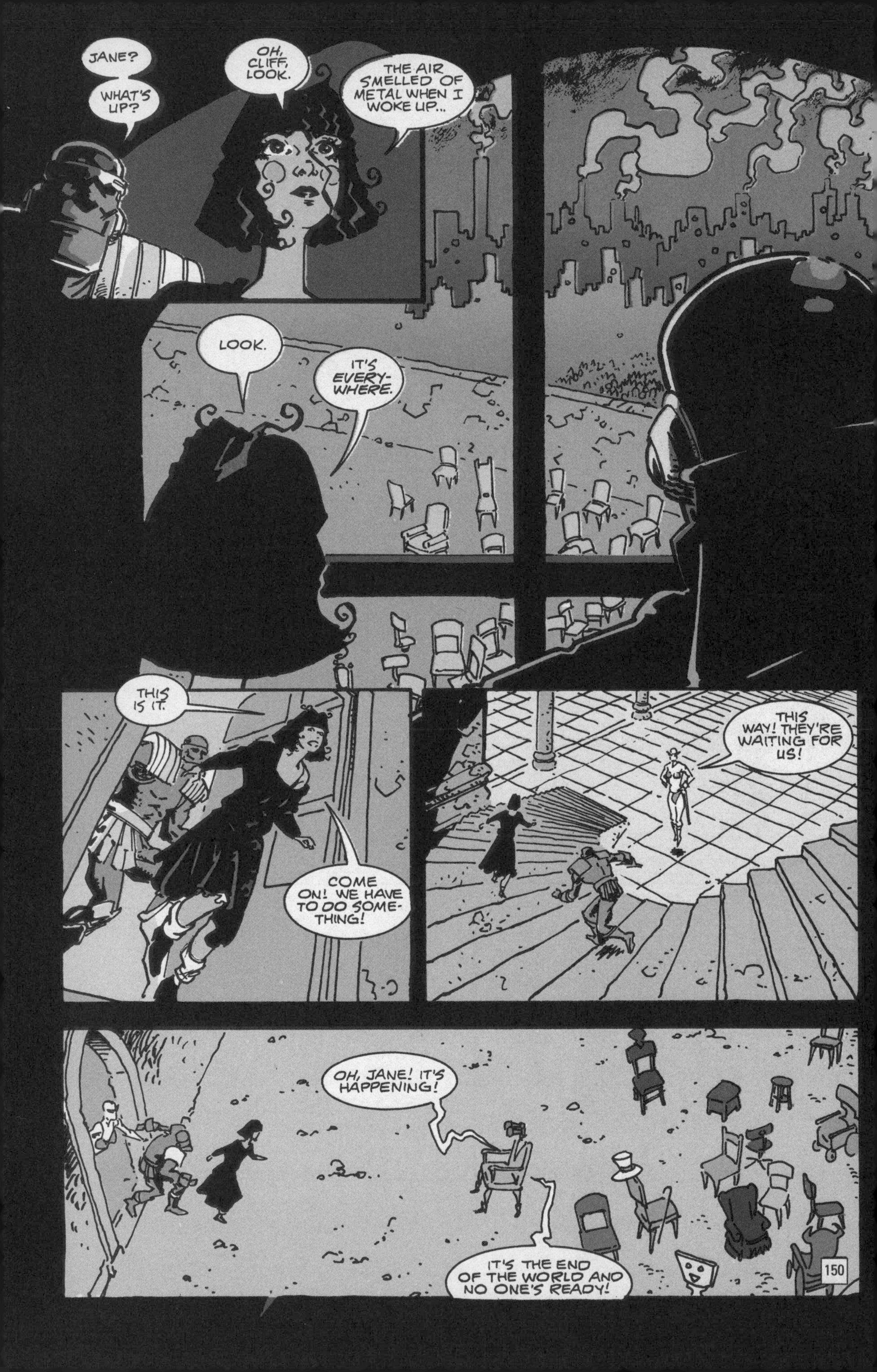
JANE?
WHAT'S UP?
OH, CLIFF, LOOK.
THE AIR SMELLED OF METAL WHEN I WOKE UP...
LOOK.
IT'S EVERY-WHERE.
THIS IS IT.
COME ON! WE HAVE TO DO SOME-THING!
THIS WAY! THEY'RE WAITING FOR US!
OH, JANE! IT'S HAPPENING!
IT'S THE END OF THE WORLD AND NO ONE'S READY!

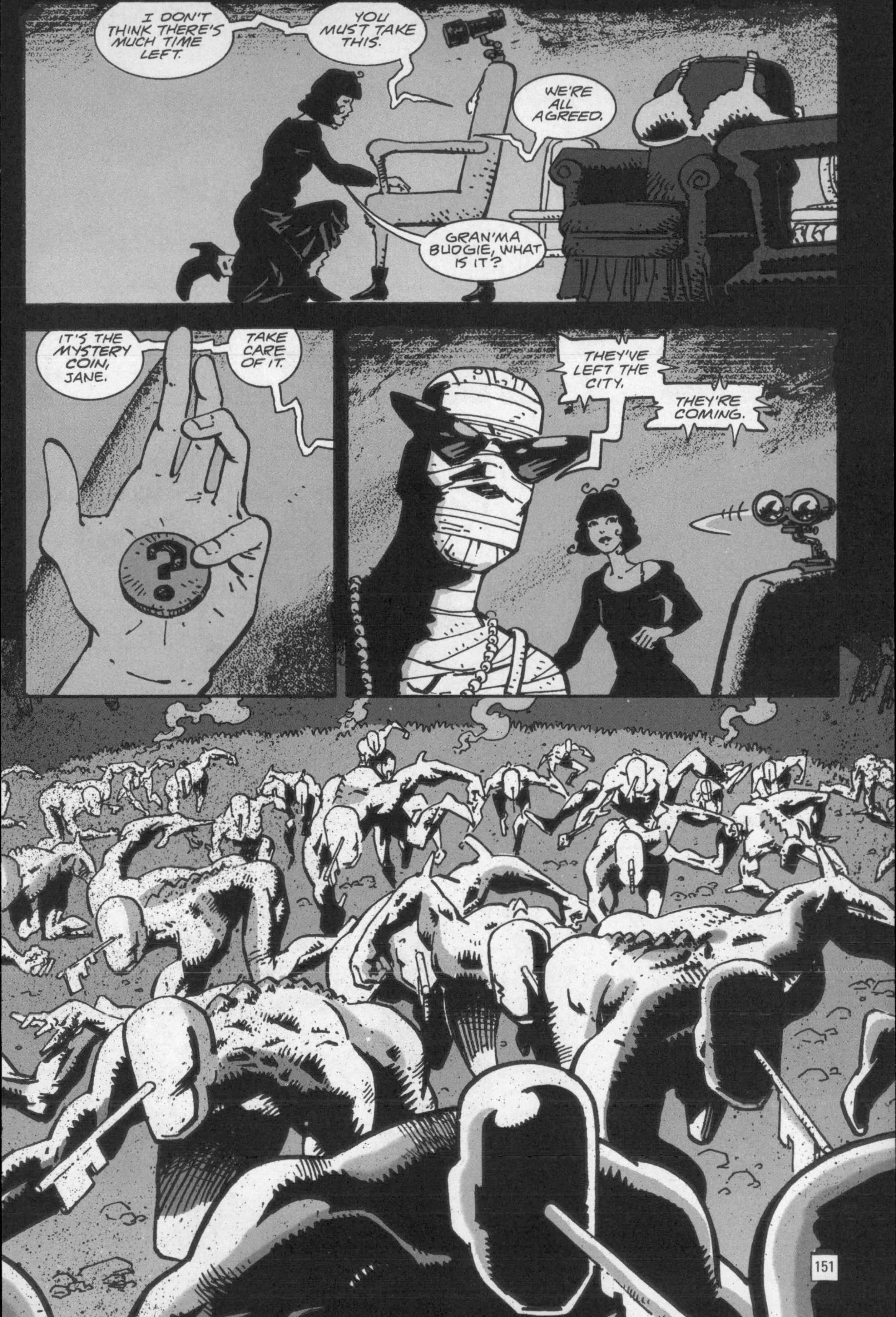
I DON'T THINK THERE'S MUCH TIME LEFT.
YOU MUST TAKE THIS.
WE'RE ALL AGREED.
GRAN'MA BUDGIE, WHAT IS IT?
IT'S THE MYSTERY COIN, JANE.
TAKE CARE OF IT.
THEY'VE LEFT THE CITY.
THEY'RE COMING.

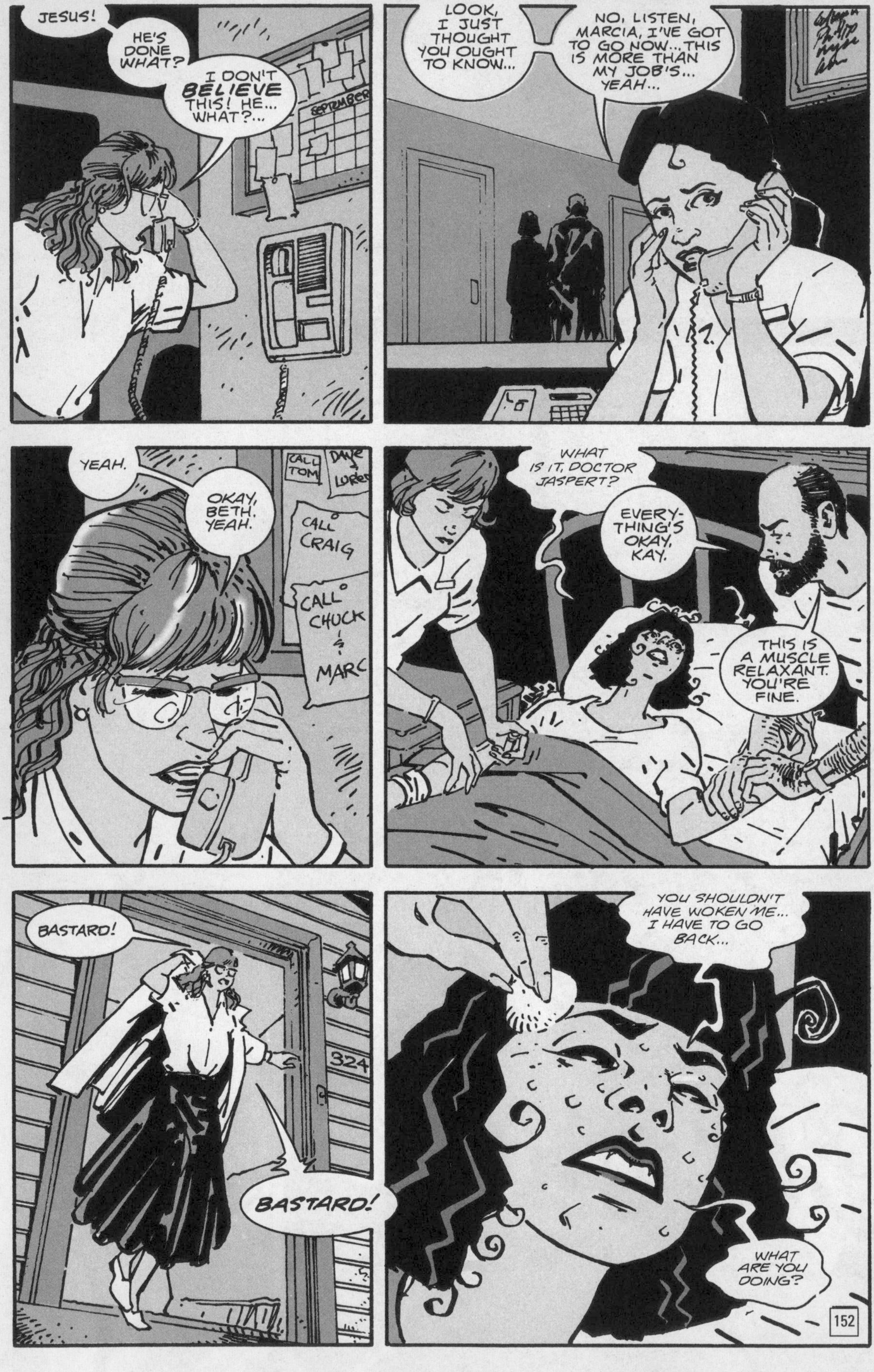
JESUS!
HE'S DONE WHAT?
I DON'T BELIEVE THIS! HE... WHAT?...
SEPTEMBER
LOOK, I JUST THOUGHT YOU OUGHT TO KNOW...
NO, LISTEN, MARCIA, I'VE GOT TO GO NOW... THIS IS MORE THAN MY JOB'S... YEAH...
YEAH.
OKAY, BETH. YEAH.
CALL TOM
DAVE & LUREN
CALL CRAIG
CALL CHUCK & MARC
WHAT IS IT, DOCTOR JASPERT?
EVERY-THING'S OKAY, KAY.
THIS IS A MUSCLE RELAXANT. YOU'RE FINE.
BASTARD!
324
BASTARD!
YOU SHOULDN'T HAVE WOKEN ME... I HAVE TO GO BACK...
WHAT ARE YOU DOING?

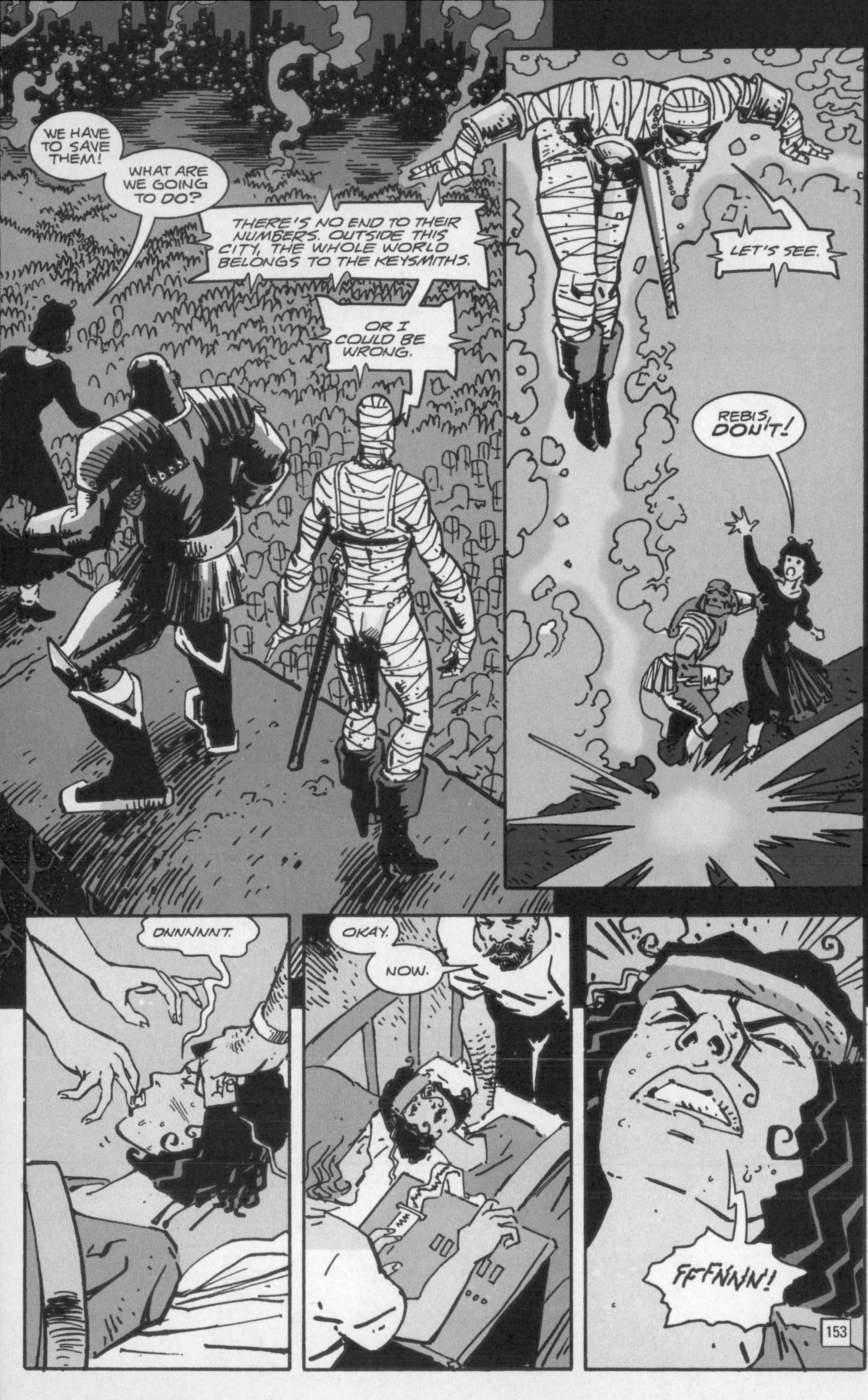
WE HAVE TO SAVE THEM!
WHAT ARE WE GOING TO DO?
THERE'S NO END TO THEIR NUMBERS. OUTSIDE THIS CITY, THE WHOLE WORLD BELONGS TO THE KEYSMITHS.
OR I COULD BE WRONG.
LET'S SEE.
REBIS, DON'T!
DNNNNNT.
OKAY.
NOW.
FFFNNN!

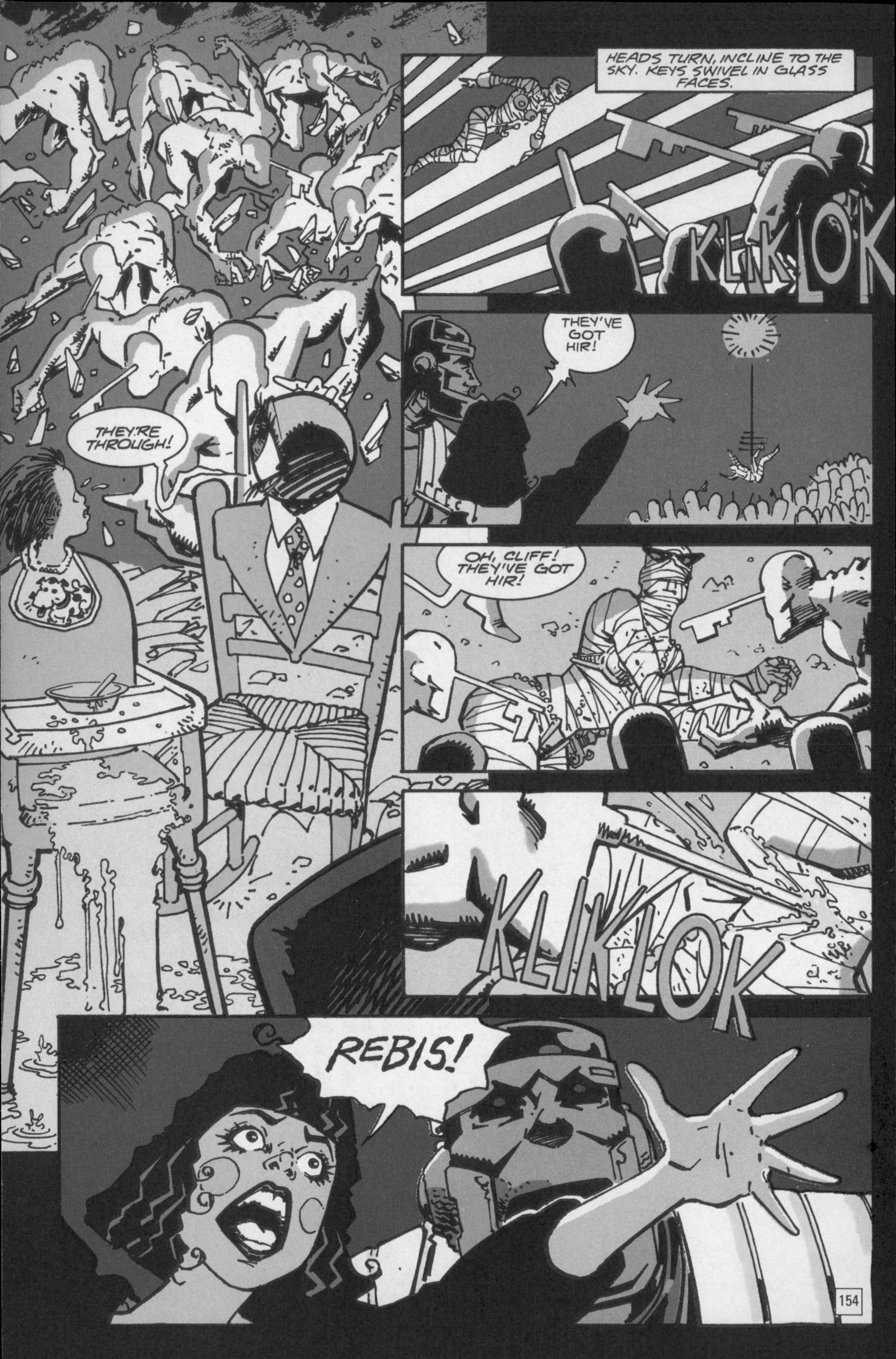
HEADS TURN, INCLINE TO THE SKY. KEYS SWIVEL IN GLASS FACES.
KLIKLOK
THEY'RE THROUGH!
THEY'VE GOT HIR!
OH, CLIFF! THEY'VE GOT HIR!
KLIKLOK
REBIS!

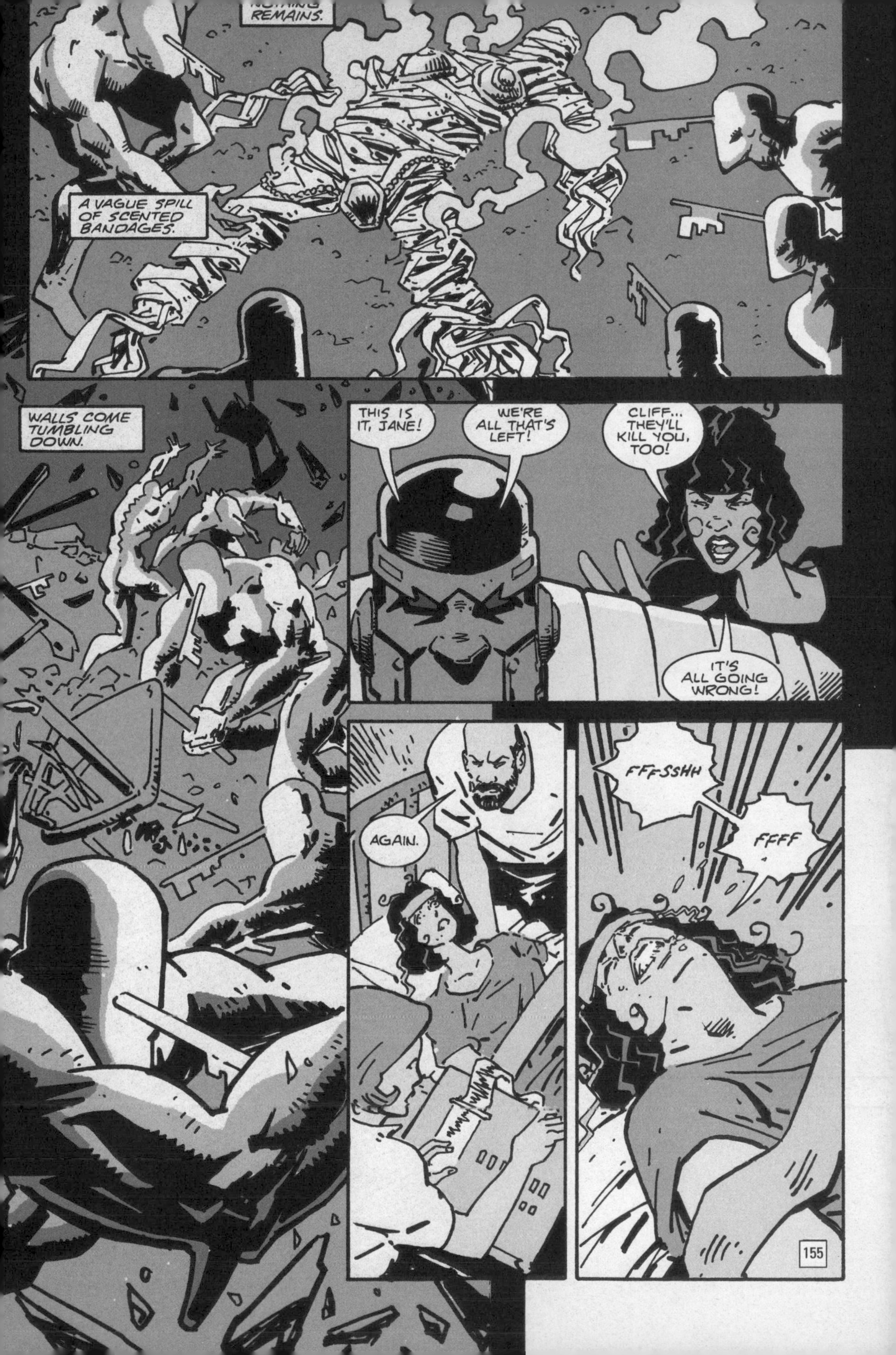
REMAINS.
A VAGUE SPILL OF SCENTED BANDAGES.
WALLS COME TUMBLING DOWN.
THIS IS IT, JANE!
WE'RE ALL THAT'S LEFT!
CLIFF... THEY'LL KILL YOU, TOO!
IT'S ALL GOING WRONG!
AGAIN.
FFF-SSHH
FFFF

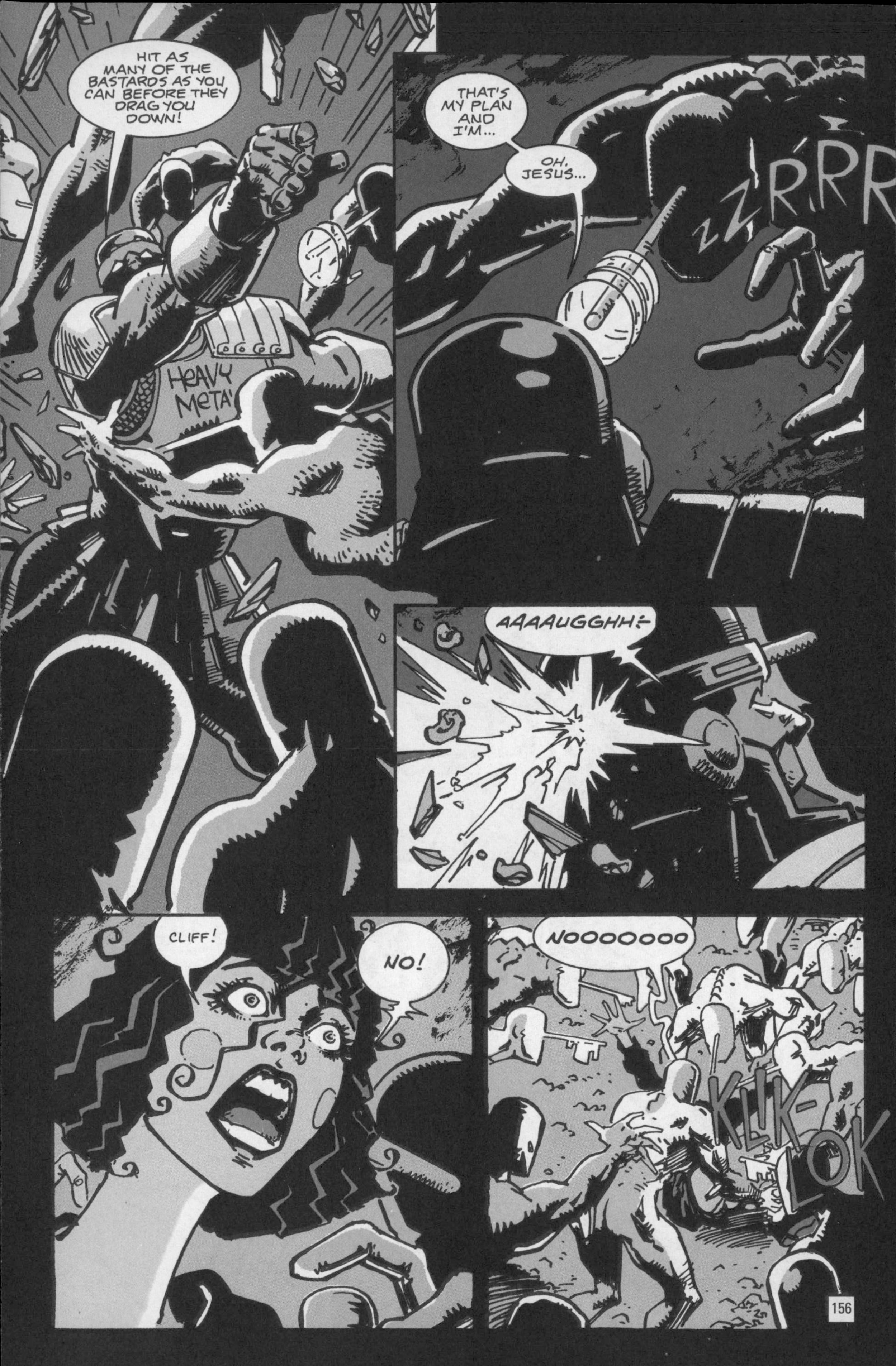

HIT AS MANY OF THE BASTARDS AS YOU CAN BEFORE THEY DRAG YOU DOWN!
HEAVY METAL
THAT'S MY PLAN AND I'M...
OH, JESUS...
ZZRRRR
AAAAUGGHH!-
CLIFF!
NO!
NOOOOOOO
KLIK-LOK

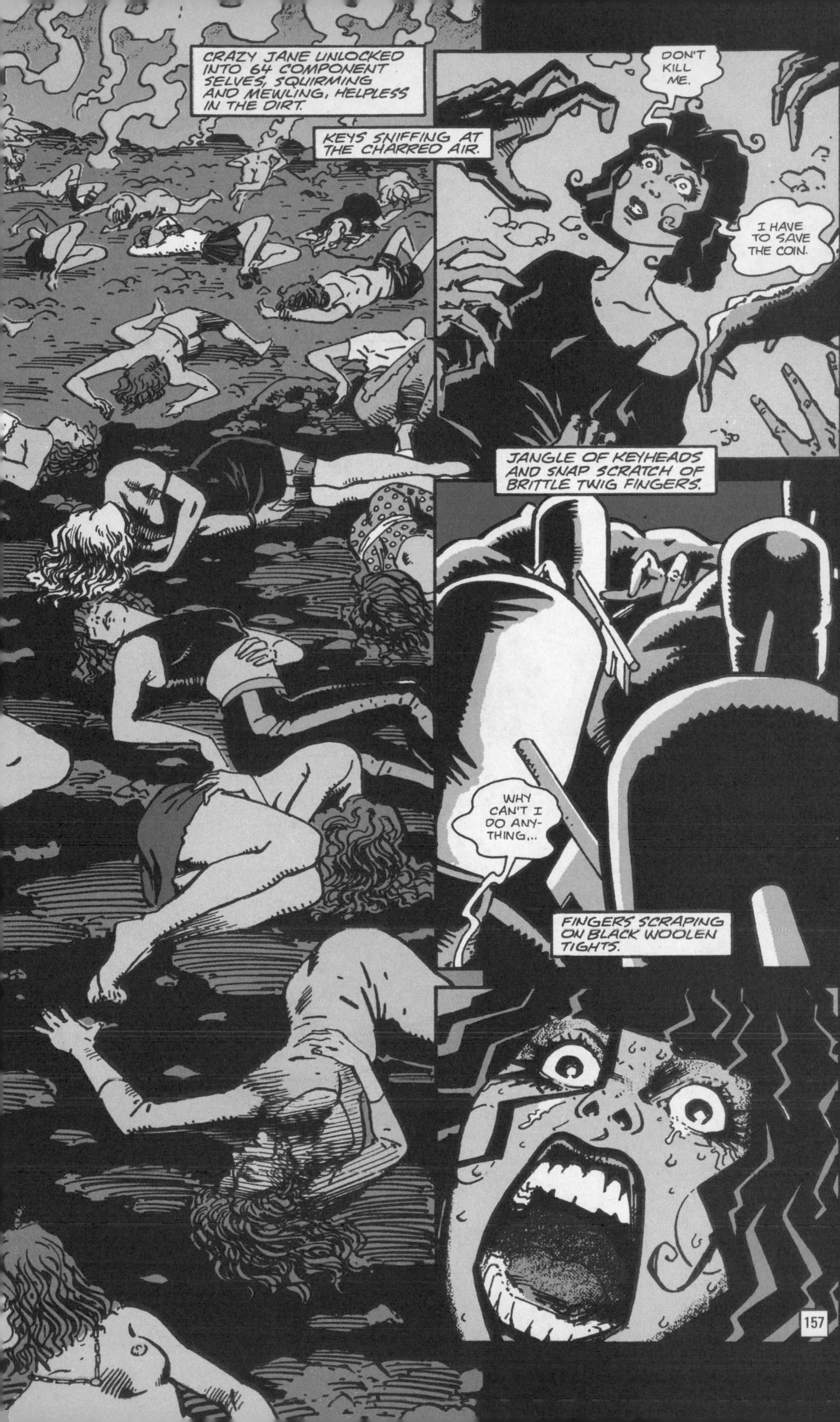
CRAZY JANE UNLOCKED INTO 64 COMPONENT SELVES, SQUIRMING AND MEWLING, HELPLESS IN THE DIRT.
KEYS SNIFFING AT THE CHARRED AIR.
DON'T KILL ME.
I HAVE TO SAVE THE COIN.
JANGLE OF KEYHEADS AND SNAP SCRATCH OF BRITTLE TWIG FINGERS.
WHY CAN'T I DO ANYTHING...
FINGERS SCRAPING ON BLACK WOOLEN TIGHTS.

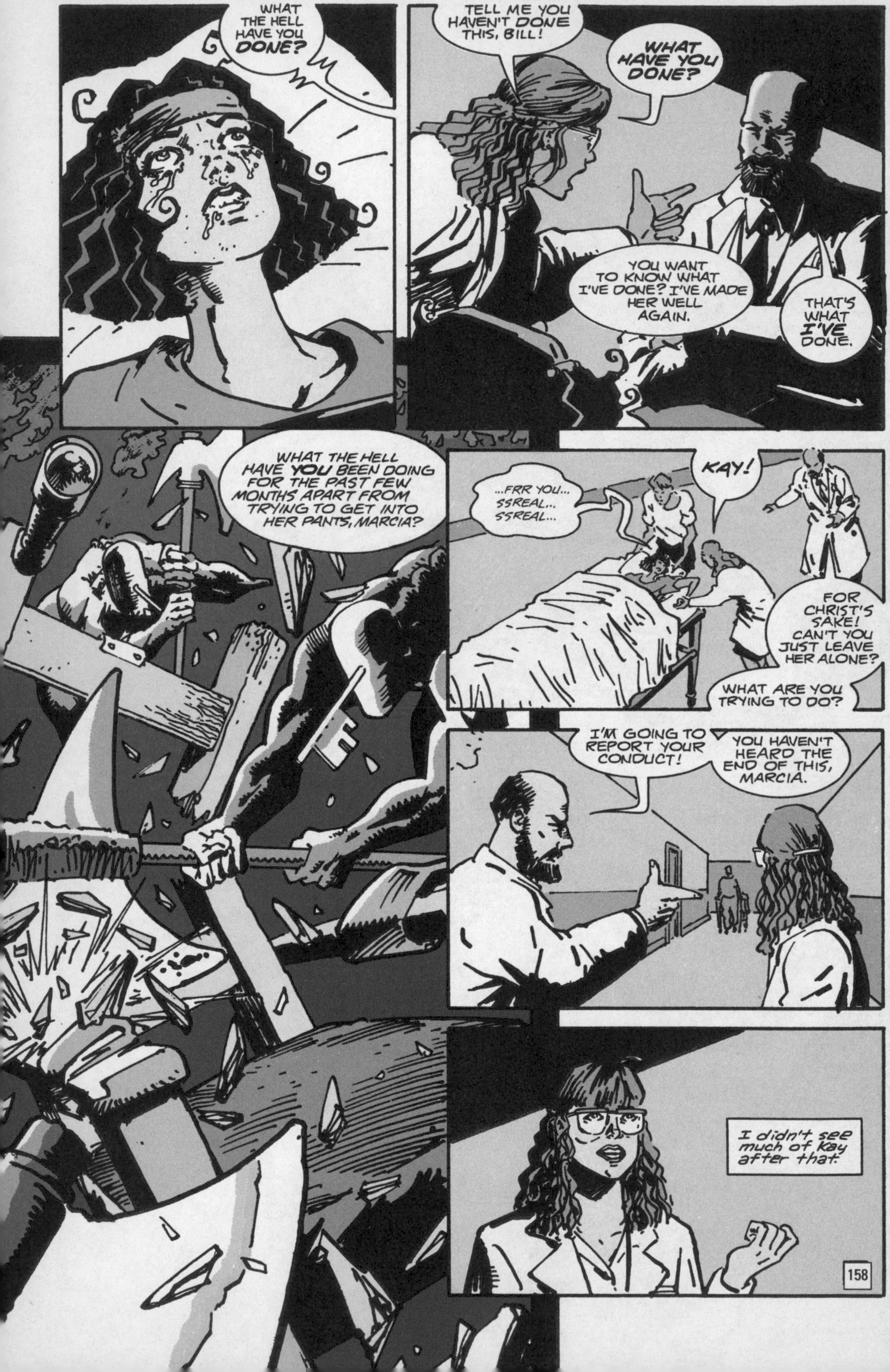
WHAT THE HELL HAVE YOU DONE?
TELL ME YOU HAVEN'T DONE THIS, BILL!
WHAT HAVE YOU DONE?
YOU WANT TO KNOW WHAT I'VE DONE? I'VE MADE HER WELL AGAIN.
THAT'S WHAT I'VE DONE.
WHAT THE HELL HAVE YOU BEEN DOING FOR THE PAST FEW MONTHS APART FROM TRYING TO GET INTO HER PANTS, MARCIA?
...FRR YOU... SSREAL... SSREAL...
KAY!
FOR CHRIST'S SAKE! CAN'T YOU JUST LEAVE HER ALONE?
WHAT ARE YOU TRYING TO DO?
I'M GOING TO REPORT YOUR CONDUCT!
YOU HAVEN'T HEARD THE END OF THIS, MARCIA.
I didn't see much of Kay after that.

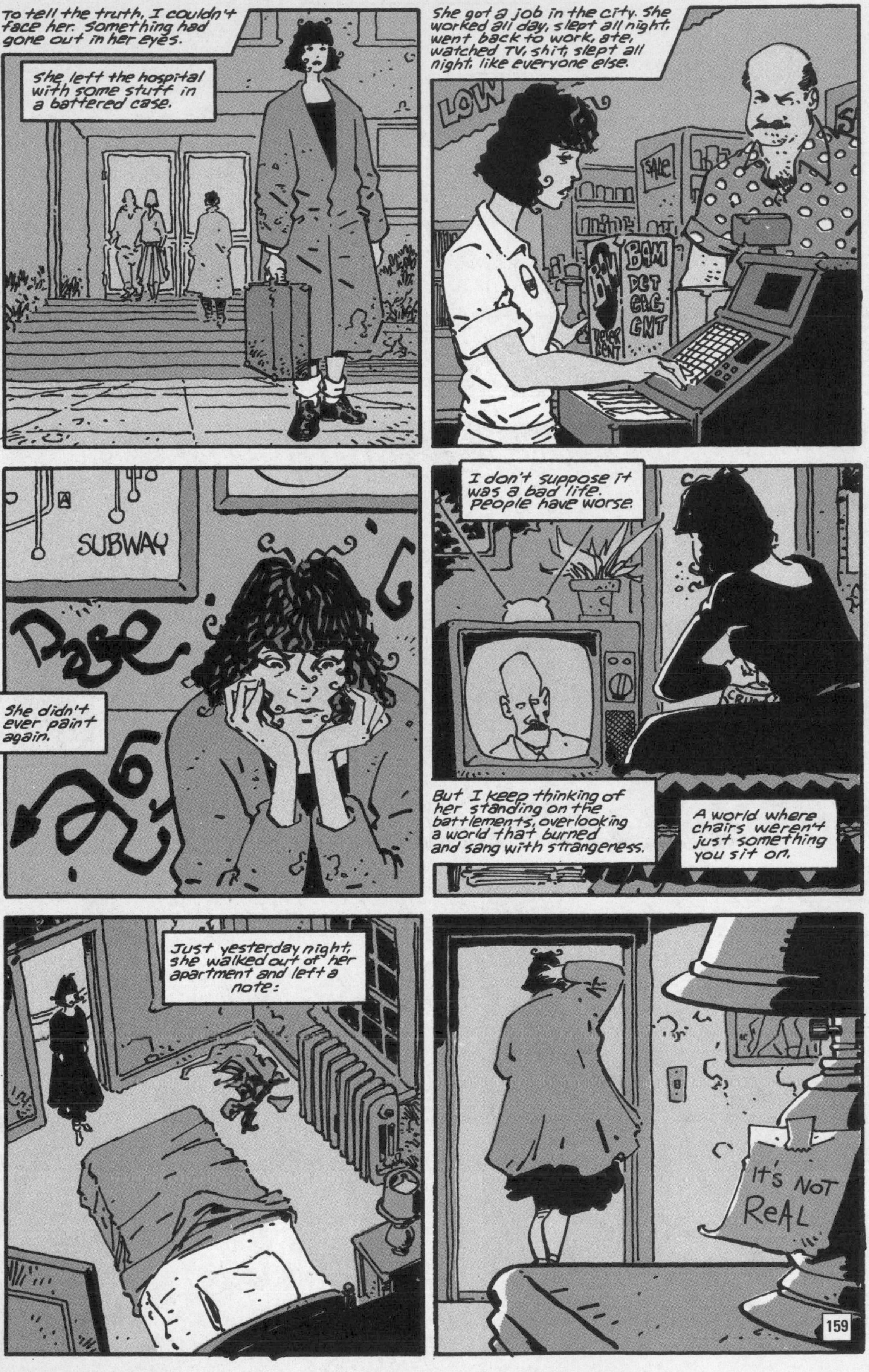
To tell the truth, I couldn't face her. Something had gone out in her eyes.
She left the hospital with some stuff in a battered case.
She got a job in the city. She worked all day, slept all night, went back to work, ate, watched TV, shit, slept all night, like everyone else.
LOW
SALE
BAM DETERGENT
SUBWAY
She didn't ever paint again.
I don't suppose it was a bad life. People have worse.
But I keep thinking of her standing on the battlements, overlooking a world that burned and sang with strangeness.
A world where chairs weren't just something you sit on.
Just yesterday night, she walked out of her apartment and left a note:
IT'S NOT REAL

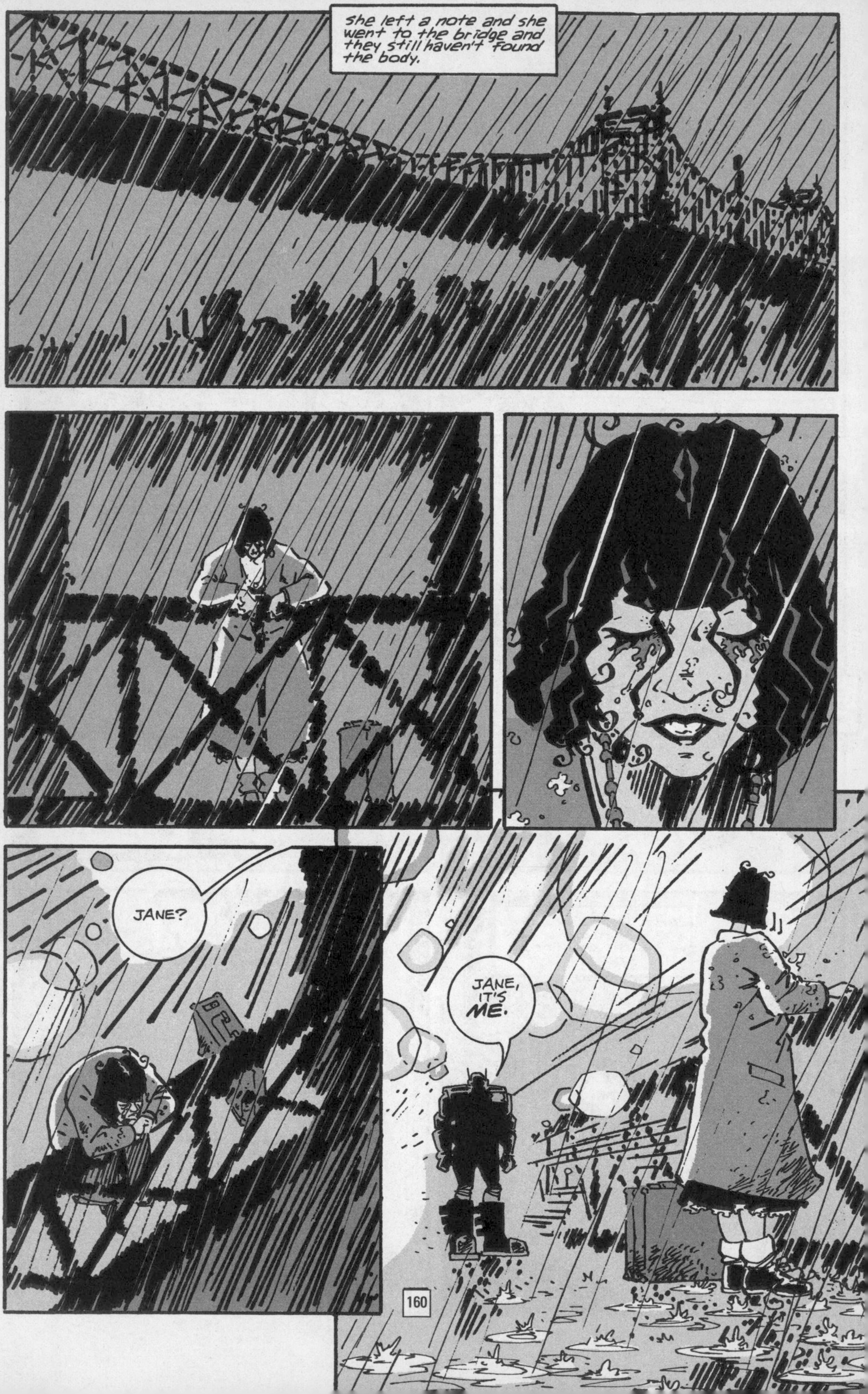

she left a note and she went to the bridge and they still haven't found the body.
JANE?
JANE, IT'S ME.

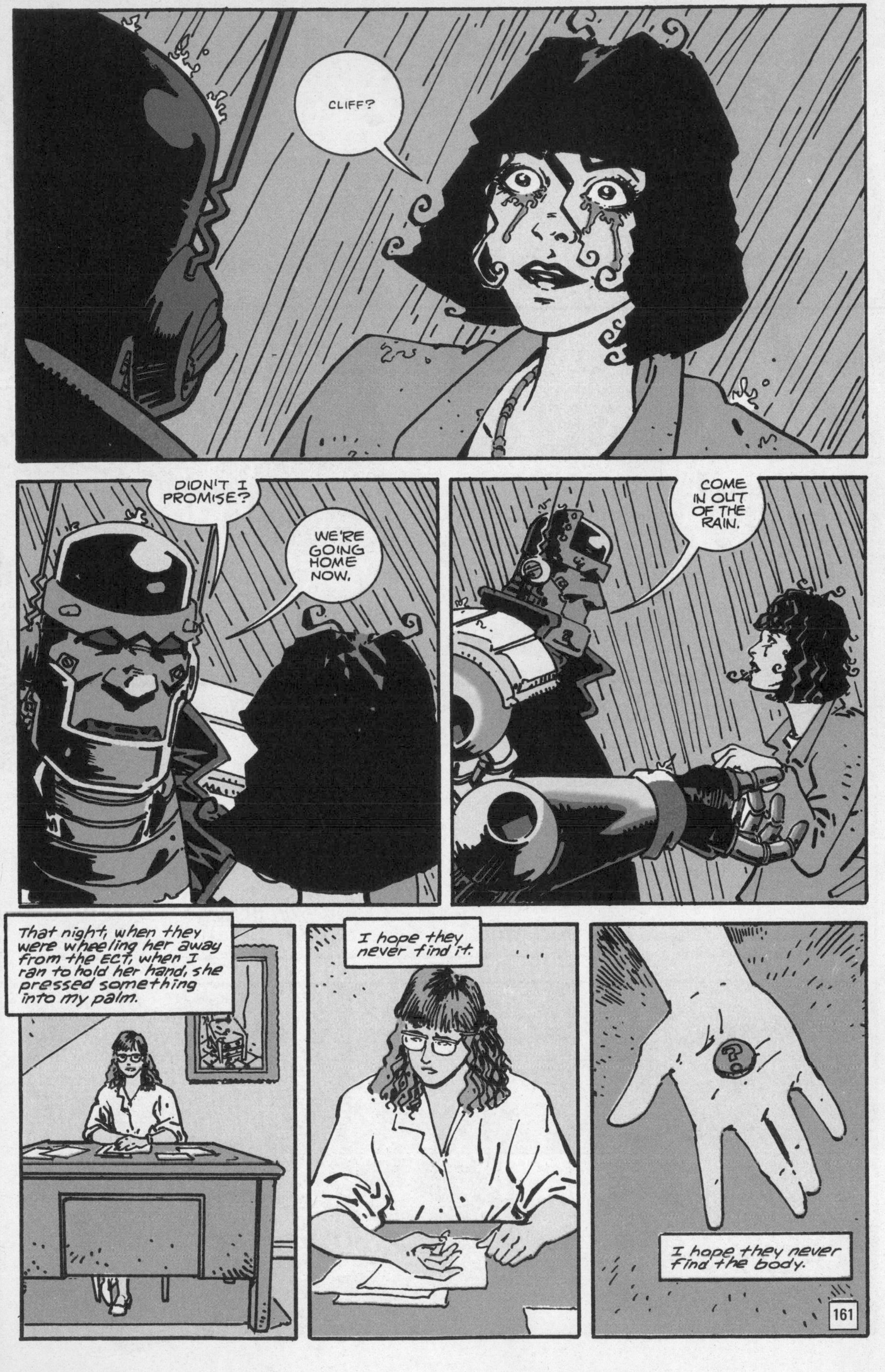
CLIFF?
DIDN'T I PROMISE?
WE'RE GOING HOME NOW.
COME IN OUT OF THE RAIN.
That night, when they were wheeling her away from the ECT, when I ran to hold her hand, she pressed something into my palm.
I hope they never find it.
I hope they never find the body.

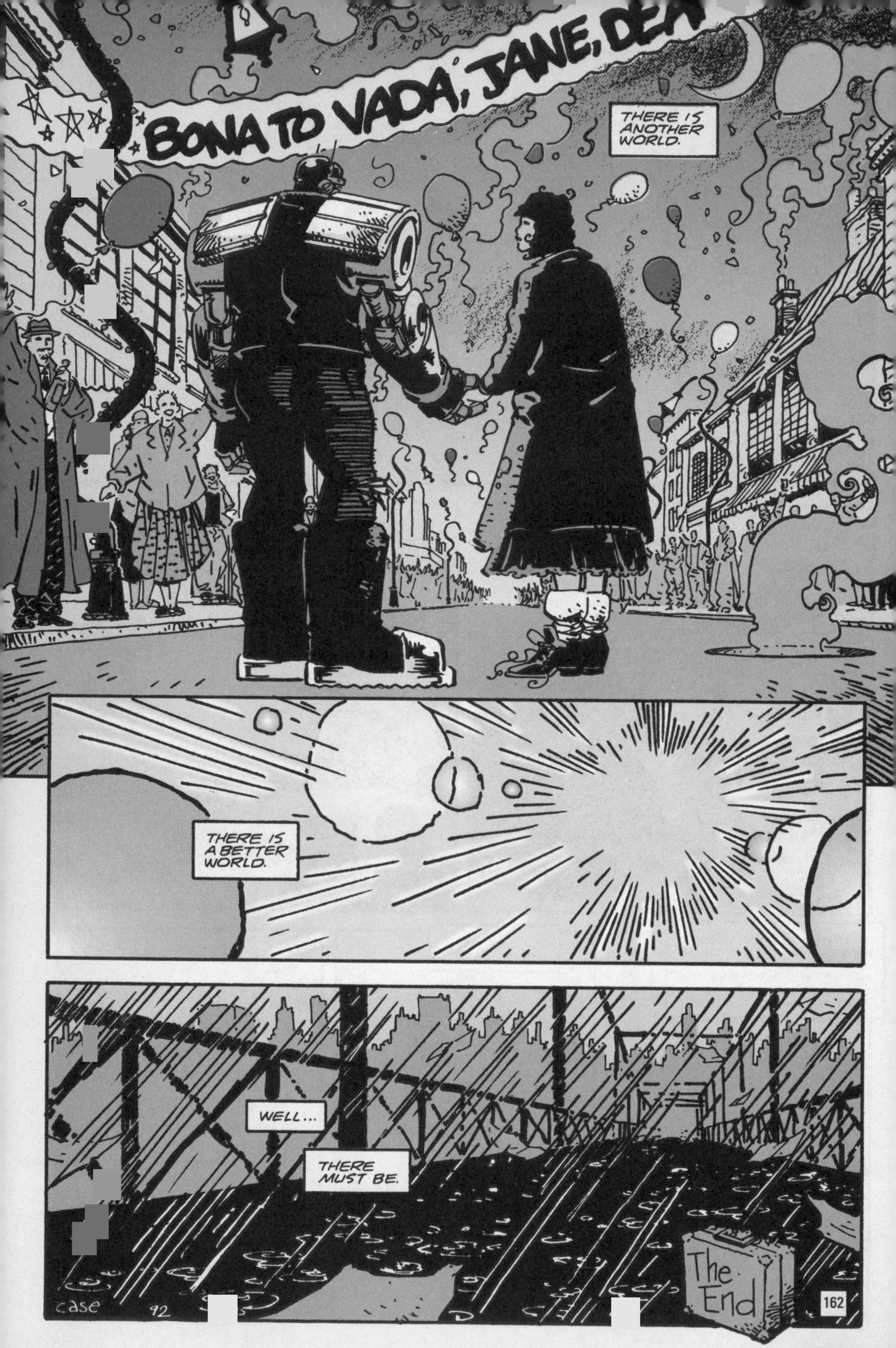

BONA TO VADA, JANE, DEA
THERE IS ANOTHER WORLD.
THERE IS A BETTER WORLD.
WELL...
THERE MUST BE.
The End
case 92

"Hurt them brutally. *Go now!*

Destroy my enemies!"

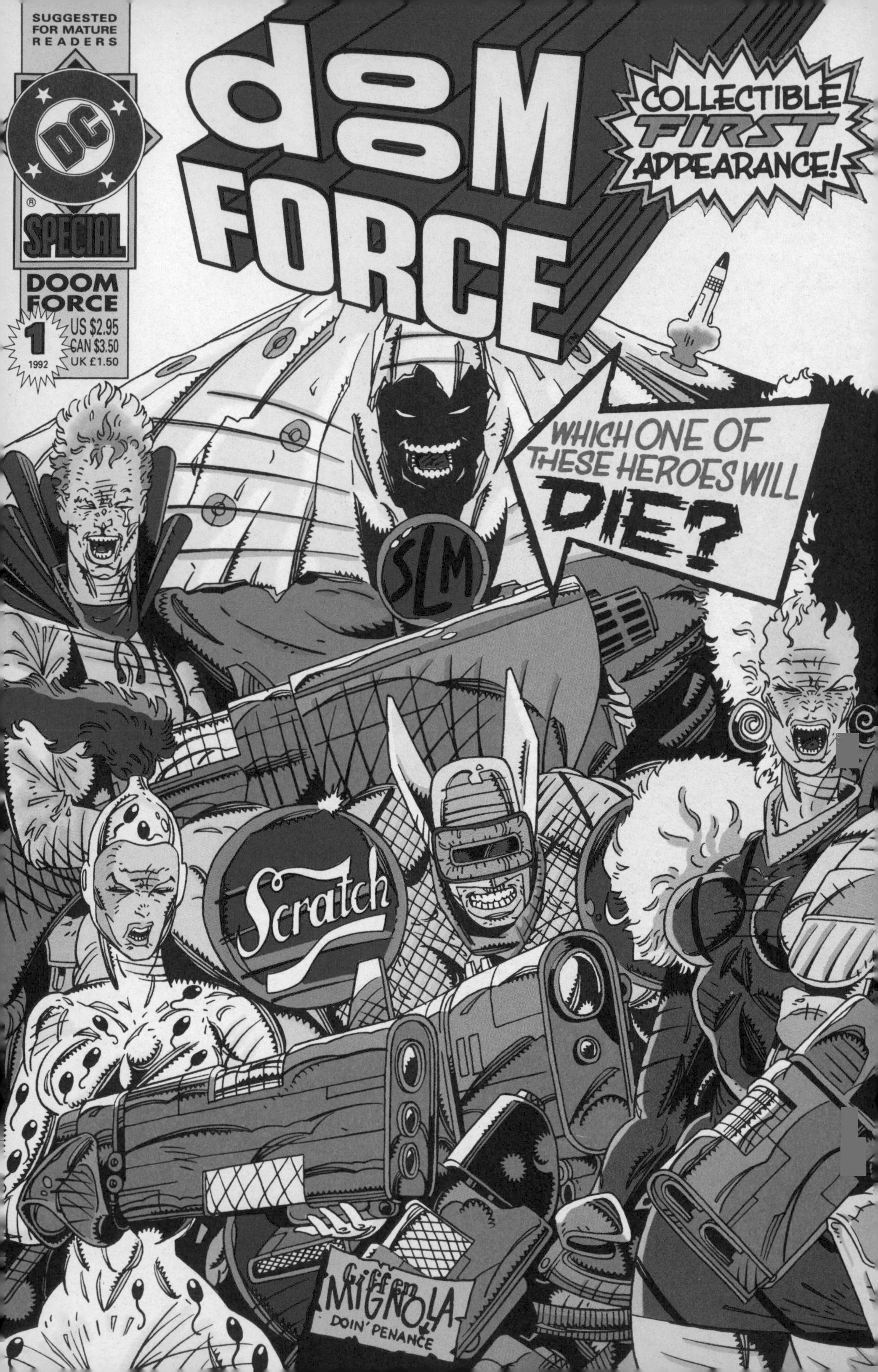
SUGGESTED FOR MATURE READERS
DC
SPECIAL
DOOM FORCE
1
1992
US $2.95
CAN $3.50
UK £1.50
DOOM FORCE
COLLECTIBLE FIRST APPEARANCE!
WHICH ONE OF THESE HEROES WILL DIE?
SLM
Scratch
Giffen
MIGNOLA
DOIN' PENANCE

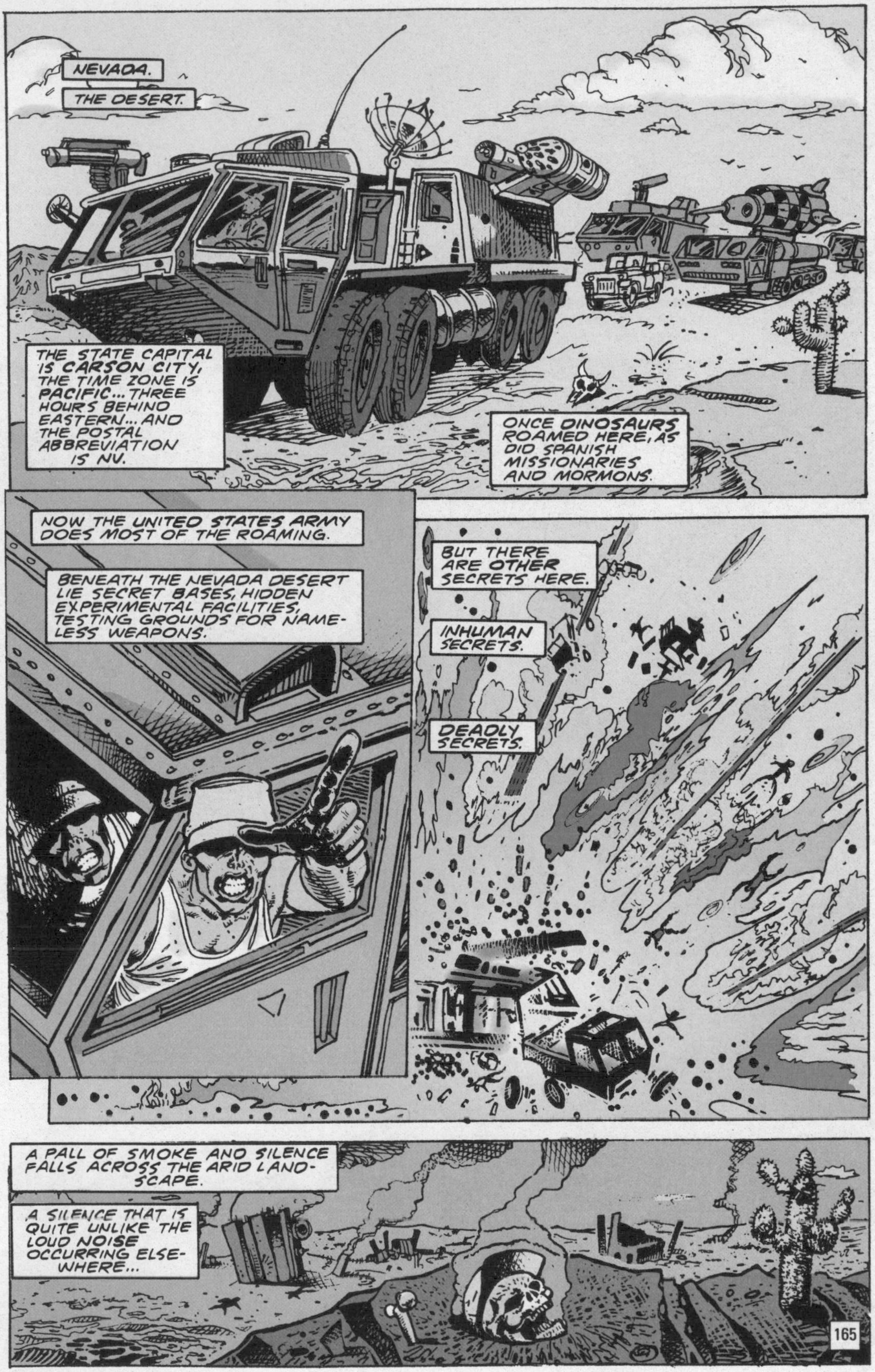
NEVADA.
THE DESERT.
THE STATE CAPITAL IS CARSON CITY, THE TIME ZONE IS PACIFIC... THREE HOURS BEHIND EASTERN... AND THE POSTAL ABBREVIATION IS NV.
ONCE DINOSAURS ROAMED HERE, AS DID SPANISH MISSIONARIES AND MORMONS.
NOW THE UNITED STATES ARMY DOES MOST OF THE ROAMING.
BENEATH THE NEVADA DESERT LIE SECRET BASES, HIDDEN EXPERIMENTAL FACILITIES, TESTING GROUNDS FOR NAMELESS WEAPONS.
BUT THERE ARE OTHER SECRETS HERE.
INHUMAN SECRETS.
DEADLY SECRETS.
A PALL OF SMOKE AND SILENCE FALLS ACROSS THE ARID LANDSCAPE.
A SILENCE THAT IS QUITE UNLIKE THE LOUD NOISE OCCURRING ELSEWHERE...

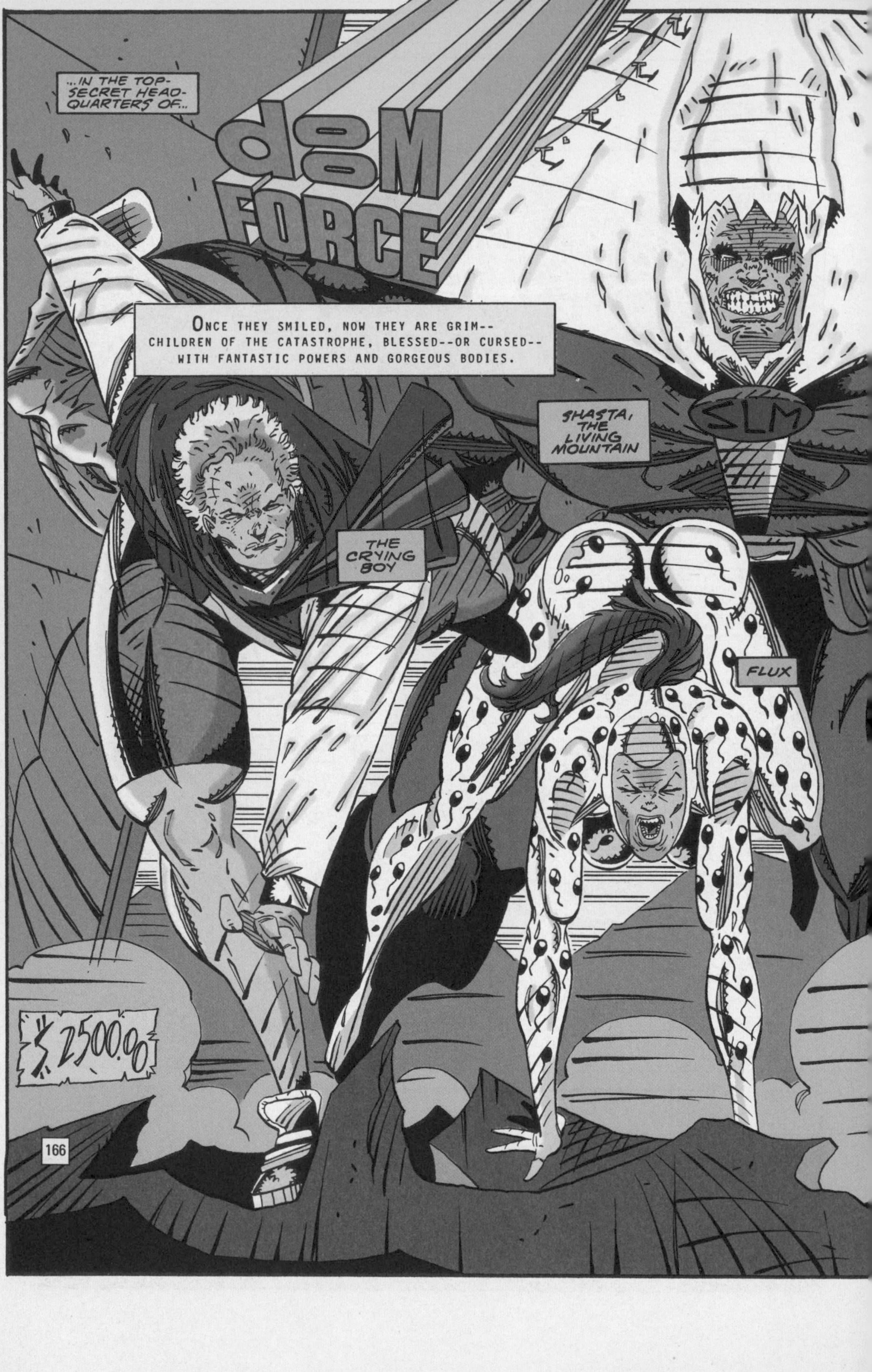
...IN THE TOP-SECRET HEADQUARTERS OF...
DOOM FORCE
ONCE THEY SMILED, NOW THEY ARE GRIM--CHILDREN OF THE CATASTROPHE, BLESSED--OR CURSED--WITH FANTASTIC POWERS AND GORGEOUS BODIES.
SHASTA, THE LIVING MOUNTAIN
SLM
THE CRYING BOY
FLUX
$2500.00

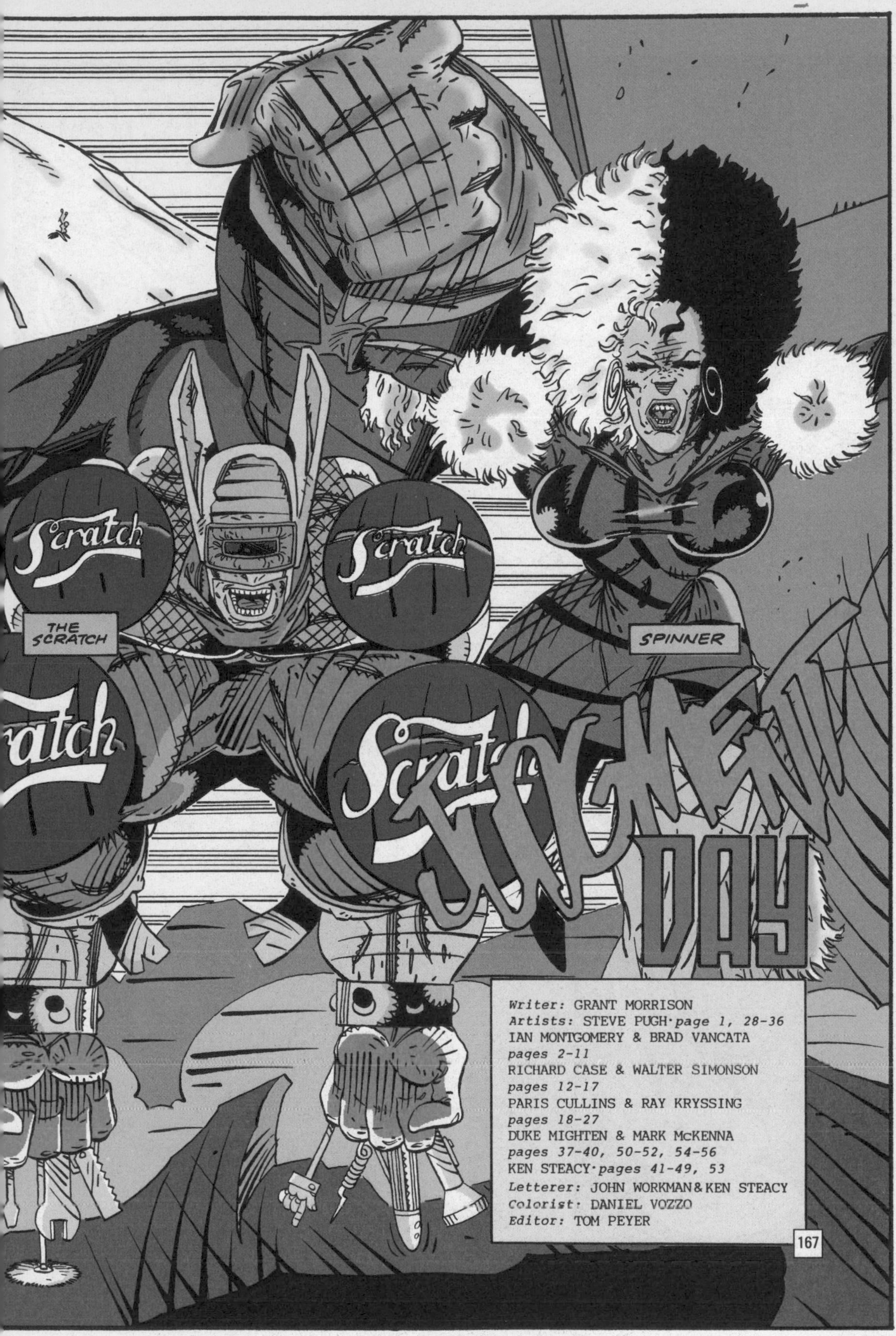
THE SCRATCH
SPINNER
Scratch
JUDGMENT DAY
Writer: GRANT MORRISON
Artists: STEVE PUGH·page 1, 28-36
IAN MONTGOMERY & BRAD VANCATA
pages 2-11
RICHARD CASE & WALTER SIMONSON
pages 12-17
PARIS CULLINS & RAY KRYSSING
pages 18-27
DUKE MIGHTEN & MARK McKENNA
pages 37-40, 50-52, 54-56
KEN STEACY·pages 41-49, 53
Letterer: JOHN WORKMAN & KEN STEACY
Colorist: DANIEL VOZZO
Editor: TOM PEYER

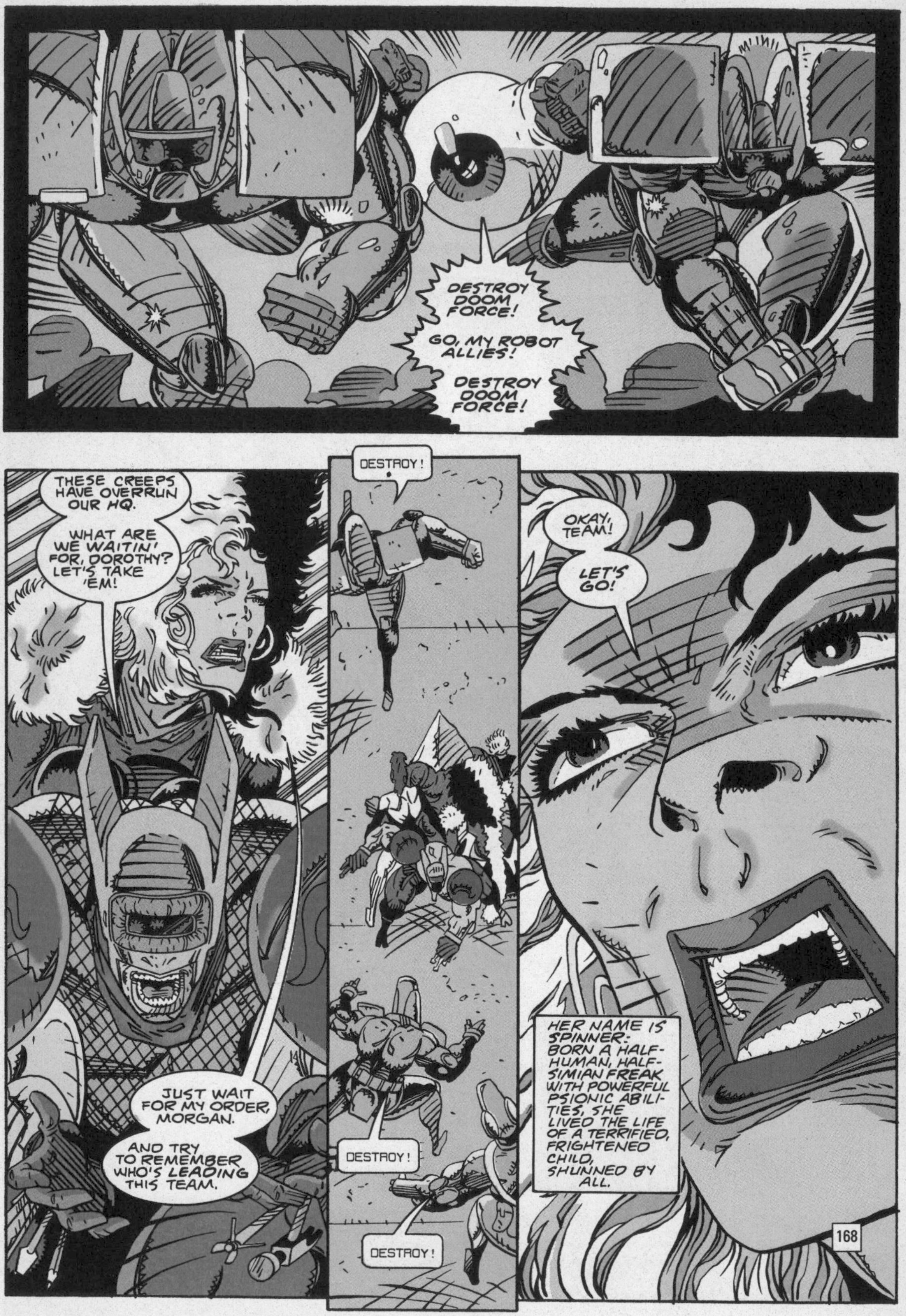
DESTROY DOOM FORCE!
GO, MY ROBOT ALLIES!
DESTROY DOOM FORCE!
THESE CREEPS HAVE OVERRUN OUR HQ.
WHAT ARE WE WAITIN' FOR, DOROTHY? LET'S TAKE 'EM!
JUST WAIT FOR MY ORDER, MORGAN.
AND TRY TO REMEMBER WHO'S LEADING THIS TEAM.
DESTROY!
DESTROY!
DESTROY!
OKAY, TEAM!
LET'S GO!
HER NAME IS SPINNER: BORN A HALF-HUMAN, HALF-SIMIAN FREAK WITH POWERFUL PSIONIC ABILITIES, SHE LIVED THE LIFE OF A TERRIFIED, FRIGHTENED CHILD, SHUNNED BY ALL.

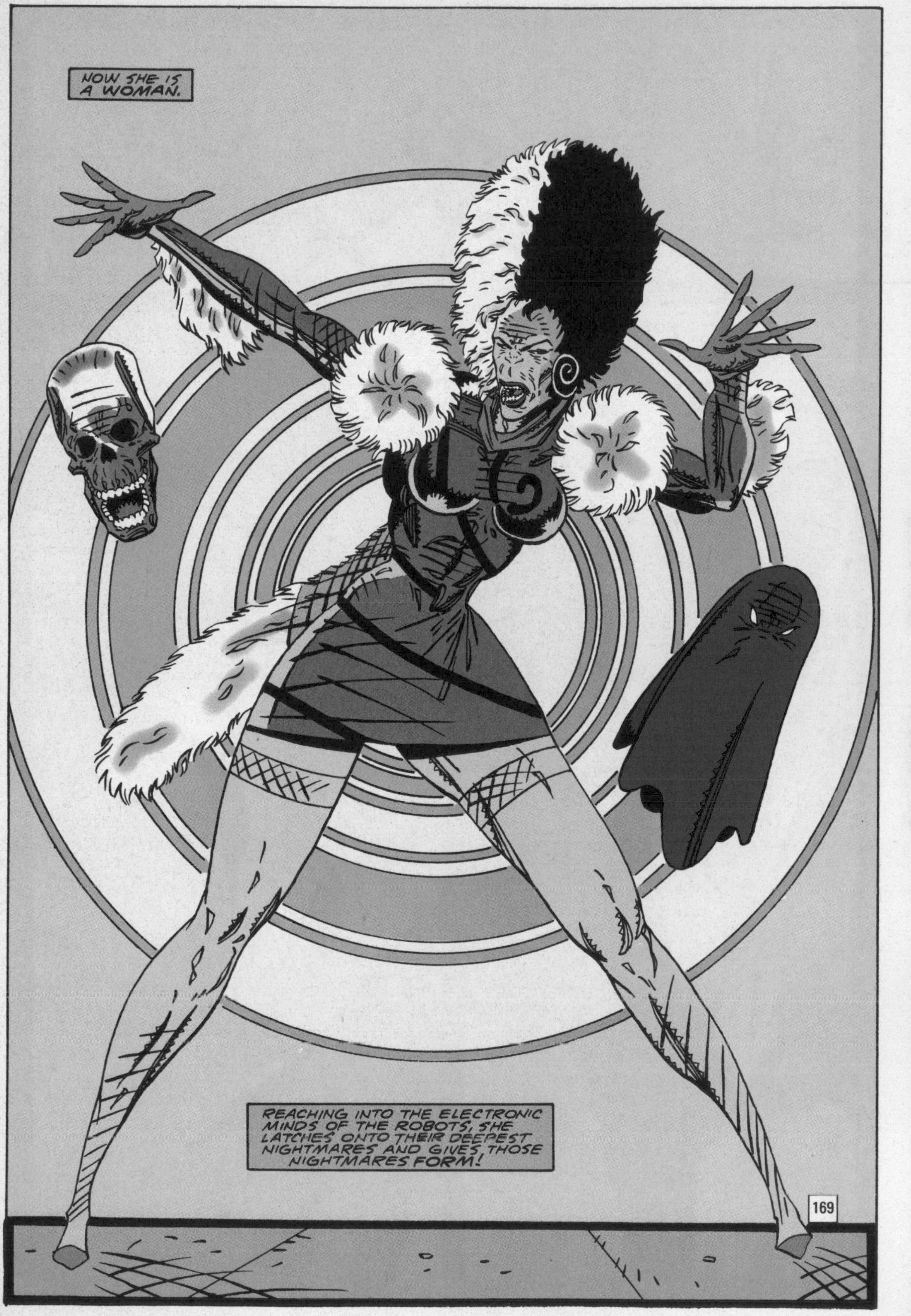
NOW SHE IS A WOMAN.
REACHING INTO THE ELECTRONIC MINDS OF THE ROBOTS, SHE LATCHES ONTO THEIR DEEPEST NIGHTMARES AND GIVES THOSE NIGHTMARES FORM!
169

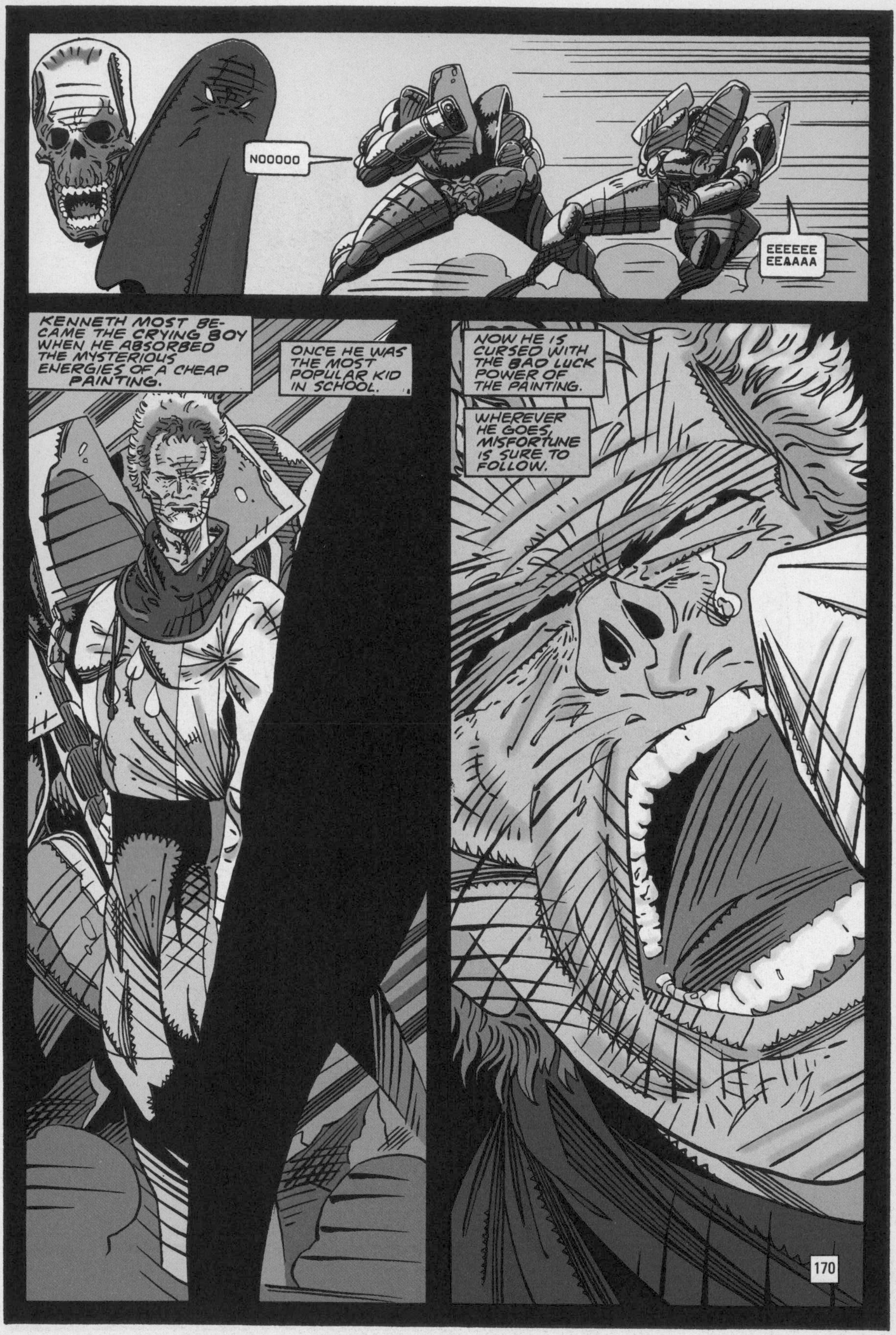
NOOOOO
EEEEEE EEAAAA
KENNETH MOST BECAME THE CRYING BOY WHEN HE ABSORBED THE MYSTERIOUS ENERGIES OF A CHEAP PAINTING.
ONCE HE WAS THE MOST POPULAR KID IN SCHOOL.
NOW HE IS CURSED WITH THE BAD LUCK POWER OF THE PAINTING.
WHEREVER HE GOES, MISFORTUNE IS SURE TO FOLLOW.
170

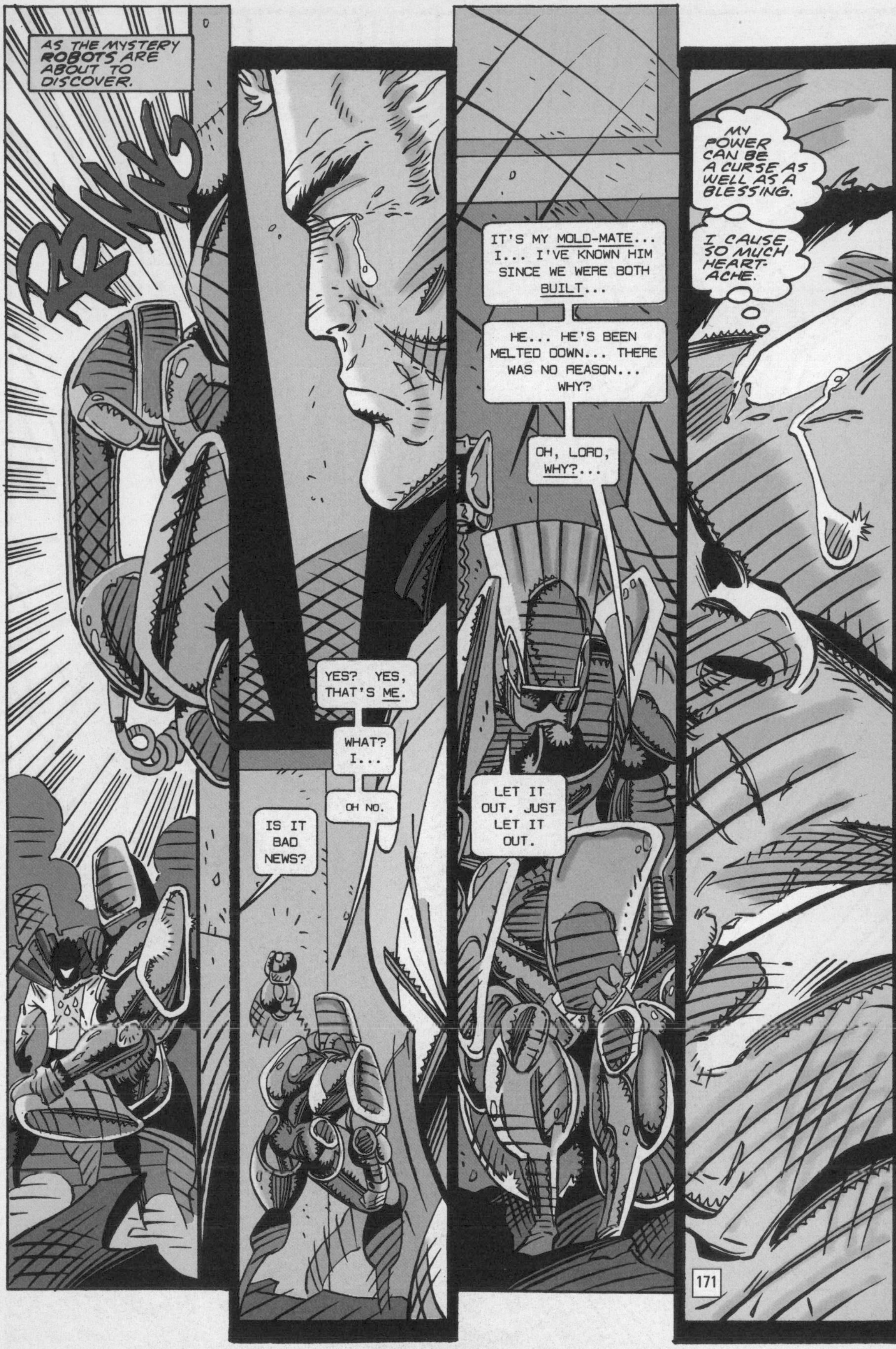
AS THE MYSTERY ROBOTS ARE ABOUT TO DISCOVER.
RANNG
YES? YES, THAT'S ME.
WHAT? I...
OH NO.
IS IT BAD NEWS?
IT'S MY MOLD-MATE... I... I'VE KNOWN HIM SINCE WE WERE BOTH BUILT...
HE... HE'S BEEN MELTED DOWN... THERE WAS NO REASON... WHY?
OH, LORD, WHY?...
LET IT OUT. JUST LET IT OUT.
MY POWER CAN BE A CURSE AS WELL AS A BLESSING.
I CAUSE SO MUCH HEART-ACHE.

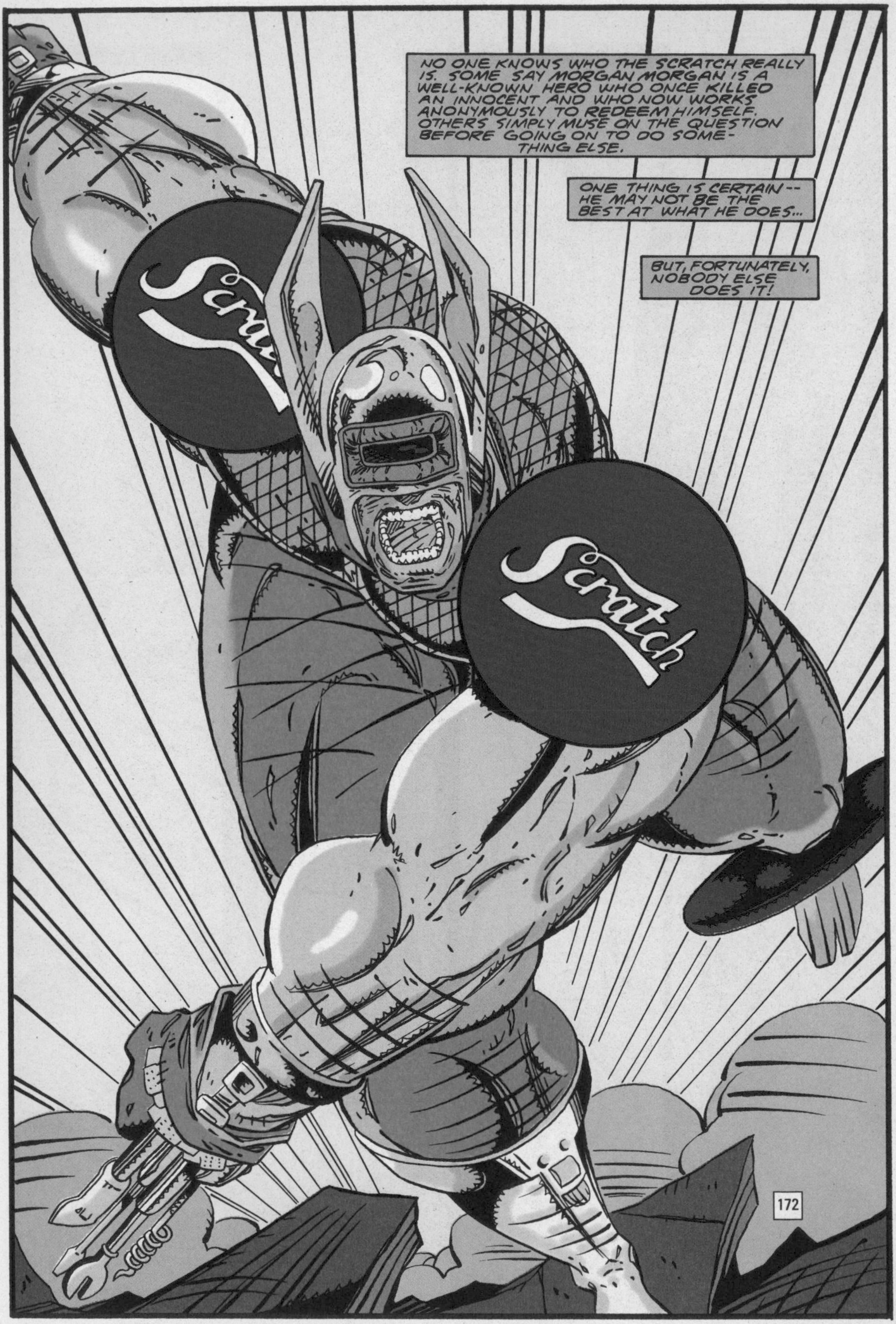
NO ONE KNOWS WHO THE SCRATCH REALLY IS. SOME SAY MORGAN MORGAN IS A WELL-KNOWN HERO WHO ONCE KILLED AN INNOCENT AND WHO NOW WORKS ANONYMOUSLY TO REDEEM HIMSELF. OTHERS SIMPLY MUSE ON THE QUESTION BEFORE GOING ON TO DO SOMETHING ELSE.
ONE THING IS CERTAIN -- HE MAY NOT BE THE BEST AT WHAT HE DOES...
BUT, FORTUNATELY, NOBODY ELSE DOES IT!
Scratch
Scratch

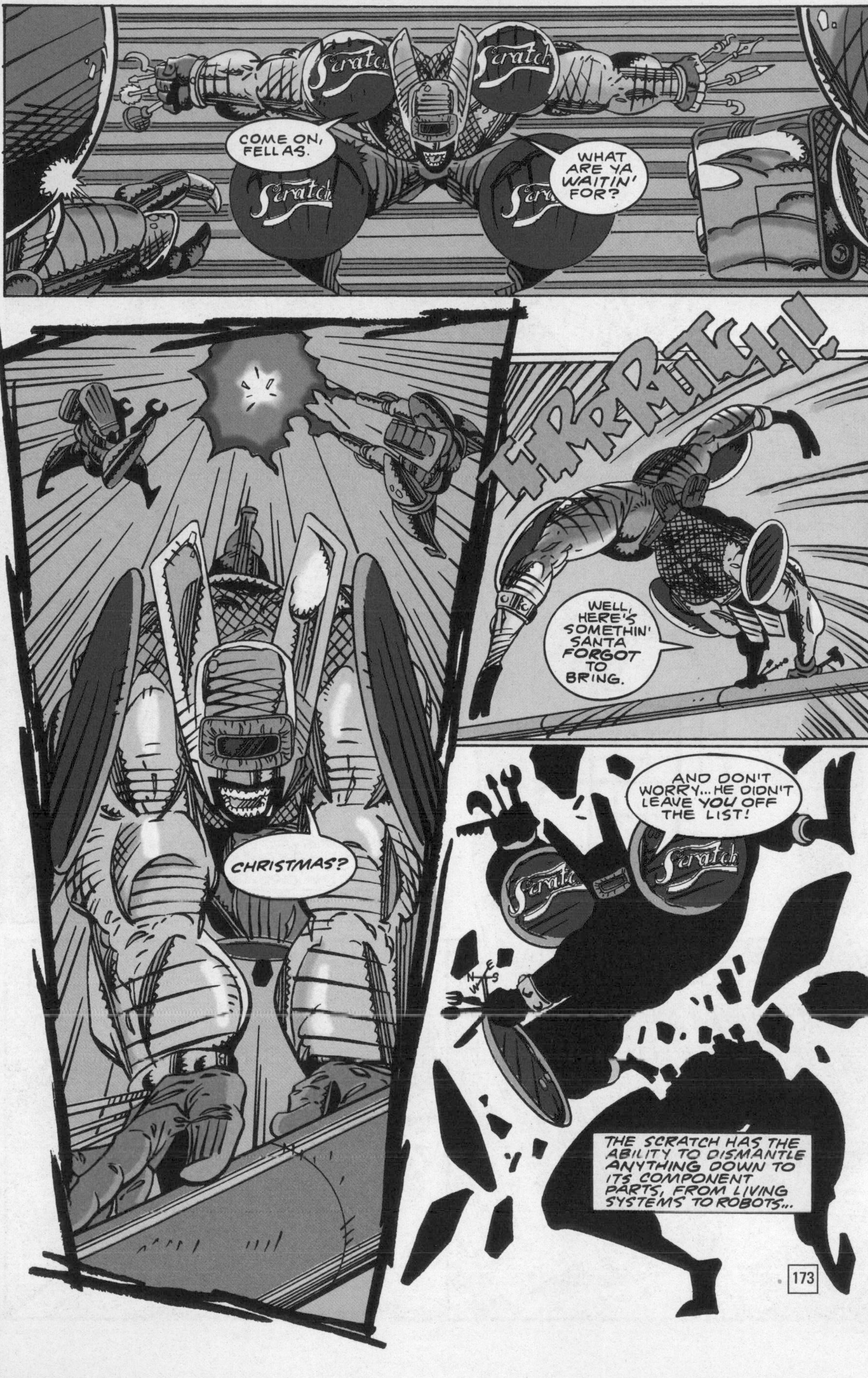
COME ON, FELLAS.
WHAT ARE YA WAITIN' FOR?
CHRISTMAS?
THRRRIKH!!
WELL, HERE'S SOMETHIN' SANTA FORGOT TO BRING.
AND DON'T WORRY... HE DIDN'T LEAVE YOU OFF THE LIST!
THE SCRATCH HAS THE ABILITY TO DISMANTLE ANYTHING DOWN TO ITS COMPONENT PARTS, FROM LIVING SYSTEMS TO ROBOTS...

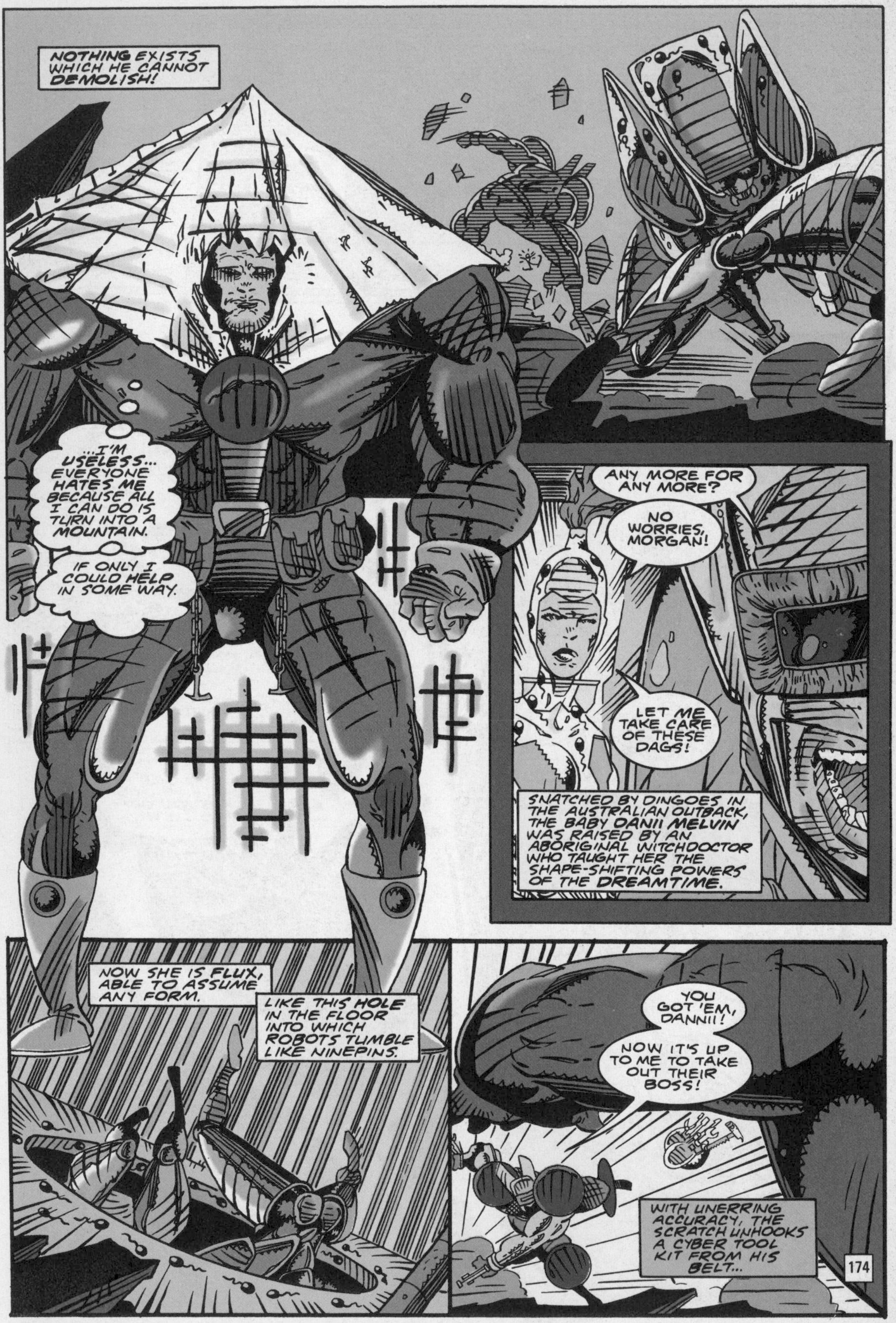
NOTHING EXISTS WHICH HE CANNOT DEMOLISH!
...I'M USELESS... EVERYONE HATES ME BECAUSE ALL I CAN DO IS TURN INTO A MOUNTAIN.
IF ONLY I COULD HELP IN SOME WAY.
ANY MORE FOR ANY MORE?
NO WORRIES, MORGAN!
LET ME TAKE CARE OF THESE DAGS!
SNATCHED BY DINGOES IN THE AUSTRALIAN OUTBACK, THE BABY DANII MELVIN WAS RAISED BY AN ABORIGINAL WITCHDOCTOR WHO TAUGHT HER THE SHAPE-SHIFTING POWERS OF THE DREAMTIME.
NOW SHE IS FLUX, ABLE TO ASSUME ANY FORM.
LIKE THIS HOLE IN THE FLOOR INTO WHICH ROBOTS TUMBLE LIKE NINEPINS.
YOU GOT 'EM, DANNII!
NOW IT'S UP TO ME TO TAKE OUT THEIR BOSS!
WITH UNERRING ACCURACY, THE SCRATCH UNHOOKS A CYBER TOOL KIT FROM HIS BELT...
174

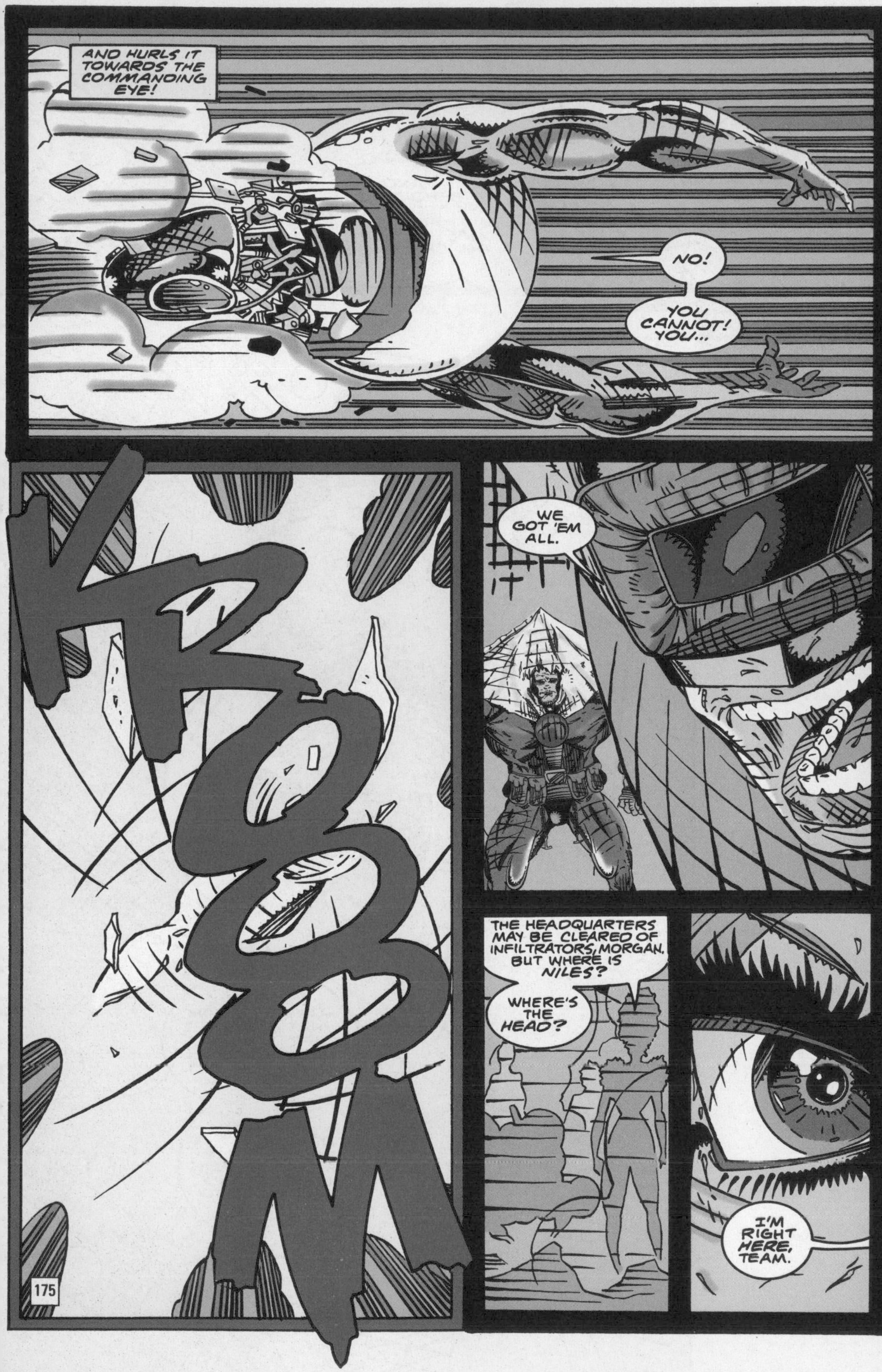
AND HURLS IT TOWARDS THE COMMANDING EYE!
NO!
YOU CANNOT! YOU...
KROOOM
WE GOT 'EM ALL.
THE HEADQUARTERS MAY BE CLEARED OF INFILTRATORS, MORGAN, BUT WHERE IS NILES?
WHERE'S THE HEAD?
I'M RIGHT HERE, TEAM.

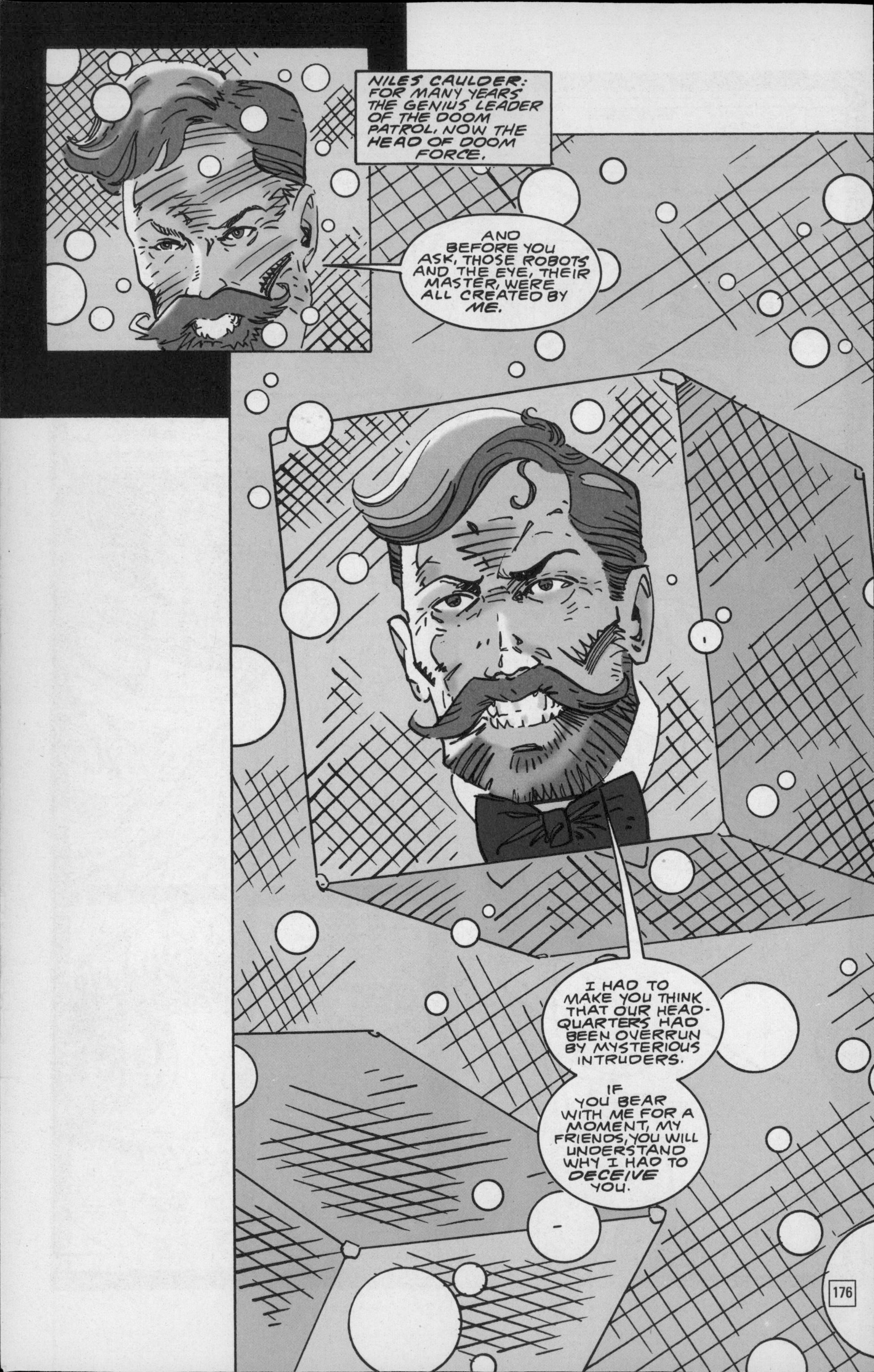
NILES CAULDER: FOR MANY YEARS THE GENIUS LEADER OF THE DOOM PATROL, NOW THE HEAD OF DOOM FORCE.
AND BEFORE YOU ASK, THOSE ROBOTS AND THE EYE, THEIR MASTER, WERE ALL CREATED BY ME.
I HAD TO MAKE YOU THINK THAT OUR HEAD-QUARTERS HAD BEEN OVERRUN BY MYSTERIOUS INTRUDERS.
IF YOU BEAR WITH ME FOR A MOMENT, MY FRIENDS, YOU WILL UNDERSTAND WHY I HAD TO DECEIVE YOU.

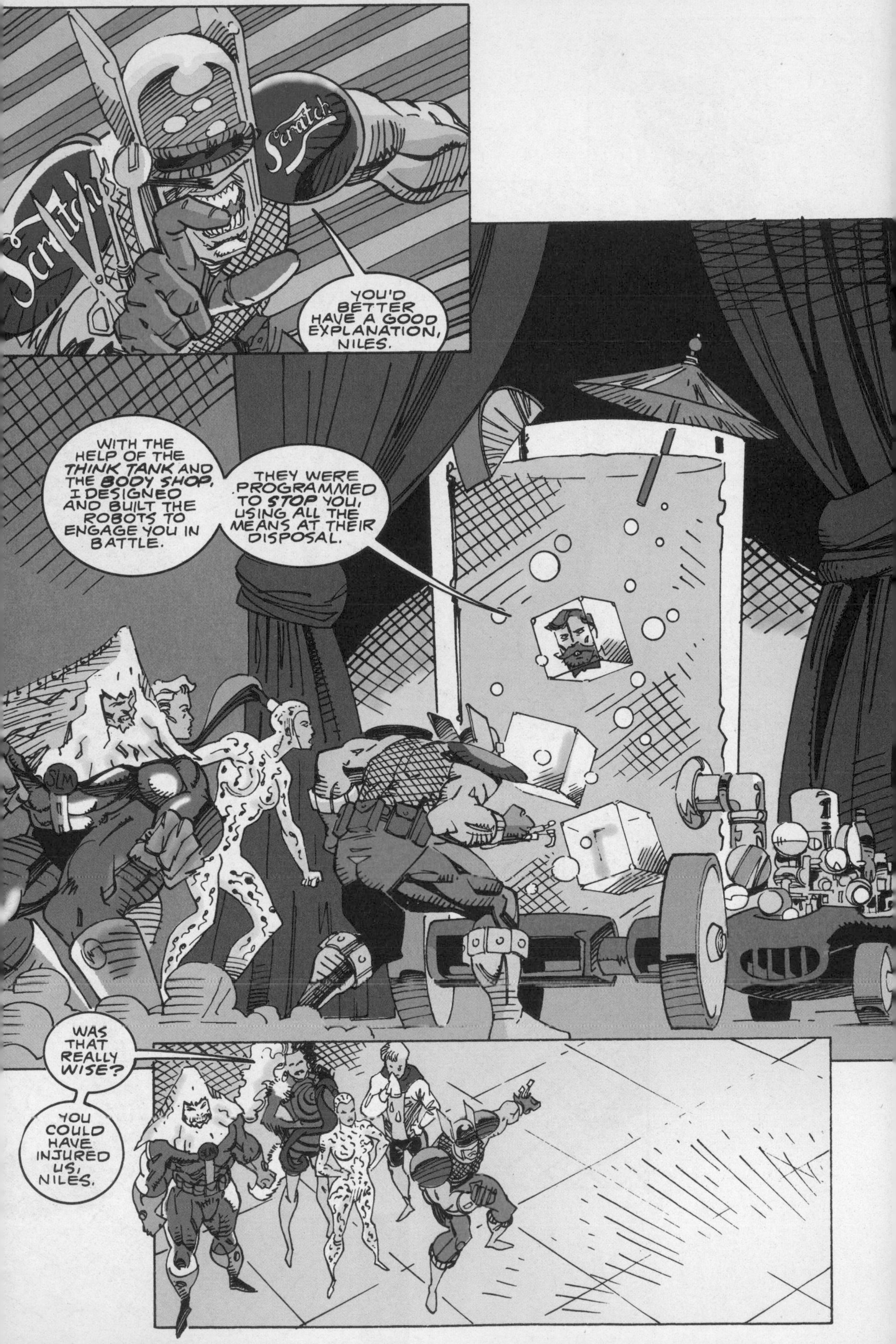
Scratch
Scratch
YOU'D BETTER HAVE A GOOD EXPLANATION, NILES.
WITH THE HELP OF THE THINK TANK AND THE BODY SHOP, I DESIGNED AND BUILT THE ROBOTS TO ENGAGE YOU IN BATTLE.
THEY WERE PROGRAMMED TO STOP YOU, USING ALL THE MEANS AT THEIR DISPOSAL.
WAS THAT REALLY WISE?
YOU COULD HAVE INJURED US, NILES.

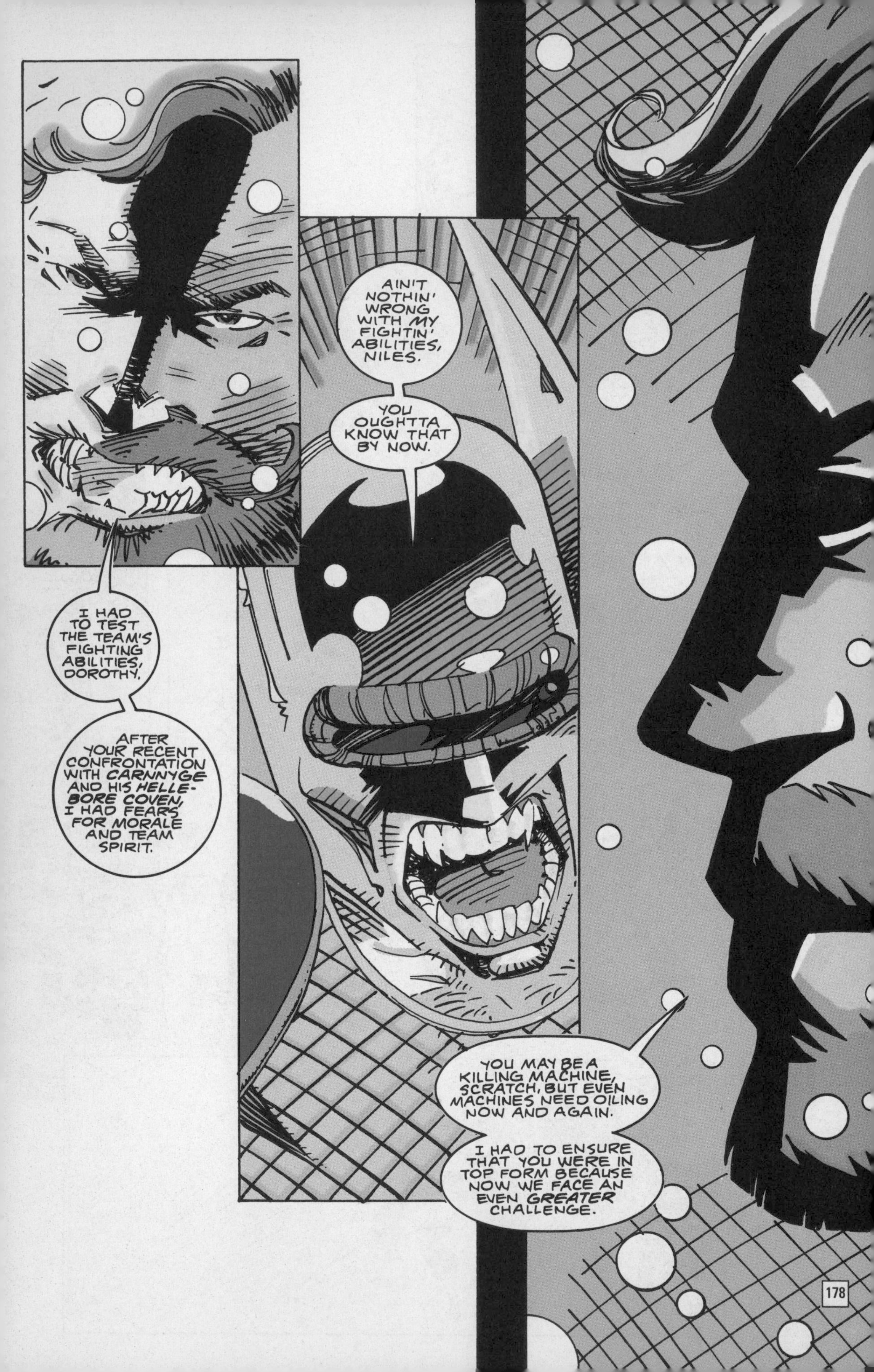
AIN'T NOTHIN' WRONG WITH MY FIGHTIN' ABILITIES, NILES.
YOU OUGHTTA KNOW THAT BY NOW.
I HAD TO TEST THE TEAM'S FIGHTING ABILITIES, DOROTHY.
AFTER YOUR RECENT CONFRONTATION WITH CARNNYGE AND HIS HELLE-BORE COVEN, I HAD FEARS FOR MORALE AND TEAM SPIRIT.
YOU MAY BE A KILLING MACHINE, SCRATCH, BUT EVEN MACHINES NEED OILING NOW AND AGAIN.
I HAD TO ENSURE THAT YOU WERE IN TOP FORM BECAUSE NOW WE FACE AN EVEN GREATER CHALLENGE.

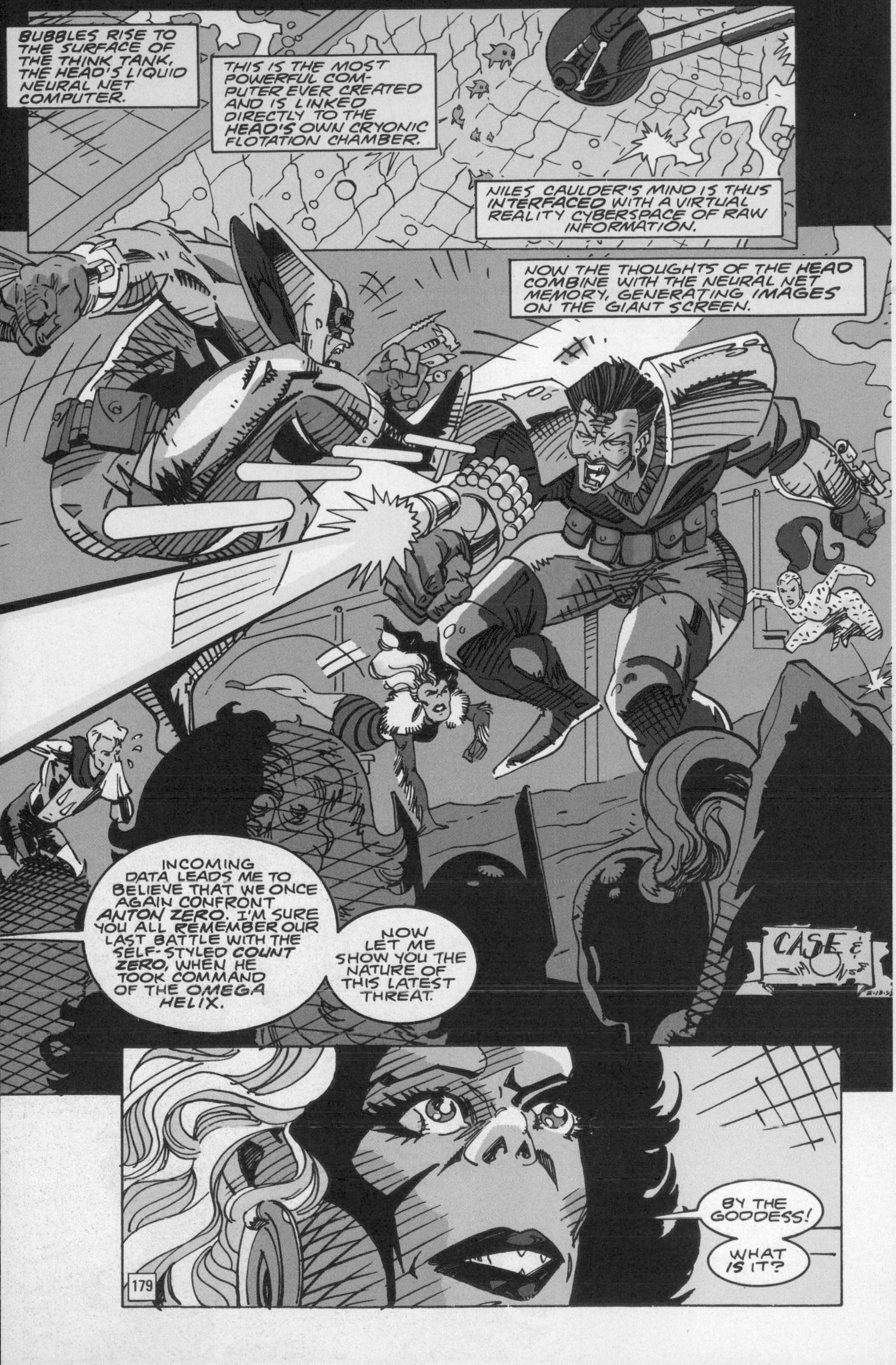

BUBBLES RISE TO THE SURFACE OF THE THINK TANK, THE HEAD'S LIQUID NEURAL NET COMPUTER.
THIS IS THE MOST POWERFUL COMPUTER EVER CREATED AND IS LINKED DIRECTLY TO THE HEAD'S OWN CRYONIC FLOTATION CHAMBER.
NILES CAULDER'S MIND IS THUS INTERFACED WITH A VIRTUAL REALITY CYBERSPACE OF RAW INFORMATION.
NOW THE THOUGHTS OF THE HEAD COMBINE WITH THE NEURAL NET MEMORY, GENERATING IMAGES ON THE GIANT SCREEN.
INCOMING DATA LEADS ME TO BELIEVE THAT WE ONCE AGAIN CONFRONT ANTON ZERO. I'M SURE YOU ALL REMEMBER OUR LAST BATTLE WITH THE SELF-STYLED COUNT ZERO, WHEN HE TOOK COMMAND OF THE OMEGA HELIX.
NOW LET ME SHOW YOU THE NATURE OF THIS LATEST THREAT.
CASE &
BY THE GODDESS!
WHAT IS IT?

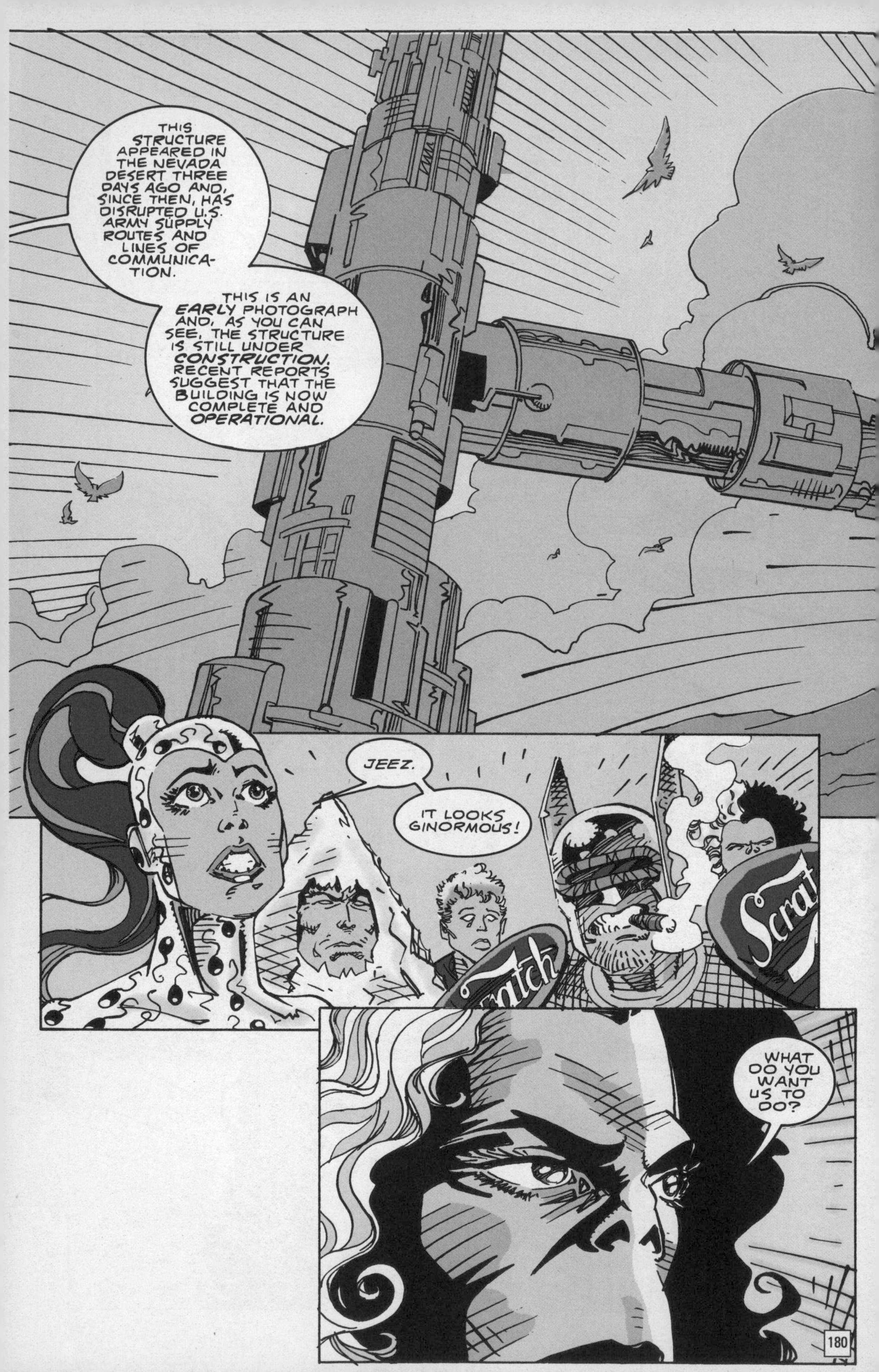
THIS STRUCTURE APPEARED IN THE NEVADA DESERT THREE DAYS AGO AND, SINCE THEN, HAS DISRUPTED U.S. ARMY SUPPLY ROUTES AND LINES OF COMMUNICATION.
THIS IS AN EARLY PHOTOGRAPH AND, AS YOU CAN SEE, THE STRUCTURE IS STILL UNDER CONSTRUCTION. RECENT REPORTS SUGGEST THAT THE BUILDING IS NOW COMPLETE AND OPERATIONAL.
JEEZ.
IT LOOKS GINORMOUS!
WHAT DO YOU WANT US TO DO?

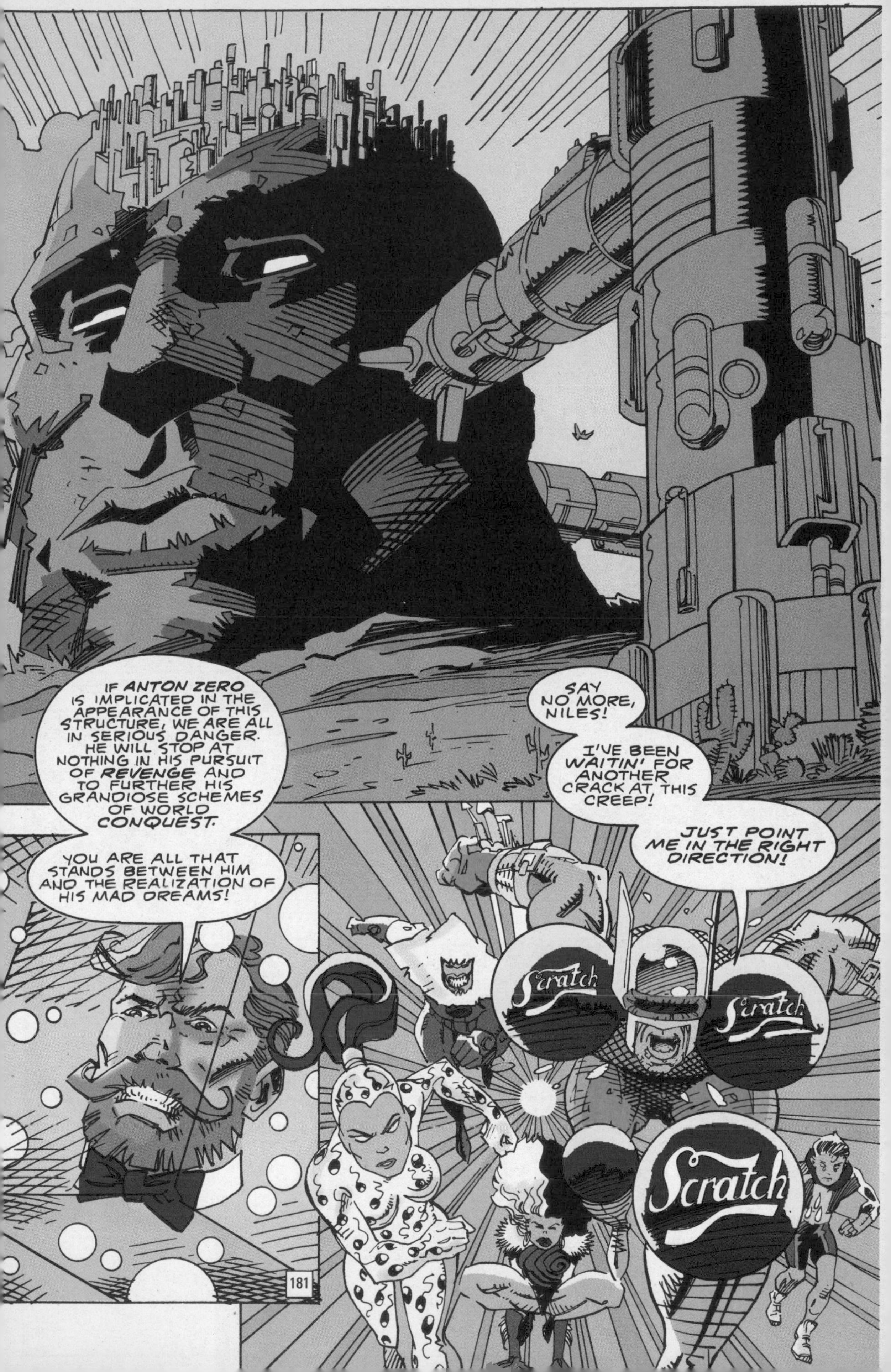
IF ANTON ZERO IS IMPLICATED IN THE APPEARANCE OF THIS STRUCTURE, WE ARE ALL IN SERIOUS DANGER. HE WILL STOP AT NOTHING IN HIS PURSUIT OF REVENGE AND TO FURTHER HIS GRANDIOSE SCHEMES OF WORLD CONQUEST.
YOU ARE ALL THAT STANDS BETWEEN HIM AND THE REALIZATION OF HIS MAD DREAMS!
SAY NO MORE, NILES!
I'VE BEEN WAITIN' FOR ANOTHER CRACK AT, THIS CREEP!
JUST POINT ME IN THE RIGHT DIRECTION!
Scratch
Scratch
Scratch

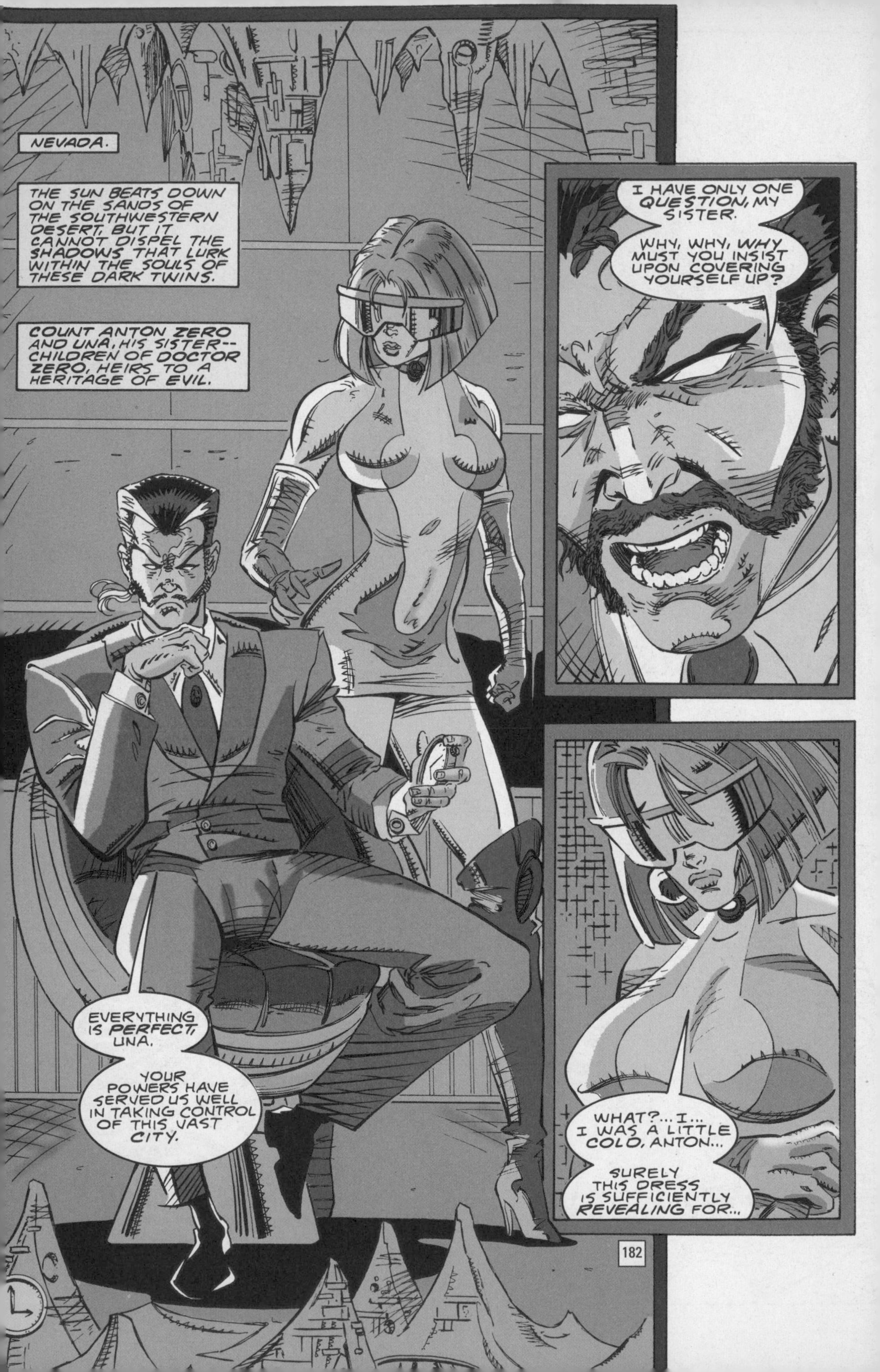
NEVADA.
THE SUN BEATS DOWN ON THE SANDS OF THE SOUTHWESTERN DESERT, BUT IT CANNOT DISPEL THE SHADOWS THAT LURK WITHIN THE SOULS OF THESE DARK TWINS.
COUNT ANTON ZERO AND UNA, HIS SISTER-- CHILDREN OF DOCTOR ZERO, HEIRS TO A HERITAGE OF EVIL.
EVERYTHING IS PERFECT, UNA.
YOUR POWERS HAVE SERVED US WELL IN TAKING CONTROL OF THIS VAST CITY.
I HAVE ONLY ONE QUESTION, MY SISTER.
WHY, WHY, WHY MUST YOU INSIST UPON COVERING YOURSELF UP?
WHAT?... I... I WAS A LITTLE COLD, ANTON...
SURELY THIS DRESS IS SUFFICIENTLY REVEALING FOR...

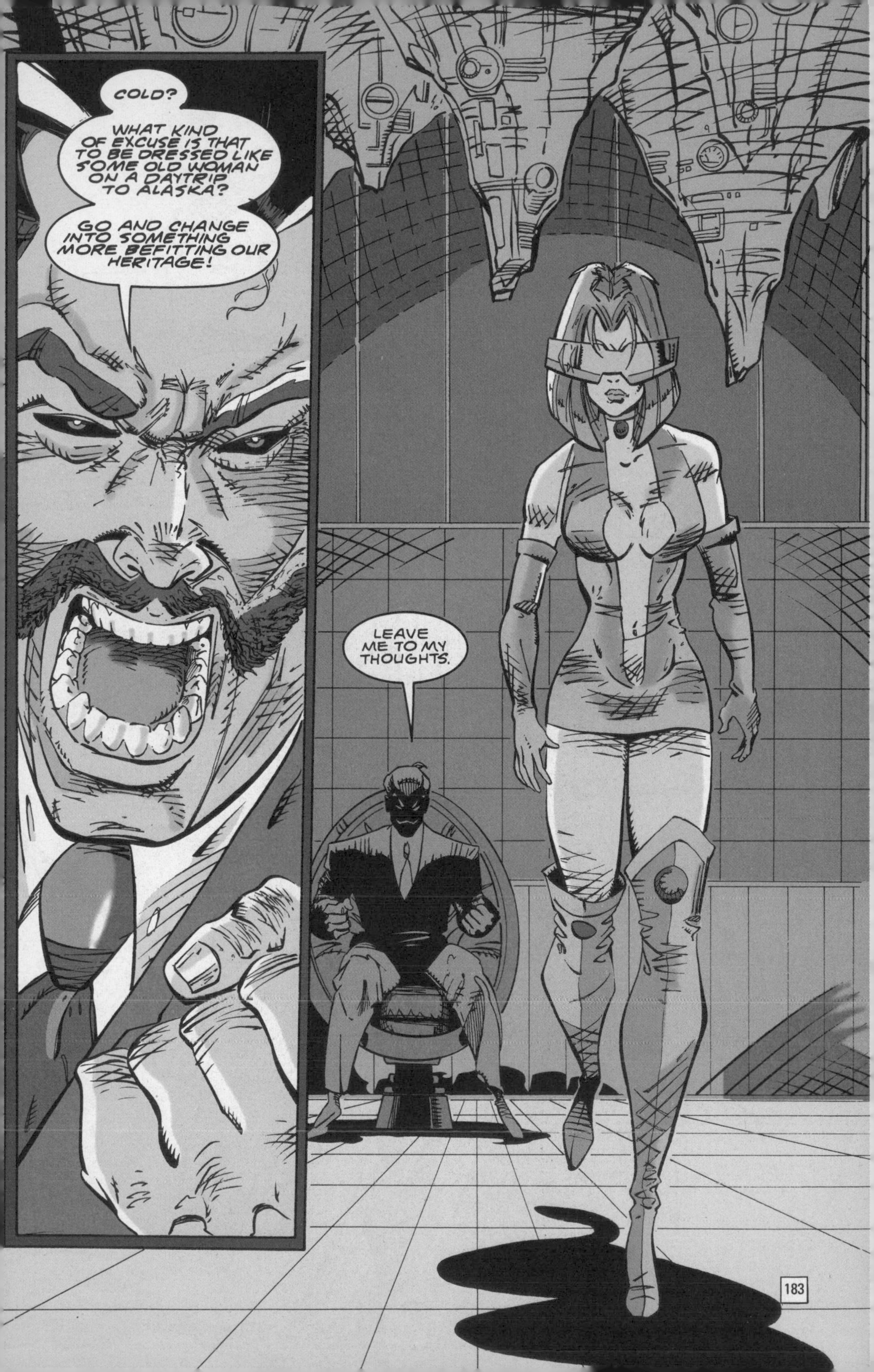
COLD?
WHAT KIND OF EXCUSE IS THAT TO BE DRESSED LIKE SOME OLD WOMAN ON A DAYTRIP TO ALASKA?
GO AND CHANGE INTO SOMETHING MORE BEFITTING OUR HERITAGE!
LEAVE ME TO MY THOUGHTS.

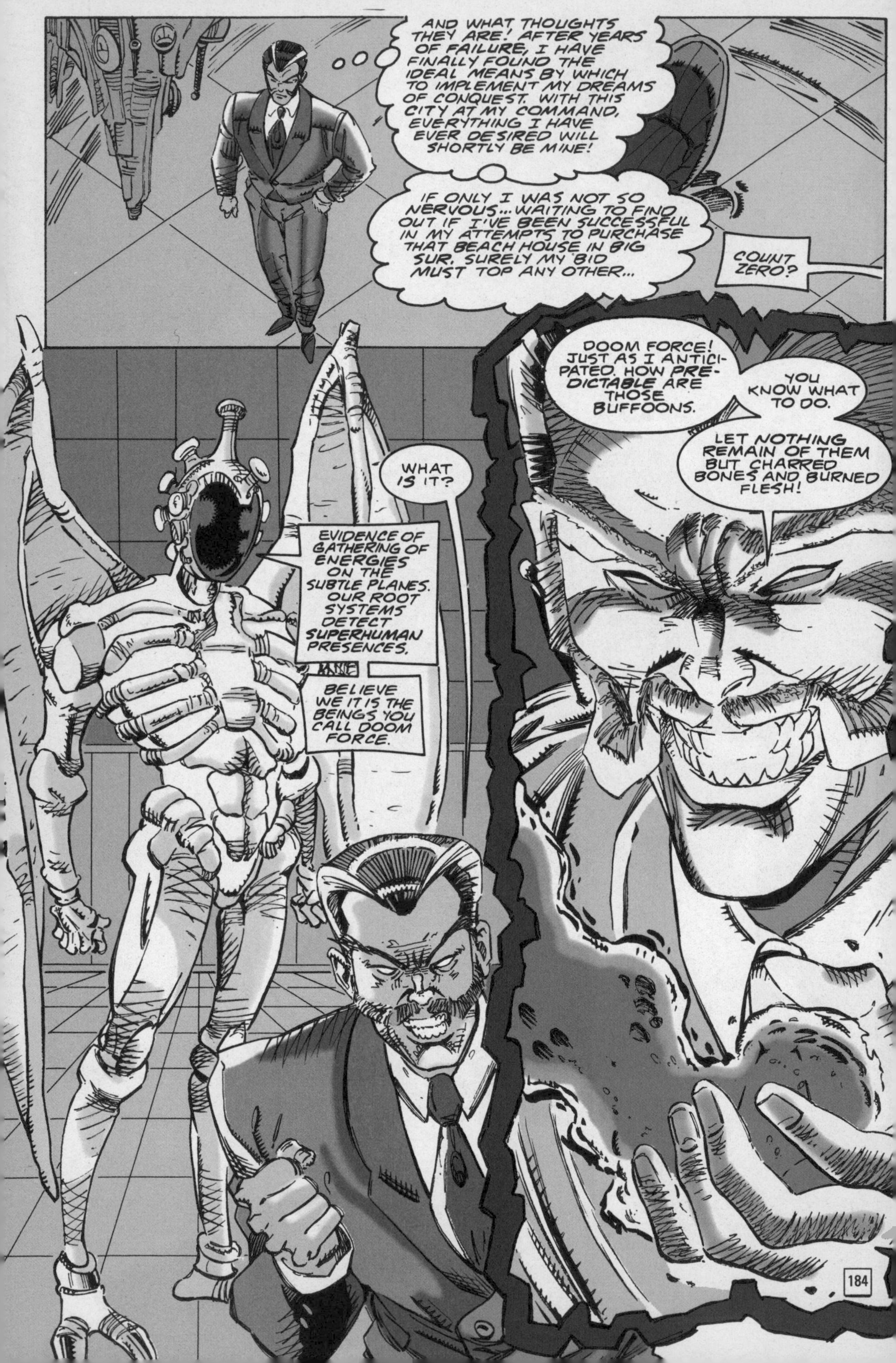
AND WHAT THOUGHTS THEY ARE! AFTER YEARS OF FAILURE, I HAVE FINALLY FOUND THE IDEAL MEANS BY WHICH TO IMPLEMENT MY DREAMS OF CONQUEST. WITH THIS CITY AT MY COMMAND, EVERYTHING I HAVE EVER DESIRED WILL SHORTLY BE MINE!
IF ONLY I WAS NOT SO NERVOUS... WAITING TO FIND OUT IF I'VE BEEN SUCCESSFUL IN MY ATTEMPTS TO PURCHASE THAT BEACH HOUSE IN BIG SUR. SURELY MY BID MUST TOP ANY OTHER...
COUNT ZERO?
WHAT IS IT?
EVIDENCE OF GATHERING OF ENERGIES ON THE SUBTLE PLANES. OUR ROOT SYSTEMS DETECT SUPERHUMAN PRESENCES.
BELIEVE WE IT IS THE BEINGS YOU CALL DOOM FORCE.
DOOM FORCE! JUST AS I ANTICIPATED. HOW PREDICTABLE ARE THOSE BUFFOONS.
YOU KNOW WHAT TO DO.
LET NOTHING REMAIN OF THEM BUT CHARRED BONES AND BURNED FLESH!

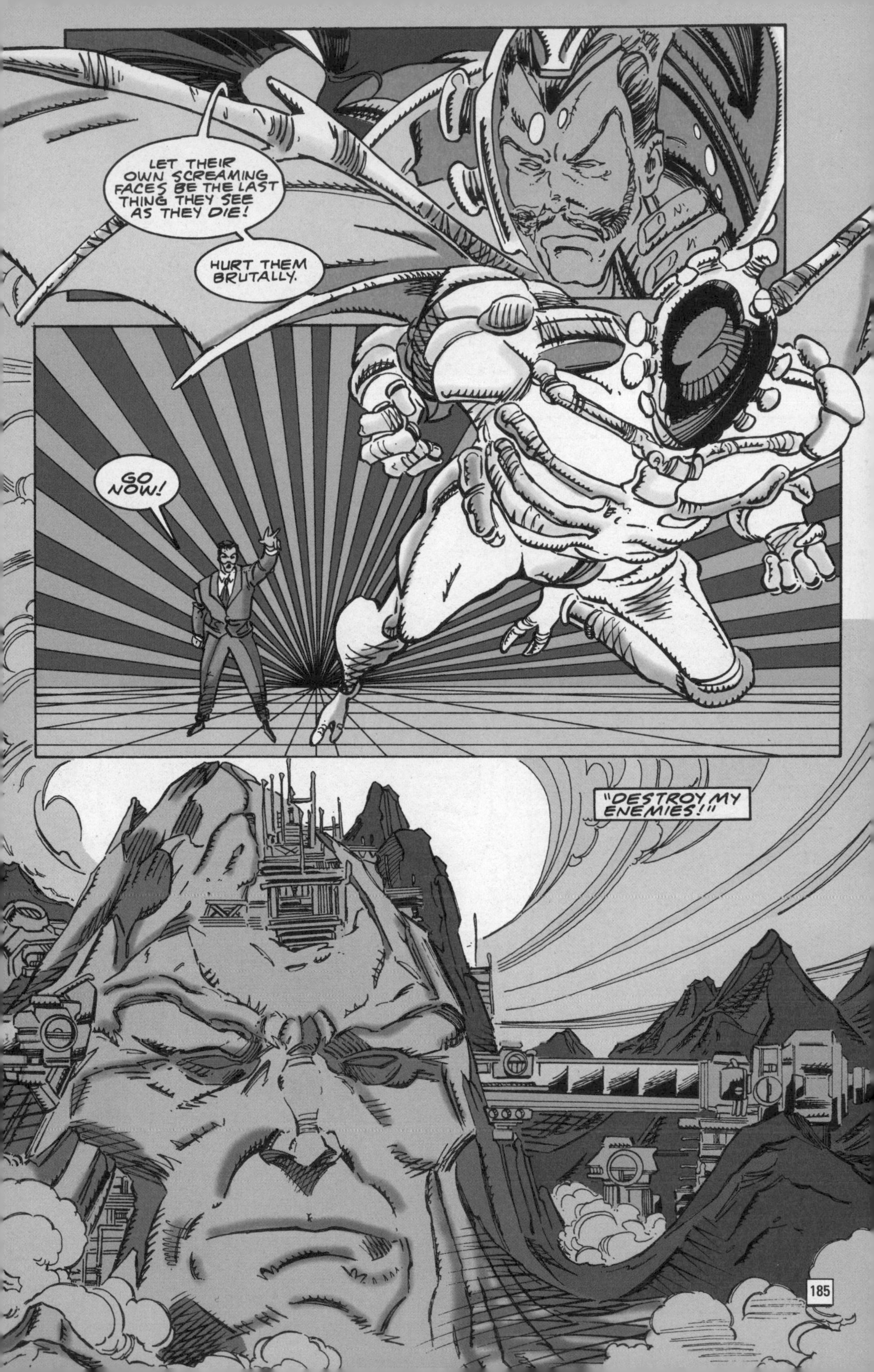
LET THEIR OWN SCREAMING FACES BE THE LAST THING THEY SEE AS THEY DIE!
HURT THEM BRUTALLY.
GO NOW!
"DESTROY MY ENEMIES!"

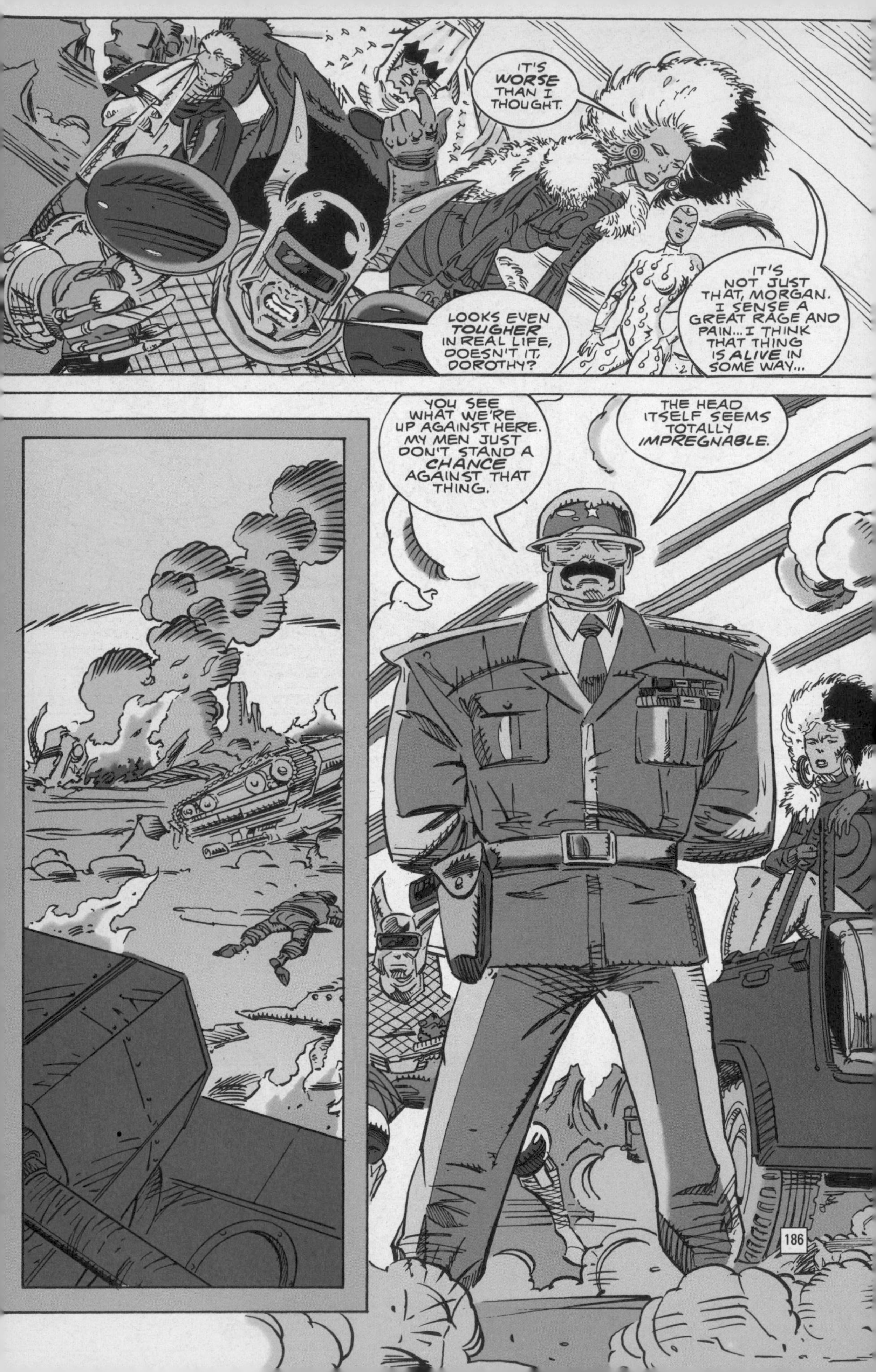
IT'S WORSE THAN I THOUGHT.
LOOKS EVEN TOUGHER IN REAL LIFE, DOESN'T IT, DOROTHY?
IT'S NOT JUST THAT, MORGAN. I SENSE A GREAT RAGE AND PAIN... I THINK THAT THING IS ALIVE IN SOME WAY...
YOU SEE WHAT WE'RE UP AGAINST HERE. MY MEN JUST DON'T STAND A CHANCE AGAINST THAT THING.
THE HEAD ITSELF SEEMS TOTALLY IMPREGNABLE.

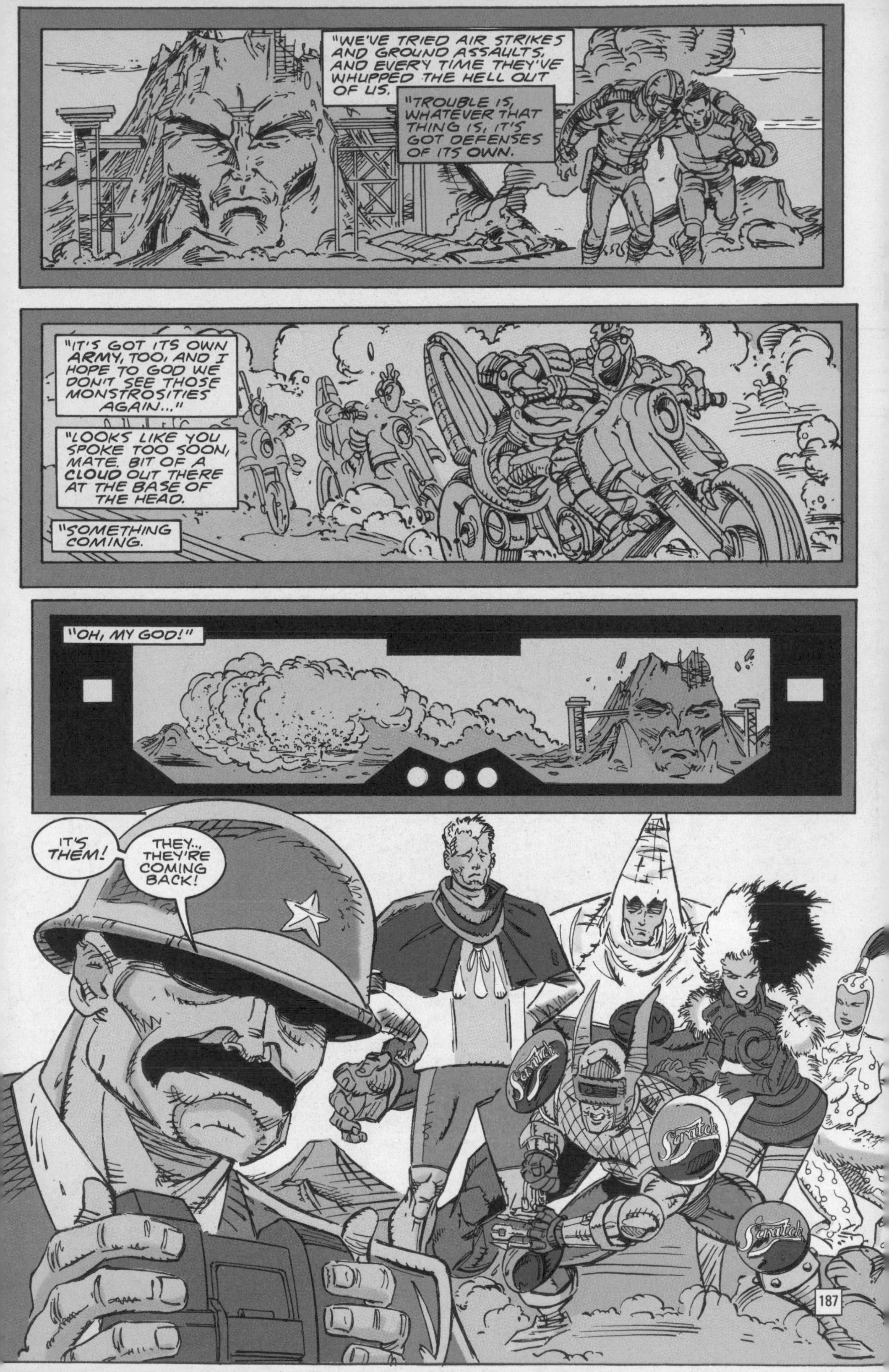
"WE'VE TRIED AIR STRIKES AND GROUND ASSAULTS, AND EVERY TIME THEY'VE WHUPPED THE HELL OUT OF US.
"TROUBLE IS, WHATEVER THAT THING IS, IT'S GOT DEFENSES OF ITS OWN.
"IT'S GOT ITS OWN ARMY, TOO, AND I HOPE TO GOD WE DON'T SEE THOSE MONSTROSITIES AGAIN..."
"LOOKS LIKE YOU SPOKE TOO SOON, MATE. BIT OF A CLOUD OUT THERE AT THE BASE OF THE HEAD.
"SOMETHING COMING.
"OH, MY GOD!"
IT'S THEM!
THEY... THEY'RE COMING BACK!
Scratch
Scratch
Scratch

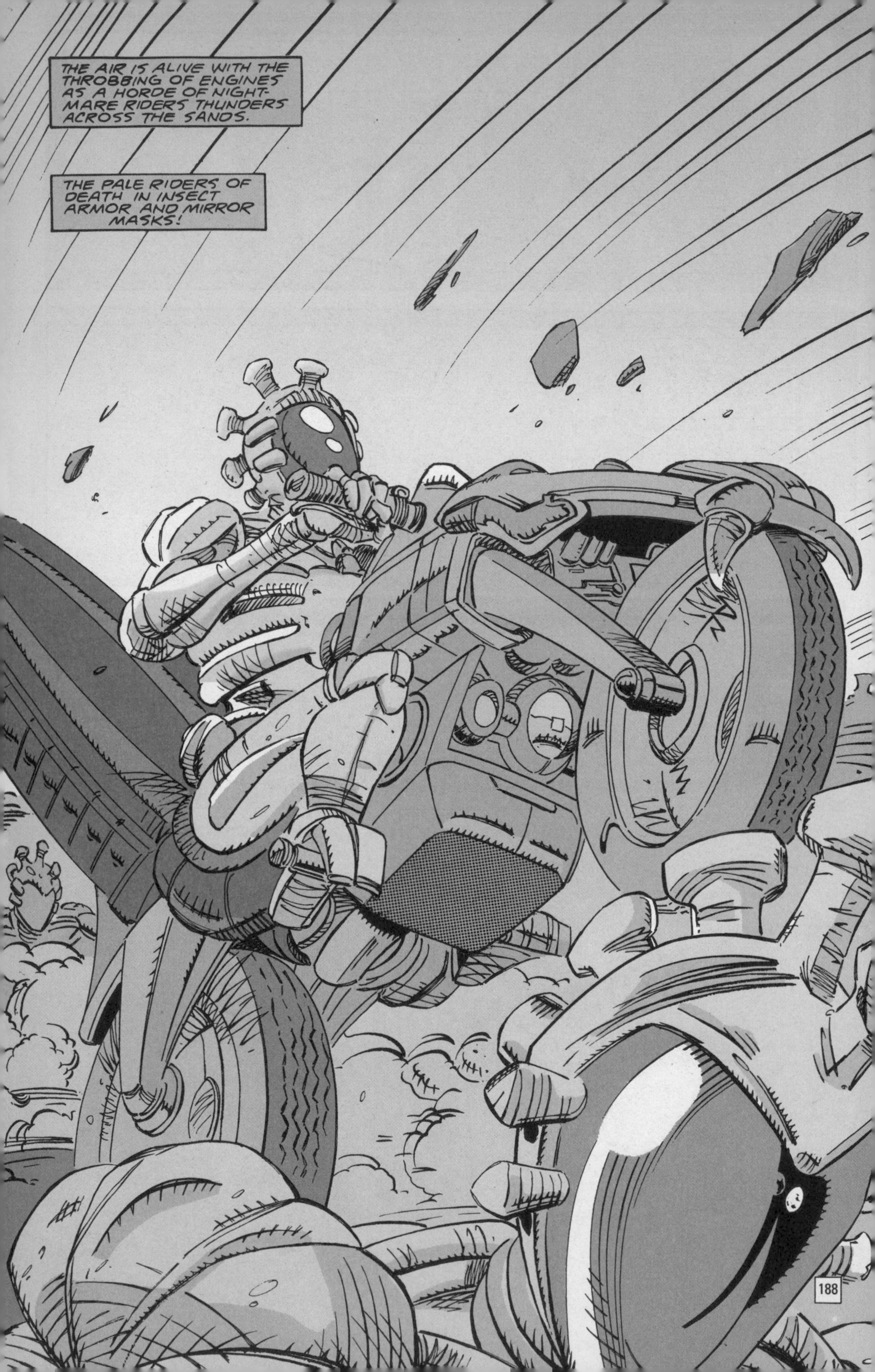
THE AIR IS ALIVE WITH THE THROBBING OF ENGINES AS A HORDE OF NIGHT-MARE RIDERS THUNDERS ACROSS THE SANDS.
THE PALE RIDERS OF DEATH IN INSECT ARMOR AND MIRROR MASKS!

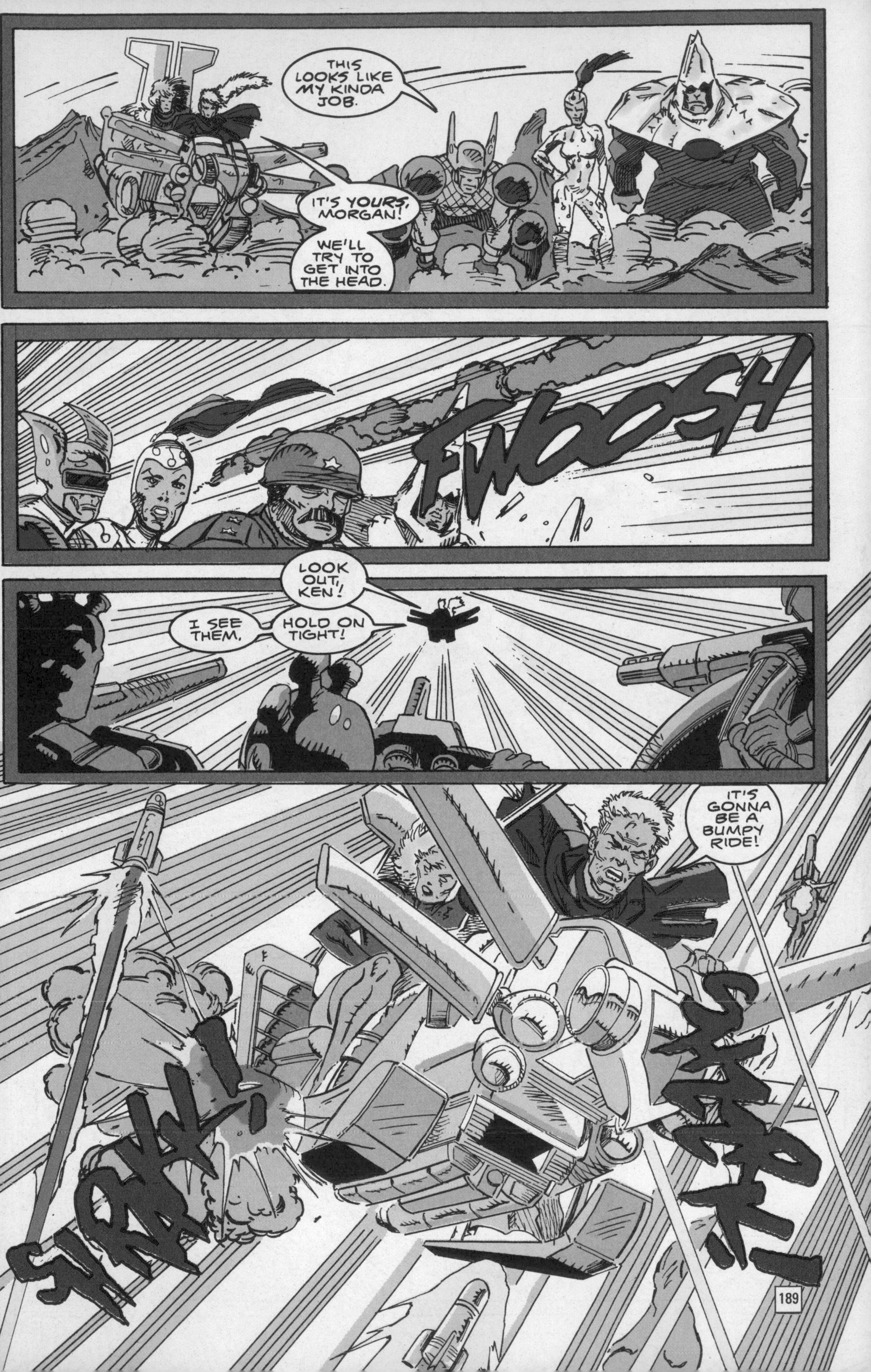
THIS LOOKS LIKE MY KINDA JOB.
IT'S YOURS, MORGAN!
WE'LL TRY TO GET INTO THE HEAD.
FWOOSH
LOOK OUT, KEN!
I SEE THEM.
HOLD ON TIGHT!
IT'S GONNA BE A BUMPY RIDE!

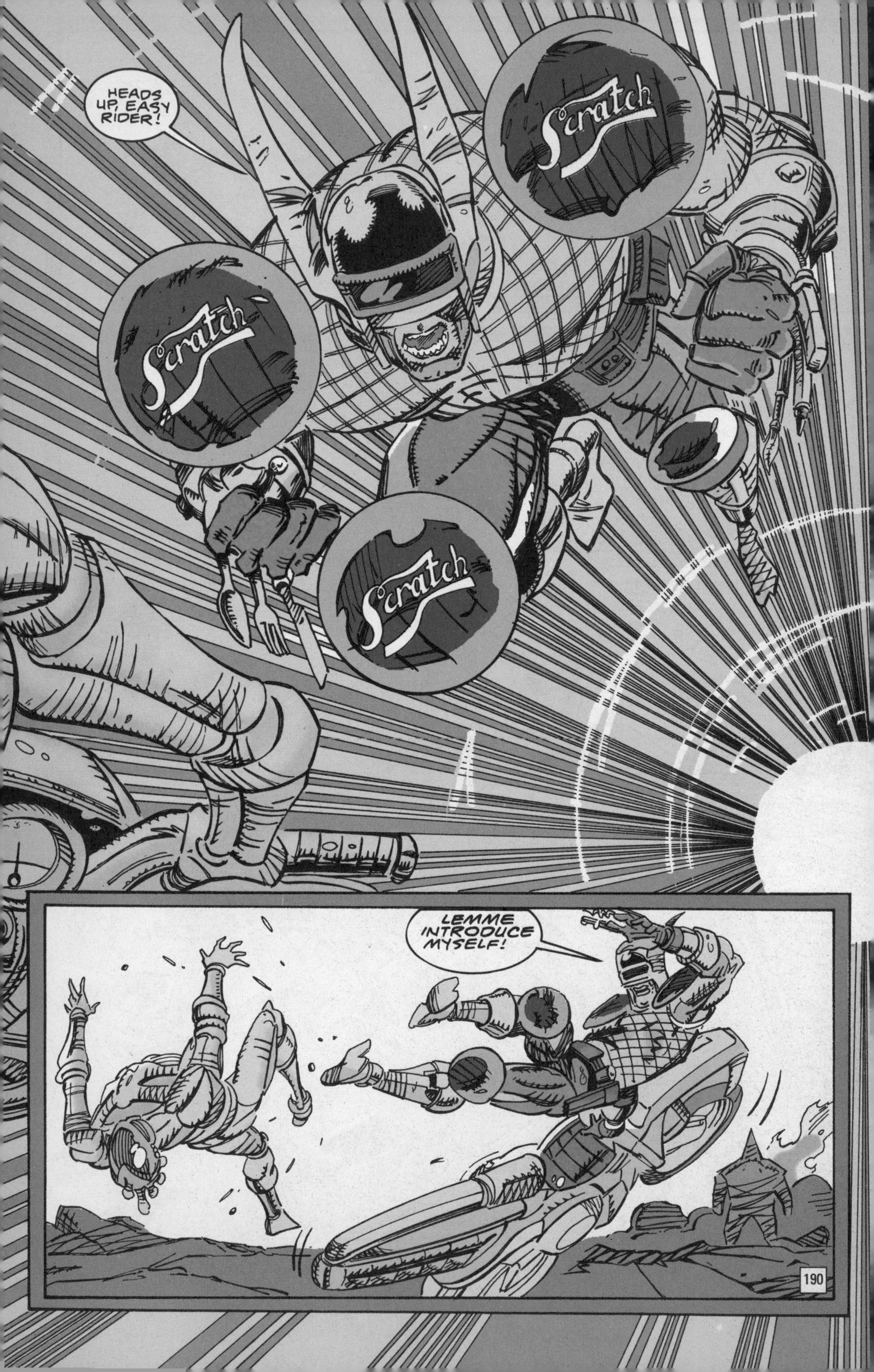
HEADS UP, EASY RIDER!
Scratch
Scratch
Scratch
Scratch
LEMME INTRODUCE MYSELF!

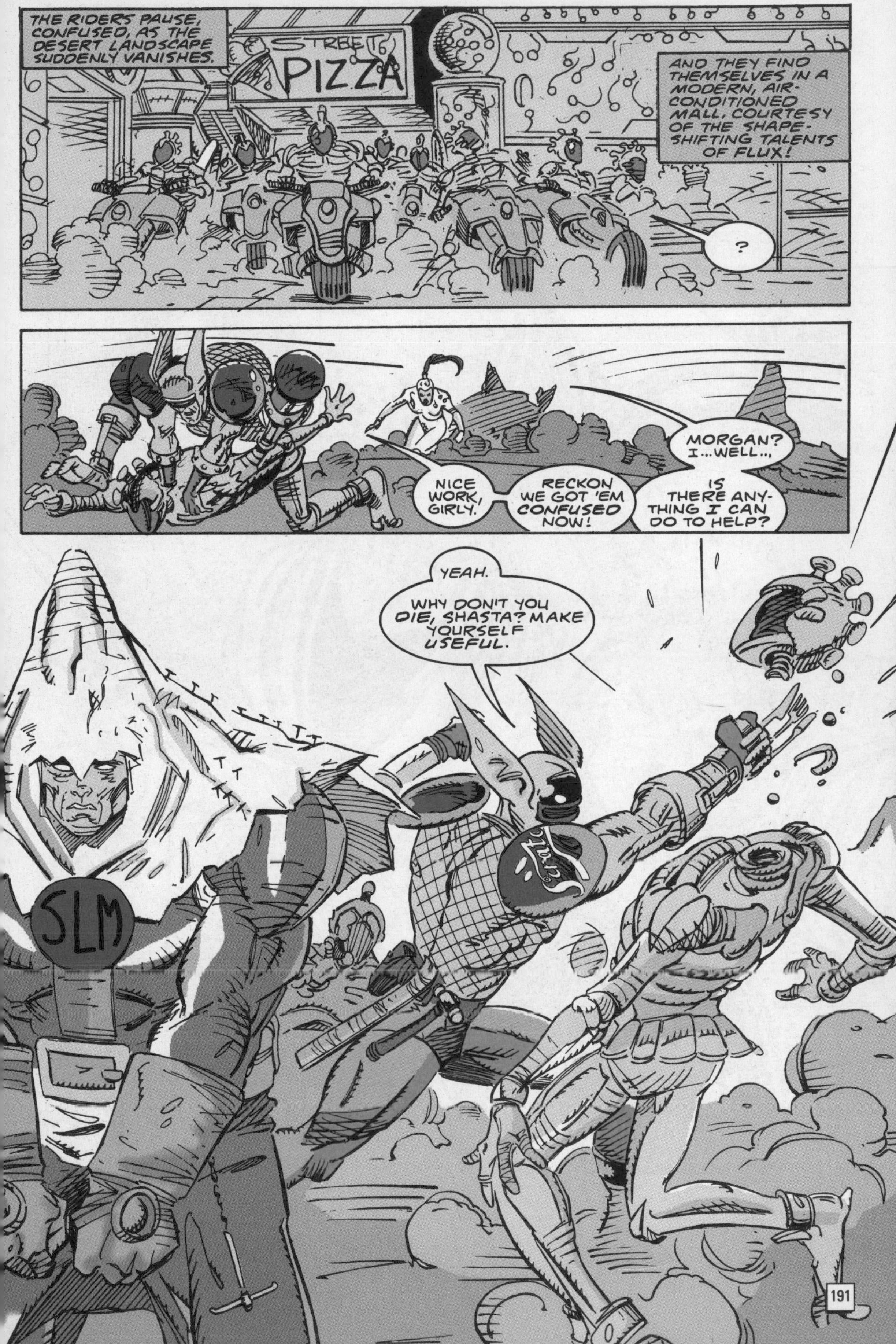
THE RIDERS PAUSE, CONFUSED, AS THE DESERT LANDSCAPE SUDDENLY VANISHES.
STREET PIZZA
AND THEY FIND THEMSELVES IN A MODERN, AIR-CONDITIONED MALL, COURTESY OF THE SHAPE-SHIFTING TALENTS OF FLUX!
?
NICE WORK, GIRLY.
RECKON WE GOT 'EM CONFUSED NOW!
MORGAN? I...WELL...,
IS THERE ANYTHING I CAN DO TO HELP?
YEAH.
WHY DON'T YOU DIE, SHASTA? MAKE YOURSELF USEFUL.
SLM

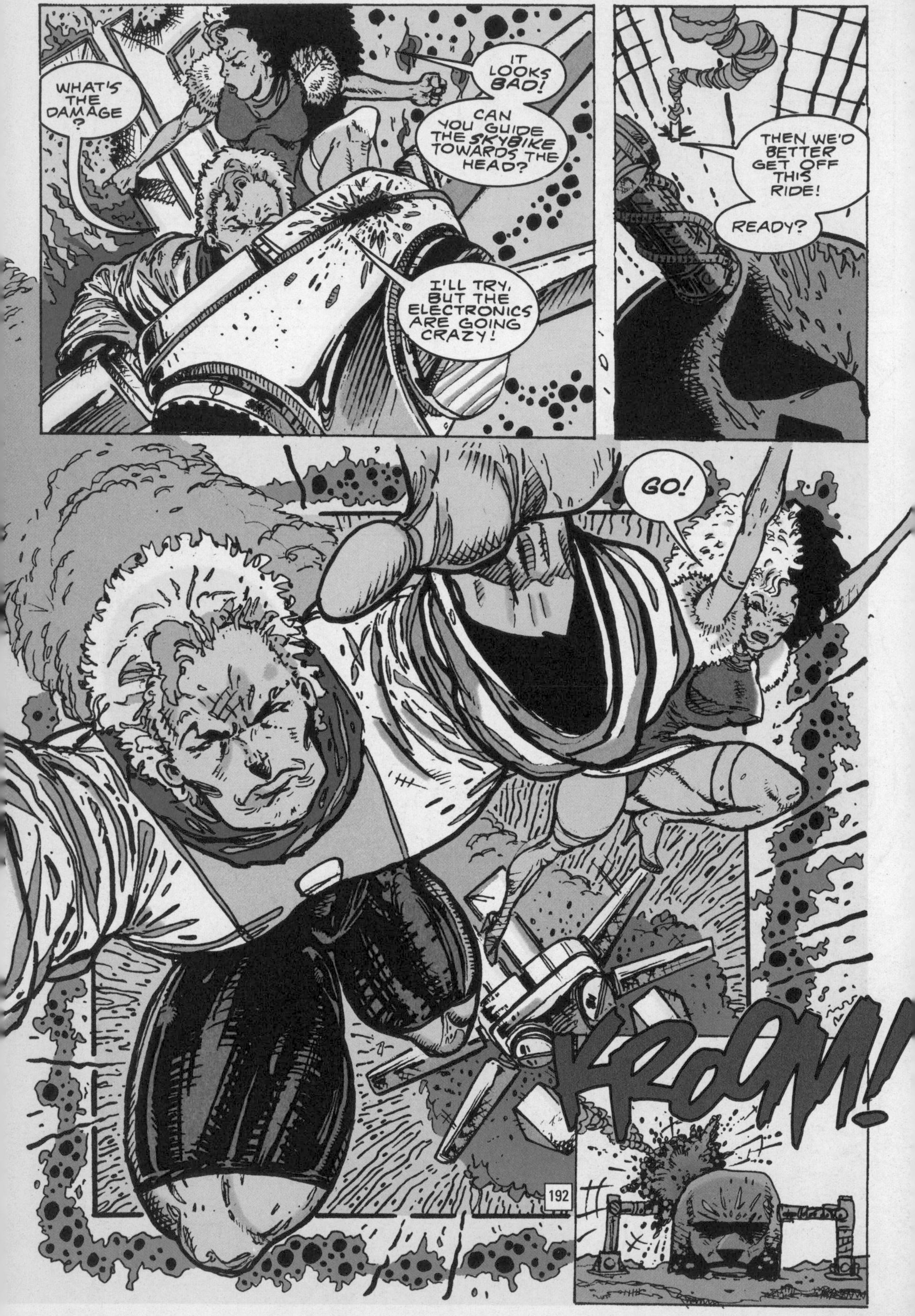
WHAT'S THE DAMAGE?
IT LOOKS BAD!
CAN YOU GUIDE THE SKYBIKE TOWARDS THE HEAD?
I'LL TRY, BUT THE ELECTRONICS ARE GOING CRAZY!
THEN WE'D BETTER GET OFF THIS RIDE!
READY?
GO!
KROOM!

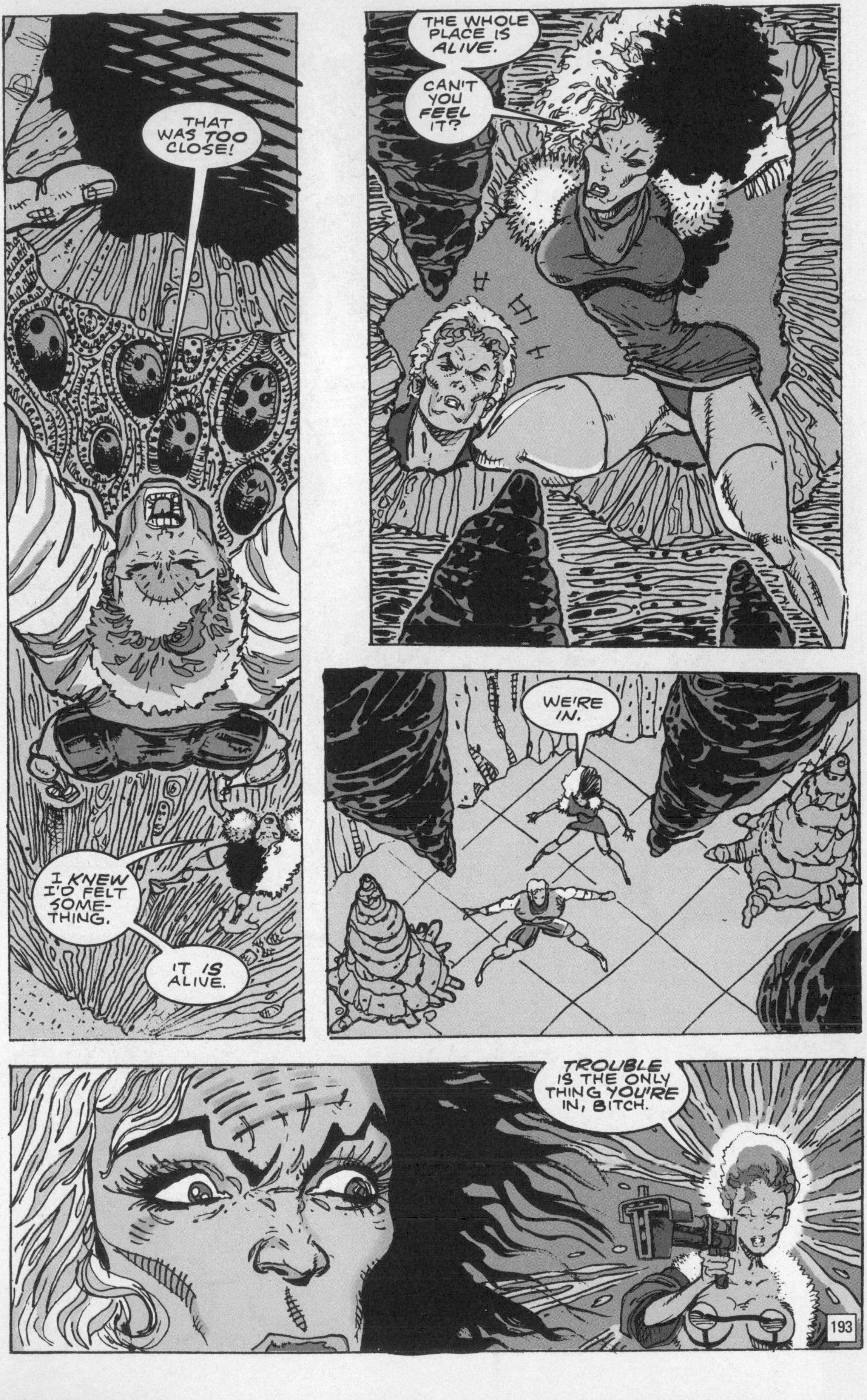
THAT WAS TOO CLOSE!
THE WHOLE PLACE IS ALIVE.
CAN'T YOU FEEL IT?
I KNEW I'D FELT SOME-THING.
IT IS ALIVE.
WE'RE IN.
TROUBLE IS THE ONLY THING YOU'RE IN, BITCH.

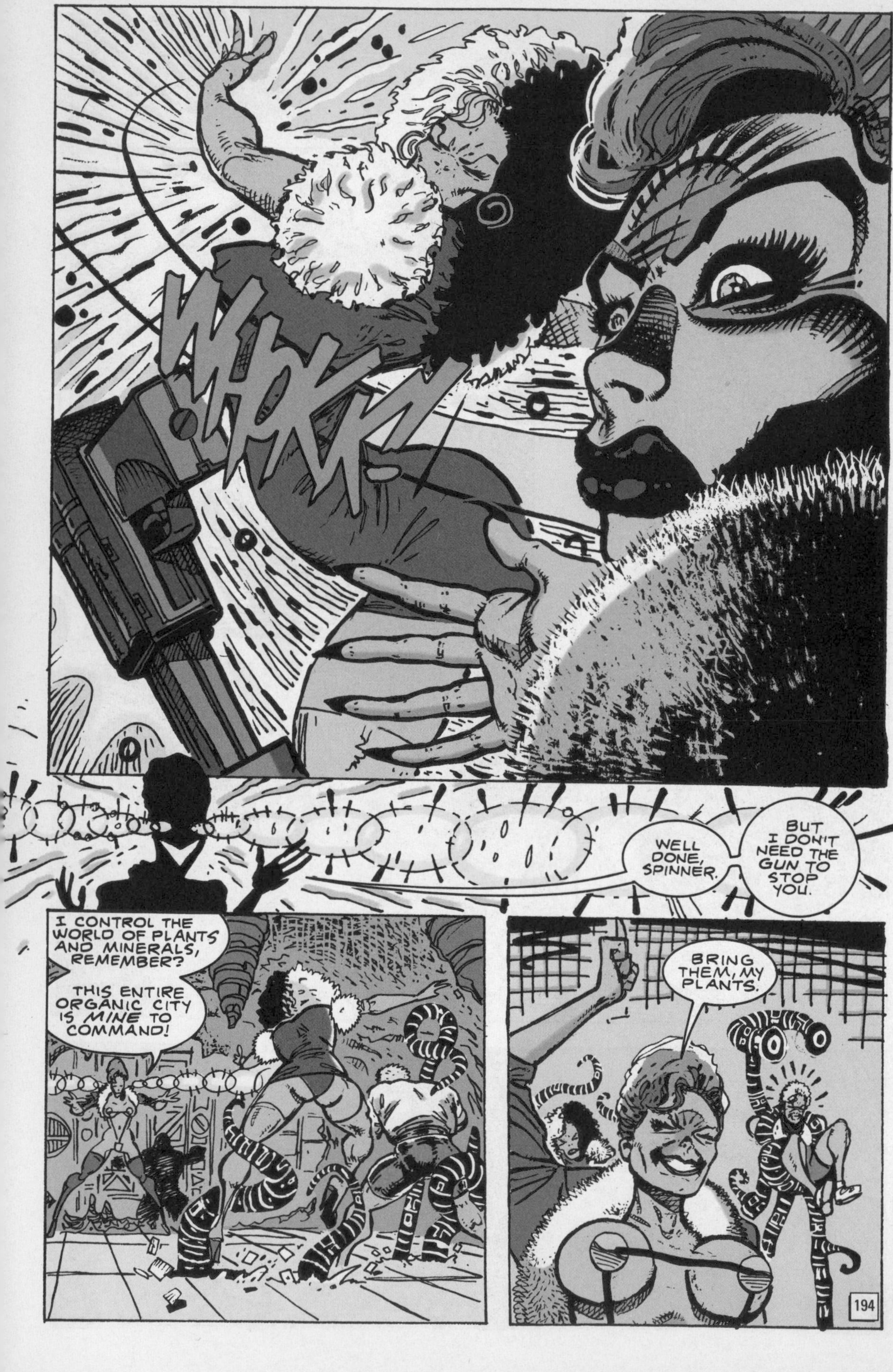
WHOOK
WELL DONE, SPINNER.
BUT I DON'T NEED THE GUN TO STOP YOU.
I CONTROL THE WORLD OF PLANTS AND MINERALS, REMEMBER?
THIS ENTIRE ORGANIC CITY IS *MINE* TO COMMAND!
BRING THEM, MY PLANTS.
194

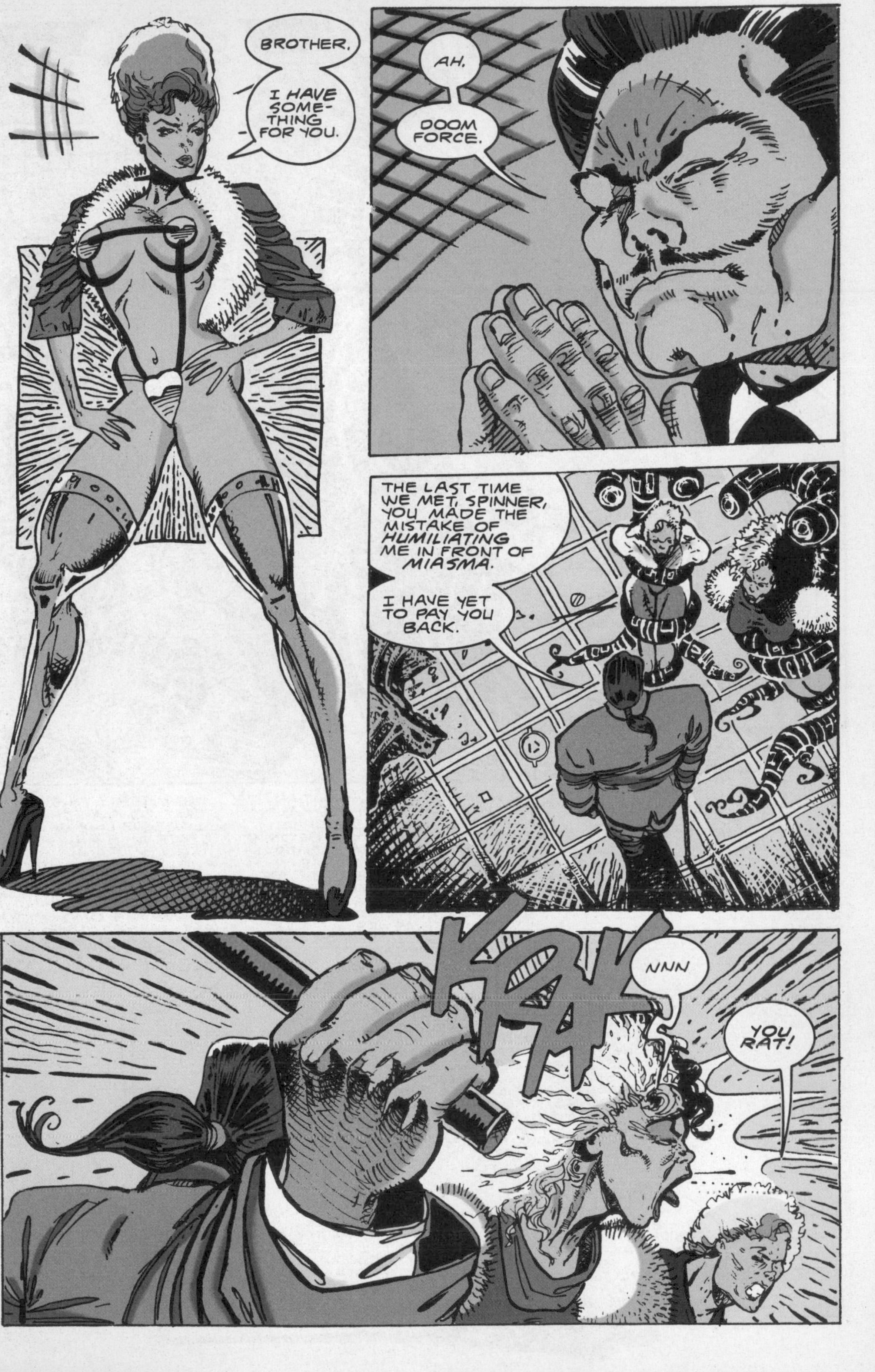
BROTHER.
I HAVE SOMETHING FOR YOU.
AH.
DOOM FORCE.
THE LAST TIME WE MET, SPINNER, YOU MADE THE MISTAKE OF HUMILIATING ME IN FRONT OF MIASMA.
I HAVE YET TO PAY YOU BACK.
KRAK
NNN
YOU RAT!

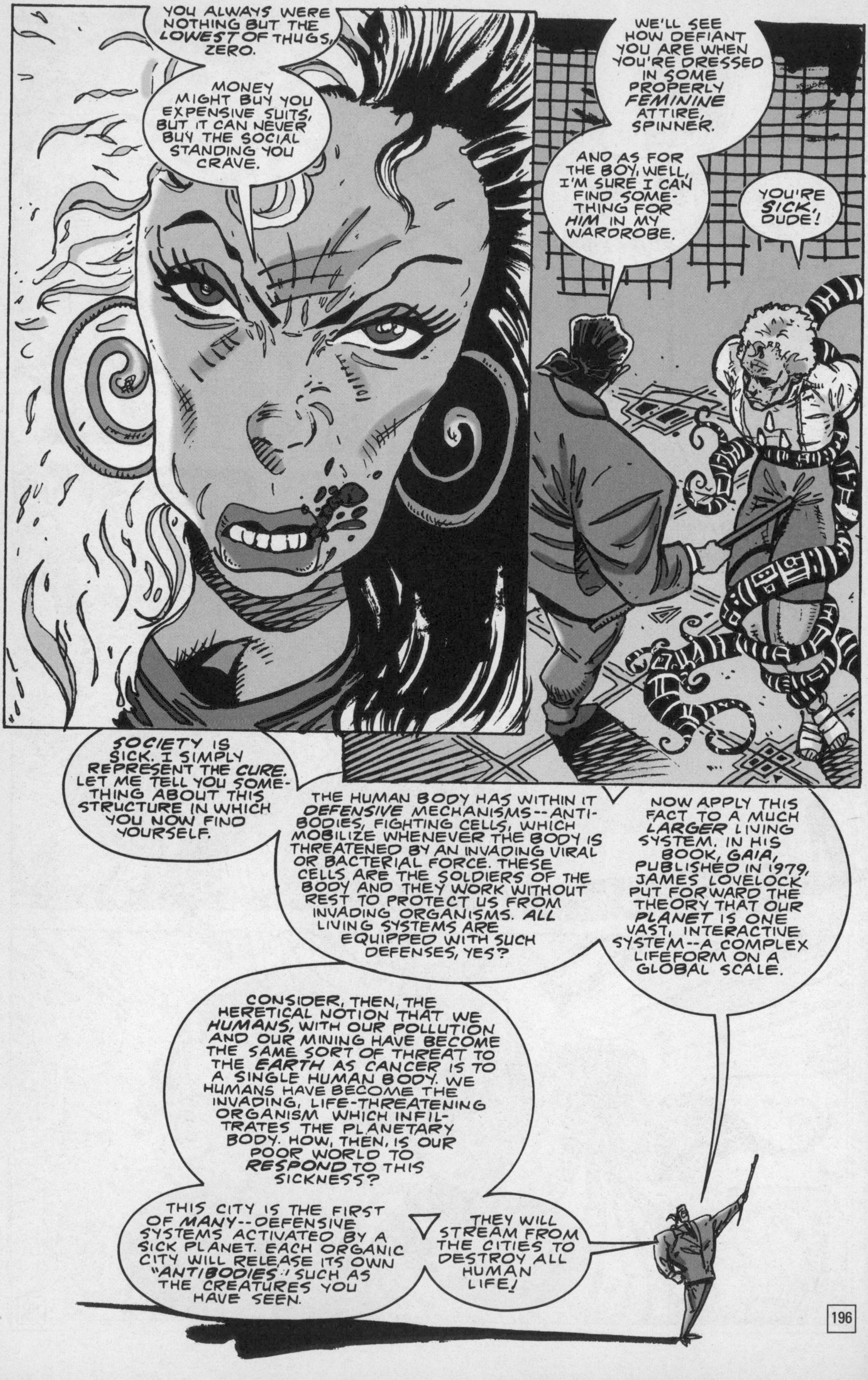
YOU ALWAYS WERE NOTHING BUT THE LOWEST OF THUGS, ZERO.
MONEY MIGHT BUY YOU EXPENSIVE SUITS, BUT IT CAN NEVER BUY THE SOCIAL STANDING YOU CRAVE.
WE'LL SEE HOW DEFIANT YOU ARE WHEN YOU'RE DRESSED IN SOME PROPERLY FEMININE ATTIRE, SPINNER.
AND AS FOR THE BOY, WELL, I'M SURE I CAN FIND SOME-THING FOR HIM IN MY WARDROBE.
YOU'RE SICK, DUDE!
SOCIETY IS SICK. I SIMPLY REPRESENT THE CURE. LET ME TELL YOU SOME-THING ABOUT THIS STRUCTURE IN WHICH YOU NOW FIND YOURSELF.
THE HUMAN BODY HAS WITHIN IT DEFENSIVE MECHANISMS--ANTI-BODIES, FIGHTING CELLS, WHICH MOBILIZE WHENEVER THE BODY IS THREATENED BY AN INVADING VIRAL OR BACTERIAL FORCE. THESE CELLS ARE THE SOLDIERS OF THE BODY AND THEY WORK WITHOUT REST TO PROTECT US FROM INVADING ORGANISMS. ALL LIVING SYSTEMS ARE EQUIPPED WITH SUCH DEFENSES, YES?
NOW APPLY THIS FACT TO A MUCH LARGER LIVING SYSTEM. IN HIS BOOK, GAIA, PUBLISHED IN 1979, JAMES LOVELOCK PUT FORWARD THE THEORY THAT OUR PLANET IS ONE VAST, INTERACTIVE SYSTEM--A COMPLEX LIFEFORM ON A GLOBAL SCALE.
CONSIDER, THEN, THE HERETICAL NOTION THAT WE HUMANS, WITH OUR POLLUTION AND OUR MINING HAVE BECOME THE SAME SORT OF THREAT TO THE EARTH AS CANCER IS TO A SINGLE HUMAN BODY. WE HUMANS HAVE BECOME THE INVADING, LIFE-THREATENING ORGANISM WHICH INFIL-TRATES THE PLANETARY BODY. HOW, THEN, IS OUR POOR WORLD TO RESPOND TO THIS SICKNESS?
THIS CITY IS THE FIRST OF MANY--DEFENSIVE SYSTEMS ACTIVATED BY A SICK PLANET. EACH ORGANIC CITY WILL RELEASE ITS OWN "ANTIBODIES," SUCH AS THE CREATURES YOU HAVE SEEN.
THEY WILL STREAM FROM THE CITIES TO DESTROY ALL HUMAN LIFE!

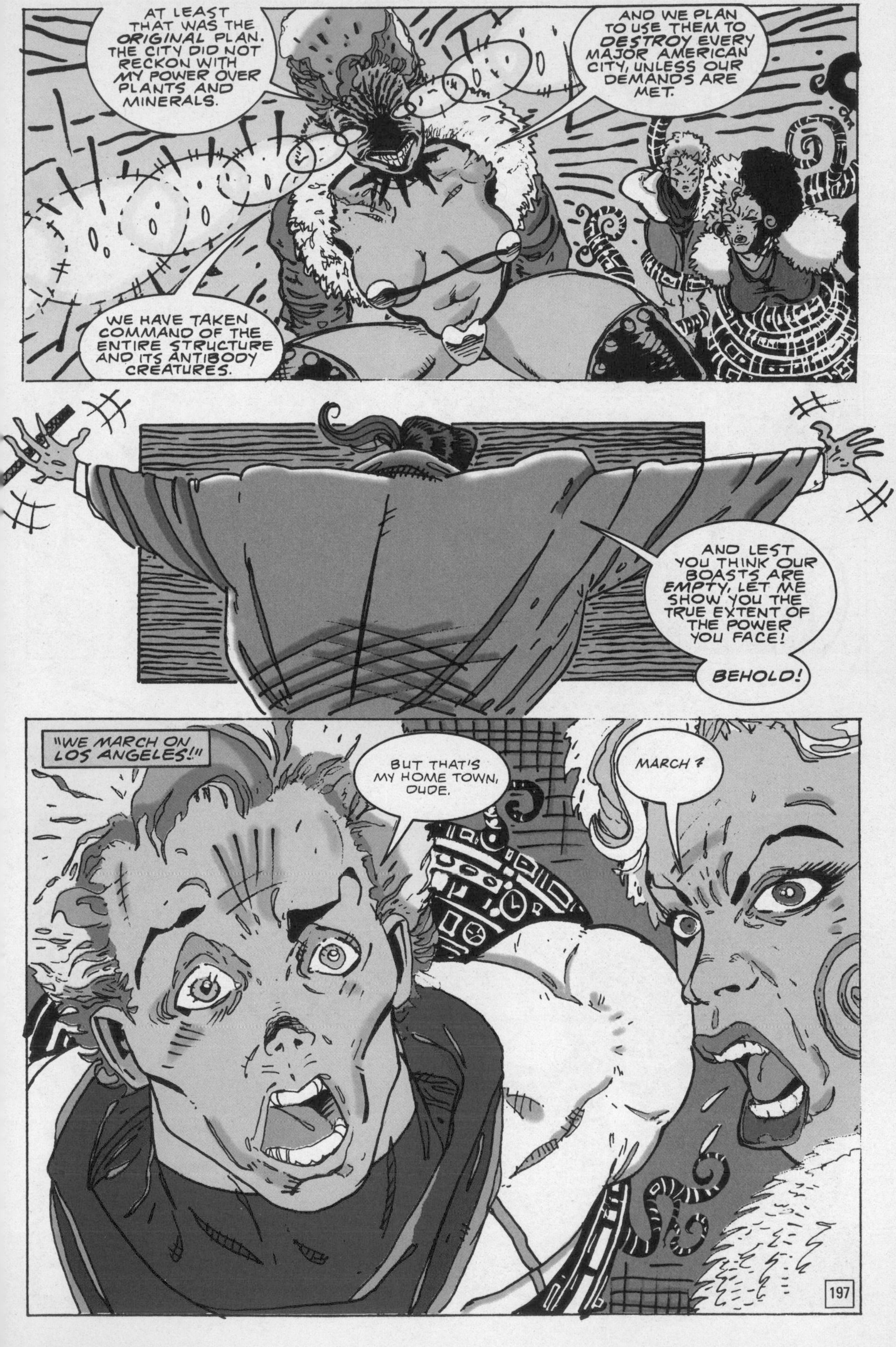
AT LEAST THAT WAS THE ORIGINAL PLAN. THE CITY DID NOT RECKON WITH MY POWER OVER PLANTS AND MINERALS.
WE HAVE TAKEN COMMAND OF THE ENTIRE STRUCTURE AND ITS ANTIBODY CREATURES.
AND WE PLAN TO USE THEM TO DESTROY EVERY MAJOR AMERICAN CITY, UNLESS OUR DEMANDS ARE MET.
AND LEST YOU THINK OUR BOASTS ARE EMPTY, LET ME SHOW YOU THE TRUE EXTENT OF THE POWER YOU FACE!
BEHOLD!
"WE MARCH ON LOS ANGELES!"
BUT THAT'S MY HOME TOWN, DUDE.
MARCH ?

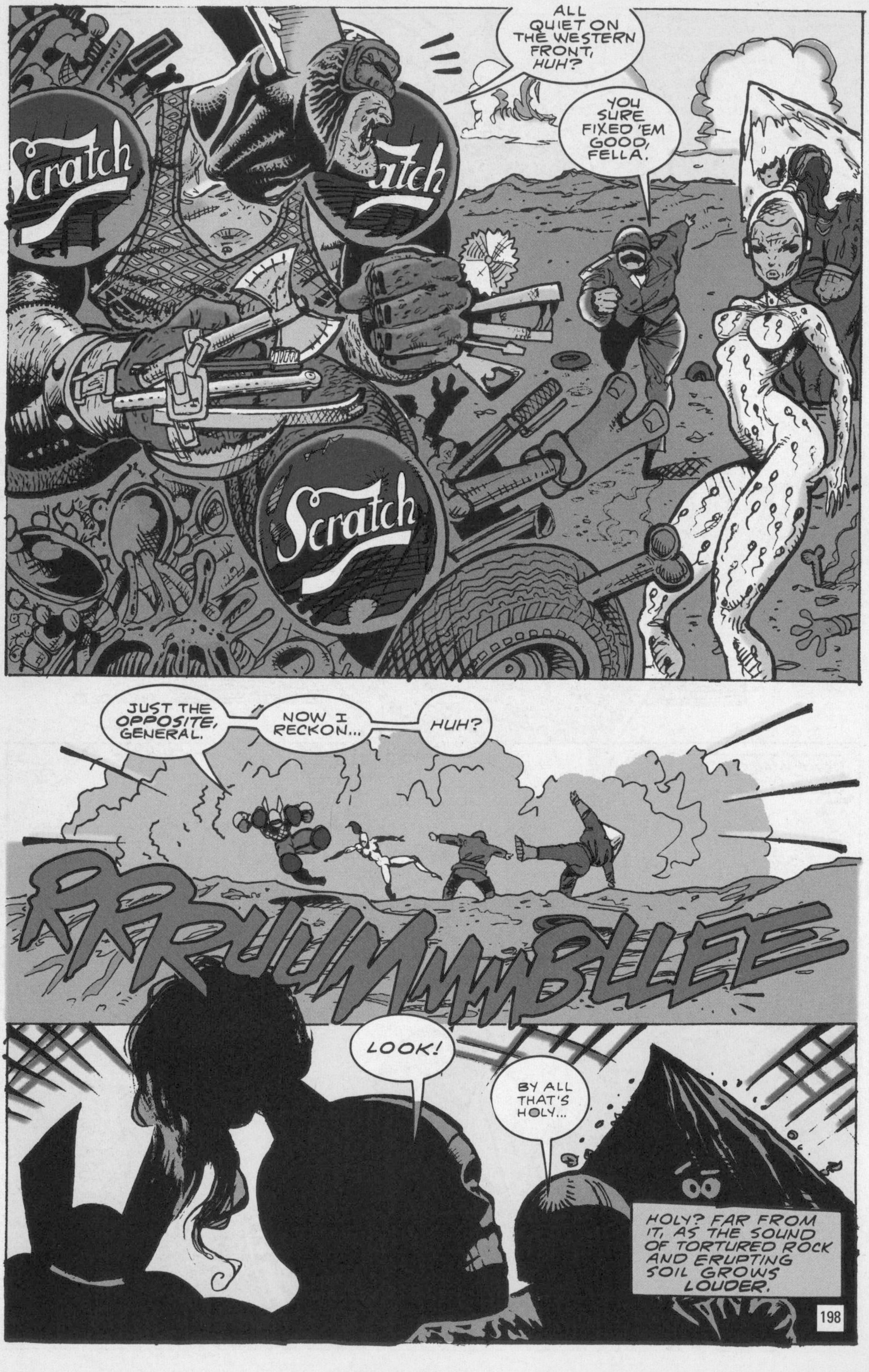
ALL QUIET ON THE WESTERN FRONT, HUH?
YOU SURE FIXED 'EM GOOD, FELLA.
Scratch
Scratch
Scratch
JUST THE OPPOSITE, GENERAL.
NOW I RECKON...
HUH?
RRRUUMMMMBLLEE
LOOK!
BY ALL THAT'S HOLY...
HOLY? FAR FROM IT, AS THE SOUND OF TORTURED ROCK AND ERUPTING SOIL GROWS LOUDER.

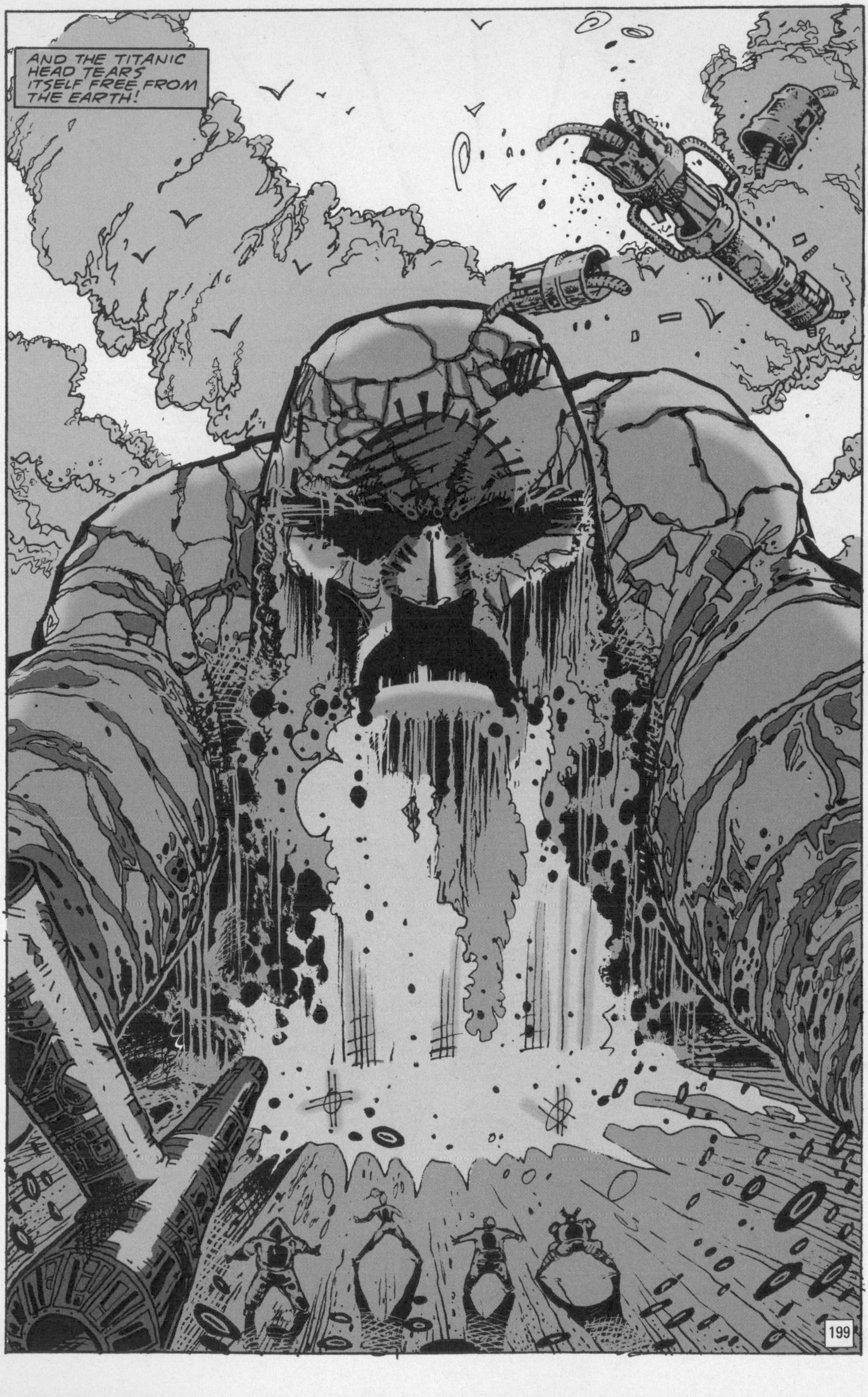
AND THE TITANIC HEAD TEARS ITSELF FREE FROM THE EARTH!

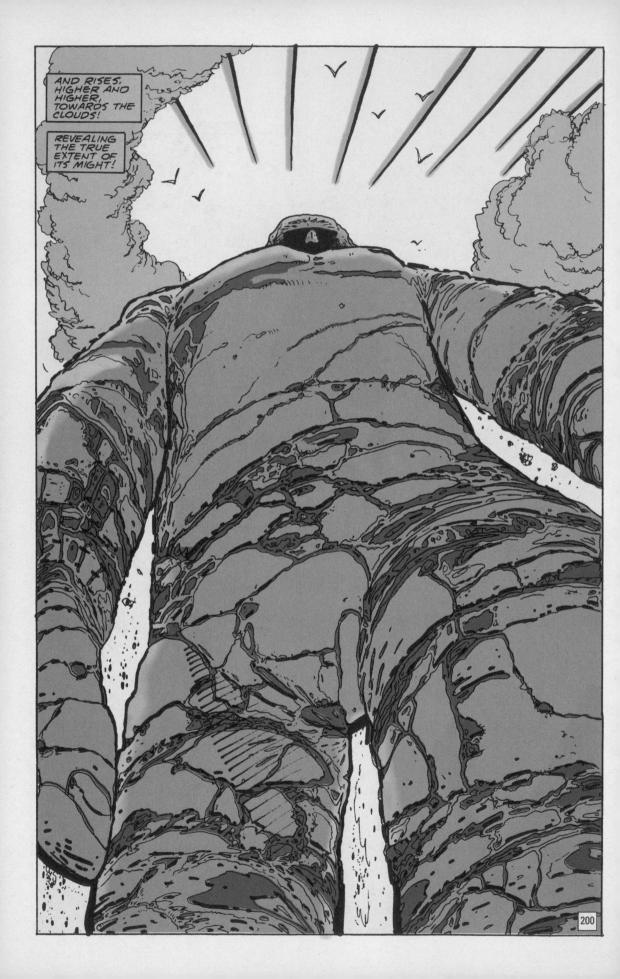

AND RISES, HIGHER AND HIGHER, TOWARDS THE CLOUDS!

REVEALING THE TRUE EXTENT OF ITS MIGHT!

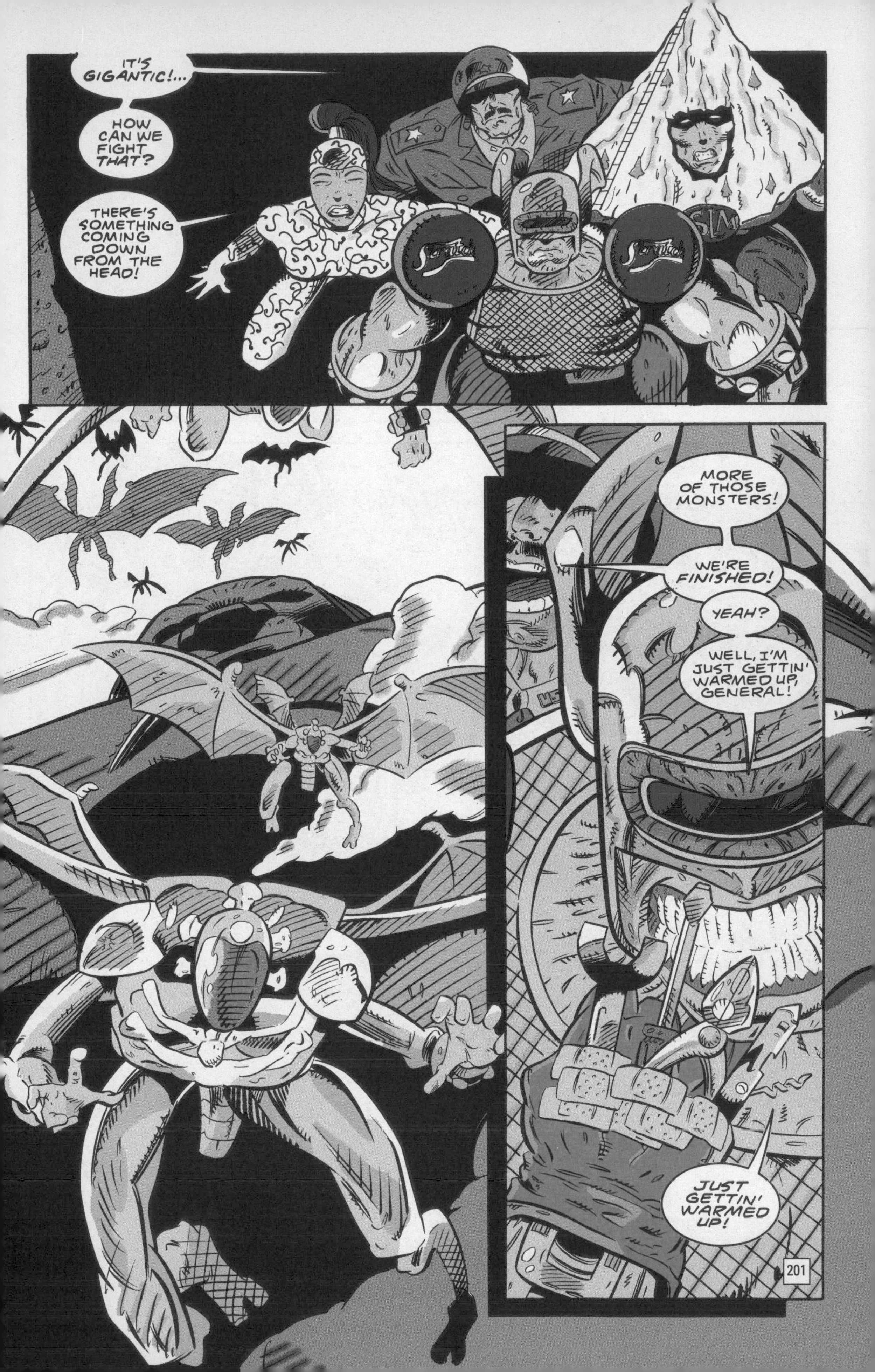
IT'S GIGANTIC!...
HOW CAN WE FIGHT THAT?
THERE'S SOMETHING COMING DOWN FROM THE HEAD!
MORE OF THOSE MONSTERS!
WE'RE FINISHED!
YEAH?
WELL, I'M JUST GETTIN' WARMED UP, GENERAL!
JUST GETTIN' WARMED UP!

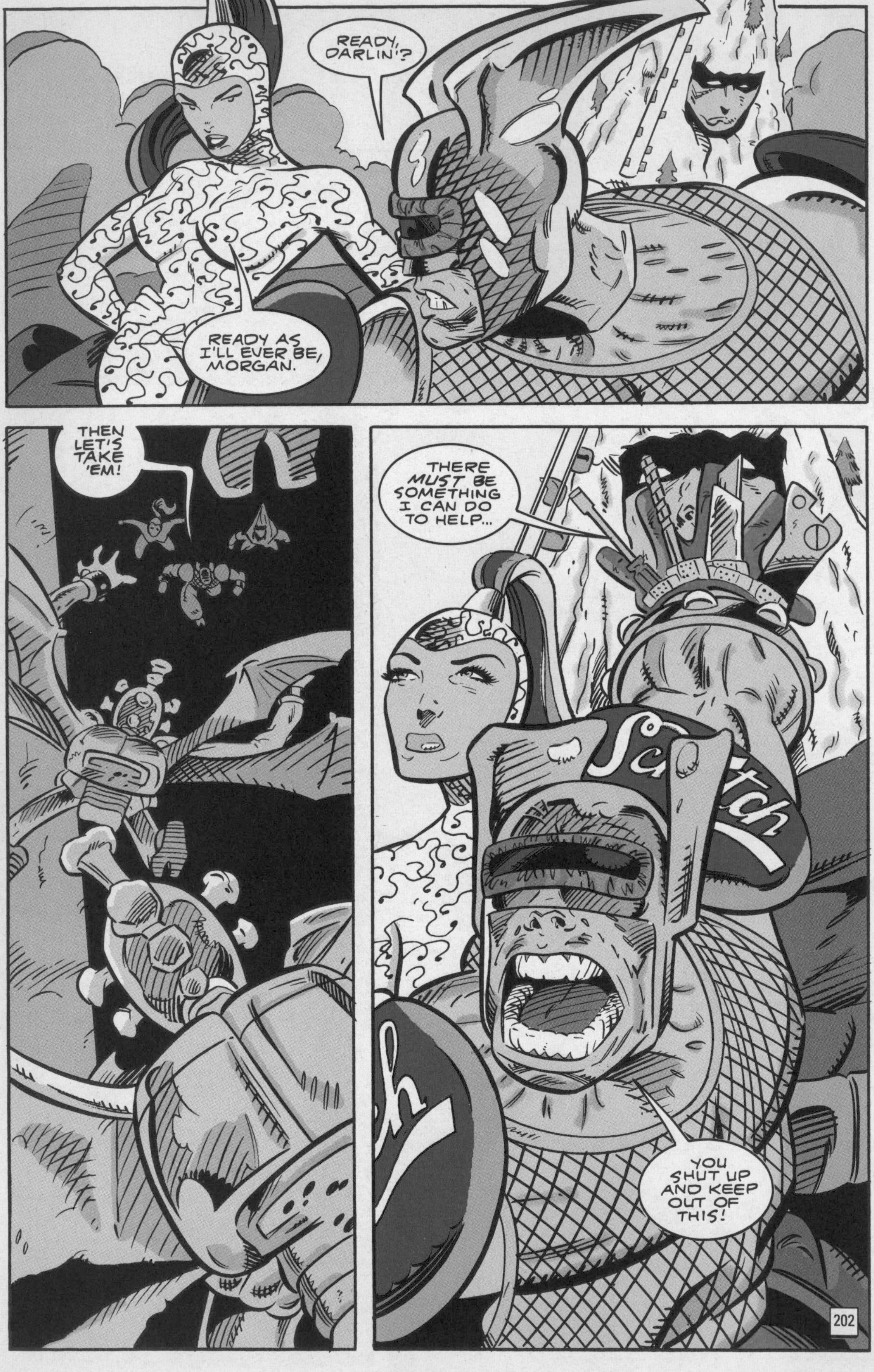
READY, DARLIN'?
READY AS I'LL EVER BE, MORGAN.
THEN LET'S TAKE 'EM!
THERE MUST BE SOMETHING I CAN DO TO HELP...
YOU SHUT UP AND KEEP OUT OF THIS!

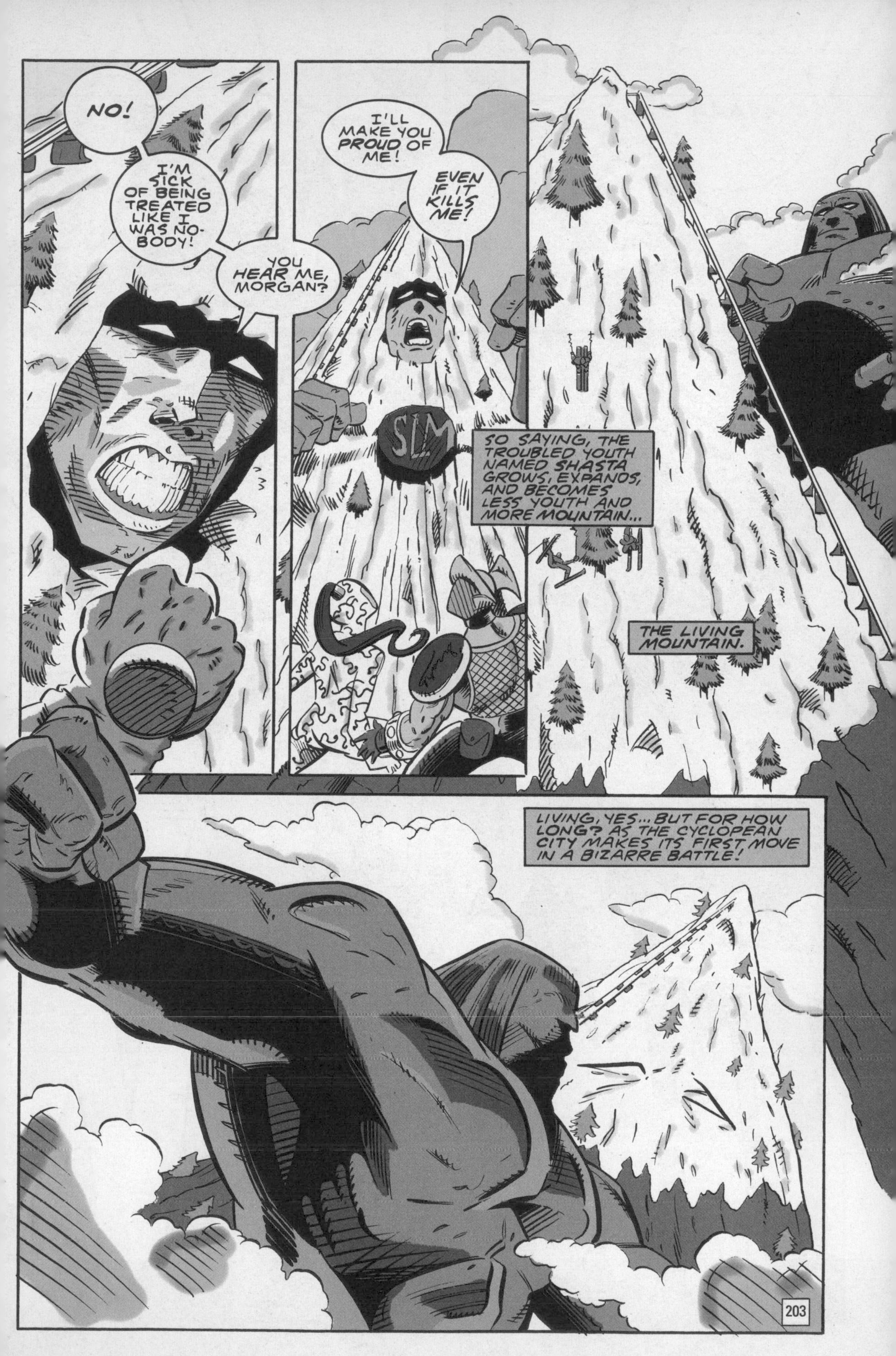

NO!
I'M SICK OF BEING TREATED LIKE I WAS NO-BODY!
YOU HEAR ME, MORGAN?
I'LL MAKE YOU PROUD OF ME!
EVEN IF IT KILLS ME!
SLM
SO SAYING, THE TROUBLED YOUTH NAMED SHASTA GROWS, EXPANDS, AND BECOMES LESS YOUTH AND MORE MOUNTAIN...
THE LIVING MOUNTAIN.
LIVING, YES... BUT FOR HOW LONG? AS THE CYCLOPEAN CITY MAKES ITS FIRST MOVE IN A BIZARRE BATTLE!

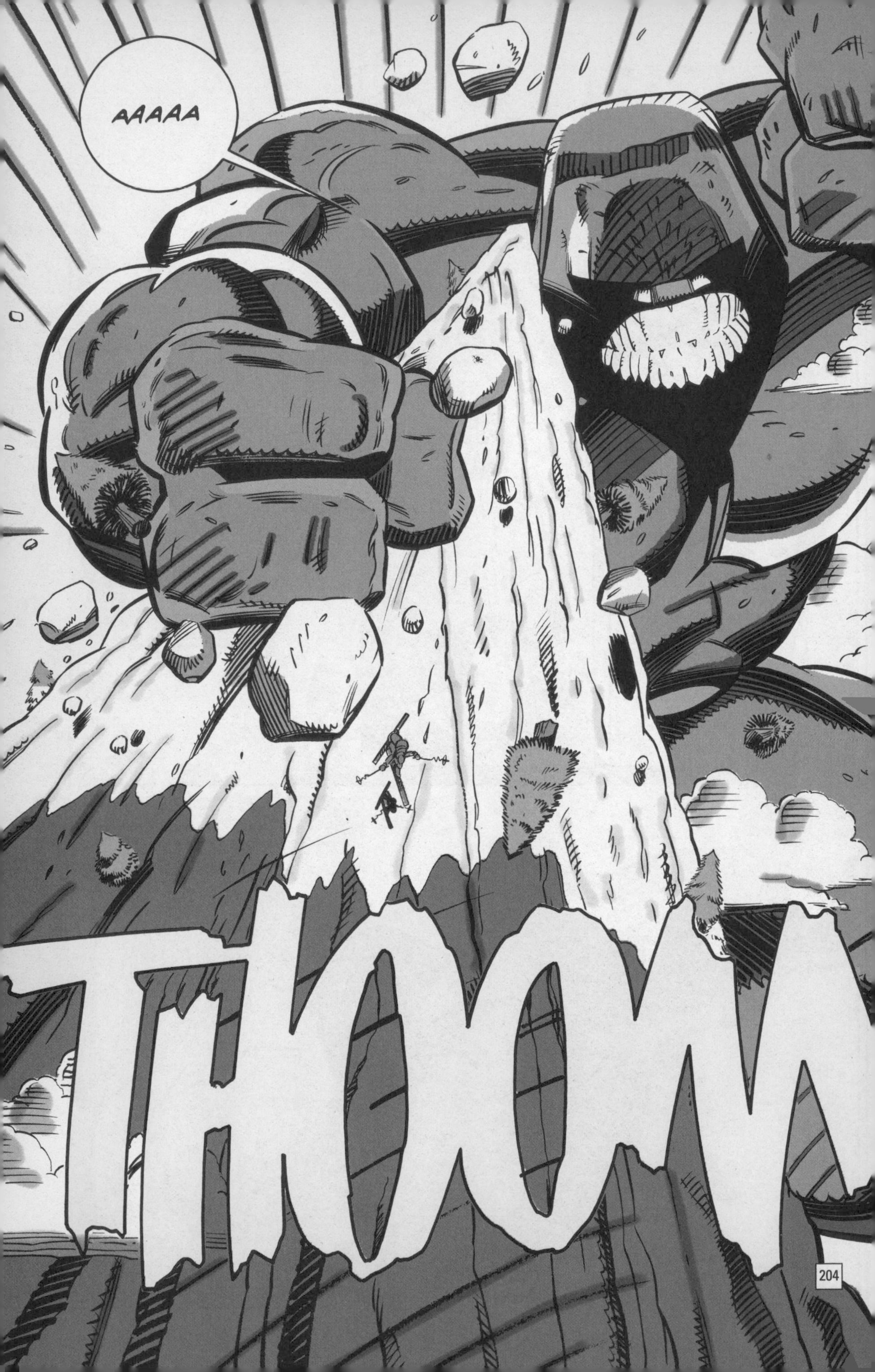
AAAAA
THOOM

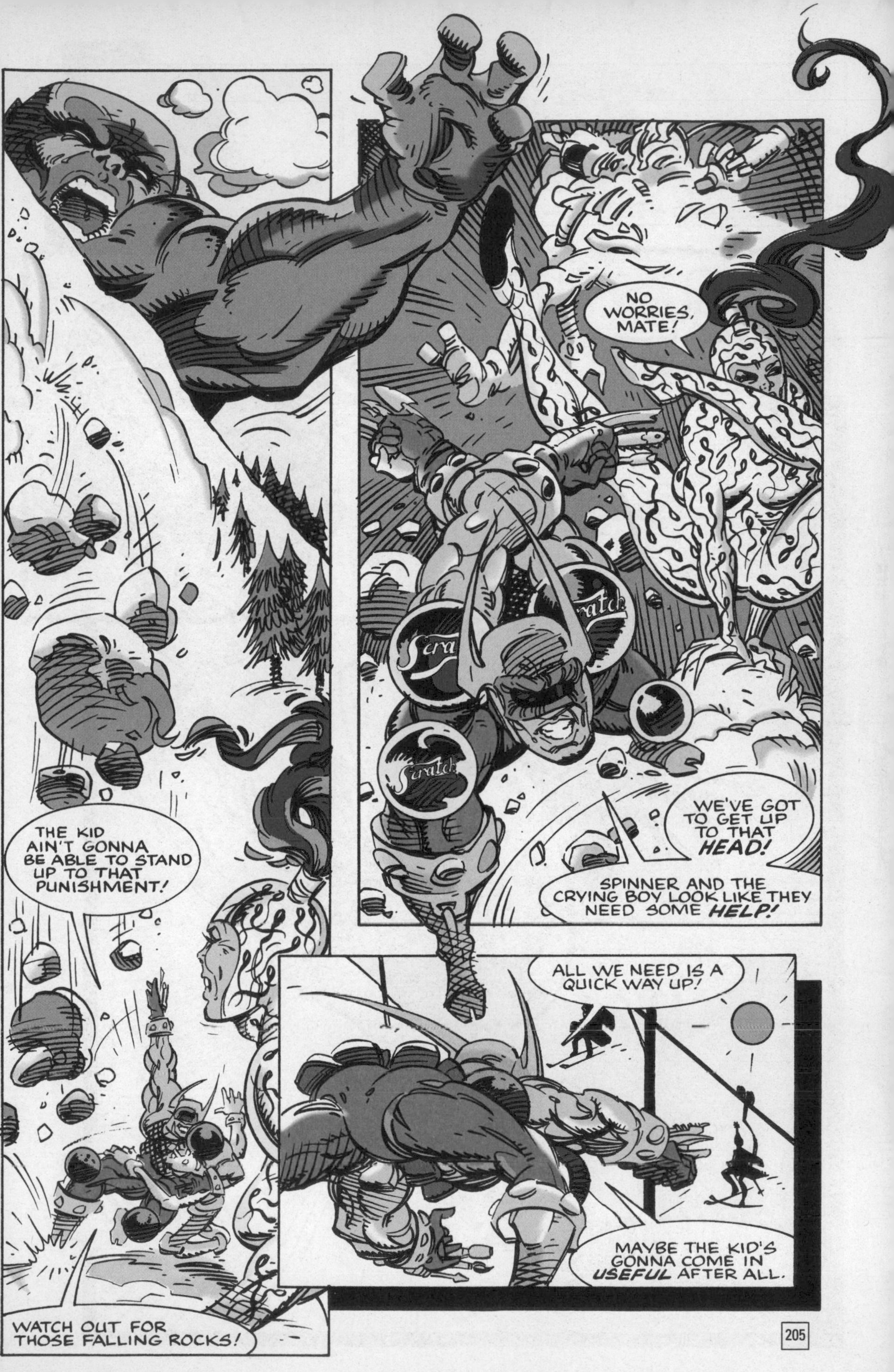
NO WORRIES, MATE!
WE'VE GOT TO GET UP TO THAT HEAD!
SPINNER AND THE CRYING BOY LOOK LIKE THEY NEED SOME HELP!
THE KID AIN'T GONNA BE ABLE TO STAND UP TO THAT PUNISHMENT!
WATCH OUT FOR THOSE FALLING ROCKS!
ALL WE NEED IS A QUICK WAY UP!
MAYBE THE KID'S GONNA COME IN USEFUL AFTER ALL.

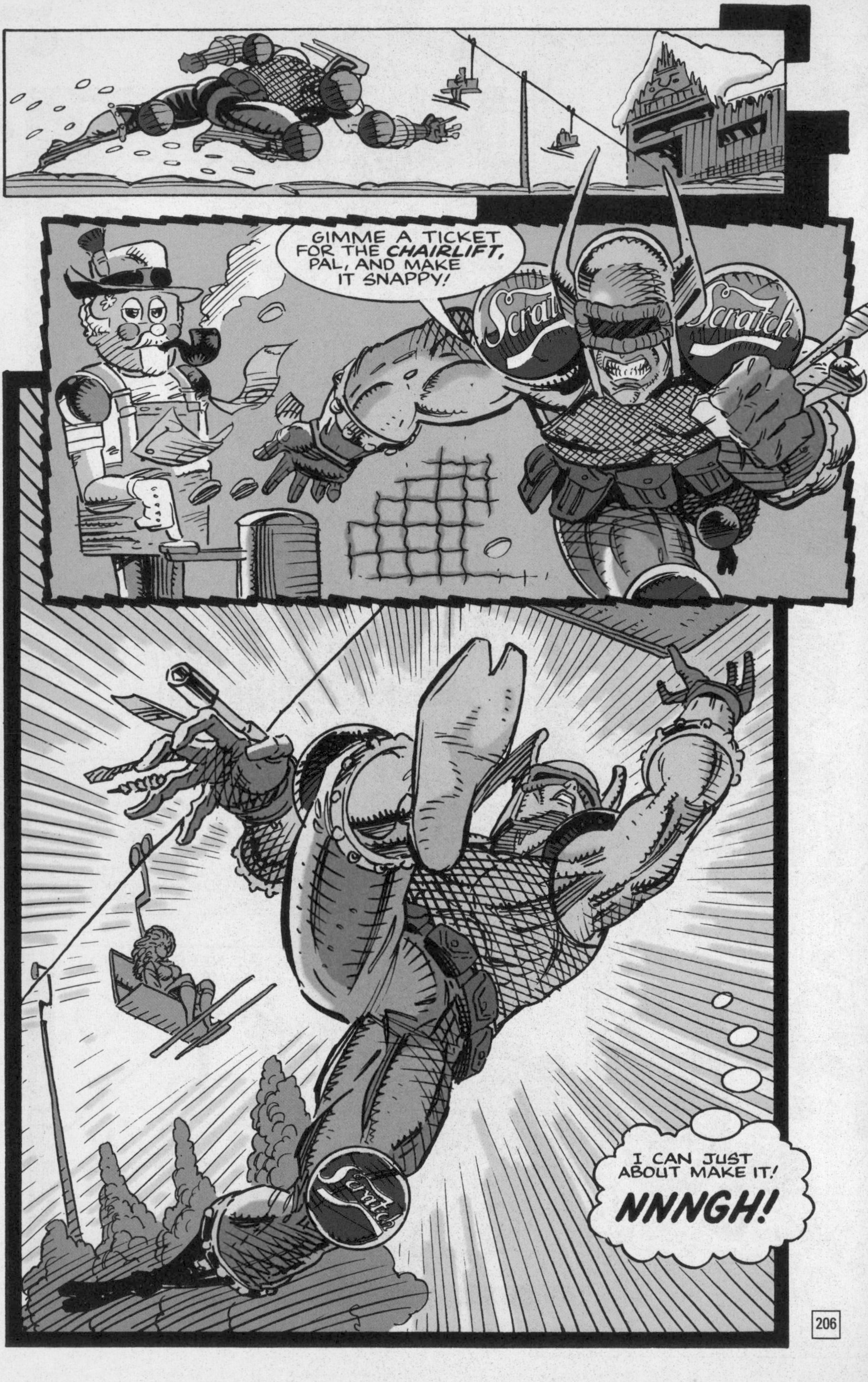
GIMME A TICKET FOR THE CHAIRLIFT, PAL, AND MAKE IT SNAPPY!
Scratch
Scratch
Scratch
I CAN JUST ABOUT MAKE IT!
NNNGH!

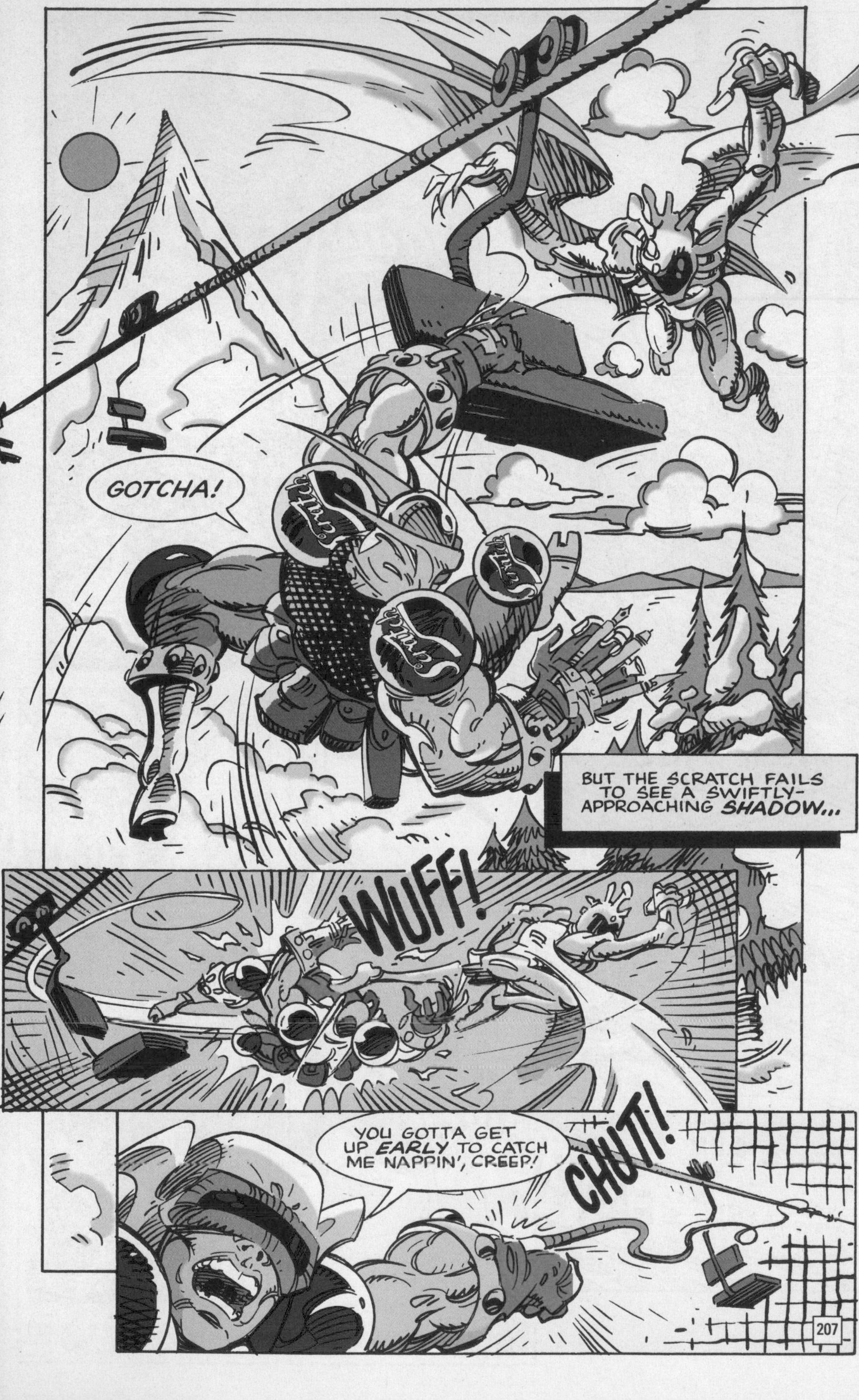
GOTCHA!
BUT THE SCRATCH FAILS TO SEE A SWIFTLY-APPROACHING SHADOW...
WUFF!
YOU GOTTA GET UP EARLY TO CATCH ME NAPPIN', CREEP!
CHUT!

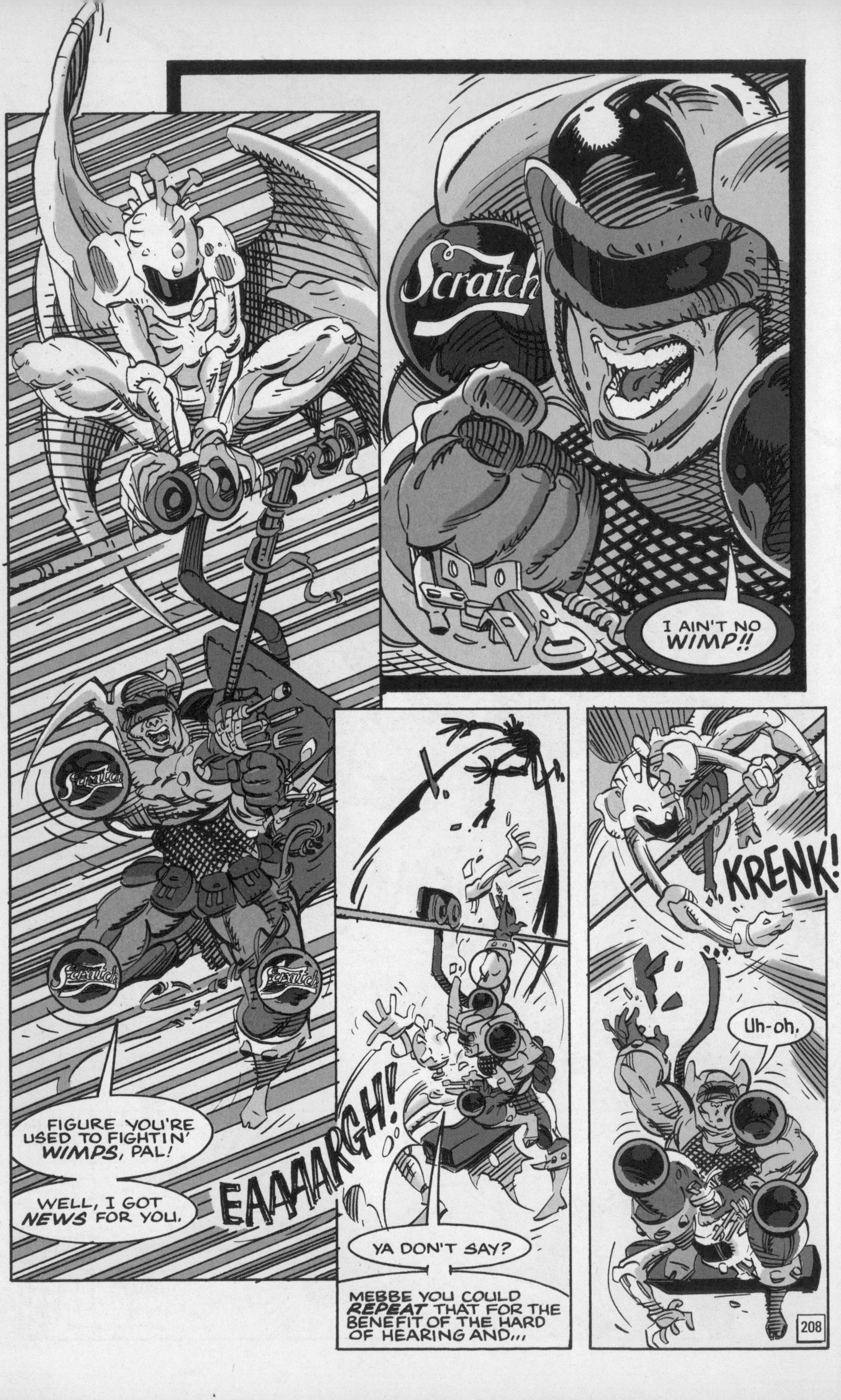
Scratch
I AIN'T NO WIMP!!
FIGURE YOU'RE USED TO FIGHTIN' WIMPS, PAL!
WELL, I GOT NEWS FOR YOU.
EAAAARGH!
YA DON'T SAY?
MEBBE YOU COULD REPEAT THAT FOR THE BENEFIT OF THE HARD OF HEARING AND...
KRENK!
Uh-oh.

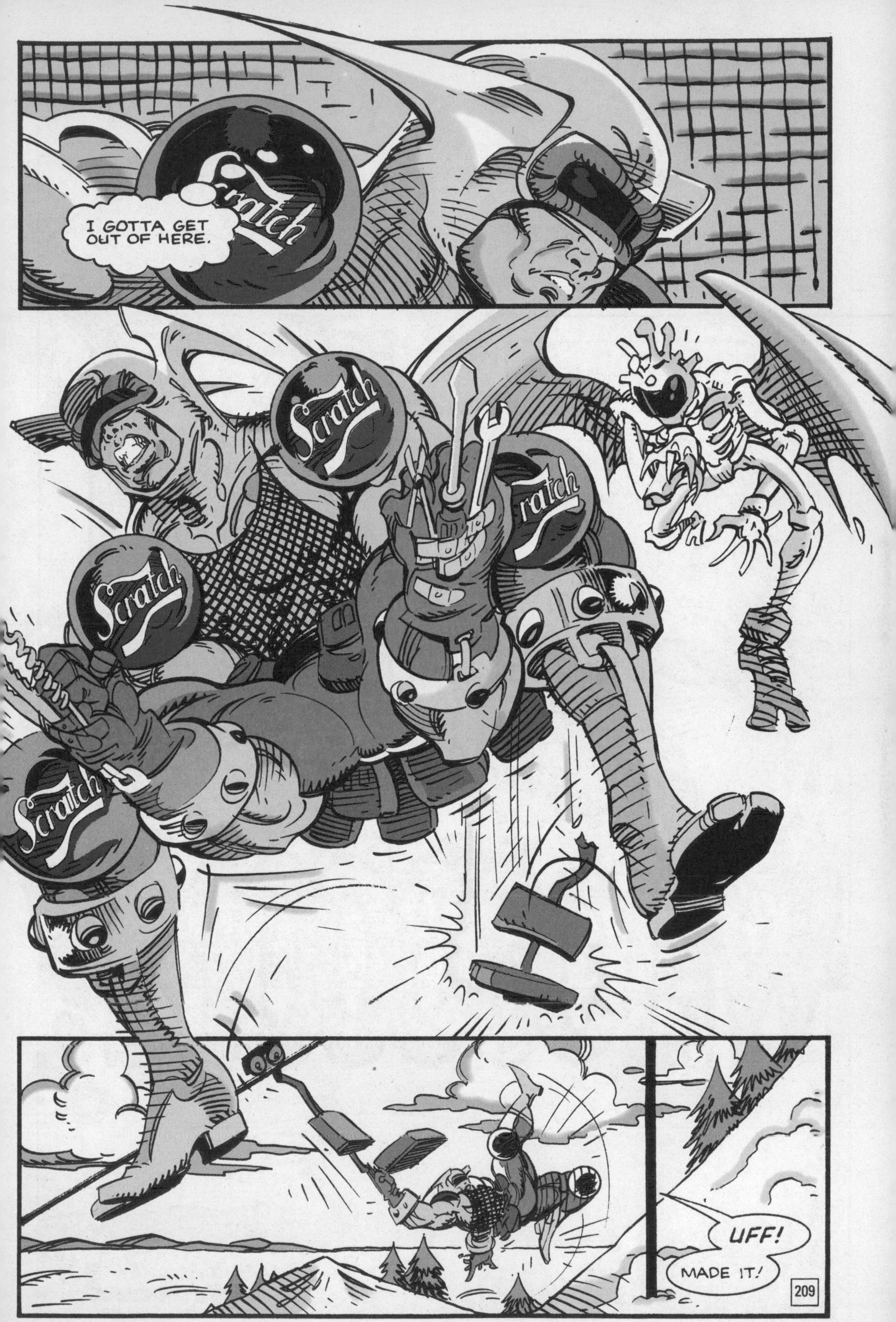
I GOTTA GET OUT OF HERE.
Scratch
UFF!
MADE IT!

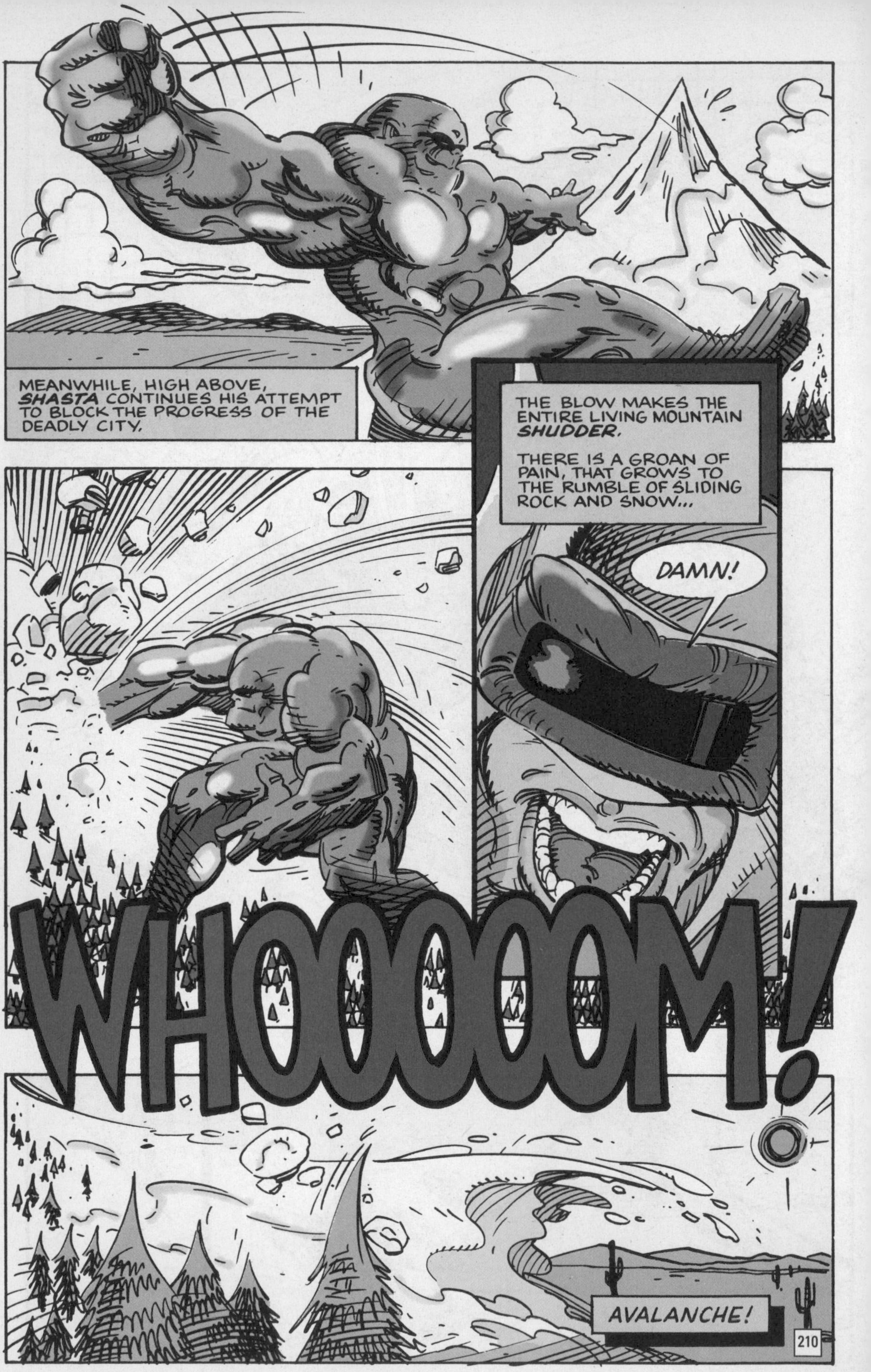
MEANWHILE, HIGH ABOVE, SHASTA CONTINUES HIS ATTEMPT TO BLOCK THE PROGRESS OF THE DEADLY CITY.
THE BLOW MAKES THE ENTIRE LIVING MOUNTAIN SHUDDER.
THERE IS A GROAN OF PAIN, THAT GROWS TO THE RUMBLE OF SLIDING ROCK AND SNOW...
DAMN!
WHOOOOOM!
AVALANCHE!

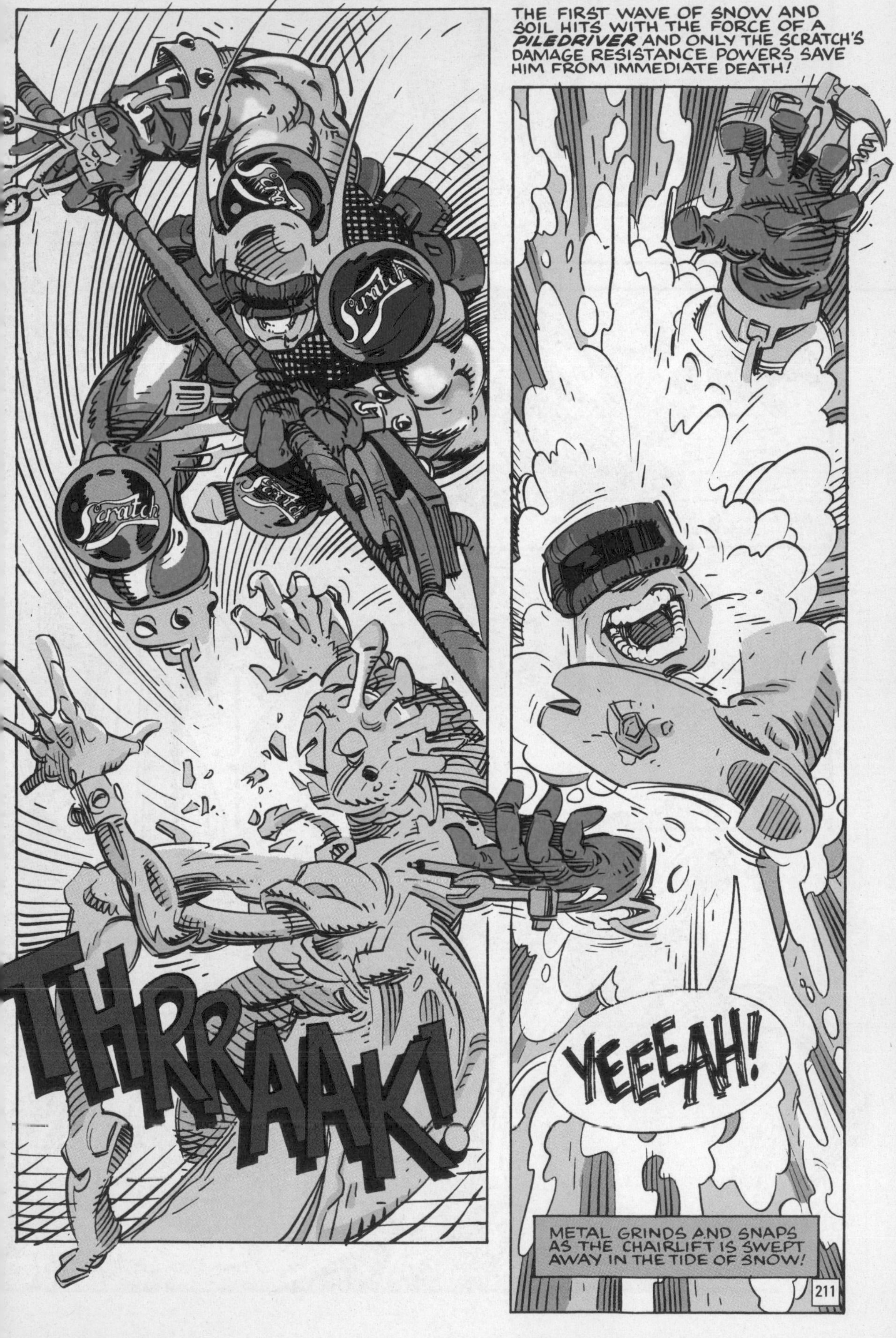

THE FIRST WAVE OF SNOW AND SOIL HITS WITH THE FORCE OF A *PILEDRIVER* AND ONLY THE SCRATCH'S DAMAGE RESISTANCE POWERS SAVE HIM FROM IMMEDIATE DEATH!
Scratch
Scratch
Scratch
THRRAAAK!
YEEEAH!
METAL GRINDS AND SNAPS AS THE CHAIRLIFT IS SWEPT AWAY IN THE TIDE OF SNOW!

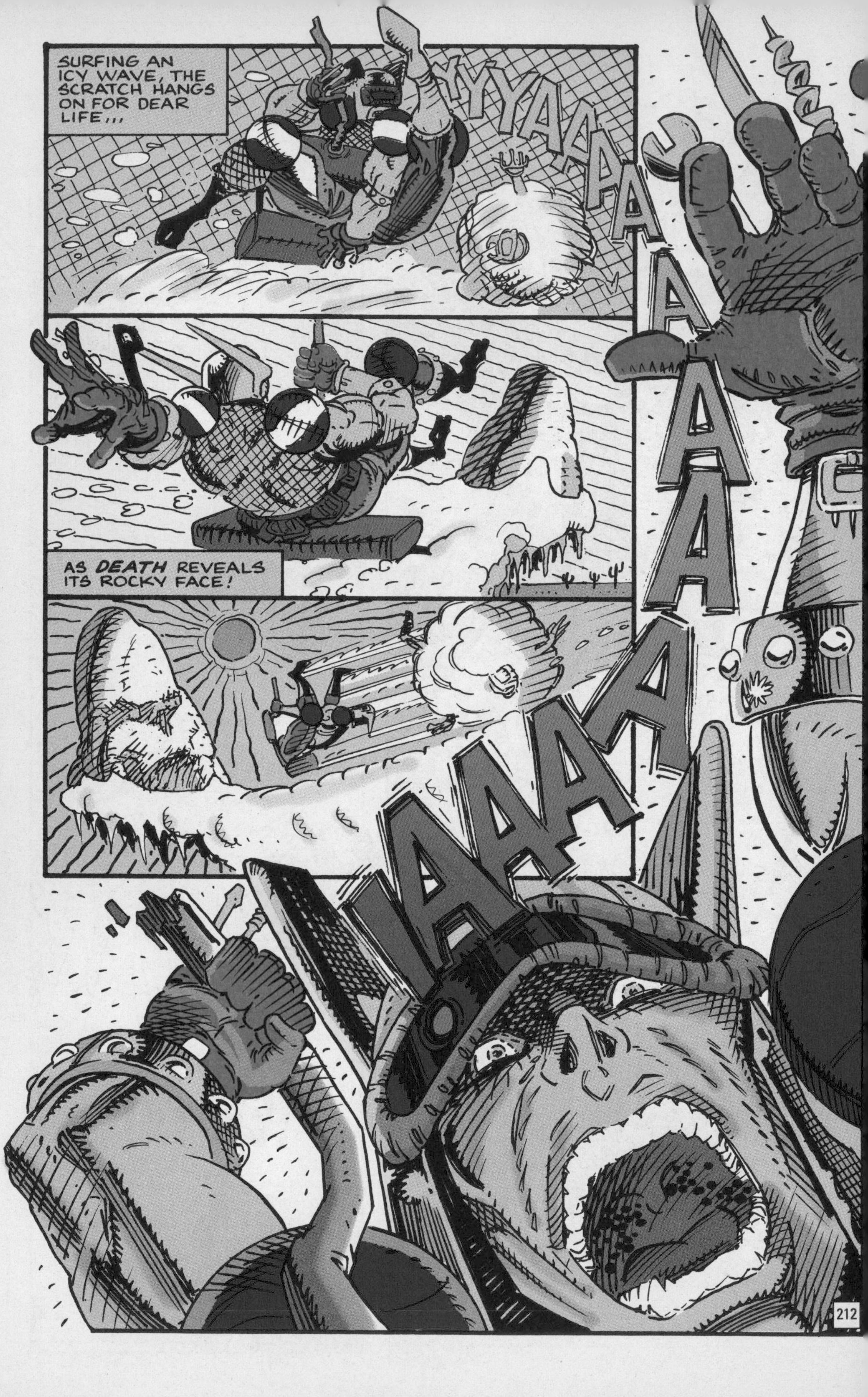

SURFING AN ICY WAVE, THE SCRATCH HANGS ON FOR DEAR LIFE...
YYYAAAAAAAAAAAAAAAAA
AS *DEATH* REVEALS ITS ROCKY FACE!

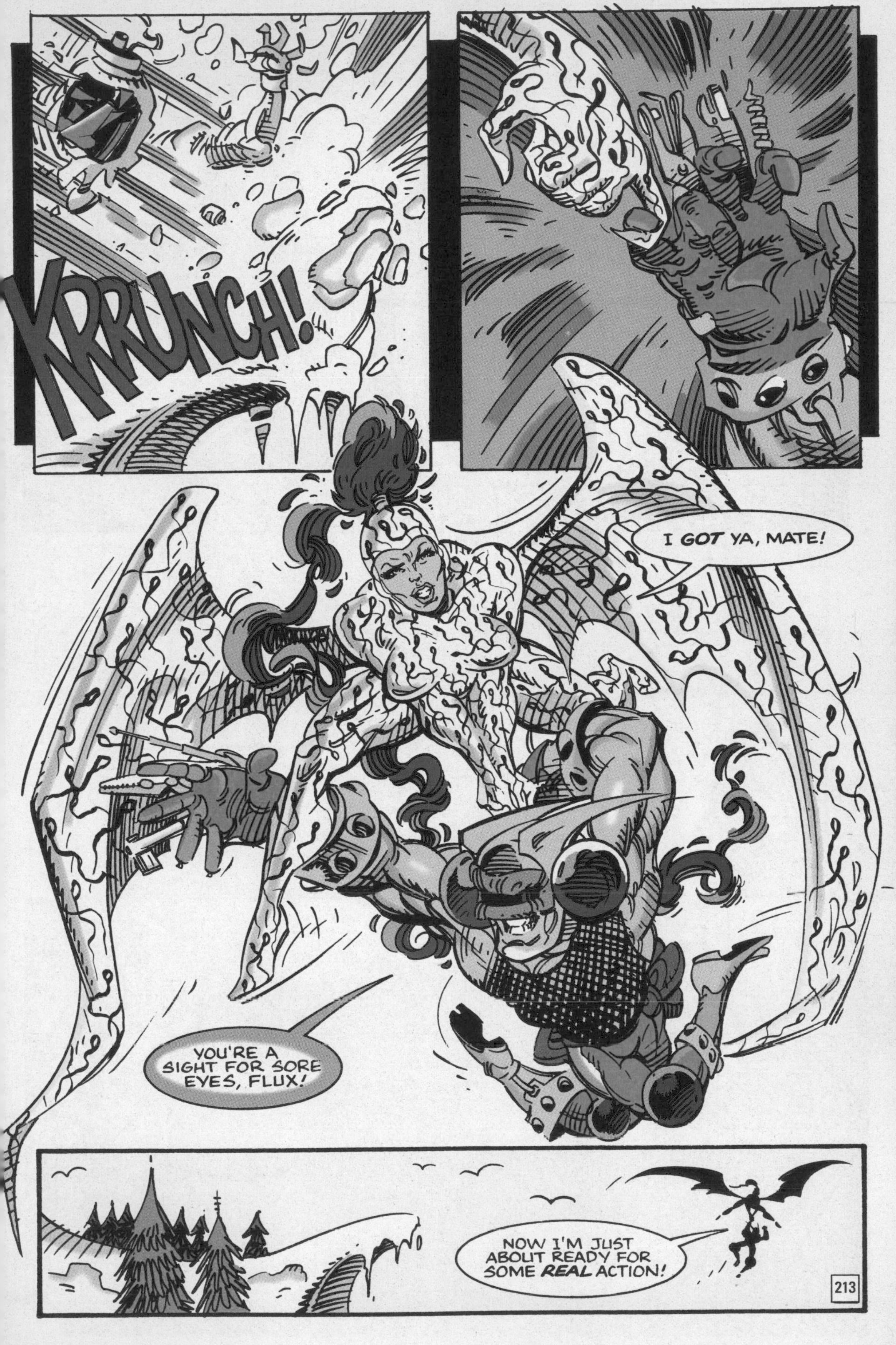
KRRUNCH!
I GOT YA, MATE!
YOU'RE A SIGHT FOR SORE EYES, FLUX!
NOW I'M JUST ABOUT READY FOR SOME REAL ACTION!

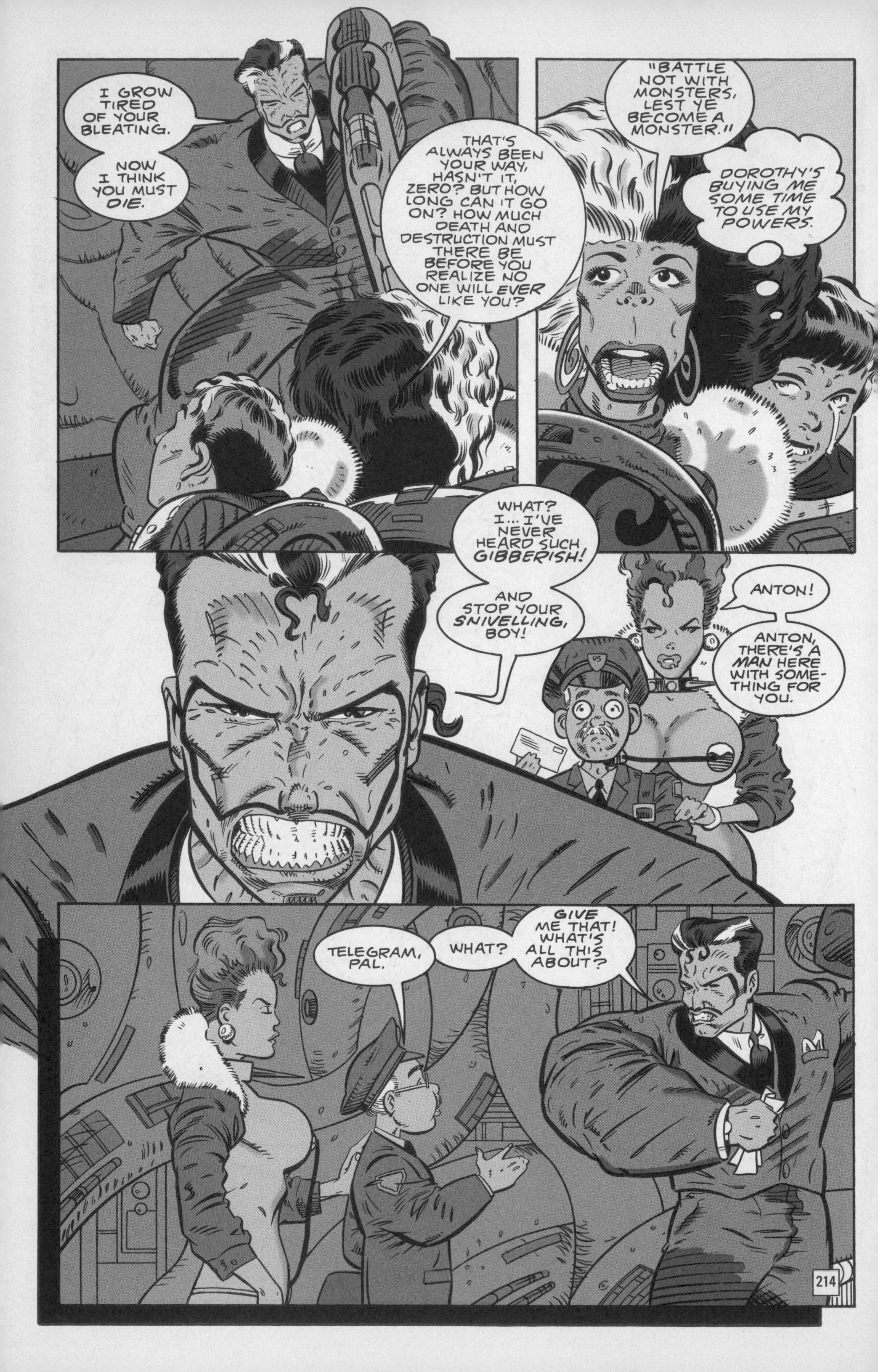
I GROW TIRED OF YOUR BLEATING.
NOW I THINK YOU MUST DIE.
THAT'S ALWAYS BEEN YOUR WAY, HASN'T IT, ZERO? BUT HOW LONG CAN IT GO ON? HOW MUCH DEATH AND DESTRUCTION MUST THERE BE BEFORE YOU REALIZE NO ONE WILL EVER LIKE YOU?
"BATTLE NOT WITH MONSTERS, LEST YE BECOME A MONSTER."
DOROTHY'S BUYING ME SOME TIME TO USE MY POWERS.
WHAT? I... I'VE NEVER HEARD SUCH GIBBERISH!
AND STOP YOUR SNIVELLING, BOY!
ANTON!
ANTON, THERE'S A MAN HERE WITH SOMETHING FOR YOU.
TELEGRAM, PAL.
WHAT?
GIVE ME THAT! WHAT'S ALL THIS ABOUT?

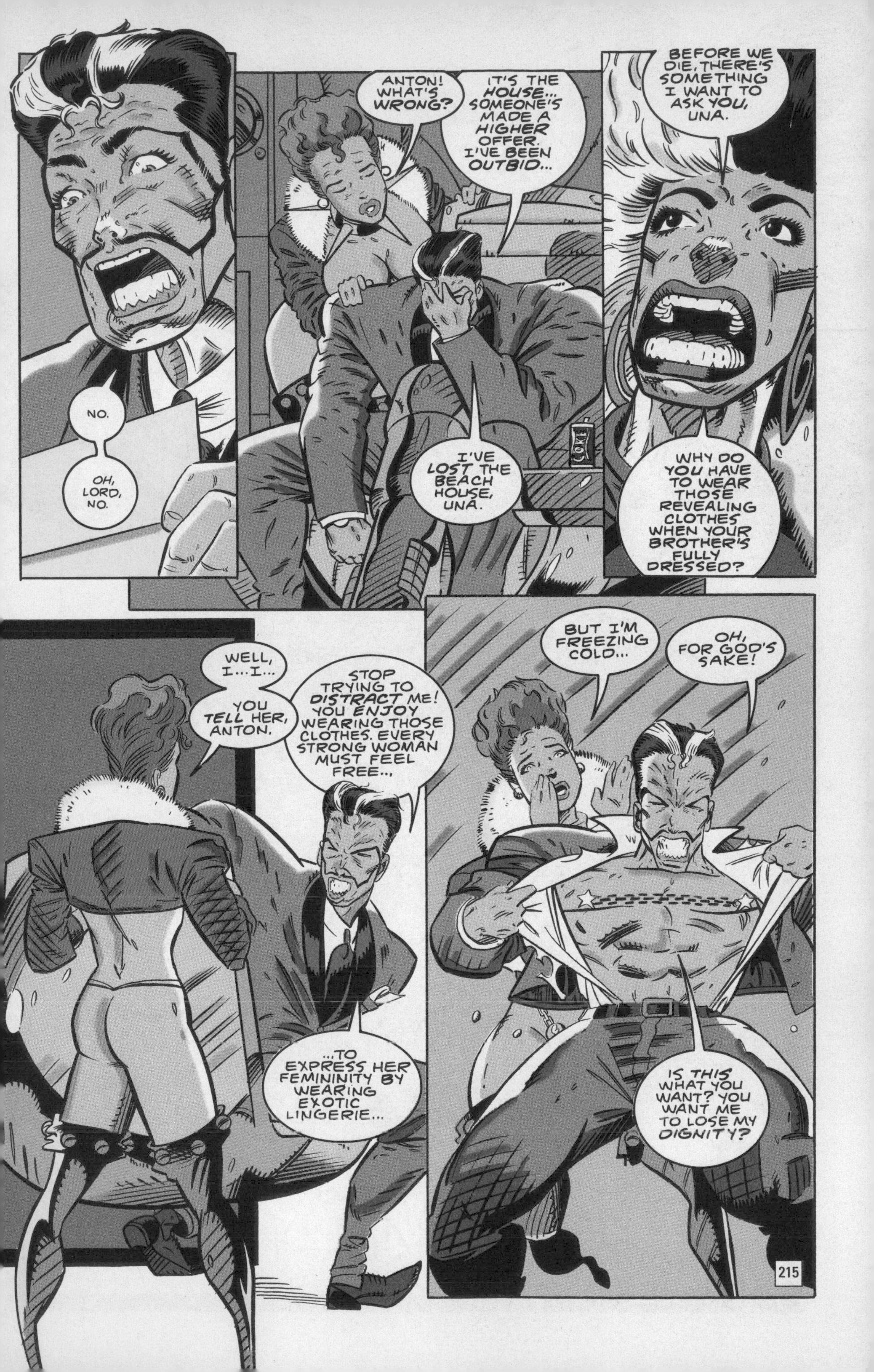
NO.
OH, LORD, NO.
ANTON! WHAT'S WRONG?
IT'S THE HOUSE... SOMEONE'S MADE A HIGHER OFFER. I'VE BEEN OUTBID...
I'VE LOST THE BEACH HOUSE, UNA.
COKE
BEFORE WE DIE, THERE'S SOMETHING I WANT TO ASK YOU, UNA.
WHY DO YOU HAVE TO WEAR THOSE REVEALING CLOTHES WHEN YOUR BROTHER'S FULLY DRESSED?
WELL, I...I...
YOU TELL HER, ANTON.
STOP TRYING TO DISTRACT ME! YOU ENJOY WEARING THOSE CLOTHES. EVERY STRONG WOMAN MUST FEEL FREE...
...TO EXPRESS HER FEMININITY BY WEARING EXOTIC LINGERIE...
BUT I'M FREEZING COLD...
OH, FOR GOD'S SAKE!
IS THIS WHAT YOU WANT? YOU WANT ME TO LOSE MY DIGNITY?

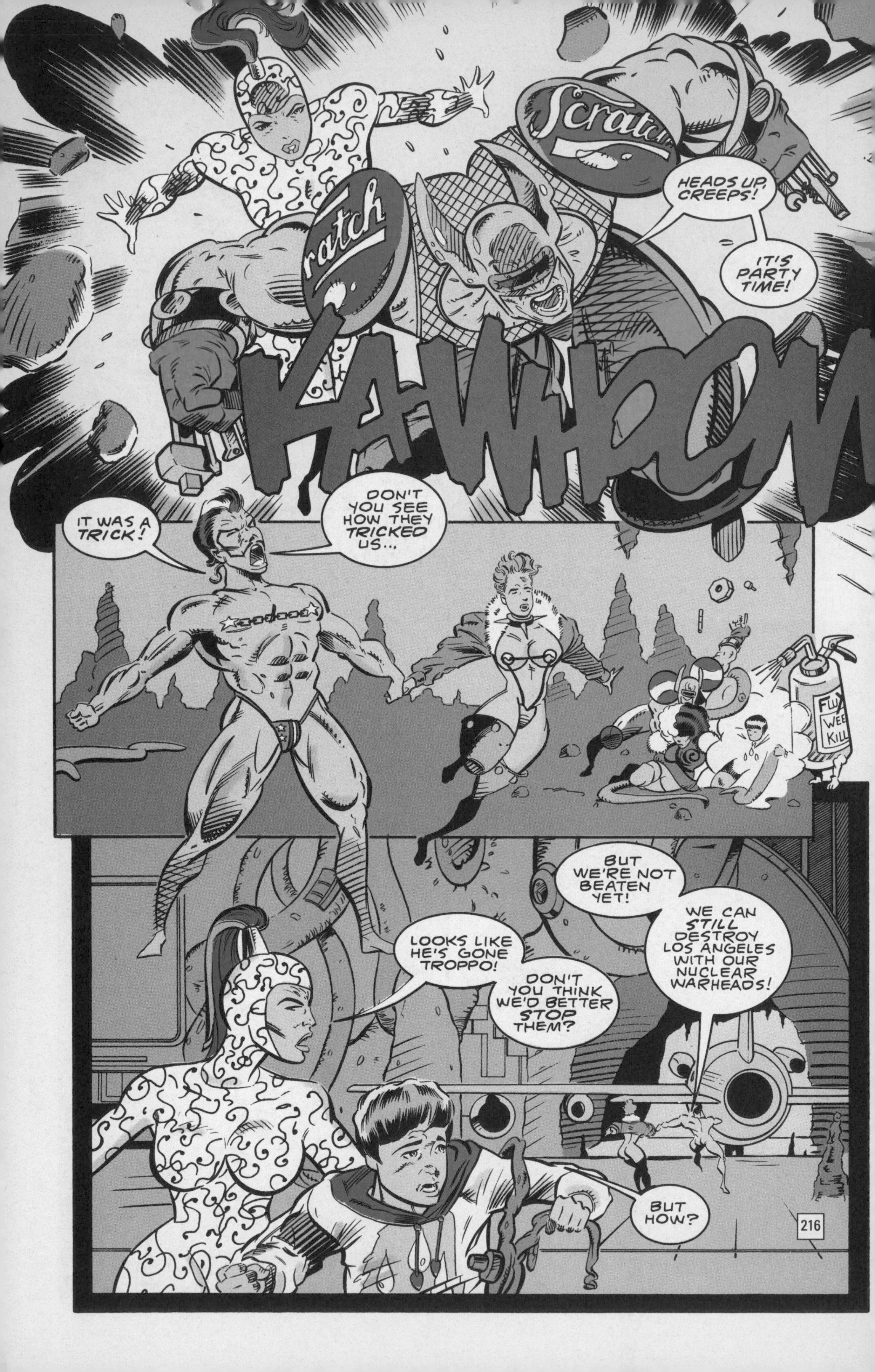
Scratch
ratch
HEADS UP, CREEPS!
IT'S PARTY TIME!
KAWHOOM
IT WAS A TRICK!
DON'T YOU SEE HOW THEY TRICKED US...
FLUX WEED KILL
LOOKS LIKE HE'S GONE TROPPO!
DON'T YOU THINK WE'D BETTER STOP THEM?
BUT WE'RE NOT BEATEN YET!
WE CAN STILL DESTROY LOS ANGELES WITH OUR NUCLEAR WARHEADS!
BUT HOW?

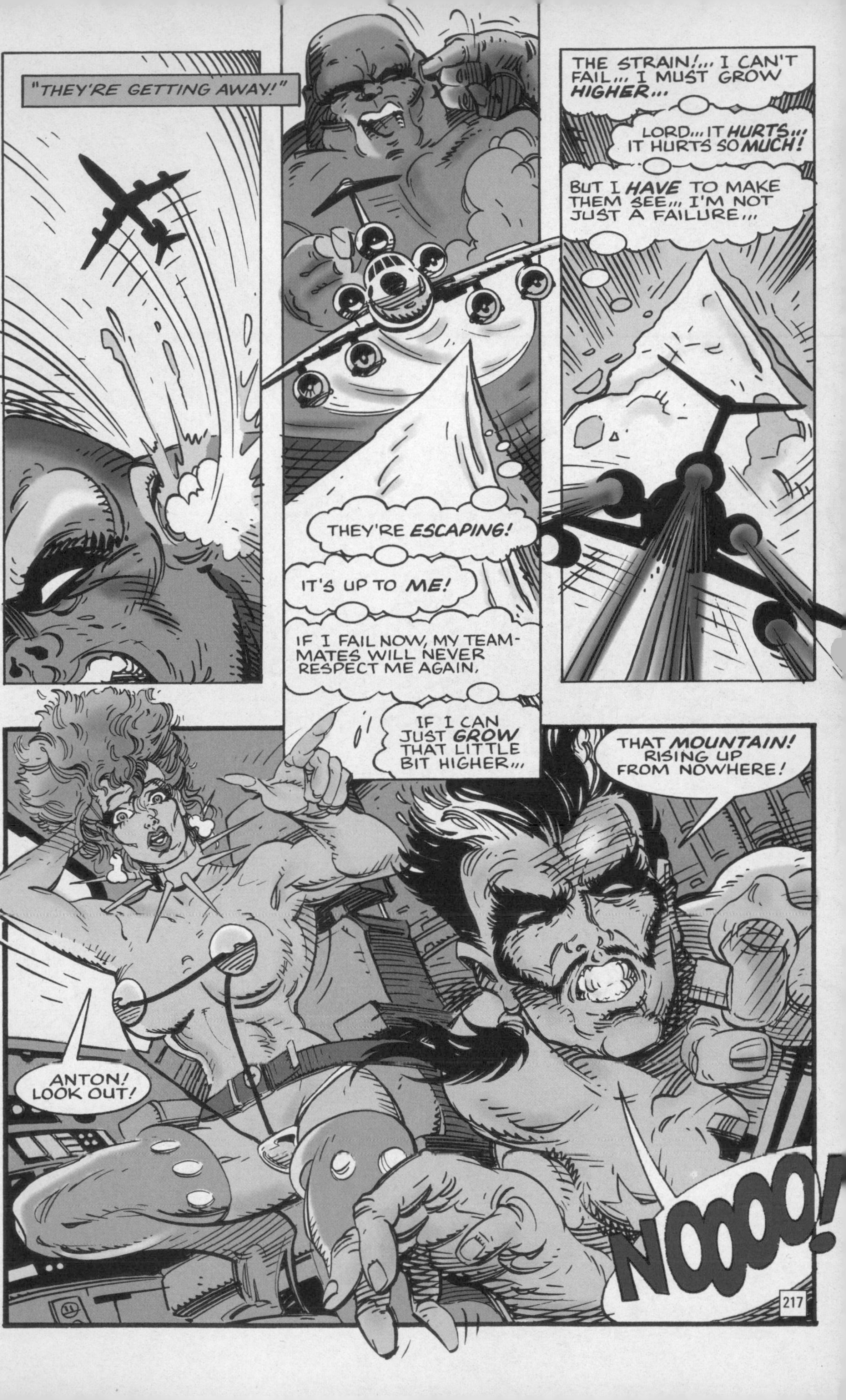

"THEY'RE GETTING AWAY!"
THE STRAIN!... I CAN'T FAIL... I MUST GROW HIGHER...
LORD... IT HURTS... IT HURTS SO MUCH!
BUT I HAVE TO MAKE THEM SEE... I'M NOT JUST A FAILURE...
THEY'RE ESCAPING!
IT'S UP TO ME!
IF I FAIL NOW, MY TEAM-MATES WILL NEVER RESPECT ME AGAIN,
IF I CAN JUST GROW THAT LITTLE BIT HIGHER...
THAT MOUNTAIN! RISING UP FROM NOWHERE!
ANTON! LOOK OUT!
NOOOO!

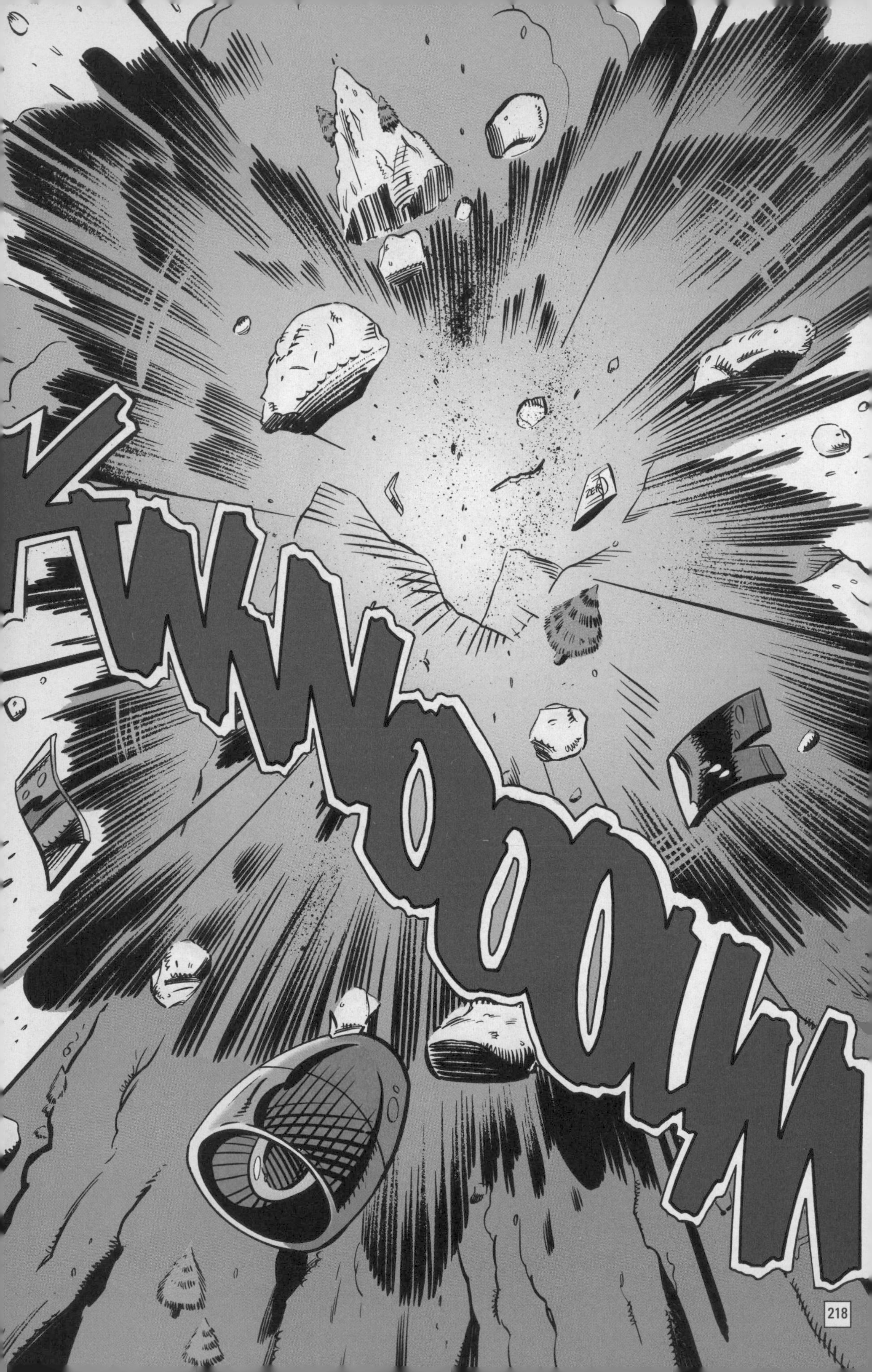
KWOOOOM

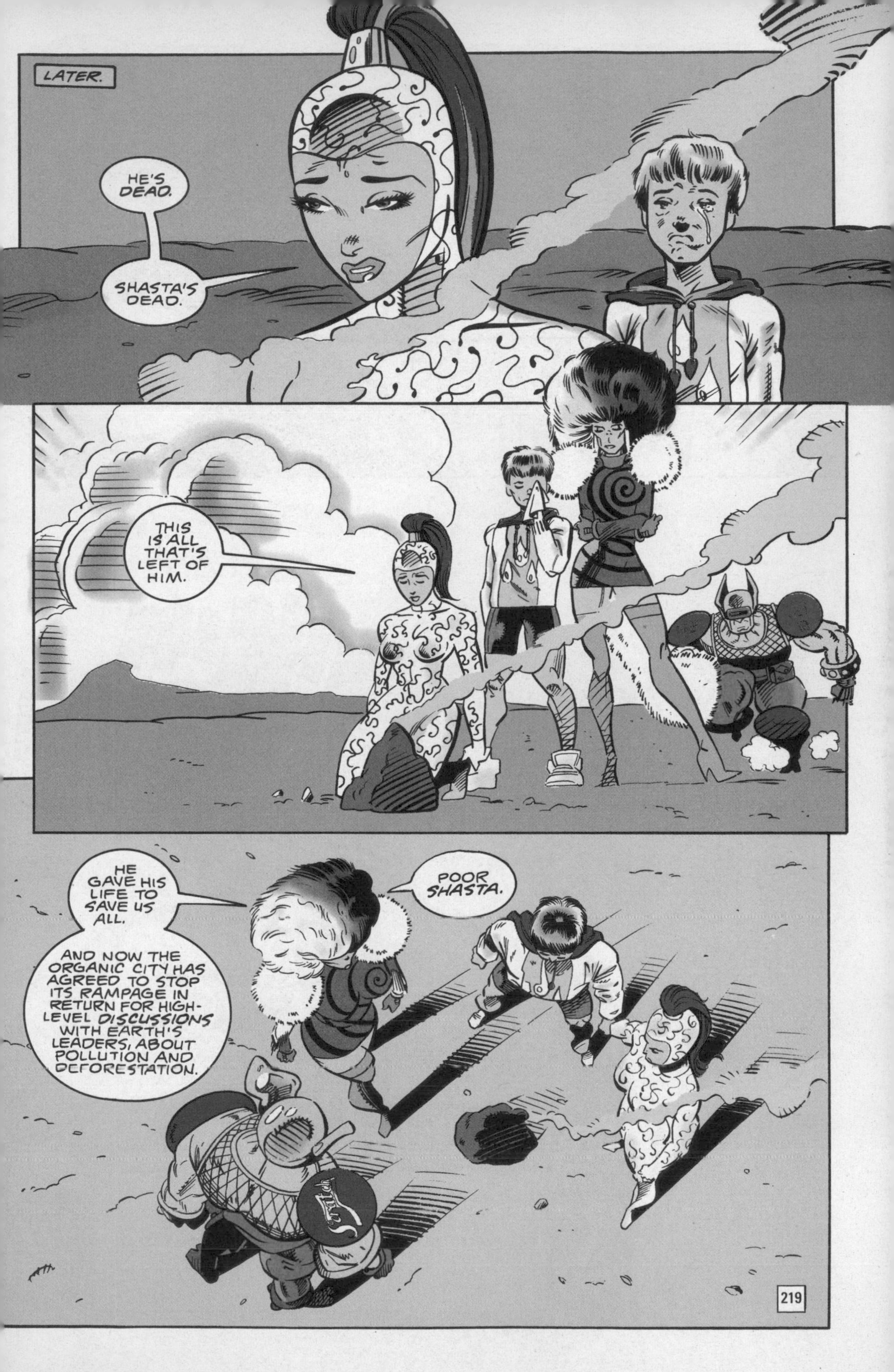
LATER.
HE'S DEAD.
SHASTA'S DEAD.
THIS IS ALL THAT'S LEFT OF HIM.
HE GAVE HIS LIFE TO SAVE US ALL.
AND NOW THE ORGANIC CITY HAS AGREED TO STOP ITS RAMPAGE IN RETURN FOR HIGH-LEVEL DISCUSSIONS WITH EARTH'S LEADERS, ABOUT POLLUTION AND DEFORESTATION.
POOR SHASTA.

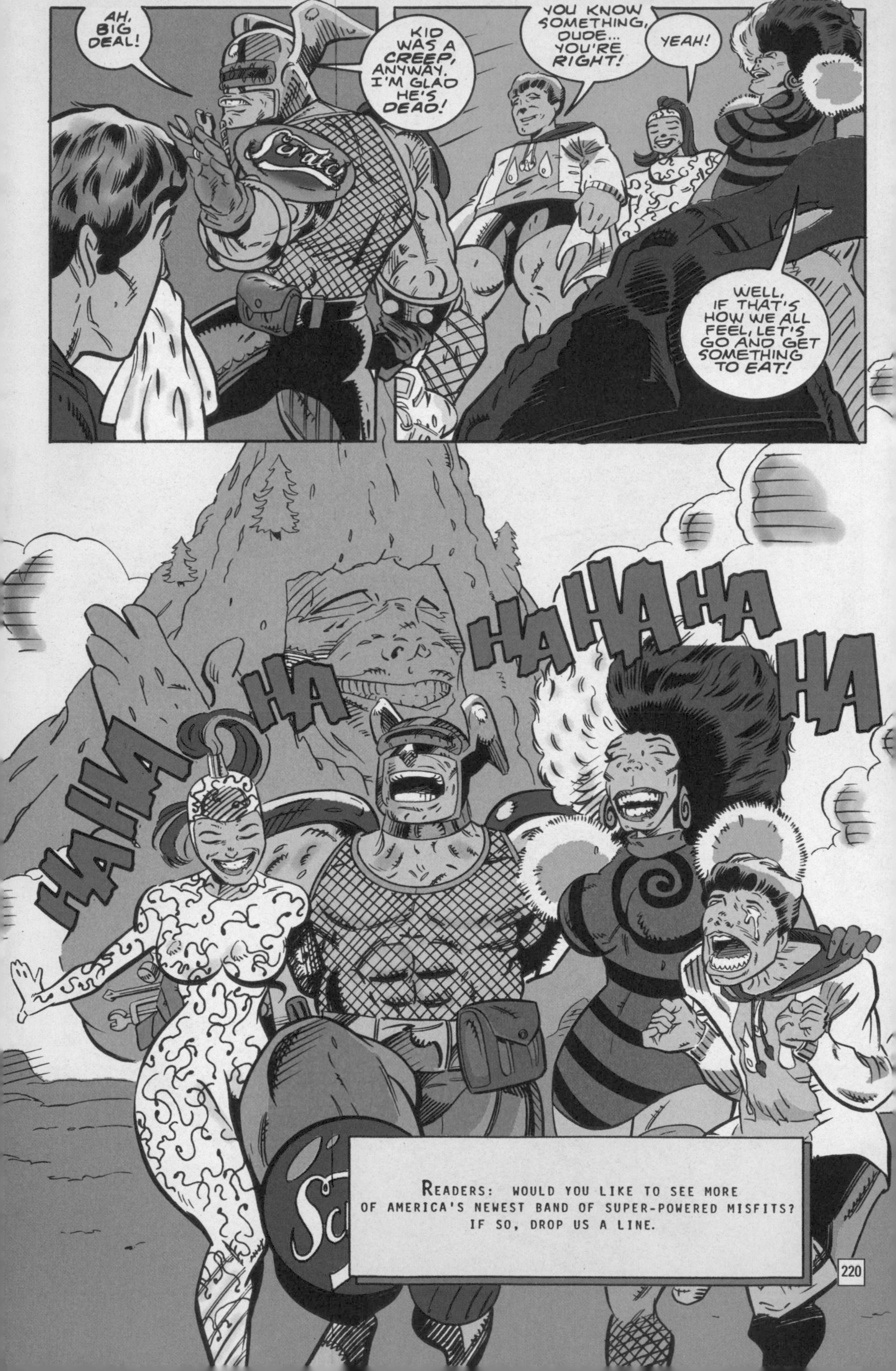
AH, BIG DEAL!
KID WAS A CREEP, ANYWAY. I'M GLAD HE'S DEAD!
YOU KNOW SOMETHING, DUDE... YOU'RE RIGHT!
YEAH!
WELL, IF THAT'S HOW WE ALL FEEL, LET'S GO AND GET SOMETHING TO EAT!
HAHA HA HA HAHAHAHA HA
READERS: WOULD YOU LIKE TO SEE MORE OF AMERICA'S NEWEST BAND OF SUPER-POWERED MISFITS? IF SO, DROP US A LINE.

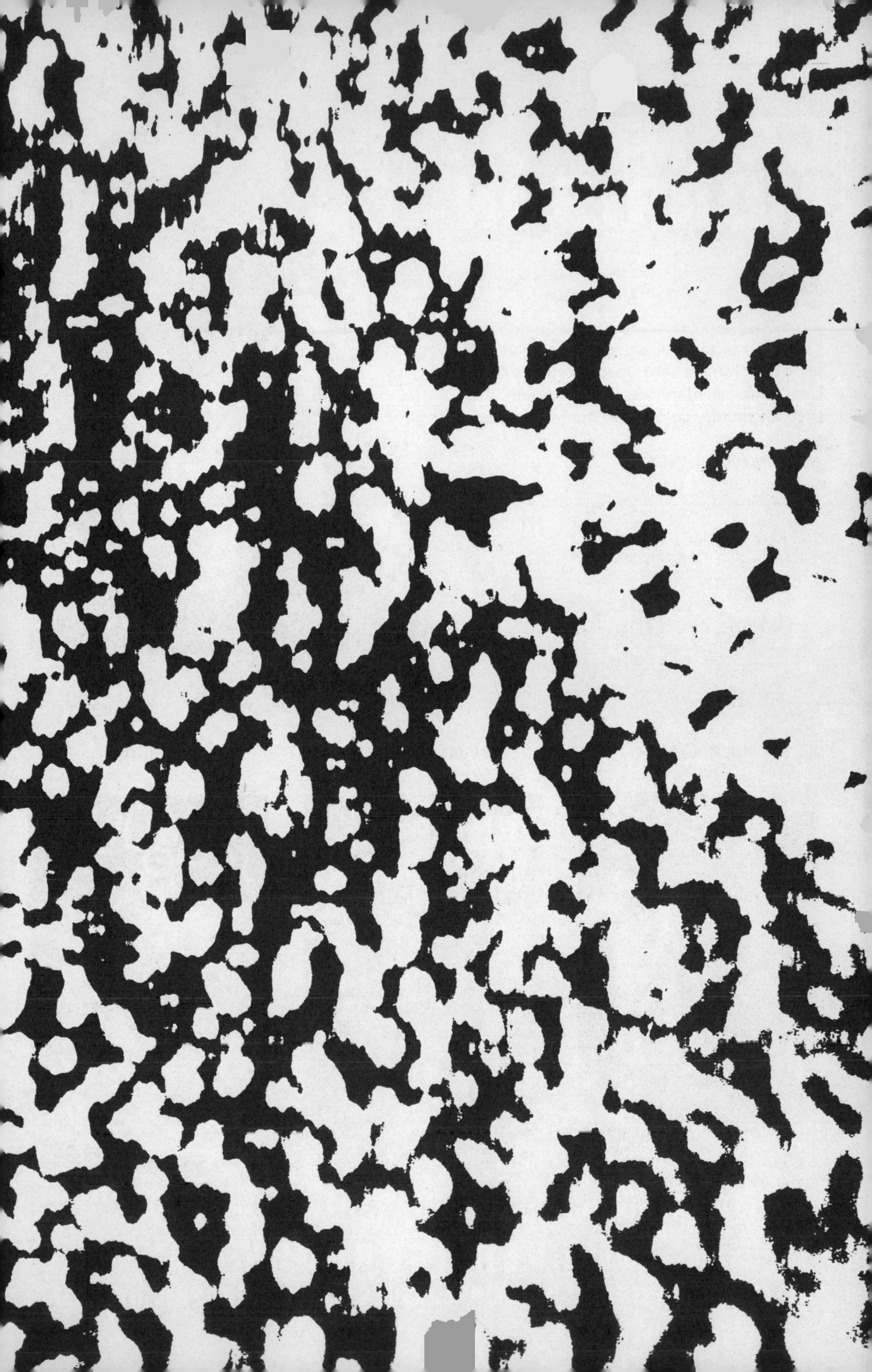

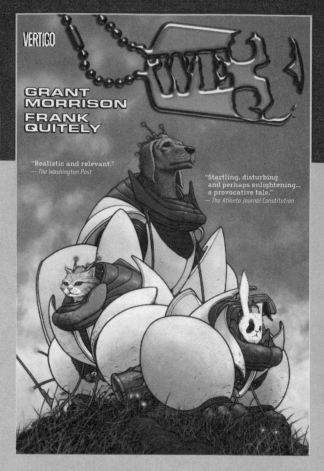
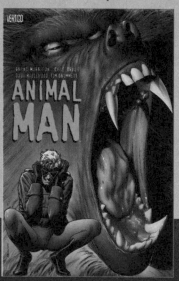  

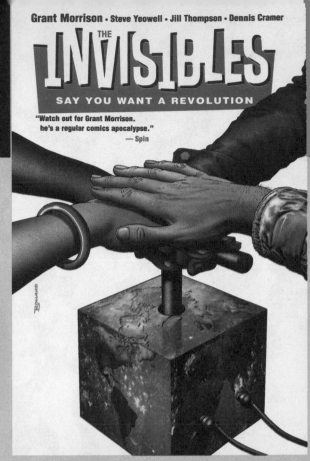
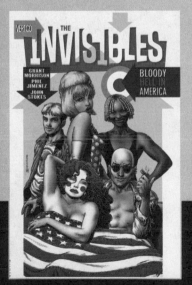